INTRODUCTION
TO ANIMAL COGNITION

John M. Pearce

Department of Psychology
University College
Cardiff
CF1 1XL

 LAWRENCE ERLBAUM ASSOCIATES, PUBLISHERS
Hove and London (UK)   Hillsdale (USA)

Lawrence Erlbaum Associates Ltd., Publishers
27 Palmeira Mansions
Church Road
Hove
East Sussex BN3 2FA

British Library Cataloguing in Publication Data

Pearce, John M.
  Introduction to animal cognition.
  1. Animal intelligence
  I. Title
  156'.39   QL785

  ISBN 0–86377–056–8
  ISBN 0–86377–057–6 Pbk

Printed and bound by A. Wheaton & Co. Ltd., Exeter

FOR MY FAMILY

Contents

v

Preface

In writing this book my aim has been to present one approach to the study of animal intelligence. It is my belief that the intelligence of animals is the product of a number of related cognitive processes. And the only way I know of understanding these processes is by studying the behaviour of animals in an experimental setting. This book, therefore, presents what is known about the intellectual processes of animals, by considering experimental findings from the laboratory and from more naturalistic settings.

Much of the book has its roots in the fields of animal learning and conditioning. I have, however, omitted a good deal of the material covered in traditional text books on these topics. Very little is said about schedules of reinforcement, or about parametric studies which show the optimal conditions for changing behaviour. Such work is of interest and importance but often the insights it provides into the mechanisms of animal intelligence are slight. Instead, I have focussed on experiments that most clearly demonstrate the operation of these intellectual mechanisms. In addition, for the sake of brevity and clarity, I have often reported only certain aspects of these experiments, and occasionally I have changed the names of groups that were included in them. I apologise to the authors for taking these liberties with their work. I can only hope that readers find the material I present to be of sufficient interest to encourage them to study directly the sources to which I refer.

The experimental study of animal intelligence spans a century, yet it is only in the last few years that there has been a substantial growth of interest in the mental processes of animals. As a result many of the topics that are discussed can still be considered to be in their infancy. Some readers may be disappointed, therefore, to discover that it is not yet possible to provide a satisfactory answer to a number of interesting theoretical questions. On the other hand, it is this lack of knowledge that makes the study of animal cognition so exciting. Many fascinating discoveries remain to be made once the appropriate experiments have been designed.

One of the rewards for writing a book is the opportunity it provides for thanking the friends and colleagues who have been so generous in the help they have given me. It is a particular pleasure to be able to thank A. Dickinson, G. Hall and N. J. Mackintosh. The way in which this book is organised, as well as the information it contains, has been greatly influenced by many discussions with them over the years. I am sure, however, that they will not agree with all that I have written. A special word of thanks is due to N. J. Mackintosh who, without apparent complaint, read an earlier version of the entire book and made numerous valuable suggestions.

And finally there is the pleasure of expressing my gratitude to my wife and children, for tolerating so patiently the demands made upon them while this book was being written. Thank you Victoria, Jessica, Alex, and Tim.

September, 1986   J.M.P.

1

The Study
of Animal Cognition

The study of animal cognition is concerned with questions of the following kind: What is animal intelligence? How does it differ from human intelligence? If there is a difference between the intelligence of humans and animals, why should this be? In what way do species of animals differ in their intelligence? How can animal intelligence be measured? None of these is an easy question to answer, and it is partly the difficulty of answering the first that makes it so difficult to answer all others.

In this book a particular account of animal intelligence will be developed. It presumes that animals, like humans, possess a number of mental or cognitive processes and that these collectively contribute to their intelligence. Thus the way animals remember, learn, reason, solve problems, communicate, and so forth will be examined in some detail. One advantage of this approach is that it may permit relatively straightforward answers to the above questions. For instance, a scale of intelligence might be constructed by ranking animals according to the number of the intellectual abilities they possess. Alternatively, it might turn out that it would be nonsensical to construct any such scale, because a species better endowed than another with one of these abilities might be less well endowed with a second. In addition, as this account is based upon a human model, it should readily permit the comparison of human and animal intelligence. The chapters that follow examine in some detail the various intellectual capacities that have been revealed in animals and to a lesser extent look at the way animals differ in their possession of these capacities.

The purpose of the present chapter is to provide a background to this discussion by considering a number of preliminary issues:

1.   An extremely popular view of animal intelligence is that there is a growth of this capacity with evolutionary development; apes are therefore seen by many as being more intelligent than most other animals. Although popular, this view deserves critical analysis, as it rests on some questionable asssumptions.

2.   The present account of animal intelligence is by no means unique. Many different approaches to this topic have been developed, and some brief justification for favouring the present one is required.

3.   Although the study of animal cognition is of interest in its own right, this may be regarded as insufficient justification for devoting a book to the topic. The study of human intelligence may be considered a more proper part of psychology. It is therefore worth identifying some of the benefits that may derive from the study of the mental life of animals.

4.   The study of mental processes in animals is difficult because the subject matter is not available to direct observation. It is certainly impossible at present to point to any event that can be regarded as a mental process in animals. As a result, special methods must be employed for the study of animal cognition, and the rationale for these needs discussion.

5.   And finally, much of the research discussed in this book relates to work conducted during the last twenty years or so, but the study of animal intelligence in the laboratory has now been pursued for nearly a hundred years. By way of providing a historical background to the rest of the book, the final section of the chapter presents a brief review of the dominant theoretical themes of this work.

THE DISTRIBUTION OF INTELLIGENCE

Banks and Flora (1977) asked college students to rank the intelligence of a variety of animals on a 10-point scale. Apes were considered the most intelligent with a rating of 9.2, then followed dogs with 7.36, cats with 6.57, horses with 5.57, cows with 3.58, sheep with 3.42, and chickens with 3.36; finally, fish were regarded as least intelligent, with a rating of 1.68. In fact, this ranking was not the principal aim of the study, and it is mentioned only because it reveals what is probably a widespread assumption: that there is a progressive development of intelligence throughout the animal kingdom, culminating in our own species, which presumably would have been awarded a score of 10 on the above scale.

I shall examine two popular justifications for the assumption that intelligence is distributed in this way. One is based upon an interpretation of evolution that presumes that animals can be arranged in a sequence according to their phylogenetic status. The other is derived from the assumption that there is a relationship between intelligence and brain size. In fact, neither of these justifies the views expressed by the students questioned by Banks and Flora (1977).

The Role of Evolution

The Great Chain of Being. Attempts since the time of Aristotle (384–322 BC) have been made to represent the animal kingdom in an orderly sequence. Such a sequence has been referred to as the *Scala Naturae*, or the "Great Chain of Being". Typically, the lower rankings of these scales are occupied by formless creatures like sponges, whereas the upper echelons are reserved for humans. Ascending through the intermediate range of these scales can be found insects, fish, amphibians, reptiles, and various mammals. According to Aristotle, elephants were placed just below humans. Although these scales generally cease with our own species, this has by no means been a universal practice. Occasionally the "Great Chain" has extended beyond humans to include angels and, ultimately, God.

Various justifications have been proposed for such a simple ordering. Aristotle based his scheme on whether or not the animals possessed blood and on the number of their legs. More recently, evolutionary terms have been used to justify what is now referred to as the phyletic or phylogenetic scale. Since the publication of Darwin's *The origin of the species by means of natural selection* in 1859, it has become accepted that all existing species have descended or evolved from different, earlier species. As a result, it is possible to envisage a chain of evolution in which the earliest animals are placed at the bottom, and the species they led to are placed above them, in the order of their appearance. *Homo sapiens* appeared some 100,000 years ago and would be very near the top of this scale. Most would accept that humans are vastly more intelligent than the protozoa to which we are distantly related, and so it is not difficult to regard the phyletic scale as roughly corresponding to the intellectual development of the species ordered along it. This interpretation could hardly be more incorrect.

While on his voyage around South America on H.M.S. *Beagle*, Darwin noted that the iguanas on the Galapagos Islands were different from those on the mainland in that only the former ate seaweed and swam in the sea. To explain this difference between such closely related species, he developed the principle of natural selection, which is based on two observations: (1) Many more animals are born than achieve reproductive success; some may die before reaching sexual maturity, others may fail to find a mate. (2) The individuals of a given species are not identical but differ from one another in a variety of ways. As a consequence, certain members of a species will be better suited than others to survive in a given environment, and they will be more likely to mature sexually and to leave offspring. If we assume that offspring resemble their parents, it follows that better-adapted characteristics will spread through a population at the expense of less well adapted characteristics. If members of the same species should occupy different environments, the different demands they face will favour the reproduction of animals with slightly different characteristics. Eventually their characteristics may have diverged to such an extent that they can no longer interbreed successfully, and they will constitute separate species.

Presumably, then, the ancestors of the iguanas observed by Darwin on the Galapagos Islands and on mainland South America were of the same stock. However, the radically different nature of these two environments—an abundance of seaweed and a dearth of vegetation on the islands, and a proliferation of vegetation on the mainland—would have favoured the gradual development of different characteristics in successive generations of offspring from the common ancestor.

One important implication of this account is that the notion of a phylogenetic scale is a gross over-simplification of the history of evolution. Instead of one species evolving from another in a strict sequence, as the "Great Chain of Being" suggests, it is now accepted that evolution has resulted in animals being related by a sort of family tree. The roots and trunk of the tree are composed of the early life forms such as protozoa and coelenterates.[1] The species that have evolved from these origins can be regarded as separate branches, which themselves branch out as later generations of their offspring evolve into new species.

Figure 1.1 shows the trunk and initial branches of a simplified version of the evolutionary tree. To give some idea of the time-scale involved, the fossil record provides evidence of animal life as long as 2,600 million years ago, yet it was not until about 450–500 million years ago that the first true vertebrates came into existence.

Figure 1.2 depicts the main branches of the evolutionary tree for the development of the vertebrates. The mammal-like reptiles that led to the mammals branched away from the reptiles approximately 200 million years ago. The birds, on the other hand, separated from the reptiles about 150

---

[1]Protozoa are single-celled organisms of varying forms which exist wherever there is water. They are capable of performing a variety of behavioural and physiological functions. Coelenterates, of which examples are jellyfish and sea anemones, are invertebrates with a sacklike body and a single opening (mouth). They possess the most primitive functionally organised nervous systems in the animal kingdom.

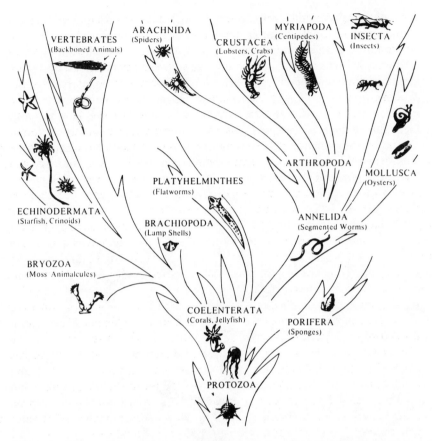

FIG. 1.1.   One possible version of the family tree of the animal kingdom (from Romer, 1966).

million years ago, via the link *Archaeopteryx*. Finally, the outer branches of the tree are presented in Fig. 1.3 for the four families of primates: prosimians, monkeys, apes, and us.

The structure of the evolutionary tree is of interest in its own right, but of more relevance to the present discussion is the fact that it is impossible to organise the relationship among the various species into any simple linear scale. Mammals and birds have both evolved from reptiles, and many of the reptiles that are alive today are only distant relatives of the reptiles that were ancestral to the birds and mammals. Given such a relationship, it is extremely difficult to imagine how the present-day animals could be placed in a sequence that mimics their evolutionary history. Evolution provides an explanation for the diversity of species—it does not provide any grounds for ranking animals according to their intelligence or, for that matter, any other characteristic.

Numerous authors have recently pursued this line of argument one step further to conclude that the evolutionary process will render futile any attempt to find common mechanisms of intelligence among animals (Hinde & Stevenson-Hinde, 1973; Seligman & Hager, 1972). It is not just the physical characteristics of animals that are shaped by evolution, but also their intellectual processes. Thus it might be expected that different species, if they inhabit different environments, will differ radically in the nature of their intelligence. For example, the habitat of a bird like the arctic tern, which spends most of its time flying between the polar regions,

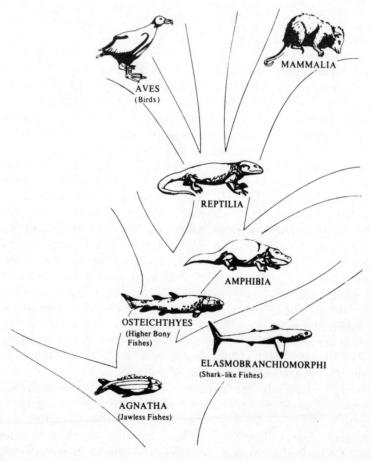

FIG. 1.2.   A simplified family tree of the classes of vertebrates (from Romer, 1955).

has very little in common with the sewer in which a rat might live. It is possible that very different intellectual processes will be possessed by animals occupying such contrasting environments. Furthermore, because the last common ancestor of the rat and the arctic tern was probably alive 200 million years ago, there has been ample time for the evolution of different mental capacities. If this argument is correct, then it is no more possible to conclude that one species is more intelligent than another than it is to say that one is more evolved than the other. All that can be said is that the species have developed different intellectual abilities that enable them to survive in their particular environments.

There is certainly some merit in this argument. Chapter 2 shows that birds that migrate great distances possess the ability to navigate by the stars. One would hardly expect to discover this skill in the sewer rat. But, at the same time, there are good grounds for believing that animals might have much in common intellectually. Despite living in radically different environments, animals face a number of common problems. Many animals must learn which foods are nutritious and which are poisonous. They must learn to identify their predators and where they can be found. They must learn the location of plentiful rather than lean supplies of food, or where water can be located. If the animals raise their young in a specific location, they must remember its position with respect to local landmarks. Given such a collection of common problems, it is at least plausible that different species employ the same intellectual processes for solving them.

Animals may, for example, have the ability to learn about recurring sequences of events, particularly when one of them is of biological significance. This would enable them, in a sense, to expect future events and to behave adaptively in anticipation of them. A simple example would be the ability to learn about the taste of a food and its ultimate gastric consequences. Animals that can learn about this relationship would then be able to restrict their diet to foods that are not harmful. There is also an obvious advantage, for virtually all animals, in being able to learn about the consequences of their actions. This will permit behaviour that has beneficial consequences to be repeated, and that which has harmful ones to be witheld. Many species might also benefit by possessing the capacity to communicate and to solve problems. The purpose of this discussion is not to argue that all animals should possess these and other abilities. Instead my aim is to indicate that although evolution will result in animals possessing very different characteristics, the common intellectual problems that confront many species may perhaps result in their sharing the same methods for solving them. If this is correct then there may be a considerable degree of similarity in the intellectual processes of different species. Of course, whether or not this is true can be discovered only by studying the animals directly.

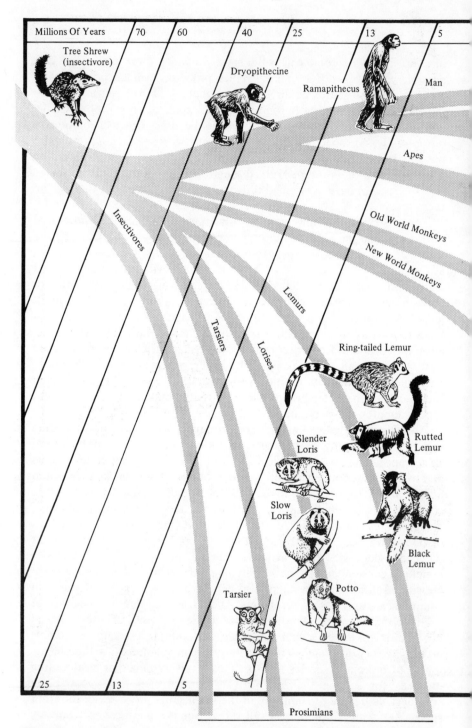

FIG. 1.3. A family tree of the primates; the details of this tree are still a matter for debate.

Australopithecus Robustus

Homo Habilis

Homo Erectus

100,000 Years

Modern Man

Neanderthal Man

Gorilla

Chimpanzee

Spider Monkey

Mandril

Pig-tailed Macaque

Gibbon

Cotton-top Monkey

Night Monkey

Rhesus Monkey

Orang-utan

Monkeys

Apes

9

Brain Size and Intelligence

One obvious candidate for providing an independent index of the intelligence of a species is its brain size. However intelligence is defined, few would dispute that the organ responsible for this capacity is the brain. It is thus reasonable to expect the species with the larger brains to possess the greater potential for intelligence. Perhaps this rationalisation was responsible for the replies to the questionnaire reported in the Banks and Flora (1977) study. There is certainly a high correlation between their ranking of intelligence and the brain size of the animals concerned: For instance, fish have smaller brains than dogs, which, in turn, have smaller brains than apes. Is it possible to rank the intelligence of species according to their brain size?

The first problem is evident when it is appreciated that elephants possess much heavier brains than humans. Few would accept that this relationship accurately indicates the relative intelligence of these species, and a moment's reflection should reveal the fallacy in the argument. The concern of the brain is not solely with such high matters as intelligence, but also with more basic activities such as respiration, digestion, reproduction, and movement—in short, all the somatic and vegetative processes of the body. The bigger the animal, the larger the volume of the brain that will be required to control these proceses. It is thus unrealistic to expect the size of the brain in absolute terms to provide an index of intelligence. A more plausible candidate is the ratio of the size of the brain to the body. If two species possess the same body size but one has a considerably larger brain, then it is plausible that this extra brain will enable it to be the more intelligent.

Figure 1.4 shows the brain weights (vertical axis) and the body weights (horizontal axis) of a variety of species, plotted in log–log coordinates. This scale is necessary because of the extremely wide range of values that must be considered. On the basis of what has just been said, it can be concluded, with some relief, that our species should be more intelligent than the ostrich. Both have the same body weight, but the weight of the ostrich brain is smaller than ours. The main problem is in deciding how species with different body weights should be compared.

One simple method is to draw polygons around the points for a collection of related species. In Fig. 1.4, Jerrison (1973), from whose book this account is taken, has drawn two polygons, one around the "higher" vertebrates (birds, mammals), and the other enclosing the "lower" vertebrates (reptiles, amphibia, fish). Because the polygons do not overlap, it is possible to conclude that in general the weight of the brain for a given body weight is greater for the higher vertebrates. In other words, the "higher" vertebrates might be expected to have a greater potential for intelligence than the "lower" vertebrates.

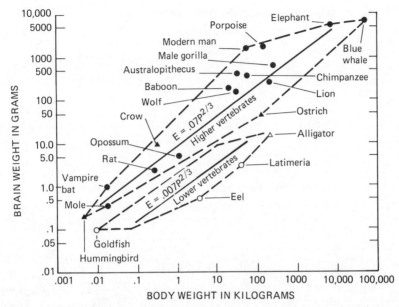

FIG. 1.4.   The brain weights (vertical axis) and body weights (horizontal axis) of a number of vertebrates. (from Jerrison, 1969).

More precise comparisons between species can be made by computing a cephalisation index (K). This essentially represents the ratio of the brain weight (E) to body weight (P), and the larger its value—we might assume—the greater the intelligence of the species concerned. Jerrison (1973) rejects the use of a simple ratio of the form E/P for determining the cephalisation index and recommends, instead, the use of the ratio $E/P^{2/3}$.[2] The solid lines in Fig. 1.4 pass through the brain and body weights that yield a K value of 0.07 (upper polygon) and 0.007 (lower polygon). Jerrison (1973) assumes that all the species that lie upon one of these lines possess an equivalent neural capacity for intelligence, irrespective of their body size. The magnitude of the vertical displacement from these lines indicates the K value for a given species. Humans and porpoises possess K values that are most displaced from the 0.07 line, which suggests they should be the two most intelligent species, with humans possessing a slight superiority.

---

[2]One justification for this ratio is the assumption that the body area is the major determinant for the amount of brain required for somatic processes. As the volume of an animal is related to the cube of its length, whereas its area is related to the square of its length, it follows that for larger animals the proportion of the brain required for somatic control is less than for smaller animals. It is to capture this relationship that the exponent 2/3 is used.

Thus, by computing a cephalisation index it may be possible to rank different species according to the volume of brain they have available for intelligence. Table 1.1 indicates that this ranking is not too unlike that proposed by the students in the Banks and Flora (1977) study. It is of interest that on this scale the elephant has a rather average potential for intelligence.

The ranking in Table 1.1 might accord with the popular conception of the way intelligence is distributed throughout the animal kingdom, but it does not confirm this view. The most that this ranking could indicate is that some animals have less brain available for intelligence than others, once account has been taken of its remaining functions. What is needed is a detailed investigation of the intellectual abilities of animals to determine whether or not they correspond with the order summarised in Table 1.1. This in turn depends upon a satisfactory definition of animal intelligence, and it is with this issue that the next section is concerned.

Before studying this problem, it is worth stating that not all authors maintain that Table 1.1 reflects accurately the distribution of animal intelligence. As early as about 500 BC, the Ionian philosopher Anaxagoras proposed that all living things possess a substance, *nous*, which is equivalent to mind. This substance has power over all things that have life; it is infinite, self-ruled, and just as good in animals as in humans. In more mundane terms, he was claiming that all animals are equally intelligent. Any apparent intellectual differences among animals were said to be due to variations in the way they can express themselves. Hence, he might have

TABLE 1.1
The Cephalization Index (*K*) for 21 Mammals
Arranged in Descending Order

1. Man	0.89	12. Dog	0.14
2. Dolphin	0.64	13. Squirrel	0.13
3. Chimpanzee	0.30	14. Wild Pig	0.12
4. Squirrel Monkey	0.28	15. Cat	0.12
5. Rhesus Monkey	0.25	16. Horse	0.10
6. Elephant	0.22	17. Sheep	0.10
7. Whale	0.21	18. Ox	0.06
8. Marmoset	0.21	19. Mouse	0.06
9. Fox	0.19	20. Rat	0.05
10. Walrus	0.15	21. Rabbit	0.05
11. Camel	0.14		

Source: Adapted from Russell, 1979.

argued that worms are intelligent, but unfortunately they lack the necessary appendages to demonstrate this capacity fully. Among Anaxagoras' other novel ideas is the proposal that snow is, in part, black.

Somewhat more recently Macphail (1982) concluded, after an extremely thorough review of a vast body of experimental evidence, that there is no difference in the intellectual capacity of vertebrates other than humans. Given that this claim is based upon the results of direct tests of animal intelligence, it merits serious attention. Although a major aim of this book is to outline a framework for the study of animal intelligence, a secondary aim is to evaluate the relative intelligence of different species. This should allow us to determine whether popular opinion is correct in assuming a progression of intelligence throughout the animal kingdom, or whether Anaxagoras and Macphail are correct in their claim concerning the equality of animals in this respect.

DEFINING ANIMAL INTELLIGENCE

Adaptability

Many authors consider that the defining characteristic of intelligence is that it enables animals to behave adaptively. Thus in a book entitled *Instinct and intelligence*, a zoologist, Barnett (1970), has proposed: "intelligence here means the ability to adapt behaviour to circumstances" (p. 59). There can surely be little to disagree with in this definition. Nonetheless, its limitations become evident when attempts are made to compare the intelligence of different species. How it could be determined whether a rat or a dog is better at adapting its behaviour to the prevailing circumstances is not immediately apparent. Nor does this definition tell us anything about the mechanisms that enable an animal to adapt its behaviour.

One solution to this problem is to acknowledge that an animal that can profit from its experiences is likely to be better at adapting to a new environment than one lacking this capacity. For example, once the location of food, water, and predators has been identified, being able to remember where they were encountered will considerably facilitate future survival. Accordingly, the animal that is faster at learning and better at remembering may be regarded as the more adaptable and hence the more intelligent. Indeed, Warren (1973) has suggested that this type of argument formed the rationale for much of the work in comparative psychology conducted during the first half of this century.

Learning

Since the turn of the century there has been an enormous number of experimental studies of learning, using animals ranging from protozoa to humans, and in a variety of tasks. One clear conclusion that can be drawn from this work is that there is definitely no relationship between the speed at which an animal learns and its cephalisation index. Evidence supporting this claim will be presented throughout the book, but at this juncture several examples will serve to make the point. Skard (1950) compared the speed at which rats and humans mastered a complex maze and found no difference whatsoever in the number of trials required to attain errorless performance. Warren (1965) reported that there was no difference in the rate at which goldfish, chickens, cats, horses, and rhesus monkeys learned a discrimination in which they were required to approach one of two stimuli to gain reward.

Perhaps even more surprising are the results of Angermeier (1984), who conducted a thorough series of experiments at the University of Cologne. Various animals were required to perform a simple response to obtain food: Mammals had to press a lever, birds peck a disc, and fish push a rod that was hanging vertically into their tank. Subjects were placed into the apparatus when hungry, and food was delivered only when the response had been performed. As his measure of learning, Angermeier (1984) recorded the number of rewards delivered before subjects reached a criterion of responding at a constant rate. The results from his studies are presented in Table 1.2, which also includes the results of other researchers using 5-month-old human infants, rewarded with food for turning their heads (Papousek, 1977), and bees rewarded for discriminating between different colours (Menzel & Erber, 1978). The remarkable feature of these data is that they are precisely the opposite of that expected if the cephalisation index of a species corresponded with its intelligence, as revealed by the speed of learning. Whatever the explanation for these intriguing results, they do suggest that it would be unwise to look to speed of learning as an index of animal intelligence.

Another reason for being wary of using speed of learning as a measure of intelligence comes from studies showing that, for a given species, the speed of learning is greatly influenced by the means used to assess it. Bolles (1971) has shown that rats will readily learn to press a lever for food, yet they have considerable difficulty in learning to perform the same response to avoid electric shock. This difficulty does not reflect an inability to perform avoidance responses, as rats find it easy to learn to jump onto a ledge or to run from one compartment to another to avoid shock (Baum,

TABLE 1.2
Number of Rewards Delivered before Criterion Was Reached
in a Simple Learning Task for 11 Animals
Arranged in Ascending Order

1. Bees	2	7. Pigeons	10
2. Triggerfish	4	8. Rats	22
3. Koi Carp	4	9. Raccoons	24
4. Silverbarb	4	10. Rabbits	24
5. Quail	8	11. Human infants	28
6. Hybrid Chickens	18		

Source: After Angermeier, 1984.

1966; Theios, Lynch, & Lowe, 1966). Similarly, in one of my experiments (Pearce, Colwill, & Hall, 1978) rats were shown to be much poorer at learning to scratch themselves than to press a lever for food. One of the clearest demonstrations of this type of effect was reported by Garcia and Koelling (1966) using an extremely simple technique. Thirsty rats were allowed to drink salt-flavoured water from a tube in the presence of a distinctive exteroceptive stimulus comprising a light and a clicker. For one group drinking was followed by an injection of a mild poison that induced illness; for another group the consequence of drinking was electric shock. After several sessions of this training the subjects were returned to the apparatus for a number of test trials; on some trials drinking salt-free water was accompanied by the light and clicker, on others these stimuli were omitted but the water contained salt. Animals that had previously been shocked showed a marked aversion to drinking in the presence of the light and clicker but they were quite happy to drink the salty water by itself. Conversely, the animals that had been made ill freely drank water accompanied by the light and clicker but rejected it when it was flavoured with salt.

This aversion to drinking on certain test trials is generally attributed to animals learning about the relationships between the stimuli and their consequences. What is important to note is that the ease of this learning depended critically upon the combination of these events. Certain pairings resulted in poor learning (salt with shock, noise and light with illness), whereas others produced very good learning (salt with illness, noise and light with shock). Some explanations for these findings will be considered in Chapter 6; for the present the principal conclusion to be drawn is that it is impossible to say whether rats are good or bad at learning, because this depends critically on the way in which they are tested. This conclusion is also true for many other species, and we must accept that assessing the speed of learning is unlikely to yield an unambiguous indication of an animal's intelligence.

But these are not the only problems with using speed of learning as a measure of intelligence. Because of the inherent difference between species, it is hard to devise a task that makes exactly the same demands on different animals. For example, in studies where the subject must learn to respond for food, the speed at which it does so is likely to be influenced by its perceptual, motivational, and motor processes. Bitterman (1965) refers to such factors as contextual variables, and as they will undoubtedly vary from one species to another, they may be responsible for any differences in learning that are exhibited. This point can be emphasised by reconsidering Angermeier's (1984) findings. He observed that rats learned more slowly than fish to perform a response for food. This might reflect the inferior learning ability of rats, but it could equally well be due to a more trivial factor—perhaps the reward given to the fish was more effective than that given to the rats, or perhaps the fish found it easier to locate the lever. Unless we can be certain that these and many other factors were equated, it would be unwise to draw any firm conclusions from Angermeier's (1984) study about the relative intelligence of the animals concerned.

In order to deal with this sort of problem, Bitterman (1965) suggested the use of a technique known as "systematic variation". This method, in essence, involves training animals from different species on the same task across a wide range of conditions. These conditions might involve variations in reward size, in the level of deprivation, in the nature of the stimuli employed, and so on. If it could be shown that despite all these manipulations one species is uniformly better at learning than another, then it would suggest that this species is the more intelligent. In principle this method should be successful, but in practice it is extremely challenging to implement. Identifying the important procedural details of an experiment is not easy, and it is therefore difficult to be sure that the relevant manipulations have been conducted. In addition, there is the practical problem that this method dictates the use of a large number of subjects being run in many possibly time-consuming experiments. Few psychologists have either the facilities or the patience to pursue this approach to the study of animal intelligence.

One final reason for being wary of using learning as a means for assessing the intelligence of animals is that it may direct attention away from other important intellectual capacities. In addition to being able to learn, animals may also be able to remember, reason, solve problems, and so on. These and other abilities should be regarded as attributes of intelligence, yet until recently they have received relatively little study. We now turn to an alternative view of animal intelligence, which takes account of such abilities.

Information Processing

The study of human cognition is characterised by the way it regards people as if they were sophisticated processors of information. Throughout our lives we are surrounded by information about the environment in which we live. Not only does this information emanate from such artificial sources as books or the radio, it is also provided by our interaction with the natural world. This information is received by all the senses, and its reception is essential for our survival. Of paramount importance is the fact that we do not receive this information passively. Of all the information that is available, we attend selectively only to a portion, and that which gains our attention may then be transformed as it passes through a variety of stages. The information may be retained so that it can be recalled on some subsequent occasion, or it may be forgotten. It may be integrated with other information, or it may be stored as a relatively discrete unit. Alternatively, it may be used as a step in a complex reasoning process. Ultimately, after passing through these stages, the information may produce a response. Given such a framework, the task of the cognitive psychologist is to identify as precisely as possible the nature and properties of the various information processing stages. There is no good reason for confining this approach to the study of humans. Animals, too, are surrounded by information that is relevant to their survival, and it is plausible that they also possess a variety of mechanisms for analysing and storing it.

From this perspective, intelligence is, then, the processing of information, and one advantage of this definition is that it points to other ways of comparing the intelligence of animals than using the speed of learning. For example, we might compare animals on the basis of the different means they have at their disposal for processing information. In this case an all-or-none comparison can be used to evaluate animal intelligence, such that species can be compared on the basis of whether or not they possess a particular information-processing mechanism. An alternative would be to focus on a specific ability, such as memory, and compare the extent to which animals differ in this respect. Thus some species may be able to store more information for greater periods than others.

In the next section the methods of investigating the information processing of animals are discussed. The remaining chapters in the book are then concerned with describing ways in which animals process information.

METHODS FOR STUDYING ANIMAL INTELLIGENCE

Physiological Techniques

Perhaps the most obvious method of studying the way in which animals process information is to study the nervous system directly. This strategy can be demonstrated by referring to the work of Kandel and his colleagues (e.g. Hawkins & Kandel, 1984), who have investigated learning in the shell-less marine snail, *Aplysia*. These invertebrates possess a gill in a respiratory chamber that is covered by a protective sheath, the mantle shelf, which terminates in a fleshy spout, the syphon. Touching this syphon results in rapid withdrawal of the gill and mantle shelf into the protection of the respiratory chamber. Repeatedly touching the syphon usually results in a progressive weakening of this withdrawal. However, if every touch to the syphon is followed by an electric shock to the tail, then no weakening of the withdrawal response occurs. Hawkins and Kandel (1984) regard this effect as evidence of a form of learning known as classical conditioning and argue that it is subject to the same principles that govern conditioning in many vertebrates.

By studying the changes in the various neurons between the syphon, gill, and tail, Kandel has been able to identify some of the physiological changes underlying this simple form of learning. In essence it appears to involve modulations of the amount of transmitter substance released by the presynaptic terminals of neurons. In a later chapter it is argued that classical conditioning can be interpreted as a form of information processing, and Kandel's work can thus be seen as a step towards the understanding of animal cognition at a physiological level.

Despite the success of this research, its limitations for the study of animal cognition are all too obvious. It is not unreasonable to believe that the cognitive capacities of many vertebrates are more sophisticated than those of *Aplysia*. Consequently, research with this animal may provide some insights into the physiological mechanisms subserving vertebrate cognition, but a full understanding will be achieved only by studying these animals directly. The much greater complexity of the vertebrate nervous system means, unfortunately, that the techniques presently developed for the study of invertebrate learning will be of only limited value.

Attempts are being made to study the physiological changes that accompany classical conditioning in vertebrates. Kettner and Thompson (1982), for example, have investigated the changes that occur in electrical activity in the cerebellum of the rabbit brain during conditioning (see also Thompson, Berger, & Madden, 1983). Their findings are, however, a long way from elucidating the changes that occur at a cellular level, which would presumably constitute a detailed physiological understanding of this form of information processing. Furthermore, we can be certain that classical conditioning does not represent the pinnacle of the intellectual achievements of animals. Admittedly, there have been some very good attempts to understand other intellectual processes at a physiological level, but we are still a long way from achieving this goal. This is not to say that physiological techniques will be of no help in unravelling the processes of vertebrate cognition, but just that it will be some considerable time before they yield an adequate account of animal intelligence.

The Study of Unobservable Processes

One alternative to studying the nervous system directly is to assume that an animal's brain constructs a perceptual world that corresponds to its environment (cf. Jerrison, 1973). This then implies that information processing by the brain can be regarded as two distinct but related processes. On the one hand there is the perceptual processing, in which information provided by the senses is integrated into units that correspond to features of the animal's environment. Very little is said about this type of perceptual processing in the present book, not because the topic is unimportant, but simply because of limitations of space. The second type of processing concerns the manner in which the brain deals with the information in the perceptual world it has constructed. It is this type of processing that is the concern of this book, and which corresponds roughly to the area studied by those psychologists interested in human cognition.

Thus if an animal is presented with a tone that signals food, we shall ignore the processes underlying the perception of these events. It will be taken for granted that their perception takes place and results in the formation of internal, central representations of the tone and food. The main focus of concern will be with such issues as identifying what information is encoded in these representations and understanding the mechanisms that enable subjects to learn about the relationship between them. In a sense, then, a central representation of an environmental event constitutes an essential component of animal cognition. The task confronting a person interested in this topic is to show what these components consist of and how they function in the higher mental processes.

The obvious problem in studying animal cognition from this perspective is that there is no direct way of observing a central representation. It is impossible to point to any feature of an animal and identify it as being a representation of food or any other event. Instead, the existence of such representations and their properties must be inferred, and for the present the animal's behaviour provides the only medium by which this can be achieved. Consequently psychologists interested in animal cognition conduct experiments in which it is hoped that the subjects act in such a way as to demonstrate unambiguously the existence and operation of a central, internal mental process. It should come as no surprise to discover that this approach is not without its pitfalls.

If the operation of a central process has to be inferred from an animal's behaviour, then it is possible that different theorists will appeal to different mental processes to explain the same activity. How is it possible to choose between a variety of accounts when they refer to events that are not open to direct observation? There are two answers to questions of this sort: the first concerns the nature of theorising in science, the second relates to the value of the experimental method.

Consider a simple experiment in which a tone repeatedly signals the occurrence of food to a hungry dog. At first there will be little reaction to the tone, but eventually the dog will salivate whenever it hears this stimulus. One explanation for this effect is that the tone arouses a memory of food, which is responsible for salivation. Another explanation, couched in terms of stimulus–response theory to be considered shortly, is that this training results in the dog reflexively salivating during the tone without any knowledge of the food that will be presented shortly.

At a theoretical level it is possible to choose between these accounts by employing what is known as Lloyd Morgan's canon: "In no case may we interpret an action as the outcome of the exercise of a higher psychical faculty, if it can be interpreted as the outcome of one which stands lower in the psychological scale" (Morgan, 1894, p. 53). In other words, the best explanation is the one that refers to the simplest psychological mechanisms. On this basis the second of the above accounts is to be preferred, because it does not assert, as the former does, that animals possess memory processes.

The other method for choosing between different accounts is to use them to generate novel predictions and to evaluate these experimentally. The best account is likely to be the one that provides the most correctly fulfilled predictions. In Chapter 4 I show that the first explanation yields a novel prediction that is confirmed and that the second explanation generates predictions that are disconfirmed. For this reason the first explanation is the better of the two.

The purpose of this brief discussion is to explain the strategy of theorists and experimenters concerned with animal cognition. A variety of explanations may be developed for a single experimental finding. They will be presented in the simplest possible terms, with little reference to sophisticated theoretical constructs. To test the explanations, experiments are conducted, which ideally will confirm one and contradict the others. Gradually this process will yield a substantial body of experimental evidence that supports a particular account of animal cognition.

WHY STUDY ANIMAL COGNITION?

Intellectual Curiosity

A major source of motivation for any scientific enterprise is the satisfaction of intellectual curiosity; the study of animal cognition is no different in this respect. As pets, as sources of food, or in the wild, animals often play a prominent role in our lives, and for this reason alone it is natural to wonder at their intelligence. This curiosity is enhanced by the occasional reports of apparently sophisticated intellectual skills being displayed by animals. At the turn of the century, there was considerable interest in a horse named Clever Hans, who, it was claimed, could count. More recently, television programmes have shown dolphins allegedly engaged in a complicated dialogue that enabled one to tell the other how to obtain food. There have also been claims that apes are capable of communicating with humans, and vice versa. Pigeons are said to be able to perform remarkable feats of navigation to return home from a distant and unfamiliar site of release; indeed, this topic has recently been the subject of correspondence to the *Times* (see Fig. 1.5). Reports such as these are bound to arouse in many a genuine curiosity concerning the intelligence of animals.

Curiosity about animal intelligence also arises from an interest in our own evolutionary history. The very name *Homo sapiens* (literally meaning "Man the Intelligent"), implies that intelligence has played a critical role in this history, but it is not clear how. Once the intelligence of animals is better understood, we may have a clearer appreciation of the evolution of our own intelligence.

Relevance to Other Disciplines

In a recent book on human cognition, Anderson (1985) considered the success of the study of artificial intelligence (AI) to mimic human intelligence. He concluded (pp. 2–3):

> Despite the fact that this has been an active area of interest for more than 20 years, A.I. researchers still have no idea how to create a truly intelligent computer. No existing programs can recall facts, solve problems, reason, learn, or process language with anything approximating human facility. This failure has not occurred because computers are inferior to human brains but because we do not yet know how human intelligence is organised.

There can be little doubt that the intellectual processes of animals are less complicated than those of humans and should therefore be easier to understand. Despite the obvious differences between humans and animals,

Pigeons in the Tube

From Mr John B. Price

Sir, Recent observations of the travelling habits of some of London's feral pigeon population suggest a level of intelligence hitherto unsuspected. Using the District Line, I have seen pigeons boarding the Underground trains at Edgware Road station and later, alighting at various points along the line. Fulham Broadway and Parson's Green seem to be favoured and also Putney Bridge if it is low water.

Usually silent and straightfaced season ticket-holders have readily responded to my enquiries and report that this practice has been continuous over a long period. Some interesting conversations have been enjoyed over the antics of our blatantly fare-dodging feathered friends.

Yours faithfully
JOHN B. PRICE,
Worcester House,
38 Alwyne Road, SW19.
August 30.

Passenger pigeons

From Mr Michael Greville

Sir, Until I read Lord Greenhill's observations in his letter to you today (September 17) on the apparently common tactics of racing pigeons, I had thought of my experience two years ago as unique.

I was sailing a 34ft yacht from Fécamp towards Beachy Head when, shortly after dropping the French coast, a number of these birds passed and one of them proceeded to join me on watch in the cockpit.

For six hours he kept me company, refusing all offers of hospitality (biscuits and beer) and declining to indulge in conversation, until he alighted from his perch, circled the mast head, presumably in appreciation, and flew off.

Within 10 minutes the Royal Sovereign Tower was sighted, and soon Beachy Head itself.

I was most impressed by this display of constructive idleness and accurate dead reckoning to boot, but not so by the mess left on the tiller.

Yours faithfully
MICHAEL GREVILLE
79A Milson Road, W14.
September 17.

Passenger pigeons

From Lord Greenhill of Harrow

Sir, Mr Price's letter (September 10) draws attention to the intelligence of pigeons. My wife wrote similarly in your columns in December, 1968, and received supporting evidence in letters from all over the world.

May I offer a further example? Some years ago I observed a flock of racing pigeons flying alongside the cross-channel steamer from Calais to Dover. At about mid-point a single pigeon at the rear detached itself from the flock and alighted on a lifeboat davit. It remained resting until shortly before Dover when it rejoined, no doubt considerably refreshed, its fellow competitors. I could think of no way of betraying its intelligent deceit.

Yours.
GREENHILL of HARROW.
House of Lords.
September 10.

Passenger pigeons

From Vice-Admiral Sir Anthony Troup

Sir, I don't know about yachting pigeons (Michael Greville's letter of September 24), but I do know about submarine pigeons.

In 1948 I took three pigeons to sea in a submarine from Gosport as an experiment. Submerging in mid-channel for several hours and after turning many circles at depth, we surfaced and released them at thirty miles, well out of sight of land.

After release they circled the submarine three times and then flew straight home to Gosport.

Yours faithfully,
TONY TROUP,
Bridge Gardens,
Hungerford,
Berkshire,
September 25.

FIG. 1.5. A selection of letters to the *Times* concerning the navigational ability of pigeons.

it is my belief that an accurate model of animal intelligence would provide a tremendous spur to its study in humans. It is not just their simplicity that makes animals attractive for study; their lack of a natural language (see Chapter 8) also makes them useful experimental subjects. To cite one example, the role that human language plays in problem solving is a matter of considerable debate. If it could be shown that animals possess sophisticated problem-solving skills without complex linguistic skills, then this would at least lend support to the view that human problem solving may not always depend on language.

One final point: The human brain contains 10 billion cells, each of which is in contact with many others. It has already been suggested that very little is known about the neural processes underlying animal cognition, and this is even more true of the way in which this complex collection of neurons and synapses controls the thoughts, actions, sensations, and experiences of humans. One approach to understanding the way in which the human brain functions is to study how this organ operates in animals. But unless brain researchers have a clear understanding of the cognitive processes of animals, the effects of their various experimental manipulations will be difficult to assess. In other words, it is essential to know *what* the animal brain is capable of achieving intellectually before it is possible to know at a physiological level *how* it is achieved. As this knowledge is acquired with animals, it is likely that considerable insights into the working of the human brain will follow.

HISTORICAL BACKGROUND

Animal intelligence has been studied in the laboratory for over 80 years, yet it is only recently that there has been a growth of interest in animal cognition. One reason is that many of the early researchers in this area were strongly opposed to the study of mental processes in animals.

Thorndike (1874–1949)

Towards the end of the last century, investigators such as Romanes (1882) regarded animals as possessing the intelligence to solve a problem by reasoning. This claim was not based upon careful experimentation but upon anecdotal evidence—for example, of cats operating the latches on gates without apparent tuition. Thorndike reacted, quite correctly, to this theorising by arguing that it provided nothing more than a sloppy anthropomorphic projection of our own mental processes onto the animals in question. He therefore began his experiments in order "to give the *coup de grace* to the despised theory that animals reason" (Thorndike, 1898, p. 39). This research entailed the study of animals escaping from puzzle boxes, and the stimulus–response theory it led to was to exert a profound influence on the study of animal intelligence.

In a typical experiment, a cat was placed into a box with a bowl of food outside (see Fig. 1.6). In order to reach the food, the cat had to respond in a specified way to open a door, perhaps by pulling a lever. Initially the cat would scratch and struggle in the box, and a considerable time elapsed before it responded correctly. Having made the response, the cat was allowed a few moments of access to food before being returned to the box for another trial. Thorndike's (1911) main concern was with the time it took the cat to escape from the apparatus across successive trials. The results from some typical studies are plotted in the learning curves in Fig. 1.7. The vertical axis of each graph represents the time in seconds that a subject took to escape from the box on any trial. The horizontal axis represents successive trials. It is evident that the time, or latency, to escape decreased over trials, and Thorndike (1911) regarded this change as evidence of learning, which raised two critically important issues: On the one hand, he was concerned with identifying what the subject had learned; and on the other, he wanted to specify as carefully as possible the conditions that promoted this learning.

Thorndike (1911) placed a great deal of emphasis on the fact that in general the decline in the latency to escape with continued training was gradual. This, he maintained, was clear evidence that animals did not use reason or thought to solve the problem. If these processes had been

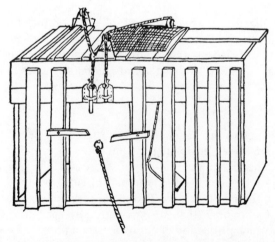

FIG. 1.6.   A sketch of a typical puzzle box used in experiments by Thorndike with cats (from Thorndike, 1898).

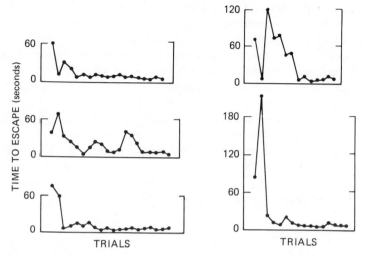

FIG. 1.7.   The time taken by individual cats to esape from a puzzle box across successive trials (from Thorndike, 1898).

employed, then the learning curve should drop suddenly at the point where the correct solution occurred to the cat. Prior to this there should have been little improvement in performance, because the subject would be ignorant of the solution to the problem. Thorndike (1911) argued from his results that learning is achieved not by a reasoning, but by a process of trial and error. That is, after being placed into the box, the subject eventually and quite by chance performed the correct response—perhaps by accidentally knocking the lever—and was able to escape. The subsequent decline in escape latencies was attributed to the food serving to stamp in or strengthen the correct response. This strengthening process was held to be gradual, which accounted for the progressive decline in latencies.

It is an oversimplification to say that Thorndike (1911) regarded the response itself as being strengthened. In fact, he proposed that the food served to strengthen a hypothetical connection between, on the one hand, the neural centre responsible for the perception of the stimuli that were present immediately prior to the execution of the response and, on the other, the centre responsible for the performance of the response itself. The greater the strength of this connection, or stimulus–response (S–R) association, the greater the likelihood of the animal responding correctly in the presence of the stimuli. These views were expressed as the Law of Effect: "Of several responses made to the same situation, those which are accompanied or closely followed by satisfaction to the animal will, other things being equal, be more firmly connected with the situation" (Thorndike, 1911, p. 244).

This law summarises Thorndike's view of animal intelligence, and it is clear that he did not regard this capacity as involving sophisticated mental processes. The only reference to such processes is the proposal that learning consists of the gradual strengthening of a connection between neural centres concerned with the perception of a stimulus and the performance of a response. This approach is nowadays regarded as too simple, but at the time it was extremely influential and, together with the proposal that reward is essential for learning, set the stage for 50 years of vigorous research and theoretical debate.

The method employed by Thorndike to study animal intelligence is now referred to either as instrumental or as operant conditioning. It is characterised by the experimenter delivering an event such as food to an animal after it has responded in a certain way.

Pavlov (1849–1936)

At much the same time as Thorndike was conducting his studies, a Russian physiologist, Pavlov, was using a fundamentally different procedure to study learning in animals. Instead of waiting for his subjects to respond before delivering food, he delivered it independently of the animal's behaviour whenever a particular signal had just been presented. This procedure is now referred to as either Pavlovian or classical conditioning. The term "conditioned stimulus" (CS) refers to the signal and "unconditioned stimulus" (US) refers to the food or other biologically significant event that follows it.

The subjects in many of Pavlov's (1927) experiments were hungry dogs. They were lightly restrained in an experimental chamber, such as that depicted in Fig. 1.8, and the CS—for example, the ticking of a metronome—was presented for a number of seconds before the delivery of the food US. At first the animal would show little reaction to the metronome, but as conditioning progressed, Pavlov (1927) noted that the dog salivated copiously during the CS even before the food was delivered. This response was defined as the conditioned response (CR). Because dogs do not normally salivate when they hear a metronome, such a change in behaviour can be regarded as evidence of learning. Pavlov's (1927) account of what this learning actually consisted of was couched in neurological terms that are no longer popular. But he also provided a less physiological account, which said, in effect, that when two stimuli, such as a metronome and food, were paired, the former came to be treated in some respects as if it were the latter. An alternative and far more influential account of the processes responsible for the appearance of the CR was provided by S–R theories of learning.

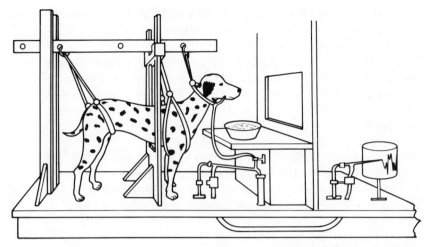

FIG. 1.8.   Diagram of the apparatus used by Pavlov for his study of classical conditioning with dogs (adapted from Yerkes & Morgulis, 1909).

The S–R Theorists

Following the publication of the work by Pavlov and Thorndike, a number of North American psychologists attempted to develop sophisticated accounts of behaviour from the premise that all learning involves the formation of stimulus–response connections. Thus despite the different methods involved in Pavlovian and instrumental conditioning, they were both assumed to result in the formation of Thorndike's S–R connections. As far as Pavlovian conditioning is concerned these connections were held to be between a representation of the CS and a component of the response elicited by the US.

Hull (1884–1952).   A weakness of the Law of Effect is that it is vague in identifying the type of event that will strengthen an S–R connection. It merely states that satisfaction will result in the growth of a connection. But what constitutes satisfaction for an animal? Hull's (1943) answer to this question was to propose that satisfaction can be regarded as a reduction in any of the animal's needs. This led him to develop a version of S–R theory that placed considerable importance on the way needs influence both what the animal learns and what it does. Hull suggested that all needs activate a single central motivational state that he termed "drive". An S–R connection was supposed to be strengthened whenever a response was followed by a reduction in the level of drive. Hence it was only responses that led to a reduction in a need that could be learned.

Although it provides a clearer specification than Thorndike of when learning will occur, there are still problems with Hull's approach. For instance, Olds and Milner (1954) demonstrated that rats can be trained to press a lever if it results in the electrical stimulation of certain regions of the brain. It is hard to identify the need reduced in these circumstances, yet learning has clearly occurred. A further property of drive is that it can energise whatever response the animal is currently performing. If it is pressing a lever for food, then the hungrier the animal is, the greater will be the level of drive and the more rapidly will it respond. Although there is some evidence to support this prediction (see Bolles, 1975, p. 95), there is much that contradicts other predictions from the theory. For example, the level of drive of an animal that is both hungry and thirsty will be greater than that of one that is just hungry. According to Hull's theory, therefore, being thirsty should enhance the rate at which an animal responds for food. In fact it is generally found that thirst has the opposite effect (e.g. Capaldi, Hovancik, & Lamb, 1975).

Guthrie (1886–1959).   One of Guthrie's (1935) main concerns was Thorndike's (1911) claim that reward, however it is defined, is essential for strengthening an S–R connection. As an alternative he made the simpler proposal that the mere pairing of a stimulus and a response is sufficient for learning to take place. Obviously when an animal is in a test chamber it makes a number of responses in addition to those that lead to reward, and it is necessary to explain why only the latter show a marked increase in frequency. Guthrie's (1935) solution to this problem was to suggest that a response will be connected to a set of stimuli only if it is the last one to occur in their presence. He further maintained that the delivery of reward will produce a marked environmental change, and this ensures that the instrumental response is connected to the stimuli that preceded its delivery. Support for this interpretation can be found in the surprising outcome of an experiment by Fowler and Miller (1963).

Hungry rats were trained to run down a straight alley for food. One group received only this treatment, whereas the others were given a mild foot shock as they were about to consume food in the goal box. For one group the shock was administered to the front paws, for the other group it was administered to the hind paws. The purpose of these different methods for delivering shock was to ensure that the shock induced different responses. When it was delivered to the front paws the rats lurched backwards, whereas they jumped forwards when the hind paws were shocked. Although the effect of such punishment in terms of the Law of Effect has not been considered, in keeping with common sense the law asserts that shock should disrupt running to the goal in both cases. In contrast, if Guthrie's (1935) claim is correct that the mere pairing of a stimulus and a response is sufficient to strengthen an S–R connection, then a different outcome is anticipated. While the rats are running down the alley for food, the lurch forward produced by shock to the hind paws will make them run faster. The pairing of this response with the apparatus cues will then strengthen an S(alley)–R(rapid running) connection, so that when placed in the alley subjects would be likely to run rapidly even before the shock is administered.

The results depicted in Fig. 1.9 support this interpretation by showing that the group receiving the hind-paw shock actually ran faster down the alley than the group receiving only food in the goal box. The figure also shows that running, relative to the food-only group, was disrupted when the shock was administered to the front paws. In this instance the jerk backwards would be the response that became connected to the alley cues, and its performance prior to the shock should disrupt running.

These findings do not challenge Thorndike's claim that all learning consists of the formation of S–R connections. They do suggest, however, that reward or punishment is not essential for this learning to take place. In the above study it was found that the mere contiguity of the alley cues and the shock-elicited response was sufficient to influence what the rats learned. Many, more recent, studies also support this conclusion, and it is now accepted that reward, however it is defined, is by no means essential for learning to occur.

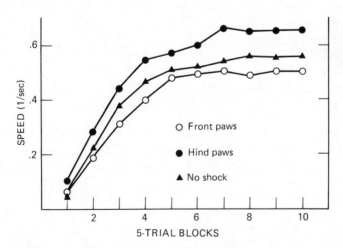

FIG. 1.9.   Speed of running down an alley for food by groups of rats that were shocked near the goal to either their front paws, or hind-paws, or that received no shock in the alley (adapted from Fowler & Miller, 1963)

Tolman (1886–1959)

For Tolman, an essential feature of instrumental conditioning is that it results in behaviour that is goal-directed or purposive. If a rat has been trained to press a lever for food, then he regards this response as being directed towards the goal of obtaining food. This seemingly obvious interpretation is completely lacking from S–R theory, which asserts that all an animal learns during instrumental conditioning is to respond in the presence of a given set of stimuli. It can even be said that because there is no mechanism in S–R theory that allows animals to anticipate the rewards of their behaviour, then whenever reward is delivered, it comes as a complete surprise.

The S–R analysis of Pavlovian conditioning is similarly counterintuitive. When a CS and a US are repeatedly paired, the theory states that animals will learn to perform a response whenever the CS is presented. No additional learning is assumed that would enable the subject to expect, during the CS, the US that is soon to follow.

Tolman (1932) viewed these as grave shortcomings of animal learning theory and developed a purposive account of behaviour, which rejected the S–R connection as the unit of learning. As far as Pavlovian conditioning is concerned, animals were assumed to learn a CS–US connection that made the CS a sign for the forthcoming US. For instrumental conditioning, the fundamental unit of learning was a S–R–US connection. The initial S–R link in this chain is similar to its counterpart in S–R theory, but the additional, final link permits the animal to know the consequences of its actions while it is responding. The precise manner in which these units operated is not of present concern; what should be stressed is that Tolman's (1932) formulation is a radical departure from S–R theory because it enables animals to anticipate stimuli that will soon be presented to them. Thus animals can be regarded as acquiring knowledge rather than responses, and it is this that marks Tolman's approach as cognitive rather than behavioural.

Tolman (1932) also objected to the claim of S–R theory that reward is essential for learning. Instead, rather like Guthrie, he suggested that for both CS–US and S–R–US learning to take place, all that was necessary was the contiguous pairing of the appropriate stimuli and responses.

Animals were not regarded as passive learners simply acquiring a collection of CS–US and S–R–US units as they interacted with their environment. They were seen, in contrast, as active processors of information integrating previously gained knowledge, as the following quotation concerning the operation of the brain (central office) indicates (Tolman, 1948, p. 192):

We assert that the central office is far more like a map control room than it is like an old-fashioned telephone exchange. The stimuli which are allowed in are not connected by just one-to-one switches to the outgoing responses. Rather, the incoming impulses are usually worked over and elaborated in the central control room into a tentative cognitive-like map of the environment. And it is this tentative map, indicating routes and paths and environmental relationships, which finally determines what responses, if any, the animal will finally release.

This excerpt captures the essence of an extremely original view of animal intelligence that anticipated by 25 years or so contemporary accounts of information processing in animals. Thus there is now abundant evidence that Pavlovian conditioning can result in the formation of CS–US connections—or associations, as they are now referred to (see Chapter 4). There is also evidence that during instrumental conditioning animals learn about the relationship between responses and their consequences (see Chapter 6). The notion that animals form cognitive maps is also growing in popularity (see Chapter 7). During his lifetime, however, Tolman's critique and experiments led to the refinement and increasing complexity of S–R theory rather than to its downfall.

In concluding this brief history, it is worth stating that the demise of S–R theory was not brought about by its failure to explain effects with which it was principally concerned, namely, instrumental conditioning. Instead, the decline in popularity of this theory was brought about by a resurgence of interest in the 1960s and 1970s in the mechanisms of Pavlovian condition-ing. It soon became apparent that attempts to explain all the effects obtained with this technique in terms of S–R learning would be unsuccessful. As a consequence, more cognitive explanations were developed to explain these findings, and this has been accompanied by a growth of interest in the cognitive mechanisms underlying behaviour in general.

2 The Representation of Stimuli

In Chapter 1 it was proposed that internal representations constitute the fundamental units of animal cognition. Once formed, these representations can be regarded as the building blocks from which other mental processes are constructed. As a prelude to studying these processes, this chapter will consider in some detail what is known of the way animals store information about the events to which they have been exposed.

An animal can be said to possess a representation if it can utilise information that is not available in its current environment. The representation may be of a specific stimulus, and here the term can be regarded as meaning no more than a memory of the event concerned. Indeed, throughout this text the terms "representation" and "memory" will often be used interchangeably. There may, however, be occasions when it is too restrictive to talk of knowledge being stored as a memory. Towards the end of this chapter I consider experiments that examine the capacity of animals to count, to time, and to form concepts of water, trees, and other natural categories. In these instances it is conceivable that the knowledge they utilise is more abstract than the memory for a concrete event, and it is to capture this possibility that the term "representation" is occasionally to be preferred.

One reason for starting an account of animal cognition with a discussion of representations is that it is likely to be the most prevalent of the cognitive capacities possessed by animals. An ability to recognise a previously encountered stimulus depends critically on the animal storing some representation of it. Unless it can do so and unless it can also compare the representation with the stimuli that currently confront it, all situations will appear to be novel. It is difficult to envisage how any animal but the most simple could survive without this ability. They would certainly be unable to profit from experience. If a rat becomes ill after consuming poisoned bait, then unless the bait can be recognised again, the rat will persist in consuming as much of this harmful substance as on the initial encounter. Without an ability to recognise landmarks from one occasion to the next, animals would be unable to learn about the permanent location of food, water, or their homes. Social animals would also be unable to identify the group to which they belong unless they can remember and recognise its members.

After describing a number of experiments demonstrating that animals store representations, this chapter looks at the information that these representations contain. It is left to Chapter 3 to discuss the processes that are responsible for the storage of a representation in the first place.

METHODS OF STUDY

In order to determine whether or not an animal has formed a representation of a previously presented stimulus, the experimenter must provide some sort of recognition test. The stimulus may be presented on a number of occasions, and, if the subject's behaviour to it should change, then this may be due to the existence of a memory of the initial exposure to the stimulus. The repeated presentations could involve the stimulus by itself (habituation); or the stimulus could serve as a signal for a biologically important event (conditioning). These are very simple techniques, and one reason for discussing them is to demonstrate that cognitive mechanisms are involved in the most elementary behavioural processes. Animal cognition is thus not to be seen as something that is involved only in sophisticated tasks.

Habituation

Hinde (1970, p. 577) defines habituation as "the relatively persistent waning of a response as a result of repeated stimulation which is not followed by any kind of reinforcement".[1] To explain this effect, several

---

[1]The term "reinforcement" is used in different ways by different authors. In this instance it refers to any biologically significant event such as food or shock. A rather different definition is developed in Chapter 6.

authors have proposed that the initial exposure to the stimulus results in the formation of a representation or model of it (Sokolov, 1963; Wagner, 1976). On subsequent trials, the stimulus is believed to be compared with this model, and if the two should correspond, then the reaction to the stimulus will be slight. In reality this is a difficult claim to substantiate, as we shall see shortly; but first a few examples should serve to demonstrate the ubiquity of habituation.

Jennings (1906) reports that paramecia react to being touched by contracting. With continued touching, however, the number of stimulations needed to produce this response increases to about 20 or 30. In a study of the Pacific sea anemone, Logan (1975) has shown that the contractions produced by a novel strong stream of water are reduced considerably in magnitude after about 30 trials. The three-spined stickleback will respond aggressively to any territorial rivals, but this weakens with the continued presence of the same rival (Peeke & Veno, 1973). Finally, sounding a relatively loud tone to a rabbit will, among other reactions, produce a pronounced change in the rate of blood flow through the ear, brought about by vasoconstriction, which diminishes with repeated exposure to the tone (Whitlow, 1975).

It is this last example that has provided some of the best evidence that habituation depends upon the existence of a representation of the repeated stimulus. Rabbits were placed into a sound- and light-proof chamber. After a while a 1-sec tone (S1) was presented, which was followed 30, 60, or 150 sec later by another 1-sec tone (S2). A resting period of 150 sec then elapsed before the next trial began; this again consisted of the presentation of the pair of tones S1 and S2, separated by one of the above three intervals. Training continued in this manner, with S1 and S2 on some trials being identical in frequency and on other trials being different. Whitlow's (1975) main concern was with the influence that S1 had on the response elicited by S2.

The principal findings of the study are depicted in Fig. 2.1. The vertical axis represents the maximum change in vasoconstriction that was recorded on any trial. It is evident that when S1 and S2 were identical (left-hand panel) and the interval between them was relatively short, the response to the second member of the pair was weaker than to the first. With a longer interval of 150 sec, however, the response to the second recovered and was much the same as to the first. Thus the repetition of a tone can result in habituation, provided that the interval between its presentations is relatively short.

According to a theory developed by Wagner (1976), the offset of S1 will leave a decaying representation of itself. If S2 is then presented before this decay is complete—that is, within 150 sec—and it matches the representation of S1, habituation will be observed. There is, however, an alternative explanation that needs to be considered. For a short while after each

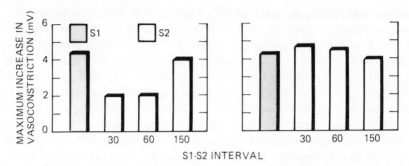

FIG. 2.1. The maximum response to S1 and S2 in the study by Whitlow (1975) on trials when they were separated by intervals of 30, 60, or 150 sec. The left-hand panel shows the results when S1 and S2 were identical, the right-hand panel when these stimuli were different. The measure of vasoconstriction is the increase from resting level in the output of a plethysmograph connected to the rabbit's ear (adapted from Whitlow, 1975).

response, the effector system may be fatigued, so that subsequent presentations of the tone will be unable to induce a large response. The simplicity of this account makes it attractive, and it may even be true for the findings with paramecia reported by Jennings (1906). But for the rabbit it is unlikely. The right-hand panel of Fig. 2.1 indicates the maximum response to S1 and S2 for the trials when they differed. Although the two different tones elicited the same response in the same effector system, on these trials the response to S2 was as strong as that to S1, no matter how short the interval between them. Hence it is only when S2 is the same as S1 that with short intervals between them the response is weaker to the second stimulus.

Yet another explanation for Whitlow's (1975) demonstration of habituation is that once a stimulus has been presented, the cells responsible for its reception become temporarily less sensitive. The occurrence of S2, when it is the same as S1, will then have less of an impact on the central nervous system and may produce a weaker response than S1. The results obtained when S1 and S2 were different are consistent with this interpretation, as the use of different stimuli will presumably excite different receptors.

Fortunately, there is an additional finding by Whitlow (1975), which allows this account to be rejected. Subjects received similar training to that described previously, but the interval between S1 and S2 was always 60 sec. On half the trials a 2-sec distractor, consisting of a flashing light followed by electrotactile stimulation, was presented 20 sec after S1; on the remaining trials this complex stimulus was omitted. On trials when S1 and S2 were identical, the response to S2 was weak if the distractor was omitted, but when this stimulus was presented, a much stronger response was elicited by S2. In other words, the distractor disrupted habituation with S2, which is an effect usually referred to as dishabituation.

This example of dishabituation is important because it suggests that S2 is capable of eliciting a strong response, even though it is the same as S1 and the interval between them is short. This in turn implies that S2 is as well perceived as S1 even when they are the same, and that sensory adaptation is not an adequate explanation of habituation. One possibility, however, is that the distractor enhances the responsiveness of the animal to any stimulus that is presented shortly after it (e.g. Thompson & Spencer, 1966). Thus S2 may have been poorly perceived by the rabbits but still elicited a strong response because of the arousing effects of the distractor. A reason for rejecting this possibility can be found in the impact of the distractor on trials when S1 and S2 were different. The arousing effects of the distractor should also be evident on these trials, yet the response to S2 was much the same on trials with and without the distractor. The account offered by Wagner (1976) for the dishabituating effect of the distractor when S1 and S2 were the same is quite straightforward. It assumes that this stimulus effectively erased the memory of S1, or made subjects forget it, so that when S2 was presented it would not match a representation left by a preceding stimulus.

Taken together, Whitlow's (1975) results strongly suggest that habituation in the rabbit depends upon the existence of a representation of the repeatedly presented stimulus. The question is now raised as to whether all instances of habituation are due to the same process. It is not possible to review the many studies investigating habituation, but most of them lack the necessary control conditions to enable unambiguous conclusions to be drawn. For the present we must therefore conclude that habituation, in at least some cases, depends upon the ability of animals to represent stimuli. But whether this is true for all, or even the majority, of instances remains to be seen.

Conditioning

As a method for studying the representational capacity of animals, habituation has its limitations. Not all the stimuli that an animal may be capable of representing will have response-eliciting properties, or, if they do, these may be so slight as to be extremely difficult to study. As a consequence a representation of a repeatedly presented stimulus may have been formed and yet result in no behavioural change to indicate its existence. An alternative method for studying this aspect of animal cognition is to endow the stimulus in question with the capacity to control a response. If on a subsequent trial the response should recur, then this may well be due to the subject possessing a relatively enduring representation of the stimulus, as well as of how to respond in its presence. Both Pavlovian and instrumental conditioning can be used for this purpose.

Recall that in Pavlovian conditioning a neutral stimulus, the CS, is used as a signal for the delivery of a biologically important event, the US. At first, the animal may not react to the CS at all, but with training a conditioned response (CR) will be elicited whenever this stimulus is presented. Unless the animal is capable of storing a representation of the CS, it will be unable to recognise this stimulus as the one that signals the US and will never perform a CR.

Similarly, it is easy to see why the success of instrumental conditioning also depends upon the formation of relatively permanent representations of stimuli. If a rat receives a reward pellet whenever it presses a lever, then unless it recognises the lever on future occasions it will be unable to benefit from this training.

The value of Pavlovian conditioning for studying the cognitive capacities of animals, especially simple ones, can be demonstrated by considering an experiment by Hennessey, Rucker, and McDiarmid (1979). Protozoa are the simplest life forms, consisting of a single, complex cell. Unlikely as it may seem, there has been considerable interest in the question of whether or not these creatures are susceptible to Pavlovian conditioning. To examine this possibility, the advanced protozoa, *Paramecia*, were individually placed into a fluid in a glass tube containing two electrodes. The tube was then put on a loudspeaker, and subjects were observed through a microscope for a number of conditioning trials that took place at regular 10-sec intervals. Each trial consisted of the presentation of a 4-sec tone, which caused the tube to vibrate. During the last 2 sec of the tone, a shock US was applied via the electrodes. At first the tone had little influence on the subjects, whereas the shock resulted in a backward jerk and axial spinning. After a number of trials the frequency of both these responses increased during the first 2 sec of the tone (see Fig. 2.2). Hennessey et al. (1979) regarded this change in behaviour during the tone as evidence of successful Pavlovian conditioning. If this interpretation is correct, then it suggests that even the paramecium is capable of storing a representation of an external stimulus for at least 10 sec.

Experiments such as that just described indicate that animals store representations, but they show us very little about the nature of the information that is stored. In order to obtain a more detailed impression of the information encoded in a representation, there are two phenomena associated with both Pavlovian and instrumental conditioning that have proved especially valuable: discrimination and generalisation.

Discrimination.   Discrimination is said to be demonstrated when subjects have been trained to respond in the presence of one stimulus but not of another. In Pavlovian conditioning, for example, this may be

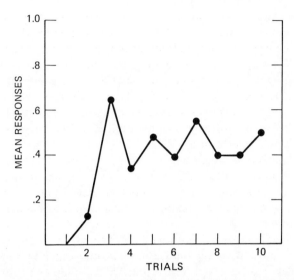

FIG. 2.2.   Acquisition by paramecia of anticipatory CRs that were recorded during the first 2 sec of a tone that signalled shock. Mean responses were calculated for each trial by dividing the total number of responses by the number of subjects (adapted from Hennessey et al., 1979).

achieved by pairing one CS with a US and a different CS with nothing. At first a CR might be observed in the presence of both stimuli, but with continued training responding will be confined predominantly to the CS that signals the US. Clearly this differentiation of responding can be achieved only if the subject possesses a representation of the CS paired with the US that is of sufficient detail to enable it to be differentiated from the other stimulus. If this were not the case, then subjects would behave identically in the presence of both stimuli. It may come as some surprise to learn that Hennessey et al. (1979) were able to demonstrate discrimination learning with their paramecia.

The method was a variant of the original and involved two different tones, one of a frequency of 300 Hz, the other of 500 Hz. For half the subjects the low-frequency tone was followed by shock (CS+), and the high-frequency tone was followed by nothing (CS−). This relationship was reversed for the remaining subjects. It is evident from Fig. 2.3 that initially this training resulted in a CR during both CS+ and CS−, but after as few as 10 trials with each stimulus responding was virtually confined to CS+.

The success of paramecia with this discrimination indicates that they must store a relatively precise representation of CS+. I do not have any idea how a single-celled animal is capable of storing this sort of information. Nonetheless, the results suggest they do, and the experiment

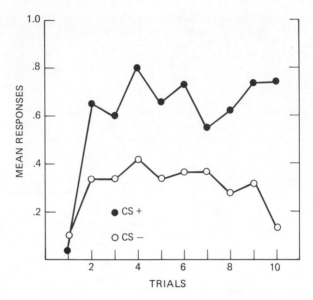

FIG. 2.3.   Acquisition of CRs by paramecia during discrimination training with one tone (CS+) that signalled shock, and a different tone (CS−) that signalled nothing (adapted from Hennessey et al., 1979).

indicates how discrimination training can provide information about the content of representations. It also provides an excellent control procedure for ruling out a number of trivial explanations of the conditioning reported by Hennessey et al. (1979) in their initial experiment. For instance, it might be argued that giving shock to paramecia enhances their responsiveness to any stimulus, whether or not that stimulus is actually paired with shock. We can, however, reject this interpretation because it incorrectly predicts that the stimuli of the second experiment should have been treated identically.

Generalisation.   The phenomenon of generalisation is demonstrated in an instrumental conditioning study by Guttman and Kalish (1956). Hungry pigeons were placed into a conditioning chamber in which a circular response key was located above a magazine to which food could be delivered (see Fig. 2.4). Pecking at the key when it was illuminated with a certain colour resulted in the occasional delivery of food. Once subjects were responding at a relatively steady rate, a period of generalisation testing was conducted. This involved the projection of different colours, as well as the training colour, onto the key. Figure 2.5 shows the rates of responding at the key for the different colours of light that were used.

FIG. 2.4.   A typical conditioning chamber for pigeons containing three response keys.

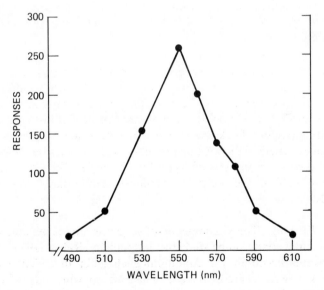

FIG. 2.5.   The mean rate of responding by a group of pigeons to a colour with which they were trained (550 nm) and to novel colours (adapted from Guttman & Kalish, 1956).

In this study the wavelength of the colour projected onto the key during training was 550 nm, and it is evident that this resulted in the highest rate of responding in the test phase. When different colours were projected onto the key, there was a decline in response rate, with the lowest rates resulting with the colours most removed from that used during training. The fact that responding occurs at all with conditions that differ from those present during training demonstrates generalisation, but the fact that animals respond less to these other stimuli demonstrates generalisation decrement.

The occurrence of generalisation, of any magnitude, indicates that subjects must have formed a representation of the training stimulus and that this has certain common features with the test stimuli. Unless this were true, the test stimuli would be treated as if they were totally unfamiliar, and generalisation would not be observed at all. Of greater interest is the demonstration of generalisation decrement. For this to occur, subjects must be sensitive to the difference between the training and test stimuli. This, in turn, depends upon the representation of the training stimulus being sufficiently detailed to permit the difference from the test stimulus to be detected. Thus by inspecting Fig. 2.6, we can conclude that the information stored in the representation of the 550-nm training light was precise enough to enable light of 560 nm to be identified as being different to the training colour.

SIMPLE REPRESENTATIONS

Having examined some techniques for studying the representational capacity of animals, the remainder of this chapter considers the nature of this capacity. My principal concern is with the range of events that animals can represent. In the first part, events that consist of only a single stimulus are considered; this is followed by a discussion of some of the more complex information that animals store.

The results from a variety of conditioning studies, both instrumental and Pavlovian, indicate that animals can represent stimuli belonging to the five principal human senses: sight, sound, taste, smell, and touch. Little is said here about such stimuli because they are frequently employed in standard conditioning studies and reference is made to them throughout this text, as well as in many others (e.g. Mackintosh, 1974). In this section I focus on the ability of animals to remember information that may be inaccessible to the human senses. An interest in this ability has arisen because many different species migrate or home over great distances in the apparent absence of cues that for humans would be essential for successful navigation. Chapter 7 considers the way this navigation is achieved; the present section determines whether or not animals are capable of storing information that is potentially of value for navigation.

Magnetic Fields

Animals might benefit from being able to detect magnetic fields, because the magnetic properties of the earth provide a pervasive source of information for orientation. Occasionally, therefore, authors have suggested that animals have a magnetic sense and use it for navigation. Yeagley (1947) and more recently Keeton (1974) made such a claim to explain pigeon homing. If magnetic fields are to provide cues for navigation, then it is insufficient for animals merely to be able to detect this source of information; they must also be able to remember the magnetic fields associated with certain locations. Without this capacity, they will be unable to infer from the present magnetic information the direction they must travel in order, say, to return home.

Despite the potential benefits of being able to store information about magnetic fields, there is just one laboratory demonstration of this capacity. Bookman (1977) placed pigeons into one end of a tunnel that was surrounded by coils that could induce a magnetic field. At the other end were two boxes, and the presence or absence of the magnetic field indicated which box contained food. As training progressed, the tendency to go directly to the correct box increased significantly. Although this improvement could be due to the animals' learning about the importance of the magnetic field, it should be borne in mind that the experiment was successful only when pairs of birds were released into the tunnel together. Why this should be necessary is not at all clear.

In contrast to the success of this unusual experiment, there has been a number of failures to condition birds with magnetic fields (Delius & Emmerton, 1978; Kreithen & Keeton, 1974). These failures are unlikely to be due to an inability by pigeons to detect magnetic fields. Pigeon homing is less accurate when there is a magnetic storm (Gould, 1982), or when they are in the vicinity of anomalies in the Earth's magnetic field (Walcott, 1978). It is, therefore, possible that pigeons possess a magnetic sense, but they have difficulty in learning about the significance of this information when it signals a US such as shock or food. After all, a change in a magnetic field is hardly likely to signal these events naturally, and it is plausible that animals lack the processes that would allow good conditioning with a magnetic field in an artificial environment. If this is correct, then it will require a particularly ingenious experiment to determine whether or not pigeons are capable of storing information about magnetic fields.

Air Pressure

A change in altitude will necessarily be accompanied by a change in air pressure. Accordingly, any animals, but in particular birds, that possess the capacity to detect and remember levels of air pressure should be able to compute their altitude. In order to examine whether pigeons are capable of utilising this source of information, Delius and Emmerton (1978) used a 10-sec change in air pressure to signal the delivery of electric shock. Initially the birds were unresponsive to the change, but as conditioning progressed, a CR of accelerated heart-rate was recorded whenever this stimulus was presented. The change in pressure was slight and indicates that pigeons can remember changes in air pressure that correspond to a vertical displacement of as little as 20 metres.

Rapid fluctuations in air pressure constitute sound, and if they are of sufficient intensity and within a range of 20 to 20,000 Hz, they will be heard by humans. Below the lower threshold of human hearing, however, there are slowly oscillating changes in air pressure with a frequency as low as 0.1 Hz that may be detected by other species. These infrasounds can be generated by thunderstorms, magnetic storms, earthquakes, and the impact of air currents on mountain ranges. One important property of infrasound is that it can travel many thousands of kilometres with little attenuation or distortion. Hence sonic booms generated by Concorde crossing the Atlantic have been recorded in New York from a distance of 1000 km (Balachandran, Dunn, & Rind, 1977).

Kreithen (1978) has noted that an ability to detect infrasound would provide valuable meteorological and navigational information for animals. In order to test whether pigeons are sensitive to this sort of stimulation, Yodlowski, Kreithen, and Keeton (1977) conducted a conditioning study in which a burst of infrasound, with a frequency of 0.1 Hz, served as a CS paired with shock. Even though the infrasound was totally inaudible to humans, conditioning with the pigeons was successful.

Pigeons are thus capable of detecting and storing information about infrasound, but there may be limitations on the use of this source of information, especially for navigation. Infrasound is prone to severe interference by local winds and turbulence, and its source would also be extremely difficult for a stationary animal to localise. Unless animals possess mechanisms for circumventing these problems, infrasound would not be a useful tool for navigation. Nonetheless, as Baker (1984) points out, it would be unlikely that pigeons can perceive infrasound unless it serves some purpose.

Polarised and Ultraviolet Light

Humans appear to be insensitive both to polarised and to ultraviolet light, and for a while it was thought that this constraint applied to all vertebrates. In contrast, insects such as bees have been known for some time to be able to detect both types of light (e.g. Von Frisch, 1950). But a recent report by Kreithen (1978) now suggests that one vertebrate, the pigeon again, can detect and be conditioned with ultraviolet as well as with polarised light. With both classes of stimuli a CR of an accelerated heart-rate was detected when they were used to signal the occurrence of an electric shock. An ability to perceive polarised light is of value for navigation, providing some blue sky is visible, because it allows the sun to be located when it is obscured by clouds. But whether pigeons use it in this way remains to be seen.

COMPLEX STIMULI

So far it has been shown that animals can represent a single stimulus like a tone or a certain colour. Very often, however, stimuli do not occur independently, but they form part of a more complex configuration, and this raises the question of whether in addition to representing individual stimuli animals can also represent combinations of stimuli. Experiments with conditional discriminations suggest, in fact, that animals often have little difficulty in representing at least simple combinations of stimuli. Rescorla (1981) conducted Pavlovian conditioning with pigeons in which the visual stimuli A and B together or C and D together signalled food, whereas the combinations of A and C, or B and D were never followed by food. With this design no stimulus is uniquely associated with food or its absence, yet the discrimination was readily mastered; and this was presumably achieved by animals remembering the different combinations of stimuli and their significance. In this section I shall examine whether animals can remember more complex visual stimuli than those composed of two elements. This will be followed by a discussion of the way animals represent patterns of auditory stimuli, including bird song. Then, after looking at the ability of animals to represent space, time, and number, the section will close with an evaluation of their concept-learning skills.

Visual Stimuli

Photographic Slides.   An experiment by Vaughan and Greene (1984), demonstrates quite clearly that pigeons have a very accurate memory for complex visual stimuli. Subjects were placed into a conditioning chamber with a clear response key that was about 5 cm in diameter. They then received discrimination training in which a series of different slides was projected onto the key. Responding in the presence of some (S+) resulted in the delivery of food, whereas responding in the presence of the remainder (S−) did not. When the slides were first introduced, subjects naturally responded at a similar rate to all of them, but as training progressed, the pigeons came to peck more rapidly at those designated as S+ and more slowly at those designated as S−. This discrimination can only be possible if the pigeons remembered the slides and how to respond in their presence.

The two remarkable features of this study are (1) that the slides between which pigeons successfully discriminated were quite complex, and (2) that there were so many of them. In one experiment, different random squiggles of the sort depicted in Fig. 2.6 were used. In spite of the large number of slides employed (80 S+ and 80 S−), performance was extremely accurate by the end of training although, it must be admitted, training continued for just on 1000 sessions. Vaughan and Greene (1984) conducted a similar study in which the pigeons were shown a large number of ordinary snapshots. Some of the slides that were used are depicted in

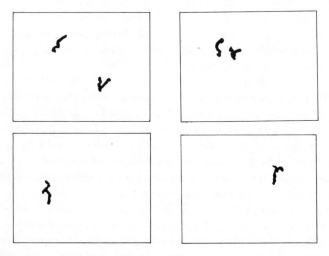

FIG. 2.6.   Examples of the slides used in a study by Vaughan and Greene (1984). Slides in the left-hand column signalled the availability of food, whereas those in the right-hand column signalled its absence (from Vaughan & Greene, 1984).

Fig. 2.7; for each pair, one picture was always associated with reward and the other with nonreward. Quite surprisingly, only 18 trials with each of the bottom pair in Fig. 2.7b were necessary before the discrimination between them was perfected.

Mental Rotation.   Considerable insight into the way humans construct and manipulate visual representations has been obtained by studying an effect known as mental rotation (e.g. Shepard & Metzler, 1971). An experiment by Hollard and Delius (1982) shows that it may also be possible to study this effect with animals. They first developed a technique for studying the phenomenon in humans under conditions analogous to those subsequently used for pigeons. A panel containing three circular response keys was placed in front of a subject. A geometric shape, the sample, was then projected onto the central key, and the subject had to tap it with a stick. The response was followed immediately by the projection of two transformations of the sample onto the side keys. One of these test shapes was identical to the sample, whereas the other was a mirror reversal of it; in addition, both shapes were rotated to an equivalent degree from the orientation of the sample (see left-hand side of Fig. 2.8). For a small financial reward, the subject had to identify as swiftly as possible the test shape that was the same as the sample. In keeping with many related studies, the right-hand side of Fig. 2.8 shows that the time taken to identify the correct shape was directly related to the extent to which its orientation differed from the sample. The generally accepted explanation for this effect is that an image is first formed of the test shape. This is then rotated mentally until its orientation corresponds to the sample, and a decision is then be made as to whether it is a copy or a mirror reversal of the sample. Such mental rotation is assumed to progress at a constant rate, so that the greater the angular displacement of the test and sample stimuli, the longer it will be before the image is in the required orientation.

The only difference in the task for pigeons was that they had to peck the response keys and the reward was food. The results, also shown in the right-hand side of Fig. 2.8, are both surprising and quite different from those of human subjects. First, at all test orientations the reaction times of the pigeons were faster than those of humans. Second, the speed at which the pigeons responded was unaffected by the size of the difference between the orientation of the sample and test stimuli.

Intriguing as these results might be, it is hard to decide what significance should be attached to them. The faster reaction times of the pigeons might be due to the fact that they found the responses easier to perform, or that they had received more training than the humans. And it is difficult to know why the pigeons' reaction times should have been unaffected by the angular rotation of the test stimuli. Perhaps they are more adept at mental

FIG. 2.7a. Examples of the photographs that were used in a study by Vaughan and Greene (1984). Pictures in the left-hand column signalled the availability of food (from Vaughan & Greene, 1984).

rotation than humans, or perhaps their perceptual world is entirely different to ours and represents objects irrespective of their angle of orientation (Hollard & Delius, 1982). Unfortunately, the vigour of the debate concerning the nature of mental imagery in humans suggests that these and related issues will not be easily resolved for animals.

Auditory Stimuli

Music. The ability of the pigeon to store complex visual representations is matched by its capacity to remember complex auditory stimuli. Porter and Neuringer (1984) describe an experiment in which pigeons had to listen to excerpts of J. S. Bach's Toccatas and Fugues in D Minor and F for organ, which alternated with Stravinsky's "Rite of Spring" for orchestra. The music was played in a conditioning chamber in which there were two response keys. Pecks on one key were occasionally rewarded during the music by Bach, whereas pecks on the other key were rewarded during the "Rite of Spring". As the excerpts of each piece were of 20 min

FIG. 2.7b. Further examples from Vaughan & Greene (1984). Pictures in the left-hand column signalled the availability of food (from Vaughan & Greene, 1984).

duration and a trial lasted on average 1 min, the exact nature of the music varied considerably from trial to trial. Nonetheless, with sufficient training all subjects were showing a clear discrimination between the music, and 3 out of 4 subjects responded almost perfectly.

It might be thought that this training resulted in pigeons learning to discriminate between an organ (Bach) and an orchestra (Stravinsky), but the results from a series of generalisation tests make this unlikely. The tests consisted of various novel pieces of music by a variety of composers. There was no indication that organ works necessarily resulted in responding on the "Bach" key, or orchestral works on the "Stravinsky" key. Instead, the fairest conclusion to be drawn from these test trials is that subjects were likely to respond on the "Stravinsky" key whenever they heard modern music and on the "Bach" key in the presence of baroque music.

One problem with the stimuli employed by Porter and Neuringer (1984) is that they are extremely complex, which makes it difficult to identify experimentally the way in which they are remembered and recognised. Consequently it is not known how pigeons are able to distinguish between

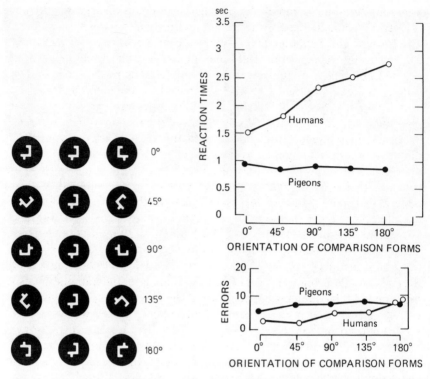

FIG. 2.8.   Examples of the stimuli used by Hollard and Delius (1982) in a study of mental rotation (left-hand side). Each row depicts a different test orientation, with the sample presented in the centre column and the two test stimuli in the side columns. In these examples the test stimuli in the left-hand column are rotations of the sample, whereas in the right-hand column they are rotated mirror-reversals of the sample. The right-hand panel shows the reaction times for humans and pigeons on this task for various degrees of rotation of the test stimuli. The percentage of trials on which an error was made by humans and pigeons is shown in the lower portion of this panel (from Delius, 1985)

baroque and modern music. A step towards overcoming this problem is to use simpler sequences of sounds that can then be carefully manipulated to provide insights into the nature of their corresponding representations. To date, the conclusions that can be drawn from such research are, it must be acknowledged, not very startling.

Artificial Tunes. D'Amato and Salmon (1982) rewarded rats and monkeys for pressing a lever in the presence of one computer-generated tune, but not while another was being played. The tunes consisted of a fixed sequence of notes that lasted for 4 sec and then repeated itself. Both rats and monkeys learned this discrimination, and, perhaps unexpectedly, it was mastered more rapidly by rats than by monkeys, suggesting that at least two mammalian species represent and recognise tunes.

D'Amato and Salmon's (1984) more recent work, however, seriously challenges this conclusion. Rats and monkeys were again trained to respond differently in the presence of two tunes. The notes of one had an average frequency of about 2.8 kHz, whereas the average frequency of the other tune was about 0.9 kHz. In addition, control groups received discrimination training with the same notes of the two tunes but presented in a random sequence from one trial to the next, thus removing their tunefulness yet retaining their average frequency. Both groups learned the discrimination at the same rate, which led D'Amato and Salmon (1984) to conclude that it is the average frequency of the notes rather than their pattern that animals use to represent tunes. In the light of this finding, considerable caution should be exercised in drawing conclusions from the Porter and Neuringer (1984) study about the musical ability of pigeons.

Whether all animals are as poor as rats and monkeys at learning tunes was questioned in a study by Hulse, Cynx, and Humpal (1984) involving starlings. Again using tones generated by computers, the authors success-fully trained their subjects to peck a key if the tune consisted of a series of tones that increased in frequency and not to peck the key when the tune was composed of a descending sequence of tones. Because the average frequency of both tunes was the same, it is difficult to explain the successful performance of the starlings in terms of the strategy proposed by D'Amato and Salmon (1984). Instead, the subjects may have learned about the relationship between the notes of the tune. But once again a degree of caution is required in the interpretation of this study. Hulse et al. (1984) report that their starlings were trained with notes taken from the same octave. When generalisation studies were conducted with ascending and descending tunes in octaves other than the one used for training, the discrimination between them was very poor indeed. This finding stands in marked contrast to the facility of humans to recognise the same tune when it is played transposed up or down an octave. At best, these results imply that starlings can recognise only the pattern of the notes with which they were trained. At worst it indicates, as Hulse et al. (1984, p. 195) point out, that starlings did not learn the tunes at all. The training tunes ended on different notes and the subjects may have solved the discrimination simply by attending to the final notes of the sequence. Thus there is currently very little evidence showing that animals can acquire and retain information about the relationship between the items of a complex auditory sequence when it is artificial.

Bird Song.   There is, in contrast, abundant evidence showing that many birds learn patterns of sound when it constitutes their natural song.

Furthermore, in certain cases it is also clear that the birds are constrained to acquiring certain songs, and this might account for the difficulty that some species have in learning artificial tunes. To give an indication of the role of learning and of these constraints on bird-song acquisition, we focus initially on Marler's (1970) work with the white-crowned sparrow. Some of the exceptions to his findings, which have been recorded from other species, are then considered briefly.

The song of the white-crowned sparrow consists of two components: a whistle, which lasts for about 500 to 1000 msec, followed by a trill of much the same length. For sparrows living in the same area there is rather little variation in the structure either of the whistle or of the trill. In the case of groups of sparrows from different areas, the construction of these components varies quite considerably. As a consequence, groups of sparrows can be said to possess their own dialects.

In nature the young male white-crowned sparrow leaves the nest at about 10 days of age, and for the next 20 to 100 days he is exposed repeatedly to the adult male song of his father and neighbours. This singing declines in the autumn and winter. The following spring, when he is about a year old and has reached sexual maturity, the young sparrow produces for the first time a good approximation to the local dialect of the adult male song.

By acoustically isolating birds of different ages for various intervals, Marler (1970) has shown that the development of the adult song depends upon the bird being exposed to it for a period between the ages of 10 to 50 days. A bird that hears the adult song during this period will produce a good copy of it on reaching sexual maturity. One that is not exposed to the adult song at all, or only after the age of 50 days, produces a song that does not correspond even to the basic structure of the species' song. The white-crowned sparrow is also constrained to the type of song it can learn. Marler (1970) found that these birds, when raised in isolation, are unable to learn the songs of other species no matter at what age they hear them.

Bird-song learning is, however, not always so constrained. As far as the time of memorisation is concerned, the chaffinch (Slater & Ince, 1982) and the marsh wren (Kroodsma, 1978) are both able to learn the adult song of their species when they are a year old; the canary can learn new songs throughout its adult life. Greater constraint does seem to apply to the song that is learnt, as in general birds learn only the songs of their species, but this is not always true. The white-crowned sparrow (Baptista & Morton, 1981) and the indigo bunting (Payne, 1981) can learn the songs of other species provided they interact with them, whereas parrots and mynahs are famous for their imitative skills. But perhaps most impressive in this respect is the marsh warbler. This bird constructs its own idiosyncratic song by mimicking and combining the components of the songs of an average of 76 different species of birds (Dowsett-Lemaire, 1979).

Given these constraints and their variety, it is likely that birds will differ markedly in the artificial tunes that they can learn and when they can learn them. It is also possible that some birds will be better at learning artificial tunes than monkeys and rats, whose vocal communications are composed of relatively simple sequences of sounds.

Spatial Relationships

Complex stimuli not only contain a number of elements, but they are often constructed in such a way as to create a fixed pattern. With the exception of bird-song learning, very little of the evidence considered thus far unequivocally demonstrates that animals are capable of learning such patterns. Thus in studies with complex visual stimuli the pigeons may simply have remembered the features that distinguished rewarded from nonrewarded slides, rather than remembering the entire pattern created by each slide. Investigations of the memory of animals for spatial relationships, however, suggest they can remember patterns.

Maze Cues. A simple demonstration that rats can represent spatial relationships comes from a study by Cheng and Gallistel (1984). The apparatus they used was an elongated X maze housed in a covered rectangular enclosure (see left-hand side of Fig. 2.9). In each corner of this enclosure was a card showing a unique pattern that served as a cue for the rat. During a pretraining phase the arm pointing to a given cue was consistently baited with a fixed quantity of food at the start of each trial. Using the terminology of Fig. 2.9, the end nearest cue A was baited with 18 pellets, that nearest C with 6 pellets, and that nearest B with 1 pellet; there were no pellets beside landmark D. A rat was then placed at the intersection of the arms and allowed to collect the food. Eventually, on

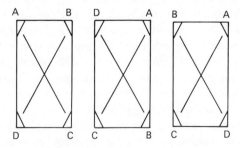

FIG. 2.9.   The relationship between the landmarks A, B, C, and D, and the arms of an elongated X maze for the various stages of a spatial learning experiment (adapted from Cheng & Gallistel, 1984).

being placed in the apparatus a rat would go directly to A; after consuming the pellets there, it would visit C and finally B.

Once they had acquired this strategy, the rats received test trials in which the cues were transposed in a variety of ways. The new positions of the cues are depicted in the centre and right-hand panels of Fig. 2.9. Two points merit emphasis: First, the quantity of food associated with each cue remained the same throughout the experiment. Hence if rats had learned solely that a given quantity of food was located near a given cue, then moving the cues should not disrupt the sequence in which the pellets are collected. Cheng and Gallistel (1984) report, in contrast, that both rearrangements resulted in a selection of arms that can best be described as random. The second point is that in one rearrangement—centre panel— the adjacent members of each cue remained the same; they had merely been rotated around the apparatus. Hence, for example, instead of a short side separating A and B, as was the case during training, these stimuli were separated by a long side. Despite the original order of the cues being retained, the distortion of their spatial relationships had a profoundly disruptive influence on performance.

The fact that both manipulations had such a disruptive effect suggests that during pretraining subjects had acquired an accurate representation of the spatial relationship between the cues. Without such a representation they would have been unable to detect the various transformations that were employed, and their performance would not have been affected by the test trials. Quite why such simple manipulations should so disrupt responding is an interesting question that is left unanswered by the present study.

Stars.   From the simplicity of an experiment that involves only four stimuli we now move to a study that involves all the stars in the northern hemisphere. Emlen (1970) was interested in the migration of the indigo bunting. These North American birds migrate southwards in the autumn and northwards in the spring. As the time to migrate approaches, they start to build up fat deposits to provide energy reserves for the forthcoming journey. They also become restless, and if they are held in a cage this restlessness is oriented towards the direction of migration. By keeping a record of this restless activity, it is thus possible to infer the direction of migration when the bird is released. The restless activity is referred to as *Zugunruhe*.

Emlen (1970) hand-reared indigo buntings in an aviary that was entirely cut off from the outside world, except that the light–dark cycle coincided with that occurring naturally. As autumn approached, two groups spent a number of nights in a planetarium, and a third group remained in the aviary. While they were in the planetarium, the buntings were exposed to a configuration of stars. For one group the configuration rotated around the normal north–south axis, but for the second group it rotated around a different axis. When it was time for the autumn migration, all three groups spent a test session of several hours in the planetarium with the stars motionless. The buntings were retained in small cages that indicated the orientation of their *Zugunruhe*.

The direction of their restless activity was essentially random for those birds that had remained in the aviary until the test session, which suggests they lacked a preferred direction for migration. The remaining birds, on the other hand, did express a preference, but it differed for the two groups. The group for which the stars had rotated around the north–south axis indicated a tendency to migrate southwards. The preferred direction for the other group was also along the axis of rotation they had experienced, but this was obviously not towards the south.

The interpretation of these results is both complex and interesting. The random behaviour of the buntings that spent all but the test session in the aviary indicates that extended exposure to the stars is essential if they are to migrate in the correct direction. As the groups that were exposed to the stars expressed different orientations of *Zugunruhe*, the movement of the stars must be an important influence on the direction of migration. Why should this be? The apparent movement of the stars is largely due to the rotation of the earth, so that the stars above the equator will seem to move a greater distance than those above the poles. Indeed, the stars that do not move at all, or at least very little, will indicate the direction of north (in the northern hemisphere). Thus by remembering the position of the stars and comparing it with their position some time later, it would be possible to determine which stars have moved the least and therefore which indicate north. Emlen (1970) argues that buntings perform precisely this process when they are in the planetarium, and, by remembering the stars located above the pole, they are able to infer the direction for migration. Of course, this will be southwards only for those birds exposed to the normal rotation of the stars.

The ability of buntings to determine the relative motion of stars provides compelling evidence that this species is capable of representing comparatively complex spatial information.

Landmarks. The final example of an ability to represent spatial relationships is provided by an invertebrate, the digger wasp. After laying her eggs in a hole that she has dug in the ground the female flies in a series of loops around the hole before departing in search of food. Once a suitable prey has been captured, it is carried some tens of metres to the hole, where it is buried with the eggs (Tinbergen, 1951). In order to determine how the wasp is able to identify the location of the hole from such a distance, several experiments were conducted with pine cones. While the wasp was in her hole, Tinbergen (1951) formed a cicle of 20 pine cones around its entrance. Then, after she had departed in search of prey, he moved the circle about a foot away from the hole without distorting its shape. On her return the wasp went to the centre of the pine cone circle, which suggests she was using the cones as landmarks to identify her nesting hole.

In a variant of this experiment, Van Beusekon (1948) also constructed a circle of pine cones around the hole while the wasp was in it, but, as soon as she flew away, he constructed either a square or an ellipse of cones beside the circle. On returning, the wasp went to the circle rather than to the square, but it selected the circle and the ellipse equally often. This discovery indicates that during her initial flight around the hole the wasp remembers the actual pattern created by the cones. Evidently the representation of this pattern is sufficiently precise to permit a distinction between a circle and a square but not between a circle and an ellipse.

Time

Most animals possess some sort of mechanism for measuring the passage of time. The polychaete worm, *Arenicola marina*, engages in a burst of feeding every 6 to 7 minutes, and every 20 minutes to 1 hour it performs a fixed pattern of activities that includes defaecation. Apparently these activities are not in response to an internal stimulus such as an empty gullet; instead, there appear to be two "internal clocks" located in the ventral nerve cord which program when the activities will occur (Wells, 1950). Some animals, such as bees and pigeons, navigate with the help of information provided by the sun, but because it is continually moving, an internal clock is required if the correct direction in which to fly is to be computed (see Chapter 7). Other evidence for the existence of internal clocks comes from the finding that many species of animals show circadian (daily) variations of general activity. On a rather grander time scale, Berthold (1978) has proposed that the annual migration of many birds is controlled by a clock that indicates when a year has elapsed.

Very often the properties of the clock are determined genetically, with experience playing a minor role in its operation. Thus when mice are reared for generations in conditions of constant light and temperature, the usual cues for the passage of time, they continue to show a circadian rhythm in activity. Of some importance is that in these cicumstances the rhythms fluctuate and settle on a value that is not exactly 24 hours (Aschoff, 1955). This suggests very strongly that the clock is not dependent on external factors for its periodicity. Such clocks do not, however, operate entirely on their own. If animals are housed in conditions where the day

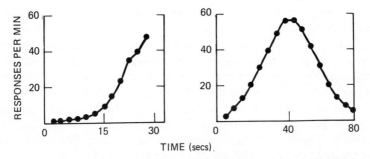

FIG. 2.10.   The gradual increase in the rate of lever pressing during the interval of a discrete trial, FI 30-sec schedule (left-hand panel, adapted from Church, 1978). The right-hand panel shows the rate of lever pressing on an FI 40-sec schedule for trials when food was not delivered (adapted from Roberts, 1981).

length is artificially set to between 21 and 27 hours, then the internal clocks readily adjust to the external conditions (see Hinde, 1970).

As well as possessing internal clocks to coordinate their daily functions, animals can represent specific intervals of time. The pattern of responding observed when rats are required to press a lever for food on a fixed interval (FI) schedule provides a simple demonstration of this ability. With a discrete trial FI schedule, a distinctive signal is presented to a rat that has been trained to lever press for food. The first response that occurs after a given interval has elapsed since the onset of the stimulus results in the delivery of food and the signal being turned off. Responses prior to this point are without effect. With extended training on this schedule, a characteristic pattern of responding develops in which the rate of responding is slow at the start of the interval but accelerates until food is delivered. The results depicted in the left-hand panel of Fig. 2.10 were obtained with a single rat trained on a FI 30-sec schedule.

To explain this type of finding, Roberts (1981) has suggested that rats possess a clock that starts when the signal commences and that they remember its value when food is delivered. Throughout a subsequent trial the current value of the clock is then compared with the memories of the intervals before food was delivered on previous trials. The smaller the discrepancy between these values, the closer in time the rat is to food and the faster it will respond.

Of course, there are alternative, simpler, explanations for the above results, perhaps the most obvious being that the procedure trains rats to increase gradually their rate of lever pressing until food is forthcoming. However, an experiment by Roberts (1982) using what he termed the peak procedure makes this account unlikely. In addition to receiving discrete-trial training with an FI 40-sec schedule, rats were occasionally given trials without food in which the signal remained on for at least 80 sec. If an FI schedule really does train animals to increase their response rate until food is delivered, then bar pressing should be very rapid indeed after 80 sec has elapsed in the presence of the signal. In contrast, if the account by Roberts (1981) is correct, then responding should be at its strongest after 40 sec and then gradually decline as the discrepancy between the current value of the clock and the remembered training values increases. The results in the right-hand panel of Fig. 2.10 show the change in response rate across these test trials, and it is quite evident that they favour the account of FI performance proposed by Roberts (1981).

Having established that rats possess an internal clock, we can go on to examine the way it changes with physical time. A linear relationship between the two would mean that increments in the internal clock correspond directly with increments in physical time. Thus if one increment of the internal clock was equivalent to 1 sec, then 5 increments would equal 5 sec. Watches and clocks hold this linear relationship with time. Alternatively, it has been suggested that the internal clock is logarithmically related to physical time, so that as time elapses the units of the internal clock represent progressively larger units of physical time (Church & Deluty, 1977). To evaluate these possibilities, experiments typically require rats to estimate the mid-point of a temporal interval. If the estimation is the same as the actual mid-point, then it would suggest, for the range considered, that there is a direct correspondence between the internal clock and physical time. On the other hand, if animals consistently underestimate the mid-point then, this would favour the claim that the two are related logarithmically. On balance the evidence favours the former of these alternatives.

In one study rats were trained with a variant of the peak procedure involving two levers in the conditioning chambers (Gibbon & Church, 1981). On some trials a light was presented and 60 sec later a response to the left lever produced food; on other trials a tone signalled the availability of food in 30 sec for responses on the right lever. After extensive training with the stimuli presented separately, the preference exhibited for the levers when the stimuli were combined was examined. When the light and tone were switched on simultaneously, there was a marked preference for the right lever, which is to be expected because responding on this lever should produce food in 30 sec, whereas a minute would have to elapse before food was made available with the other lever. On other trials the tone commenced 45 sec after the onset of the light, and here the preference was reversed. For this to have occurred, the rats must have calculated that the interval before food was available was less for the left (15-sec) than the right (30-sec) lever. A preference for neither lever was revealed on the remaining trials, when the tone commenced 30 sec after the light. This last finding is of interest because it suggests that subjects had estimated correctly that the tone was turned on at the mid-point of the interval signalled by the light and that both stimuli signalled the availability of food at the same time. This accurate estimation of the mid-point of an interval indicates that there is a direct correspondence between the internal clock and physical time.

At first sight the results of a study by Church and Deluty (1977) point to a different conclusion. Rats in Skinner boxes received either short (2-sec) or long (8-sec) signals. As soon as the signal had finished, two levers were inserted into the box. Presses on one resulted in food if the short signal had been presented, whereas after the long stimulus, presses on the other lever produced food.

Once this discrimination had been learned, generalisation test trials were given with signals of intermediate durations to the training values. With durations that were near one or other training value, responses tended to be directed towards the appropriate lever; but with intermediate values there was a reduction of this preference. The odd feature of the results concerns the point at which the levers were equally preferred. Instead of being at the mid-point of the interval between 4 and 16 sec, that is, 10 sec, the equal preference was at the lower value of 8 sec.

Although this outcome is consistent with the proposal that the internal clock and real time are related logarithmically, Gibbon and Church (1981, 1984) have developed an alternative explanation. They start with the reasonable assumption that rats are not perfect at representing the durations of the short and long training stimuli, which implies that both stimuli will be represented by a range of values rather than by a specific value. It is also claimed that the extent of this range will be greater for the longer stimulus. Thus when a generalisation trial is conducted with a 10-sec signal, it will more closely resemble a remembered value of the long than the short signal and produce a slight preference for the lever on which presses after the long stimulus are rewarded.

Number

At the beginning of the century there was a horse named Clever Hans, who, it was claimed, possessed considerable arithmetic skills (Pfungst, 1965/1908). His trainer would write a simple sum on a blackboard, and Hans would then tap his foot for the number of times that indicated the answer. Very often he was correct, and for a while this behaviour was seen as evidence that horses can do mental arithmetic. A more detailed examination of the conditions in which Hans performed has, however, yielded a different interpretation. Apparently, Hans' trainer calculated the answer to the sum himself, and after the correct number of taps he unconsciously moved. This movement, albeit slight, was a sufficient cue for Hans to stop tapping his foot and coincidentally provide the correct answer.

An impressive display of counting in birds, and one that has also been criticised (Wesley, 1961), can be found in the work of Schieman (1940; see Thorpe, 1963, for a summary). A jackdaw was required to lift the lids off a row of boxes that contained food. Once five pieces of food had been collected, any further attempts to remove a lid were punished by a mild tap on the back. Thorpe's (1963) account of the events on one trial makes interesting reading (pp. 346–347):

> Thus a jackdaw, given the task to raise lids until five baits had been secured (which in this case were distributed in the first five boxes in the order 1,2,1,0,1) went home to its cage after having opened only the first three lids and having consequently eaten only four baits. The experimenter was just about to record "one too few, incorrect solution" when the jackdaw came back to the line of boxes. Then the bird went through a most remarkable performance: it bowed its head once before the first box it had emptied, made two bows in front of the second box, one before the third, then went further along the line, opened the fourth lid (no bait) and took out the last (fifth) bait. Having done this, it left the rest of the line of boxes untouched and went home with an air of finality.

Wesley's (1961) criticism of this study is that the bird was always required to collect five baits. Perhaps, therefore, it was the cues provided by visceral feedback, rather than counting, that informed the subject when the task was completed.

An experiment by Chen (1967) using a somewhat unusual design suggests that rats can count. Subjects were placed in a straight arm that was attached to a circular runway. They were required to enter the runway from the arm and perform a number of circuits before leaving via the straight arm to obtain food. Nine out of an original 12 rats solved this task when only 3 circuits were required, but only one was able to perform this task when it involved 6 circuits. Given the rat's skill at timing, it is quite possible that instead of counting the circuits as they performed them, the subjects learned to run for a specified duration before going to the goal.

A rather different method for studying counting in rats has been developed by Meck and Church (1983, see also Church & Meck, 1984). In principle, the method is similar to that employed by Church and Deluty (1977) described previously. The insertion of two levers into a chamber was preceded either by a "few" signal, composed of two pulses of white noise, or by a "many" signal, composed of 8 pulses. Food was delivered for pressing the left lever immediately after the "few" signal, or the right lever after the "many" signal. Although the discrimination was mastered with little difficulty, it is not clear whether this was due to counting. For both signals the pulses of white noise, each lasting for 0.5 sec, were separated by an equivalent period of silence, so that they differed in total duration (2 or 8 sec) as well as in the number of pulses.

In order to confirm that animals had learned about the numerical attributes of the signals, a test session was conducted with 4-sec signals. The "few" signal was thus composed of alternating intervals of noise and silence, each lasting 1 sec, whereas this value was reduced to 0.25 sec for the "many" signal. Subjects showed a clear preference for the left (few) lever when 2 pulses had been presented and a marked preference for the right (many) lever after 8 pulses. Because the duration of the signal was the same in both cases, this finding confirms that the rats solved the discrimination by counting rather than by timing.

Categories

The experiments discussed in this chapter demonstrate that animals are capable of storing memories of unitary events such as tones or a particular photograph. But for people there is evidence that the storage of knowledge about stimuli can involve an additional process. Not only are unitary events remembered, they are often integrated into a larger body of knowledge that is composed of categories. To take a frequently cited example, cricket, marbles, tennis, chess, and golf differ in many ways, but they possess certain features that enable them all to be regarded as examples of a particular category: games. In this section it will be argued that animals are also capable of forming categories. This, then, raises the problem of specifying the way in which a category is represented. In fact, this is not a simple issue even where humans are concerned. For example, try to identify what it is about the above instances that makes most people accept they are games, yet would lead to the exclusion of gambling and jogging from this category.

In a study of category learning by pigeons, Herrnstein, Loveland, and Cable (1976) presented subjects in each session with a set of 80 different slides, half of which contained pictures of trees. The trees were not especially prominent in the slides—rather, the slides were of scenes that contained trees. The remaining slides were of similar scenes but without trees. Slides were shown one at a time, and subjects were rewarded for pecking a response key whenever one showing a tree was present (S+). Responses in the presence of slides without a tree (S−) were never rewarded. The slides were selected from a pool containing more than 500 pictures, and after a considerable number of training sessions most subjects were discriminating accurately between the two sets of slides. As well as trees, Herrnstein et al. (1976) report that pigeons can respond according to the categories of water and a specific person.

Although such results suggest that pigeons can form a category of trees and use this to govern their responding, another explanation should be considered. We saw earlier that Vaughan and Greene (1984) have demonstrated that pigeons have an accurate memory for specific pictures they have seen. Conceivably, instead of using the category of tree to identify the slides associated with reward, the pigeons might have remembered each of the slides that had been paired with food. The principal reason for rejecting this interpretation is that on occasional test sessions novel slides were used, but this did not reduce the accuracy with which the subjects identified those belonging to the category. This would not be possible if pigeons solve the discrimination by remembering each of the slides associated with food.

Before considering the ways in which pigeons may represent a category like "tree", some results reported by Cerella (1979) merit attention. These add little in substance to the findings of Herrnstein et al. (1976), but they demonstrate better than most studies the remarkable ability of pigeons to utilise categories.

In one experiment the 40 slides constituting S+ were all silhouettes of oak leaves (see upper row, Fig. 2.11), and the 40 items presented as S− were silhouettes of other leaves (see lower row, Fig. 2.11). It required only 24 sessions before the birds were responding nearly perfectly. The correct pattern of responding also generalised very well to 40 novel silhouettes of oak leaves. Other pigeons were trained with one oak leaf as S+ and 40 other leaves as S−. Even in these circumstances pigeons learned to respond to the category of oak leaf, because a generalisation test with 40

FIG. 2.11.   Silhouettes of oak leaves (upper row) and non-oak leaves (lower row) that are representative of the stimuli used in a category learning experiment by Cerella (1979) (from Cerella, 1979).

slides of different oak leaves intermixed among the original S— slides revealed an excellent level of discrimination.

In order to confirm that the pigeon's ability is not without limit, it should be mentioned that Cerella (1980) had difficulty in training them to distinguish one oak leaf from 40 other oak leaves; indeed, two of the four pigeons trained in this manner were unable to learn the discrimination. Thus pigeons are able to distinguish oak leaves from other leaves, yet have great difficulty in acquiring a representation that would enable them to distinguish one oak leaf from other oak leaves.

In discussions of category learning by people, at least three different accounts have been developed that can be applied to the analysis of the results just described: instance theory, prototype theory, and feature count theory.

Instance Theory.   According to this approach (e.g. Medin & Schaffer, 1978), subjects remember all the instances to which they are exposed. In order to explain how they will behave when confronted with a novel item, instance theory proposes that the tendency to respond to the examples to which they have already been exposed will generalise to a similar, novel stimulus when it is first presented. In a sense this is no different from training a pigeon to peck a key for food in the presence of a tone of one frequency and then discovering that it will also respond to a tone of a slightly different frequency. A difficulty with this theory is that it is not clear how similarity can be computed so as to ensure that responding generalises only to instances of the category. Presumably a slide of a scene with a small tree in it is very similar to the same scene but with the tree removed. It is likely that pigeons trained with the tree category would respond in the presence of the former but not of the latter, but how this would be achieved is hard to specify. Considerably more needs to be known about the way in which responses generalise between complex stimuli before this account can be of much value.

Prototype Theory.   Prototype theory stands in virtually direct contrast to instance theory because it holds that subjects just remember the ideal instance of a category (Reed, 1972; Franks and Bransford, 1971). It is the extent to which a test slide matches this ideal that determines how subjects will respond on a trial. The problem confronting this type of account is to identify the origin of such a prototype. One possibility considered by Herrnstein et al. (1976, p. 301) is that categories are natural, meaning that "pigeons tend innately to infer a tree category from instances of trees". This proposal may not be too unreasonable as far as trees and leaves are concerned. In addition, pigeons appear to have difficulty in learning categories that for them would not be expected to be natural: chairs, food cups, bottles, and wheeled vehicles (Herrnstein, 1984, p. 249). It is also unlikely that they would possess a natural category for a single oak leaf, and this would explain their difficulty in distinguishing one oak leaf from many.

On the other hand, there is sufficient evidence to make one question seriously the merits of prototype theory. Herrnstein and DeVilliers (1980) have demonstrated that pigeons can readily discriminate between under- water scenes that contain the presence rather than the absence of fish. As Herrnstein (1984) himself acknowledges, it is unreasonable to assume that such a category as fish is natural for the pigeon, either by dint of previous experience or because it is inborn. Possibly even more problematic for the view that prototypes are natural are the findings by Morgan, Fitch, Holman, and Lea (1976), which indicated that pigeons are able to respond as if they possess categories for the shapes of "2" and "A". It is hardly necessary to point to the unlikelihood of these categories being inborn.

Of course it is possible that the prototype is formed as a result of the training given during the experiment. This, in fairness, is the view expressed by those who have proposed the existence of certain prototypes in humans (but see Rosch, 1973). The way in which animals form such prototypes, however, remains to be specified.

Feature Theory.   One method for comparing the similarity between two scenes is to break each down into a number of component features and to count the number they have in common. At a relatively coarse level, then, trees can be said to consist of such features as trunks, bark, leaves, branches, twigs, and so on. According to a feature theory, any instance that possesses a sufficient sub-set of features will be treated as a member of the tree category (Anderson, Kline, & Beasley, 1979). Thus instead of a category being represented by a protoype, this approach assumes that a collection of features will be used to evaluate whether an item belongs to a category. An advantage of this account is that it readily explains why pigeons have no difficulty in responding correctly to a novel stimulus once a category has been formed: if some of the correct features are present, it will be treated as a member of the category. Additional support for this view may be found in the study by Morgan, Fitch, Holman, and Lea (1976), which demonstrated that pigeons can discriminate between slides containing various forms of A and those containing variants of 2. After this phase, a number of generalisation tests containing letters of the alphabet were presented. The letters containing most features in common with A were treated like this stimulus, whereas those with more features in common with 2 were treated like the number.

Feature theory is also supported by the results from a study by Cerella (1980) who trained pigeons to peck a key for food in the presence of

FIG. 2.12.   Examples of the slides used in the generalisation tests by Cerella (1980) (from Cerella, 1982).

Charlie Brown cartoons but not when they were shown other cartoon characters. Once this was achieved, albeit with considerable difficulty, they received generalisation tests with unusual slides of Charlie Brown (see Fig. 2.12). These were treated as if they were quite normal instances of the training category. Because each of the unusual views contained many of the features embodied in the training slides, it is easy to understand this performance in terms of feature theory.

Support for feature theory can also be found in a study with monkeys by Schrier, Angarella, and Povar (1984). For their original training, subjects were shown a set of photographic slides, of which half were scenes with humans. To obtain a reward they had to press one button whenever a slide showing a person was projected onto a screen, and another when a slide without a person was shown. Figure 2.13 shows the percentage of trials on which a typical subject, Evan, responded correctly on each of the 45 training sessions of this stage. In contrast to the occasional reports of rapid category learning by pigeons, the performance of Evan is rather disappointing. For example, Herrnstein (1985) reports that in some of his experiments pigeons have shown a statiscally reliable discrimination by the second session of training.

A transfer test was then conducted which was similar to the original training except that a new set of 80 slides was used. On the first session the discrimination was better than for the equivalent session of the original training, but it was also substantially inferior to the transfer shown by pigeons (Herrnstein & Loveland, 1964; Malott & Siddall, 1972; Siegel & Honig, 1970). The rate of improvement thereafter was much the same as for the initial stage (see Fig. 2.13).

The third stage of the experiment consisted of a random test with yet another novel set of 80 slides, half of which included a person. Responding on one button was rewarded in the presence of a randomly selected 20 human and 20 nonhuman slides, whereas for the remaining slides responses on the other button were rewarded. Thus in this phase of the study the concept of a person would hinder the discrimination if it was used to choose the correct response. In spite of this potentially disruptive

influence it is apparent from Fig. 2.13 that the rather different requirements of this task resulted in the same rate of discrimination learning as the
original training.

To explain these findings, Schrier et al. (1984) suggested that for the
first stage the monkeys did not use a category, but, as they must have done
for the final stage, they learned how to respond to the individual slides.
The slight benefit of the original training on the transfer test is attributed to
some of the second set of slides containing features that were present in the
original set—for example, colour of skin or black dots (eyes). Whether or
not this analysis is correct remains to be seen; for the present, the relatively
poor performance of monkeys does suggest that interpretations of category
discrimination learning that refer to more sophisticated processes than
those involved in feature theory should be treated with caution.

Despite these successes, feature theory does have its problems. It must
explain how the animal identifies those features that the experimenter has
chosen to regard as "correct". At the beginning of training various slides,
each containing a large number of features, are presented. How is it that
the subject is able to identify, occasionally rapidly, the features that are
relevant to successful performance on the discrimination? Why, moreover,
are some categories easier to identify than others?

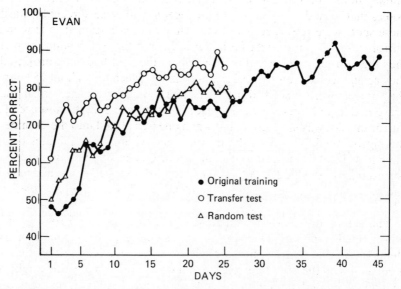

FIG. 2.13. Percentage of trials on which a single monkey responded correctly for each
session of the three stages of a concept learning experiment by Schrier et al. (from Schrier et
al., 1984).

Self-Concept.   Before leaving this discussion of concept learning, some comment is needed concerning Gallup's (1970, 1983) suggestion that a few animals can form a concept of self. He observed that when chimpanzees first look in a mirror, they treat their reflection as if it were another chimpanzee, but after several days these reactions are replaced by more self-directed activities, such as grooming and inspecting hitherto unseen regions of their bodies. Once some chimpanzees had reached this stage, Gallup (1970) anaesthetised them and marked their foreheads and ears with a non-irritating dye. On seeing their reflections in the mirror, following recovery, the subjects all showed a great deal of interest in the marks by touching themselves on the appropriate regions. This finding has been reliably demonstrated with chimpanzees and orangutans (Gallup, McClure, Hill, & Bundy, 1971; Lethmate & Ducker, 1973; Suarez & Gallup, 1981) but not with the gorilla (Ledbetter & Basen, 1982; Suarez & Gallup, 1981), or monkeys (Anderson, 1983). Gallup (1983) draws two conclusions from these reports. First, that self-directed behaviour guided by a mirror demonstrates the existence of self-awareness and second, that apart from humans this awareness is to be found only in chimpanzees and orangutans.

The results from a study by Epstein, Lanza, and Skinner (1981) seriously question the second of these conclusions. Pigeons were trained initially in the following manner: Small dots were placed on parts of their bodies that were directly visible to the pigeon, and pecks directed towards these spots were rewarded with food. They were also trained to look in a mirror to see a spot of light flashed briefly onto the wall behind them. If they then turned and pecked the wall where the light had been projected, they again received reward. After this training, which took about 15 hours, the subjects were placed into the chambers wearing a paper collar that prevented them from seeing a dot placed on their chest. In the absence of a mirror this dot was ineffective, but when one was placed into the chamber, the pigeon would approach the mirror, "and within a few minutes begin moving its head downward repeatedly toward the position on the bird that corresponds to the hidden dot. . . . The last bird we tested continued to bob and peck in this manner for more than 6 minutes" (Epstein et al., 1981, p. 47).

This quotation clearly reveals that pigeons can use a mirror to guide self-directed responses. Does this mean, as Gallup (1983) claimed for the chimpanzee, that pigeons, too, are self-aware? Certainly, if self-awareness is equated with the use of mirrors, then it does, but for many this would be an unduly limited definition of self-awareness. As far as humans are concerned, this term implies that we can experience mental states of the sort, "It is me looking in the mirror". Whether animals experience similar states when they look into mirrors is something that psychologists are unable to answer. It is impossible to assess by any objective, experimental test what animals are experiencing, and thus it is impossible to know whether they have an awareness of self that is akin to our own. In view of this obstacle I suspect it would be less misleading if terms like self-awareness were avoided in discussions of animal cognition.

Perhaps the most noteworthy feature of the study by Epstein et al. (1981) is that it shows that the use of mirrors is not confined to one or two species. The reasons why chimpanzees and oragutans have so far been the only animals to display a spontaneous use of mirrors remain to be identified. One possibility is that where animals have failed to use mirrors it is because they lack the incentive rather than the ability to do so. Gorillas may well touch a spot of dye on their forehead if this produces a tangible reward.

THE STRUCTURE OF REPRESENTATIONS

There can be little doubt that animals store representations of a wide range of stimuli. The problem that now arises is to identify the way in which the stored information is encoded. This is a difficult issue about which a great deal of controversy persists as far as human cognition is concerned. It is also a topic that is only infrequently considered in discussions of animal cognition (but see Premack, 1983a,b). Nonetheless, I suspect that until we have discovered how information is stored in animals, we shall remain a long way from understanding their cognitive abilities.

Concrete Representations

Perhaps the simplest account of the way in which a representation is structured is that it is a direct copy of the event to which it relates. The term "concrete representation" can be used to refer to this means of storing information. Of course, the copy need not be perfect—a concrete representation may store only a fraction of the information that is available. One way of activating such a representation would be to excite at least a portion of the neurons that are responsible for the perception of the event itself. This idea has been proposed for certain aspects of human memory (e.g. Farah, 1985) and hinted at by several authors interested in animal memory. Konorski (1967), for example, maintains that the cells responsible for the perception of a stimulus are also activated whenever a memory of that event is recalled.

As an alternative to physiological accounts of concrete representations, some psychological accounts assume that any external event will excite a collection of elements (Atkinson & Estes, 1963; Blough, 1975). These elements correspond to all the physical attributes of the stimulus concerned, and their pattern will alter whenever there is a change in the stimulus. A memory of an event can then be excited by activating some or all of the elements that the event itself activates. The reason for this seemingly complex approach is that it provides a ready explanation for generalisation and generalisation decrement. Put very simply, the more elements two stimuli have in common, the greater will be the generalisation between them.

In the case of spatial representations, it would be reasonable to assume that they consist not only of a copy of the stimuli concerned but also of a copy of their position relative to one another. Indeed, just such a proposal has been made by O'Keefe and Nadel (1978), who have gone further to suggest that the place in which these elaborate concrete representations are stored is the hippocampus.

Amodal Representations

When a stimulus is presented to an animal, its physical attributes may vary along a number of dimensions that will apply to stimuli of any modality. For instance, it will be of a particular intensity and of a given duration, and, if it is intermittent, it will have a certain on–off frequency. A concrete representation can readily encode this information—for example, intensity might be represented by the number of elements that a stimulus activates. However, the intriguing question is raised as to whether animals can abstract information about an attribute of a stimulus and store it independently of the modality to which it originally related. If this can be demonstrated, then it will indicate that the representation is not a direct copy of the original training experience but something more abstract. To accommodate this possibility, the term "amodal representation" refers to any stored information that can be used in situations that extend beyond the modality of the original training.

Evidence that rats store amodal representations can be found in a study by Meck and Church (1982, Experiment 2). Subjects were trained in a temporal generalisation task in which they were rewarded for pressing a lever after they had been exposed to a light of medium—but not short or long—duration. The solid line in Fig. 2.14 indicates that with sufficient training rats learned the discrimination because they pressed the lever more rapidly after the medium stimulus than after the short or long one. This finding suggests that the rats had formed some sort of representation of the medium-duration stimulus. To test whether this representation was concrete or amodal, Meck and Church (1982) changed the procedure by using white noise rather than light as the temporal signal. The effects of

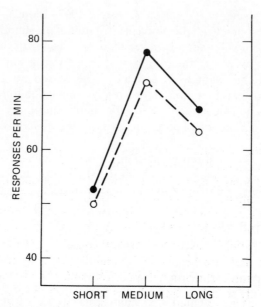

FIG. 2.14. Average number of responses per minute following the short-, medium-, and long-duration stimuli in the experiment by Meck and Church (adapted from Meck & Church, 1982).

this change are shown by the dotted lines in Fig. 2.14, and it is quite evident that their discrimination was as good with this stimulus as with the light. Because there is physically little in common between a tone and a light, it is likely that an amodal representation of duration gained control over responding and permitted the excellent transfer between the two stimuli.

Other findings suggest that animals are also able to form amodal representations of intensity (Over & Mackintosh, 1969), frequency (Ward, Yehle, & Doerflein, 1970), and shape (Weiskrantz & Cowey, 1975). These experiments were conducted with rats, bushbabies, and monkeys, respectively. Whether other vertebrates such as birds or invertebrates possess this representational ability is not yet known.

CONCLUSIONS

Considerable attention has been paid in this chapter to the ability of simple creatures to store information. Thus it has been argued that even paramecia can retain a representation of a tone, whereas the digger wasp can remember a pattern made by pine cones. These findings are of interest in their own right, but they also emphasise two important points concerning the study of animal cognition.

First, they indicate that cognitive processes play an important role in the behaviour of so-called primitive animals, and in the most basic of experimental tasks. Animal cognition is thus not to be found in a restricted selection of species, nor is it confined to methods designed to tax the higher mental capacities. The focus of this area of study is, instead, with the mechanisms that enable animals to store and utilise information gained from their experiences, wherever this may occur.

The second point concerns the tendency, when considering the cognitive processes of animals, to anthropomorphise by imagining that their mental experiences are much the same as our own. An instance of this tendency is provided by Herrnstein (1979) when considering the success of pigeons with discriminations based on natural concepts: "Their performance suggests that they are seeing the stimuli approximately as we do, as representing a three-dimensional space containing solid objects" (p. 125). We have already seen how difficult it is to evaluate the claim that animals are self-aware, and a similar caution applies when considering the visual experiences of animals. It is very much harder, if not impossible, to believe that paramecia have a mental life resembling our own. A discussion of their cognitive processes, therefore, draws attention to the fact that the study of animal cognition is concerned with information processing, not with the experience or consciousness of animals.

An extremely wide range of species can be said to possess some sort of representational ability; but is there any evidence that animals differ in this respect? Because this question is rarely asked, it should not be too surprising to discover that there is no certain answer to it. In fact, for the present it is difficult to do more than speculate on the likely outcome of future research. One possibility is that animals with a higher cephalisation index (brain-to-body ratio) may form more elaborate representations than their smaller-brained counterparts. Thus dolphins might be better than ostriches at remembering the relationships within a pattern. Evidence that seems incompatible with this prediction comes from the indigo bunting's memory for the pattern created by the stars, or the digger wasp's memory for a circle of pine cones. In these instances, however, as we saw in the case of the white-crowned sparrow, this ability may be confined to a restricted range of stimuli. And this suggests the possibility that the representational abilities of many animals are circumscribed by the circumstances to which they are naturally adapted. Although this seems plausible, a further possibility is that some animals may be less constrained in this way than others and thus able to represent a wider range of stimuli. A final possibility is that the abstraction of amodal stimuli may be found only in a selected range of animals. Unfortunately, given our present knowledge, these ideas are no more justifiable than the alternative possibility that, in general, animals differ little in their possession of the capacities considered in this chapter.

3 Memory Processes

Animals are evidently capable of storing information about a wide variety of events. Our concern now is with understanding the processes that are responsible for this storage. Where humans are concerned, it is customary to distinguish between at least two sorts of memory: There is believed to be a transient, or short-term memory (STM), which consists of information about the immediate past and which will be soon forgotten unless special strategies such as rehearsal are employed. There is also a long-term memory (LTM), which comprises all the knowledge we have acquired and which can, hopefully, be recalled whenever it is needed. In recalling any fact, it is generally accepted that this will result in the information being transferred temporarily to STM, from which it will soon disappear and revert to its normal state in LTM.

This distinction between STM and LTM for humans has influenced considerably the study of animal memory, and it has also determined the way in which this chapter is organised. In the first section we look at the ability of animals to store information over relatively long retention intervals and also look at some of the factors that are responsible for the forgetting of this information. The second, and larger section, then examines what is known about short-term retention in animals.

PART 1: LONG-TERM RETENTION

CAPACITY

For humans the outstanding features of LTM are its capacity and durability. The amount of information that a person can retain is enormous, comprising the memories of a life-time. Moreover, some of this knowledge will have been stored for very long periods, such as an elderly person's memories of childhood. With some animals, at least, it seems that these general principles are also true.

As far as the amount of information that can be retained is concerned, the record, at present, probably resides with the Clark's nutcracker. Every autumn these birds collect as many as 33,000 pine seeds and bury them in shallow holes (caches) at an average of 4 seeds per cache. Throughout the winter and spring they retrieve these hidden supplies to feed both themselves and their offspring. According to Vander Wall (1982), this requires the nutcrackers to revisit between 2,500 and 3,750 different caches. Because the seeds are most frequently recovered from caches made by the retriever, it suggests that these birds can store sufficient information to be able to identify well over 3,000 different locations. Even though strategies might be employed to reduce the amount that must be remembered—for instance, by burying a number of seeds close to one another—this still provides a most impressive demonstration of animal memory.

Almost equally remarkable are the results of a laboratory study involving pigeons. In an experiment that was referred to in Chapter 2, Vaughan and Greene (1984) trained pigeons on a discrimination involving pictures of natural scenes. Initially, they were presented with 80 different pictures, projected one at a time onto a response key. Responding on the key in the presence of a randomly selected 40 of these slides resulted in the delivery of food, whereas food was never made available in the presence of the remaining 40 pictures. Once the subjects were discriminating accurately between the slides they were put to one side and a new set of 80 slides was introduced. Training with these was conducted in a similar manner until the discrimination had been learned, whereupon subjects were again exposed to a new set of 80 slides. The experiment continued in this way until the pigeons had been exposed to 320 different pictures, half of which were associated with food. At this point the birds were exposed to all 320 slides—separately of course—and their discrimination between them was very accurate indeed.

Vaughan and Greene (1984) also investigated the length of time for which the memory of these pictures can last. After the experiment just described, the pigeons were retained in their home cages for a period of 2 years before being returned to the experimental apparatus and reexposed to the original pictures. Even after this interval the discrimination between the two categories of pictures was still far in excess of that expected by chance. Further evidence of the durability of the pigeon memory is provided by Skinner (1950), who demonstrated that they may retain information for as long as five years.

The considerably shorter life-span of the rat (2–3 years) than of the pigeon (more than 15 years) means that demonstrations of a long memory with rats are of necessity less impressive. Nonetheless, there is ample evidence that they are capable of storing information for considerable periods—Gleitman (1971) found no forgetting by rats of a conditioned response they had acquired 90 days previously.

A rather different demonstration of the robustness of animal memory comes from a creature known as the African claw-toed frog (*Xenopus laevis*). This animal undergoes a metamorphosis, over a period of 35 days, from a limbless tadpole to a young frog that differs only in size from an adult, and this change is accompanied by considerable neural growth. In one study Miller and Berk (1977) trained subjects to move from a black to a white compartment in order to reduce the severity of an electric shock. Both tadpoles and young frogs learned this task with equal facility, but the remarkable finding is that they also showed excellent retention of the task when tested 35 days later. In the former case, of course, they had metamorphosed into frogs by the time of the retention test, but the changes associated with this metemorphosis did nothing to disrupt memory.

Animals can therefore remember things for a remarkably long time. But is there any loss of the information that is stored over such periods? One of the surprisingly few studies to look for such forgetting is by Thomas and Lopez (1962), who trained pigeons to peck a key illuminated by a monochromatic light of 550 nm for food. The memory for this training stimulus was then tested in different groups after retention intervals of 1 min, 1 day, or 1 week. The method of testing was to present the subjects with the key illuminated by light varying in wavelength from 500 to 600 nm. As reported in Chapter 2, such a procedure results in responding being most rapid to the original training colour and slowest to the colours most removed from this value. The results from this study are depicted in Fig. 3.1.

The group tested within a minute of being trained responded more rapidly to the original training colour than to any other employed during testing. This indicates that the memory for the original training stimulus remained intact for at least 1 min. The results from the other groups show that this memory soon decays to some extent. Both groups responded no more rapidly to the original training colour than to its nearest neighbours

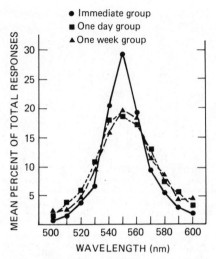

FIG. 3.1. Mean stimulus generalisation gradients for three groups of pigeons tested at different intervals after they had been trained to peck a key for food when it was illuminated with light of wavelength 550 nm (adapted from Thomas, 1981).

(540 and 560 nm), which suggests that with the passage of time the exact value of the stimulus employed during training was forgotten. This conclusion has been confirmed with a variety of species and training procedures (e.g. Thomas, 1979). The implication from all these studies is that with the passage of time subjects forget the specific attributes of the training stimulus but not the response that is required in its presence.

In addition to the passage of time, a number of other factors have been shown to influence how well material is remembered or recalled. These demonstrations have generally been conducted with the aim of evaluating different theories of long-term retention and will be considered next, along with the theories they were designed to test.

THEORETICAL INTERPRETATION

Two rather different theoretical frameworks have been developed to explain the way in which long-term storage of information takes place. Using the distinction made at the start of this chapter, consolidation or rehearsal theory stresses that information must be rehearsed in STM immediately after it has been presented if it is to be stored adequately in LTM. Retrieval theory, on the other hand, holds that information is stored virtually instantaneously in LTM and assumes that forgetting is due principally to a failure to find the information at the time of testing.

Consolidation Theory

One reason for studying animal memory has been the hope that it will lead to an understanding of the neural processes subserving the acquisition and storage of knowledge in both humans and animals. The assumption underlying much of this work has been that any long-term retention of information must be due to an equally long-term change in the nervous system. According to Hebb (1949), memory storage depends upon the virtually permanent formation of circuits of interconnected neurons. These were assumed to be only partially formed at the end of a training trial, and for learning to be complete a period of sustained reverberatory activity (consolidation) in the neural circuit after the trial was deemed essential. Should this activity not occur, or be disrupted, then permanent links in the network would not be formed, and the memory of the trial would be incomplete.

Originally, the most compelling evidence to support this type of theory came from studies investigating the influence of electro-convulsive shock (ECS) on animal memory. ECS involves the passage through the brain of an electric current of sufficient intensity that it would presumably disrupt any reverberatory activity in a localised collection of cells. Administration of ECS shortly after a training trial should, therefore, inhibit the processes necessary for producing a normal memory of that trial. An experiment by Duncan (1949) was among the first to test this prediction. Rats were placed in a box with a metal grid floor that could be electrified. A light was then turned on for 10 sec, and this was followed by foot shock (not ECS). To prevent the shock occurring, the rat was required to move from one end of the box to the other while the light was still on and unless this response was made, shock was automatically delivered as soon as the light was turned off. There were 9 groups in the study, 8 of which received ECS at intervals varying from 20 sec to 14 hr after each daily trial. A control group, which did not receive ECS, quickly learned to avoid the shock, but this learning was very much poorer for the group that received ECS 20 sec after every trial. Moreover, as the interval between the end of each trial and the administration of ECS was extended, the disruptive influence of this treatment diminished (see Fig. 3.2). One explanation for these findings is that ECS immediately after a trial prevents the consolidation of the learning necessary for the successful prevention of shock. Postponing the ECS for a period after each trial would reduce this disruptive influence and allow more effective learning. A review of more recent experiments on this topic is presented in Lewis (1979).

The generality of these findings has been shown by Wagner, Rudy, and Whitlow (1973), but the rationale behind their experiment was based more on information processing than on neurological considerations. Rabbits

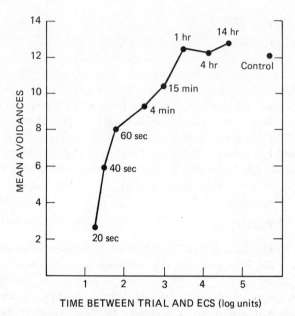

FIG. 3.2.   Mean number of avoidance responses made by groups of rats that differed in the interval for which the delivery of electroconvulsive shock (ECS) was delayed after each of 18 avoidance training trials. Group Control did not receive ECS (from Duncan, 1949).

first received conditioning trials in which one stimulus, A, was paired with a shock US and another stimulus, B, was presented alone. As a result of this training, subjects were expected to learn that A predicted shock and B its omission (see Chapter 4). For the test phase all subjects received conditioning trials with a third CS, C, which was consistently paired with a shock US, and followed 10 sec later by a post-trial event. For Group Congruent this event consisted of a conditioning trial that was identical to those of the initial stage, either A paired with shock or B alone, whereas for Group Incongruent the post-trial event consisted of the opposite treatment, A presented alone or B paired with shock.

For conditioning with C to be effective, Wagner et al. (1973; see also Wagner, 1976, 1978) proposed that a period after each trial is necessary in which representations of C and the US are rehearsed simultaneously in STM. STM is seen as being of limited capacity and, of equal importance, to give priority to recent, surprising events. During the test phase the trials with A and B were designed to be surprising for Group Incongruent, as they were different from those experienced during pretraining. Their occurrence was thus expected to command access to STM and disrupt rehearsal of the immediately preceding trial with C. Such a disruptive effect was not expected for Group Congruent as the post-trial events were the same as during pretraining and should not be surprising. In support of this analysis, Fig. 3.3 confirms that conditioning with C was more effective for Group Congruent than Incongruent.

Because the account by Wagner et al. (1973) assumes that rehearsal is necessary for only a limited period after a conditioning trial, it follows that incongruent trials with A and B will be most disruptive when they occur shortly after a trial with C. This prediction has been confirmed in another study by Wagner, Rudy, and Whitlow (1973, Experiment 5). They demonstrated that conditioning was much less effective when each trial with C was followed by an incongruent post-trial event after 3 rather than 10 sec.

Retrieval Theory

In essence, the long-term retention of information can be subdivided into three stages, the first involving the formation of a memory trace of a particular training episode, the second involving the storage of that information for some interval, and the third consisting of retrieving the trace when it is required. Consolidation theories place most emphasis on the first two of these stages. They assume that a poor memory is due either to inadequate storage because of insufficient rehearsal at the time of

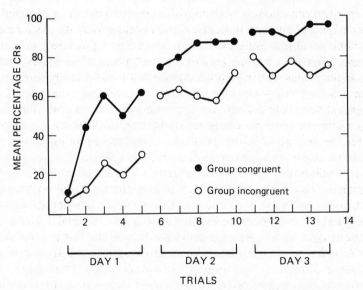

FIG. 3.3. Mean percentage of subjects in Groups Congruent and Incongruent for which an eyeblink CR was recorded on each of the 15 conditioning trials with CS C (adapted from Wagner et al., 1973).

training, or to a decay of the trace due to the passage of time. In contrast, retrieval theories of memory (Spear, 1973; Lewis, 1979) maintain that the formation of memories is more-or-less instantaneous and that once formed they remain permanently intact. To account for forgetting and the amnesic effects of ECS, these theories place greatest emphasis on the retrieval process.

Of the various accounts of a retrieval theory of memory that have been proposed, the one considered here is that by Lewis (1979) because it provides the most explicit framework into which a variety of experimental findings can be accommodated. He maintains that the formation of the memory trace is very rapid and once formed it can reside in either Inactive or Active Memory.[1] At the time of acquisition, information is held in Active Memory, where it is assumed to be swiftly coded and elaborated before being stored permanently in Inactive Memory. The purpose of this coding and elaboration is to aid the efficient retrieval of the information from Inactive Memory when it is needed. In order for this retrieval to take place, subjects must be in the presence of some of the stimuli that were present at the time of the training trial. These stimuli serve to retrieve the memory of the entire trial into Active Memory, and once in this state the information can be further elaborated as well as influence the subject's behaviour. It is important to emphasise that unless information is retrieved from Inactive into Active Memory, it will be of no use to the animal.

A simple study supporting many of these proposals is reported by Spear, Smith, Bryan, Gordon, Timmons, and Chiszar (1980), which also shows that the room in which the training was conducted can serve as a retrieval cue. The apparatus was a two-compartment shuttle box with an open top so that subjects could observe the room in which the experiment was conducted. One compartment was white with a grid floor through which an electric shock could be passed, the other compartment was black; to cross between the two it was necessary to jump over a small hurdle. For the initial stage of the experiment all animals received avoidance training in which they were placed into the white compartment and were given an electric shock if they did not step into the black compartment within 5 sec. After a number of such trials, subjects rapidly jumped from the white compartment whenever they were placed into it. Some time after the completion of this training the rats were again placed into the white compartment, and the time taken to leave it was recorded. For Group Same the test trials were conducted with apparatus in the same room as that used during training, whereas for Group Different another room was

---

[1]This distinction between Active and Inactive Memory is similar to that made by other theorists between STM and LTM.

employed for the test trial. According to retrieval theory, the sight of the features of the room, which were visible during training, should immediately retrieve the memory of their training for Group Same and result in a rapid exit from the white compartment. On the other hand, the cues provided by the new room for Group Different will not aid such efficient retrieval, and these subjects should take longer than those in Group Same to escape from the white compartment—which is exactly what Spear et al. (1980) observed.

Further support for retrieval theory comes from two additional groups, trained on opposite tasks in the two rooms. Their initial training, in Room X, was designed to teach them to stay in the white compartment: they were placed into this compartment at the outset of each trial, and they were shocked only if they left it. Having learned this, they were then transferred to Room Y, where they had to learn to leave the white compartment in order to avoid shock. Not surprisingly, there was initially some interference from the the previous, opposed training, but subjects eventually learned to leave the white compartment rapidly whenever they were placed in it. At the end of this training the rats were again placed into the white compartment for a test trial. Group X–Y–X received this trial in the room used for the original training, Room X, and Group X–Y–Y was tested in the room where the animals had been trained to leave the white compartment. Retrieval theory predicts that these different rooms should retrieve memories of the different training that was conducted in them: Group X–Y–X should retrieve a memory of being trained to remain in the white compartment, whereas Group X–Y–Y should retrieve a memory of its more recent training and move swiftly to the black compartment. In keeping with this analysis, it was found that Group X–Y–X remained in the white compartment for much longer than Group X–Y–Y.

Reactivation Effects.   Some surprising results that are consistent with retrieval theory concern the effects of what have come to be known as reactivation treatments. After training on a particular task, retrieval theory asserts that exposure to even a fraction of the cues that were present at the time of training will retrieve or reactivate information about that episode into Active Memory. Once reactivated, this information can be modified in a variety of ways and thus effectively alter the animal's memory of the original training.

A series of experiments summarised by Gordon (1981) supports this type of analysis. In one experiment (Gordon, Frankl, & Hemberg, 1979, Experiment 1) rats were initially trained to leave a white compartment to avoid shock with a procedure identical to that used by Spear et al. (1980). Three days after the successful completion of this training, the subjects were returned to the experimental room for what may be termed reactivation treatment. For one group this consisted of being confined in the white compartment for 15 sec, and for another group for 75 sec. In both cases crossing to the black side was impossible, and shock was never delivered. A third group was not placed into the apparatus for this stage of the experiment. Finally, on the following day all three groups received a single test trial in which they were placed into the white compartment and the time taken to cross to the black side was recorded.

The reactivation treatment had a profound effect on the performance of the three groups (see Fig. 3.4). Subjects that had received a 15-sec exposure to the apparatus were the fastest to leave the white compartment, those receiving no exposure were somewhat slower, whereas the subjects given 75 sec of reactivation treatment revealed little concern about being in the white compartment. Gordon (1981) interpreted his findings in the following way. Exposure to the apparatus for 15 sec should reactivate the memory of the avoidance training and may very well result in further elaboration and coding of this memory. On the test trial the memory of the

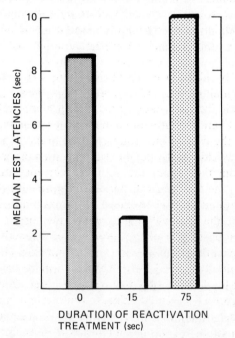

FIG. 3.4.   Median latency to leave a white compartment for three groups of rats that had previously been trained to jump from the compartment to avoid shock. The groups received reactivation treatment of being placed in the white compartment without shock for 0, 15, or 75 sec before the test trial (adapted from Gordon, 1981).

original training should then be rapidly retrieved and result in a swifter avoidance response than for the group that did not receive the reactivation treatment. A similar effect would not be expected for the group that received the reactivation treatment for 75 sec, as the extended exposure to the white compartment will have modified the memory of the original training to incorporate the information that shocks are now unlikely to occur in the apparatus. The retrieval of this modified memory on the test trial would not produce a particularly vigorous avoidance response.

This may strike the reader as a rather arbitrary explanation. Why is it that a period of elaboration for 15 sec in the absence of shock should facilitate the retrieval of information on the test trial? One possibility is suggested by the idea that the internal state of an animal provides a component of the information that can be used to retrieve the memory of a training episode (e.g. Spear, 1981). When the interval between the training and test episodes is short, there will be little change in the internal state of the subject and this should not influence the retrieval process. On the other hand, when there is a longer interval between the two episodes, there may very well be a change in the animal's internal state and this will make it more difficult to retrieve the memory of training. In support of this claim Spear et al. (1980) have shown that drugs such as pentobarbitol, which can alter an animal's anxiety level, can serve as influential retrieval cues in memory tasks.

In the study by Gordon et al. (1979) there was a reasonable delay between the original training and testing. Perhaps the subjects experienced a change in their internal state across this period, and for those that received no reactivation treatment memory retrieval on the test trial would be hindered. In the case of the group exposed to the apparatus for 15 sec this treatment would reactivate the training memory and enable it to incorporate infomation about the subject's current internal state. The internal state on the test trial will thus correspond with the internal state recently incorporated into the memory of the training trial, and this will serve to facilitate the retrieval of the training memory.

A further demonstration of the influence of a reactivation treatment comes from an experiment by Deweer, Sara, and Hars (1980, Experiment 2). Rats were initially trained to run through a maze containing 6 choice points to collect food. After only five trials the three groups were making as few as two errors a trial, and the time to run through the maze had fallen from some 300 sec on the first trial to about 50 sec on the fifth trial. One group (Group Immediate) was given a test trial on the next day, whereas the remaining subjects were not exposed to the apparatus for a retention interval of 25 days. Then, on the test session, one of the remaining groups (Group Delay) was run in the maze in the same manner as during training.

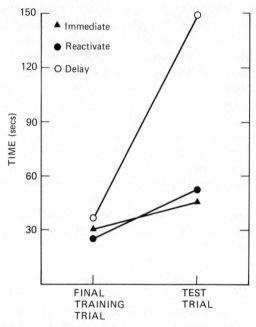

FIG. 3.5 .   Mean time taken by three groups of rats to run through a maze on the final training trial and on a subsequent test trial. For Group Immediate the interval between these trials was 1 day, for the other two groups it was 25 days. Group Reactivate was given reactivation treatment immediately before the test trial (adapted from Deweer et al., 1980).

The other group also received this test procedure, but immediately prior to it the rats were placed into a wire mesh cage beside the maze for 90 sec (Group Reactivate).

The results from the study are depicted in Fig. 3.5, which indicates the average time it took the three groups to run through the maze on the final training trial and on the test trial. The first feature to note is that on the test trial Group Immediate ran through the maze considerably more rapidly than Group Delay. This difference demonstrates forgetting by Group Delay. The more important point to note is that there was a similar difference between Group Delay and Group Reactivate on this trial. One explanation for this finding is that the exposure to the room cues prior to testing reactivated a memory of the original training. The presence of this information in Active Memory when the animal was placed into the maze itself should then facilitate running through the maze relative to Group Delay. For the latter subjects a period would be required to reactivate the training memory before they could negotiate the maze successfully.

By using reactivation treatments it has also proved possible to understand why ECS has such a disruptive influence on memory. Gordon and Mowrer (1980) trained rats to jump from a white compartment with an avoidance task similar to that described previously and tested their retention 3 days later. Animals that received ECS immediately after the initial training were much slower to respond on this retention test than controls given no ECS. But the deleterious effects of this ECS treatment were completely abolished if animals received a reactivation trial, consisting of brief exposure to the test apparatus, 15 min before the retention test.

According to retrieval theory, ECS acts by reducing the elaboration of memory necessary to ensure successful retrieval. The reactivation trial should—albeit with difficulty—have retrieved a memory of the original training and thus allowed it to undergo further elaboration to make it readily available at the time of testing. In keeping with this analysis it was found that reactivation not only alleviated the effects of ECS, but also improved performance relative to the group that had received neither ECS nor the reactivation treatment.

Concluding Comments

Taken together, the foregoing results provide impressive evidence that reactivation treatments can improve the efficiency of memory recall. Moreover, the finding that these treatments can counteract the effects of ECS suggests that this manipulation does not prevent the storage of information, as was originally claimed. It needs to be acknowledged, however, that our understanding of the way retrieval operates is still incomplete. Thus although efficient retrieval might depend on a period of elaboration after a training trial, it is not yet clear what this consists of or how long it should take. There is also some uncertainty about the way in which reactivation is effective. If exposure to the apparatus just before a test trial can activate a training memory, why should this not also occur on the test trial and result in normal performance? Perhaps the main advantage of retrieval theory is that it provides a framework in which issues such as these can be addressed.

PART 2: SHORT-TERM RETENTION

Various tasks have been used to study short-term retention in animals, and they reveal the common outcome that after being exposed to a source of information, subjects are able to utilise it for only a restricted period.

Human STM is said to hold 7 ($\pm$2) items of information (Miller, 1956), which can remain there for up to about 20 sec unless they are rehearsed. If there is any parallel between the short-term retention of information by animals and humans, then we should expect to find that this store also is capable of holding small amounts of information for relatively short intervals. In fact these properties seem to depend very much on the nature of the task that is used to study them.

METHODS OF STUDY

Habituation

In the experiments by Whitlow (1975) described in Chapter 2, the response to the second of a pair of identical tones was found to be weaker than to the one presented first. I argued that this effect was due to the presence of a representation of the initial member of the pair being stored in memory until its partner occurred. Of importance to the present discussion is the additional finding by Whitlow (1975) that this effect could only be found when the interval between the tones was less than 150 sec. This suggests that the memory of the initial tone persisted for a limited period, and thus Whitlow's study provides a relatively simple demonstration of short-term retention in the rabbit.

There has been a large number of investigations of habituation, using many species, but as noted in Chapter 2 the majority of these have lacked the appropriate controls to establish that the habituation reported did indeed depend on a memory of the test stimulus. It is therefore not possible to draw firm conclusions about short-term retention from many of these studies, and little more will be said about this method.

Conditioning

Typically in Pavlovian conditioning the CS remains on until at least the onset of the US. This technique is known as delay conditioning. With trace conditioning, the US is presented after the CS has been turned off, and for this training to be successful a memory of the CS must persist until the US occurs. Because trace conditioning is generally ineffective with relatively long trace intervals, it provides us with a method for studying short-term retention. In fact, it was thought originally that trace conditioning could only be effective with intervals extending up to a minute or so. More recent studies, however, have shown that this is incorrect and that the short-term retention of some animals can extend up to several hours. A study by Smith and Roll (1967) demonstrates this point.

Thirsty rats were permitted to drink saccharin solution from a tube in a test chamber for several minutes. At varying intervals after this treatment different groups were exposed to X-irradiation to induce illness. Two days later the animals were returned to the chambers, where they could drink either from a tube containing saccharin or from one containing water. Evidence of successful taste aversion conditioning was revealed by a low consumption of the saccharin solution. The results from this test are shown in Fig. 3.6, which indicates that even with a trace interval of 12 hours the consumption of saccharin was less than for a control group that was treated identically except that it never received X-irradiation.

In several experiments of this sort rats have been given either water or some other flavour to drink in the interval between consumption of the flavour CS and the onset of illness, so it is quite implausible to suppose that the original flavour could have lingered in the mouth throughout the trace interval (Revusky, 1971). Instead, the more plausible interpretation of taste aversion learning over long delays is that a memory trace of the CS persists until the US occurs, and it is the existence of this trace that is responsible for successful conditioning.

The discovery that taste aversion conditioning is possible with extensive trace intervals prompted a number of authors to suggest that taste aversion learning is not typical of conditioning in general. Seligman (1970) regards successful conditioning over such long delays as being due to the existence

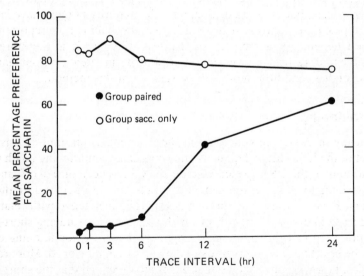

FIG. 3.6.   The preference of rats for drinking from a spout containing saccharin solution rather than water after they had previously received X-irradiation at different trace intervals following the consumption of saccharin solution (Group Paired). For Group Sacc Only, the consumption of saccharin was never followed by X-irradiation (adapted from Smith & Roll, 1967).

of a specialised taste-learning process. According to Garcia, McGowan, and Green (1972), the mechanism responsible for this learning resides in a neural region that is relatively insulated from stimuli arising in the external environment and is specialised to handle long trace intervals.

A variety of arguments have been offered to counter this suggestion (see, for example, Revusky, 1977), but perhaps the most convincing is that other, quite different preparations have also resulted in learning over surprisingly long trace intervals. In an experiment by D'Amato and Buckiewicz (1980), monkeys were allowed to explore a T-maze with a black arm and a striped arm. The next day they were confined in one arm for a minute and then placed into a holding chamber for 30 min. Upon their release they were put into the start box of the T-maze and allowed to consume 12 raisins. The monkeys were then given a test trial in which they could choose between the two arms of the maze. A control group was treated identically, except that the raisins were not available on their return to the start box. On the choice trial the monkeys that had been fed the raisins showed a significantly greater preference than the controls for the arm in which they had been confined for a minute. The implication from this study is that the monkeys had retained, at least for 30 min, a memory of the arm in which they had been confined (CS) and that this became associated with the raisins (US) by the experimental group. D'Amato and Buckiewicz (1980) regarded the preference for the arm in which they had been confined as an example of conditioned attraction consequent upon this trace conditioning.

A similar finding has been reported by D'Amato, Safarjan, and Salmon (1981), except that the subjects were rats and they were held and fed in a waste-paper basket before the choice trial in a T-maze. One group was confined in an arm of the T-maze for 40 min before being placed into the basket for 2 hr. After they had been fed, they were allowed to choose between the two arms of the maze. As with the monkeys, these subjects exhibited a greater preference for the arm in which they had been confined than a control group that was treated identically except that they were not fed in the waste-paper basket. Once again the explanation offered for this finding is that the memory of the arm of the maze was sustained for 2 hr and associated with the food that was eaten in the basket.

An intriguing study by Thomas, Lieberman, McIntosh, and Ronaldson (1983; see also Lieberman, McIntosh, & Thomas, 1979) identifies one factor that may be important in promoting learning across delays. Rats in Group Control were trained to run through a maze similar to that depicted in Fig. 3.7. After entering the choice box from the start box, they were permitted to enter either the black or the white side arm and then pass into the delay chamber, where they were confined for 2 min before being allowed to enter the goal box. Food was available in the goal box only on

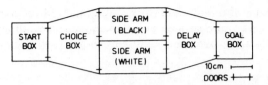

FIG. 3.7.   Ground plan of the maze used by Thomas et al. (from Thomas et al., 1983).

those trials when the rat had passed through the white arm. The results for this group are presented in Fig. 3.8, which shows that despite a large amount of training there was virtually no increase in the preference for the white arm.

A second group in this study, Group Marker, was treated in much the same way except that both correct responses, of entering the white compartment, and incorrect responses, of entering the black compartment, were "marked" by being followed immediately with a two-sec burst of white noise. This modest procedural change was sufficient to produce a substantial improvement in performance (see Fig. 3.8). To explain this finding, Thomas et al. (1983) suggested that each burst of noise surprised the rat and resulted in the formation of a relatively salient memory of the response that had produced it. As a consequence, when food is delivered some 2 min later, subjects should be more likely in Group Marker than Control to remember their choice response and learn about its significance.

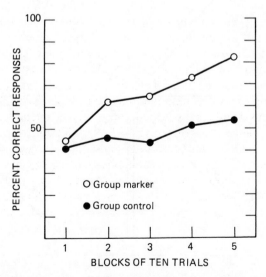

FIG. 3.8.   Percentage of correct responses by Group Control and Group Marker, in 10-trial blocks, in the marking study by Thomas et al. (adapted from Thomas et al., 1983).

In addition to this work with rats, Lieberman, Davidson, and Thomas (1985) have also demonstrated an improvement in learning over a delay with pigeons as a result of marking their choice response.

The Radial Maze

A diagram of a radial maze, together with the dimensions of its various components, is presented in Fig. 3.9. A trial typically starts with a rat being placed in the arena at the centre of the apparatus and with a pellet of food in a hole at the end of each arm. The rat is then allowed to explore the maze and remains in it until it has visited the eight arms and collected all the available food. After a number of such trials with this task rats become very efficient at collecting food and rarely visit the same arm more than once per trial. In order to perform with this accuracy it has been claimed that the rat remembers either the arms that have been visited, or those that remain to be visited.

There are a number of rather obvious alternative explanations for successful performance with this maze, and these must be discounted

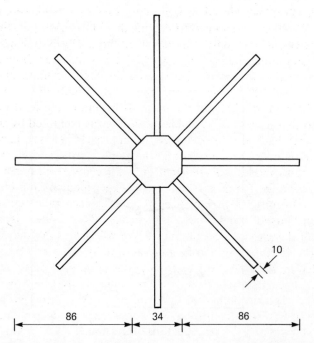

FIG. 3.9.   Top view of an 8-arm radial maze (dimensions in cm) (from Olton & Samuelson, 1978).

before we accept this explanation too willingly. The rat may adopt a stereotyped pattern of responding, such as always selecting the adjacent unvisited arm. Alternatively, it may be able to detect by the smell of food which arms remain to be visited. Finally, it could mark with a secretion the entrance to the arms that have been visited and avoid this substance in the future. Olton (1978), who developed the radial maze, cites several convincing aruments against these accounts (see also Roberts, 1979), but perhaps the clearest case is made by Suzuki, Augerinos, and Black (1980, Experiment 2).

Rats were trained with an 8-arm radial maze located in a vertical, black cylindrical chamber. At the end of each arm, on the walls of the cylinder, was suspended a distinctive stimulus such as a toy bird, christmas tree lights, and so on. Once the rats were performing efficiently on the maze, the task was modified slightly. At the start of a trial subjects were confined to the central arena with doors blocking access to the arms. One door was then opened, and the rat was able to run down the arm to collect food. On returning to the arena the door was closed and another opened, and the rat could collect the next pellet. After three such forced trials all the doors were opened, and the subject was expected to go to the arms it had not been forced to in order to retrieve food.

Training continued in this manner until very few errors were made. At this point in the experiment, after making three forced choices, the animals were confined in the central arena for 2.5 min. During this interval the experimenter either did nothing, switched the distinctive stimuli around in an unsystematic fashion, or else rotated the entire cylindrical chamber, thus retaining the original configuration of stimuli but altering their relationship with the arms of the maze. In addition, the food was moved around so that it was not available in those arms identified by the stimuli that the rat had just been forced to approach. These changes were conducted without the animal's knowledge. After the entire cylinder had been rotated it was discovered that the subjects were just as accurate at choosing the baited arms as when the the experimenter did nothing to the apparatus. In contrast, their choices were far less accurate after the stimuli had been moved around unsystematically. This failure is important because, if rats choose arms on the basis of whether or not they can detect food at the end, they should respond accurately no matter what changes are made. In addition, both manipulations resulted in rats returning to arms they had already visited. It is thus unlikely that their performance was based upon whether or not an arm had been marked by a secretion. It is also difficult to explain these findings by assuming that rats adopt a stereotyped response pattern in the radial maze. If this were the case, they would be unable to perform correctly when the cylinder was rotated.

Taken together, the results from this study suggest that rats identify and remember arms on the basis of the stimuli at their ends. However, this is not achieved by associating each arm with a single stimulus, because this strategy would allow accurate performance when the stimuli were moved around unsystematically. Instead, the most likely interpretation is that rats identify the arms on the basis of the configuration of the stimuli surrounding them. If this conclusion should seem unreasonable, recall that it was also prompted by the findings of Cheng and Galistel (1984) that were discussed in the previous chapter.

In order to examine how long information relevant to the solution of radial maze problems can reside in memory, Beatty and Shavalia (1980a) returned rats to their home cage after they had made four choices in an 8-arm maze. After a given period had elapsed, they were allowed to complete the trial. When this period of removal was four hours or less, subjects were still very accurate in selecting the arms they had not previously visited. There was, however, a marked and systematic decline in this accuracy when the delay was extended to 8, 12, and 24 hours.

There have also been attempts to establish how much information can be remembered when animals are solving radial maze problems. Olton (1978) has suggested that with an 8-arm maze the animal must remember 7 locations in order to perform perfectly, but this may not be the limit of the rat's memory capacity. Olton, Collison, and Werz (1977) employed a 17-arm maze and found that even in these circumstances rats performed well above a level predicted by chance. Roberts (1979) constructed an 8-arm maze in which 3 subsidiary arms branched off from the end of the principal arms. On every trial, therefore, the subjects had to visit 24 different locations to collect food, and even in these circumstances they soon learned to perform with very few errors. Although these latter findings might suggest that rats can remember something approaching 24 different locations, there was evidence in both studies that they adopted some sort of response strategy that may have reduced the burden on their memory. Thus whereas the results show that rats are very good at performing on complex mazes, they may not provide unambiguous information about the capacity of their memory.

Before leaving this discussion of the radial maze a report by Roberts and Van Veldhuizen (1985) merits brief mention. They examined the performance of pigeons in the radial maze. With appropriate training this species made no more errors than rats in an 8-arm maze, and there was no evidence that they adopted a stereotyped response pattern to aid their memory. In addition, in one experiment subjects were forced to select 4 arms before they were confined to the central arena for intervals up to 6 min. When they were then allowed to choose from the 8 arms, they reliably selected those that had not previously been visited. Performance at all delays was above chance, but there was some evidence of forgetting with longer intervals. Thus, as with the rat, pigeons demonstrate a reasonably capacious memory when solving radial maze problems, but it may not be as durable.

Delayed Matching to Sample (DMTS)

In contrast to the robust effects just described, the implication of studies with DMTS is that short-term retention is rather poor. Subjects are presented with one of two stimuli at the beginning of a trial. In the case of pigeons, this could be the illumination of a response key by either red or green light. After a while this "sample" stimulus is turned off and nothing is presented for a period known as the "retention interval". At the end of this interval two different response keys are illuminated, one with red the other with green light. These are referred to as the "comparison stimuli". To gain reward, the pigeon must peck the comparison colour that is the same as the sample presented on that particular trial. Pecks to the other colour normally result in both keys being darkened and no reward. After the completion of the trial, whether the subject is correct or not, there is a period in which nothing happens—the "intertrial interval"—before the sample is presented for the next trial. In order to gain reward, then, the subject must store information at the time the sample is presented and use it to select the correct response when the comparison stimuli are subsequently available.

Unlike the tasks already considered, DMTS is extremely difficult to learn. Subjects must first be trained with the single sample and two comparison stimuli presented simultaneously. Once they have learned to peck the comparison that matches the sample, the comparison stimuli are presented as soon as the sample is turned off. After considerable training, this 0-sec retention interval is gradually extended, but rarely to very long intervals. For example, most researchers use delays of 5 to 10 sec when pigeons are subjects. In one study, Grant (1976) obtained reasonably accurate performance by pigeons on DMTS with a 1-min retention interval. This was achieved at the expense of considerable effort by both experimenter and subjects, as it required some 17,000 training trials.

Other species fare little better when this technique is adapted for them. D'Amato and O'Neill (1971) found with monkeys that accurate retention was possible for 2 min, and with careful training this can be extended to 9 min (D'Amato & Worsham, 1982). Using dolphins, accurate DMTS has been achieved with a 4-min retention interval (Herman & Thompson, 1982).

There has been relatively little research into the question of how much information can be stored during the retention interval with DMTS. But that which has been conducted suggests it is very limited. Riley and Roitblat (1978; Riley, 1984) employed a version of DMTS in which two samples were projected simultaneously onto the same key at the outset of a trial. Pigeons were required to remember information about both in order to perform accurately. Performance in this instance was inferior to that when only a single sample was used. The unlikely implication of this finding is that the memory of pigeons is stretched when they must retain simultaneously information about two items, even for short periods. Both Riley (1984) and Cox and D'Amato (1982), however, have provided entirely plausible alternative explanations for this decrement with 2 samples, and at present there is little that can be said with confidence about the capacity of memory as revealed by DMTS.

The most obvious account of successful delayed matching is that subjects remember the sample until the the comparison stimuli are presented, whereupon the comparison stimulus that matches the memory of the sample can be selected (see, for example, Roberts and Grant, 1976). The memory of the sample in this instance is referred to as a retrospective code, because it is of a stimulus that has already occurred.

More recent evidence suggests that this attractively simple view may be wrong, at least under certain circumstances (Gaffan, 1977; Honig, 1978; Roitblat, 1980). As an alternative it may well be that at the time the sample is presented subjects store an instruction of the form "peck the green comparison stimulus". Obviously the memory of an inarticulate animal would not encode the information in precisely this way, but the point should be clear that it is knowledge about a mode of responding that is being stored. Because this knowledge relates to how the subject should respond in the future, it is referred to as a prospective code.

Much of the evidence that relates to this proposal is based upon experimental procedures that are not among the easiest to describe, or comprehend. In addition, as Grant (1981) concludes from his review of these studies, their interpretation is difficult as they occasionally yield ambiguous findings. Little space is therefore devoted to this issue, except to describe one experiment that is at least consistent with the claim that pigeons can employ a prospective code. Roitblat (1980) conducted a matching study with three different coloured samples and three line orientations as the comparison stimuli. On any trial a single sample was shown and followed after a retention interval by the simultaneous presentation of the comparisons on three different keys. Table 3.1 shows the colours and line orientations used, and the way they were paired. Hence, on trials with a blue sample, the subject had to peck the comparison key with a vertical line on it to obtain food.

With extended retention intervals, Roitblat (1980) discovered that pigeons made more errors when the blue and orange samples were used

TABLE 3.1
Sample Stimuli, Presented Individually,
and Comparison Stimuli,
Presented Simultaneously,
Used in the Study by Roitblat (1980)

Sample stimuli	Comparison stimuli
Blue	Vertical (0 degrees)
Orange	Slant (12.5 degrees)
Red	Horizontal (90 degrees)

Note: After being exposed to a sample, pigeons were expected to peck the comparison with which it is paired in the table in order to gain food.

than when red was the sample. This effect, he proposed, suggests that they stored a prospective code during the retention interval. The prospective codes on trials with the blue and orange samples will involve information about the vertical and slanting lines. Because these stimuli are rather similar, differing by only 12.5 degrees, any deterioration of the prospective memory during the interval would make it difficult to identify the correct comparison at the end of the trial. On the other hand, when red is the sample, a deterioration of the prospective code for the horizontal comparison might still be expected to permit identification of the correct key, because this comparison stimulus is so different from the other two. Furthermore, if subjects employed a retrospective code, then a different outcome to this study would be anticipated. Any forgetting about the samples would lead to more errors on trials when red and orange rather than blue were used.

Theoretical Interpretation

Thus far relatively little has been said about the processes that are responsible for the findings of short-term retention in animals that we have considered. The simplest approach would be to adopt the distinction made for humans and assume that STM is responsible for the temporary storage required in all of the above tasks. If this is correct, then we might expect animals to remember similar amounts of information for similar intervals, irrespective of the task employed. But this has not proved to be the case. Using the radial maze, for example, the impression would be gained that STM is both durable and of large capacity. In stark contrast, if the results from studies of DMTS are taken at face value, then STM would seem to be a rather poor store for information. The question is thus raised as to whether the different procedures that have been discussed utilise different memory processes. I do not believe it is possible to answer this question with complete certainty, but I favour the possibility that all the findings we have been reviewing are due to the operation of the same memory system. To account for the variety of outcomes that have been reported, we must look to differences in the procedures that led to them.

One reason for the excellent memory revealed by the radial maze is that there are many features that enable the different arms to be identified. They occupy different spatial locations, they will be placed next to different features of the room housing the equipment, and they may even differ in the way they look, feel, and smell. In contrast, with DMTS the samples are generally presented in a very similar manner and differ in only a single attribute: usually colour. Perhaps it is easier to remember items that are composed of many distinctive attributes. Support for such a possibility comes from a study by Mazmanian and Roberts (1983) who trained two groups of rats on a radial maze. One group was permitted unrestricted views of the room while running in the maze; for the other, the careful placement of screens allowed only a restricted view of the room. In the latter case, the information available to identify the arms must have been considerably reduced, and, as evidenced by the number of errors, they were very much harder to remember. Surprisingly, no one has attempted to demonstrate the converse of this effect of improving DMTS with the use of radically different samples.

A further difference between the various techniques we have discussed is the frequency with which the trials are conducted. Typically, conditioning with long trace intervals is successful only when there is a very long interval between the trials, or in the limiting case when only a single trial is given (e.g. Smith & Roll, 1967; Kaplan, 1984). Trials with the radial maze tend to be performed once a day. In the case of DMTS, 60 or more trials may be presented in a single session with an average intertrial interval of only 30 sec. It turns out that massing trials in this way can have a profoundly disruptive effect on performance on this kind of task and may well contribute to the difference between DMTS and the other tasks. To understand why this should be, it is necessary to discuss the factors that are responsible for forgetting.

Before we turn our attention to forgetting, however, one further factor that may be responsible for the diversity of findings described previously needs to be considered. Lett (1978) has suggested that in some short-term retention tasks information is held temporarily in LTM and transferred to STM only when it is needed. This suggestion has by no means gained universal acceptance; but if it is true, then until we can identify when this strategy is being used it will be difficult to draw any meaningful conclusions about the properties of STM.

FORGETTING

In all of the experiments considered in the previous section the retention of information may be short-term simply because it decays with the passage of time. More detailed consideration of such forgetting, however, suggests an alternative or at least additional explanation. Items are not remembered in isolation—instead they are presented against a backgound of many other events. It may be that this additional material is responsible for forgetting, either because its presence in memory serves as a source of confusion, or because it displaces the representation of the target from memory. In either case the material can be said to induce forgetting by interference.

At a procedural level it is possible to identify two potential sources of interference. "Proactive interference" is said to occur when information acquired prior to the target item disrupts its retention. "Retroactive interference" is used to describe the forgetting of information that occurs because it is followed by something distracting. Although both types of interference may be due to the same process, this distinction is useful, if only because it serves to organise a rather large body of diverse experimental findings. After examining a number of demonstrations of proactive and retroactive interference, we consider the various theories that have been offered to explain these effects.

Proactive Interference

A modified DMTS design was adopted by Grant and Roberts (1973) to study proactive interference with pigeons. On control trials, straightforward DMTS with only a single sample was conducted, but at the start of other trials two possible samples were presented in succession, separated by a gap of either 0 or 10 sec. For these trials subjects were rewarded if they pecked the comparison stimulus that was the same as the more recently presented sample. When the interval between the two samples was 10 sec, subjects chose the correct comparison with an accuracy equivalent to that when only a single sample was presented. But when the interval between the samples was 0 sec, there was a significant reduction in the accuracy of matching. Thus the presence of the first sample can be said to have interfered proactively with the memory of the second one, but only when the interval between them was minimal.

A between-trials demonstration of proactive interference with DMTS is provided by Grant (1975). Pigeons were given a single delayed matching trial with two stimuli, X and Y, serving as the comparisons, and X as the sample. Immediately following this trial they received another trial with the same comparison stimuli, but on this occasion Y served as the sample. Performance on the second trial was less accurate in these circumstances than when the first trial was omitted. This finding suggests that when the first trial was given, the memory of the sample persisted into the second trial and made it harder for subjects to identify the correct comparison.

A similar effect has been reported by Olton (1978), who demonstrated that the choices on one trial with the radial maze can influence the errors made on the subsequent trial. (Recall that a trial is defined as being completed when all the arms have been visited). During a trial the subject must keep a record of the arms it has already visited or has still got to visit. If this information should be retained, then its presence at the start of a new trial could be extremely disruptive. Normally, trials with the radial maze are conducted at the rate of one a day, and this problem does not occur, because the information about one trial is likely to have disappeared long before the start of the next trial. But if the interval between trials is reduced, then the potential for the memories of one trial to interfere proactively with performance on the next one will be increased. In order to test this possibility, Olton (1978) conducted 8 radial maze trials a day with 1 min between each trial. Figure 3.10 shows the results plotted for 8 successive trials in one day. On Trial 1 rats made very few errors, and it was only when they had visited 7 of the 8 arms that they occasionally made a mistake by revisiting one of the arms. With an increase in the number of trials, performance on the latter part of each trial showed more errors than on the first trial. This deterioration in performance can be regarded as an effect of proactive interference due to the initial training trials.

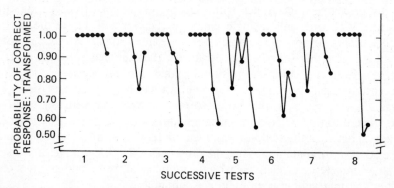

FIG. 3.10.   The corrected mean probability of a correct response for choices on an 8-arm radial maze when 8 test trials were given in succession (from Olton, 1978).

Retroactive Interference

A straightforward demonstration of retroactive interference comes from the study by Whitlow (1975), discussed on page 36, who found that the presentation of a 2-sec distractor in the 60-sec interval between two identical tones eliminated the habituation normally observed to the second tone. Because it has been argued that habituation results from the persistence of a memory for the first tone, the distractor can be said to have interfered with this memory. The term "retroactive interference" is used to refer to this effect because the distractor disrupted the memory of a previous event.

Retroactive interference has been revealed with pigeons by Grant and Roberts (1976) using DMTS. During the interval between the offset of the sample and the onset of the comparison stimuli there was a change in the illumination of the test chamber. This manipulation appears to have interfered retroactively with the memory of the sample because subjects found greater difficulty in identifying the correct comparison stimulus than when the change in illumination was omitted. Similar effects have been observed with dolphins (Herman, 1975), and monkeys (D'Amato, 1973). A surprising finding is that for monkeys and pigeons the only effective distractor for DMTS is a change in illumination (D'Amato, 1973; Grant & Roberts, 1976; Kraemer & Roberts, 1984). Thus, for example, retroactive interference does not occur when sounds are presented in the retention interval. This is true for monkeys even when the sounds consist of the vocalisations of other members of the species.

It is also possible to observe retroactive interference with radial maze tasks, but here the distracting event must be quite substantial. A typical experiment involves confining a rat to the central arena after it has made 4 forced choices on an 8-arm maze (Maki, Brokofsky, & Berg, 1979; Beatty & Shavalia, 1980b). A variety of events such as lights, sounds, odours, and food are then presented to the subject before it is allowed to continue the trial. Very often, such treatment has no influence at all on the 4 remaining choices, and more dramatic means of demonstrating retroactive interference are required. One technique that has been tried is to remove the animal from the radial maze after it has made 4 choices and to give it a trial with a different piece of apparatus. Such an interpolated trial can involve another 8-arm maze and be conducted in either the same or a different room. When conducted in the same room, the second maze may be physically superimposed upon the first. Despite the similarity of the distracting interpolated trial with the original trial, it is still difficult to demonstrate retroactive interference. Indeed, Roberts (1981) reports that it is necessary to expose subjects to three identical mazes in different rooms before they display any significant decline in accuracy on the remaining 4 choices of the target trial.

THEORETICAL INTERPRETATION

Two accounts have dominated theorising about short-term retention. They both maintain that STM is responsible for this retention, but they ascribe different properties to it. One asserts that STM is of limited capacity and that an item is forgotten because it is displaced by more recent events. According to the other, information gradually decays, quite spontaneously, from STM, and this is the reason for forgetting. By using these simple principles theorists have been able to account for many of the effects outlined previously. Nonetheless, it will be argued that both accounts are contradicted by recent evidence.

Decay Theory

Roberts and Grant (1974, 1976) proposed that the presentation of a stimulus activates a representation, or trace, which persists in STM even after the stimulus has been removed. But traces do not last indefinitely; as soon as the stimulus ends, the trace starts to decay. The initial strength and persistence of this trace is determined by the intensity and duration of the stimulus concerned. An important feature of this theory is that the strength of a trace is not influenced at all by other traces currently residing in STM. The theory asserts, therefore, that STM is of unrestricted capacity and the number of items it stores is determined by the frequency with which they occur in the environment.

In a task such as DMTS, it is assumed that if a number of items are in memory when the comparison stimuli are presented, then the one with the strongest trace will determine the subject's choice. Errors will occur if the traces of two samples are present and of equal strength, because it will be difficult to identify the relevant one. This outcome would be expected to occur in the study by Grant and Roberts (1973) when a target sample was preceded immediately by one that was irrelevant. Increasing the interval between the two samples will enhance the discrepancy in the strength of their traces and make it easier to identify the trace of the correct sample, and this account thus correctly accounts for the finding that a distracting sample produces most proactive interference when it is presented immediately before the sample. In a similar way, decay theory can also account for the proactive interference produced by one trial that shortly precedes another (Grant, 1975; Olton, 1978).

A problem with decay theory, as Grant (1981, p. 229) has pointed out, is that it does not provide a very good account of the sort of retroactive interference effects reported by Whitlow (1975). In that study presentation of a distractor between a pair of identical tones attenuated habituation to the second tone. Because the distractor should not influence the memory of the preceding tone, it is hard to understand why it resulted in dishabituation. For similar reasons it is not clear why a change in illumination should interfere retroactively with DMTS. As we shall see, limited capacity theories provide a much better account for this type of interference.

Limited Capacity Theory

Wagner (1976, 1978, 1979, 1981) has also proposed that STM contains a number of decaying memory traces. In addition, this store is assumed to be of limited capacity. The introduction of a stimulus, therefore, will not only result in a representation of itself being formed, it will also weaken or displace any previously formed traces. These principles have already been introduced to explain Wagner, Rudy, and Whitlow's (1973) finding that a surprising event after a CS–US pairing can disrupt conditioning.

The retroactive interference effects that posed a problem for decay theory can also be understood within this framework. Presenting a distractor after a target, such as a sample in DMTS, will weaken the trace of the target and make it that much harder for it to be effective at the time of testing. The retroactive interference observed with the radial maze is also consistent with this account. Furthermore, by adding the assumption that items already in STM can restrict the strength of new traces, this theory can account for many of the effects of proactive interference. Thus it would be difficult to store a list of arms that have been visited during a trial with the radial maze if STM is already full with information from previous trials.

Despite these successes there remain problems for decay theory. It does not explain why, for pigeons and monkeys, DMTS is susceptible to retroactive interference only when the distractor is a change of illumination. The use of other distractors should also reduce the trace strength of the sample and result in forgetting. In addition, it is not immediately clear why immunity to retroactive interference should be so much greater for tasks such as the radial maze than, say, habituation.

Deliberate Forgetting

As it has been described, STM is rather a passive repository for information, with the duration of a trace being determined solely by its intensity and the number of other traces that are present. Recently a number of different authors have suggested that the storage of information may be more flexible than this account implies, and when information is irrelevant to a task it might be discarded by a process of deliberate or active forgetting.

Olton (1978) was among the first to suggest that rats actively forget information that is no longer relevant, supporting this claim by his study of proactive interference which we considered earlier. Olton (1978) was impressed by the small amount of proactive interference when rats were given a series of massed trials on the radial maze—that is, by the accuracy of his rats when they were given several trials in succession (see Fig. 3.10). Accordingly, he proposed that rats can erase or reset the contents of memory at the end of each trial. In this way the memory of arms visited on one trial would not be able to interfere with the task of trying to remember which arms had already been visited on a subsequent trial.

More recent evidence has suggested that Olton (1978) may have greatly exaggerated his rats' efficiency. Roberts and Dale (1981) repeated Olton's study, and at the same time they kept a record of the pattern of responding within each trial. Although they were able essentially to replicate Olton's (1978) findings, they discovered that the use of massed trials resulted in rats adopting the response strategy of always choosing the adjacent arm. This outcome indicates that the memories formed on one trial may not be reset at the end of a trial. Instead, in order to overcome the potentially interfering effects of these memories, the rats were forced to find a method that did not involve remembering the arms they had visited. A further observation by Roberts and Dale (1981) is consistent with this interpretation. At the start of a trial rats showed a marked tendency to avoid the arm selected last on the preceding trial. This bias should not be evident if information about the preceding trial had been erased from memory upon its completion.

Although there may be little evidence for the deliberate forgetting of information from one trial to the next, it is possible that rats employ deliberate memory strategies within a radial maze trial. Thus far I have followed Olton (1978) and others in assuming that the radial maze task imposes an increasing burden on memory as each trial progresses. After 7 choices, for example, the rat must remember all 7 arms if it is to choose the one unvisited arm. A moment's thought, however, suggests that this is an uneconomical strategy. At this point in the trial, the rat need only remember the one unvisited arm. The most efficient strategy, in terms of minimising the burden on memory, is to remember the arms already visited, in order to avoid them, for the first half of the trial, and the arms that have not been visited, in order to select them, for the second half of the trial. In this way the subject could perform the entire task without having to remember more than half the arms of the maze.

A study by Cook, Brown, and Riley (1985), using a 12-arm radial maze, suggests that rats do indeed adopt this sensible strategy. Once they had learned the problem, they were occasionally removed from the apparatus for a period of 15 min after the 2nd, 4th, 6th, 8th, or 10th choice. If they were always remembering which arms they had already visited on a trial, then this additional delay should be most difficult to cope with when their memory is most overburdened—that is, after 10 choices. On the other hand, if they remembered the arms that remained to be visited, then the delay should be most disruptive after 2 choices. Instead, they made most errors when the delay was imposed after 6 choices. The implication of this finding is that the subject's memory is most burdened at the half-way point in a trial, and this is exactly what would be expected if they adopted the strategy just outlined.

Turning now to the pigeon, it has also been suggested that this species is capable of deliberate forgetting. After giving subjects standard DMTS training, Maki and Hegvik (1980) introduced trials in which the sample was immediately followed by one of two stimuli. One stimulus, known as the "remember cue", signalled that the comparison stimuli would be presented at the end of the retention interval. The other stimulus, the "forget cue", signalled that the comparison stimuli would not be presented. On these latter trials, then, there was no need to remember the sample, and the forget cue could serve as a signal for the sample to be forgotten. To examine whether the forget cue did serve this function, subjects were occasionally tricked by being presented with the comparison stimuli at the end of the forget cue trials. If this cue does make pigeons actively forget the sample, then on these test trials they should be very poor at identifying the correct comparison. The results were consistent with this prediction (see also Colwill, 1984; Grant, 1984).

The issue of whether or not animals are capable of deliberately forgetting information is one that has been raised only recently. We should not be surprised, therefore, to find that the interpretation of many of the results in this area is still a matter for debate (e.g. Kendrick, Rilling, & Stonebraker, 1981). But if it should be discovered that animals are capable of deliberately forgetting, and perhaps also deliberately remembering, then this would have important implications for our understanding of forgetting in general. We should have to acknowledge that neither decay nor interference theory by themselves can provide an adequate account of forgetting because, superimposed upon these processes, would be deliberate memory strategies that greatly influenced their outcome.

SERIAL POSITION EFFECTS

When humans are given a list of words and asked to recall them immediately, they typically get the first and last few items correct but are more likely to make mistakes with the middle of the list. This pattern is referred to as the serial position curve. The good recall of early items is referred to as "primacy", whereas the term "recency" refers to the good recall of the later items. These effects have been extensively studied with humans, but they still remain a matter of theoretical debate. One suggestion is that they reflect the combined influence of proactive and retroactive interference (e.g. Baddeley, 1976). Memory for the items in the middle of the list is said to be poor because of proactive interference from the items they follow, and retroactive interference from the items they precede. In contrast, recall of the extremes of the list should be somewhat better because they will suffer from only one source of interference. If this interpretation is correct, then it implies—as animal memory is disrupted by both proactive and retroactive interference—that animals too should manifest serial position effects when required to remember lists.

Recency effects have been relatively easy to demonstrate with a variety of species. Thompson and Herman (1977) presented bottle-nosed dolphins with a list of 6 sounds, after which they were presented with a test sound. On some trials the test sound was different to those in the list; on others, it was identical to a member of the list, but the position of the one to which it corresponded varied from trial to trial. The task confronting the dolphin was to indicate whether or not the test sound had occurred in the list.

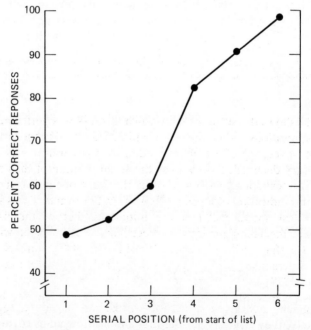

FIG. 3.11.   Percentage of correct recognitions, by dolphins, of a probe that had previously been presented in a list of 6 items, according to its serial position (adapted from Thompson & Herman, 1977).

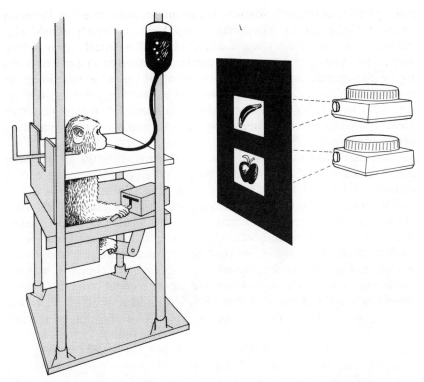

FIG. 3.12.   Physical arrangement of the monkey, primate chair, response lever, stimulus panel and projectors used in the study by Sands and Wright (from Sands & Wright, 1980).

Figure 3.11 shows the accuracy with which this task was performed for the various list positions. When the test sound was identical to the last member of the list, a recency effect of responding very accurately was revealed. This accuracy declined, however, as the serial position of the sound that matched the test sound moved towards the front of the list. There was, however, no indication of a primacy effect, as performance was very poor when the test sound matched the initial member of the list. Using variations of this technique similar effects have been revealed with rhesus monkeys (Gaffan, 1977; Gaffan & Weiskrantz, 1980), squirrel monkeys (Roberts & Kraemer, 1981), pigeons (Macphail, 1980), and rats (Roberts & Smythe, 1979).

Successful demonstrations of a primacy effect in list learning have been reported by Dimattia and Kesner (1984) and Wright, Santiago, Sands, and Urcuioli (1984). The apparatus employed by Wright et al. (1984) was similar to that depicted in Fig. 3.12. A monkey was seated in front of a screen onto which pictures could be projected, either to the upper or lower half. For the first part of each trial a list of four different pictures presented in succession was projected onto the upper part of the screen. After a retention interval, which varied from trial to trial, a picture was presented on the lower panel of the screen. If this picture was the same as one in the list, then subjects were required to push the lever in one direction; otherwise, the lever had to be pushed in a different direction. Correct responses in both cases were rewarded with a squirt of orange juice or a banana-flavoured pellet. After a short interval the next trial commenced with a new set of pictures.

The results from one monkey, Joe, are summarised in the upper row of Fig. 3.13. The figure shows the percentage of trials on which Joe accurately identified the test picture as being identical to one in the list, according to list position. The three graphs depict the results obtained with three different retention intervals. When the test picture followed immediately after the list, Joe's performance was similar to that of the bottle-nosed dolphin: there was a strong effect of recency but not of primacy. With a retention interval of 10 sec a serial position curve was obtained, with the initial and later items being remembered more accurately than those in the middle of the list. Finally, with a retention interval of 30 sec there was evidence of a primacy but no recency effect. This abolition of accurate recall of the last members of the list with a long retention interval has also been reported by Gaffan and Weiskrantz (1980), also using monkeys.

The middle row of Fig. 3.13 shows the striking similarity between the performance of Joe and that of a 13-year-old boy when tested on a similar task. The task was made harder by—among other changes—using longer retention intervals. Despite these changes, the similarity of the performance of these subjects as the retention interval lengthens hardly needs emphasising.

Turning, finally, to the lower row of Fig. 3.13, we see the results from a pigeon, who was trained in a similar manner to the monkey but obviously in a different apparatus. The retention intervals were also shorter for the pigeon. Once again, the results bear a striking similarity to the serial position curves of the boy and Joe. Taken together, these results lend compelling support to the suggestion by Wright et al. (1984) that similar processes underlie list learning in humans, monkeys, and pigeons.

One issue left unresolved by the studies of Wright et al. (1984) is that of explaining why the retention interval should exert such an influence on the primacy effect. I am not sure that it is yet possible to answer this question correctly, but Wright et al. (1984) have suggested that it is due to the passage of time reducing retroactive interference from the later members of the list.

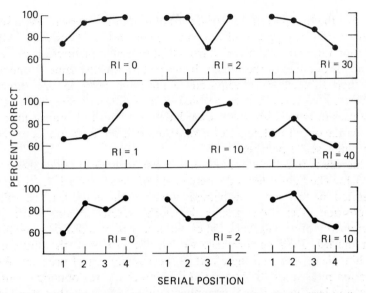

FIG. 3.13.   Serial position curves for a monkey (upper row), a boy (middle row), and a pigeon (lower row) when they were required to identify whether or not a probe had occurred in a previously presented 4-item list. For each subject, a number of different retention intervals (RI) between the last item of the list and the presentation of the probe were employed; these intervals also differed across species (adapted from Wright et al., 1984).

CONCLUSIONS

The findings by Wright et al. (1984) suggest that there is a striking similarity between the memory processes of different species, and in general the results from many studies of animal memory are consistent with this conclusion. For example, using spatial learning tasks, such as the radial maze, short-term retention has been found to be both capacious and durable for rats (Olton, 1978), pigeons (Roberts & Van Veldhuizen, 1985), chimpanzees (Menzel, 1978), a species of the Hawaiian honeycreeper (Kamil, 1978), and the savannah sparrow (Moore & Osadchuk, 1982). Similarly, when memory is investigated with DMTS, the results are not very different for species as diverse as pigeons and dolphins. Perhaps even more remarkable is the finding by Menzel (1979) that ECS has the same sort of disruptive influence on learning in bees as it has with rats. Conceivably species differ in the degree to which they use deliberate memory strategies; but because interest in this topic has arisen only recently, it is not yet possible to evaluate it.

One finding that is inconsistent with the tone of the above paragraph is provided by Roitblat, Tham, and Golub (1982). They trained Siamese fighting fish in an aquatic 8-arm radial maze and found that successful performance depended on the development of response strategies of swimming down adjacent arms in a clockwise or anti-clockwise direction. When steps were taken to disrupt this strategy, there was a marked deterioration in the efficiency of responding. This finding may be due to the memory system of the Siamese fighting fish being radically different to anything that has been considered so far. But given the generality of the findings discussed in this chapter, it is just as plausible that some more trivial factor was responsible for the inability of these fish to perform efficiently on the maze. Perhaps the construction of the maze was such that it prevented subjects from seeing the spatial cues that surrounded it. We have already seen that such a restriction will impair the performance of a rat on the radial maze, and the same may also be true for Siamese fighting fish.

4 Associative Learning

Often in an animal's environment one event will reliably predict another. The ingestion of some flavours will be followed by illness, whereas others will lead to beneficial consequences. Some environments will frequently be visited by predators, others will not. In addition, the action of the animal itself may result in consistent consequences: Following a certain route might take it to food or water, whereas different paths might lead to danger. Any animal that knows about these relationships will benefit because it will be able to anticipate future events and behave appropriately in preparation for them. But how can this knowledge be acquired? In an unchanging world animals could be born with it so that, for instance, the consumption of a certain flavour would automatically and consistently result in it being consumed or rejected. The world, however, is not unchanging: At the very least the location of food will change from generation to generation, and so too might the relationship between the taste or sight of food and its gastric consequences. Accordingly, animals must themselves discover which events reliably signal important consequences, and one way of achieving this is by the process of associative learning.

Methodologically, it is possible to distinguish between two sorts of associative learning. There is that which occurs when one stimulus reliably predicts another, as exemplified by Pavlovian conditioning in which a neutral conditioned stimulus (CS) signals a biologically significant unconditioned stimulus (US). There is also the learning that occurs during instrumental conditioning when an animal's behaviour results in a consistent outcome. In the present chapter we shall focus principally on what has been discovered about the mechanisms of associative learning by the study of Pavlovian conditioning. It is left to Chapter 6 to consider instrumental conditioning.

At first sight there may seem to be little of interest in studying the process that enables a dog to salivate in the presence of a light paired with food, or a rabbit to blink whenever it hears a tone that signals a mild cheek shock. But once it is acknowledged that these conditioned responses (CRs) are a product of a process that is essential for learning about the sequential structure of the environment, then they become of fundamental importance. Their occurrence allows us to study in detail a basic process of animal cognition.

The first part of this chapter introduces three first-order conditioning techniques, in which the CS is paired directly with the US. These have proved particularly useful in the study of associative learning and are mentioned often in the forthcoming sections. But it is not only with first-order conditioning that associative learning has been studied. This sort of learning should take place whenever one stimulus reliably follows another, and to explore this possibility the effects of serial and second-order conditioning, where two CSs are paired, are also examined.

Any training in which one stimulus predicts the occurrence of another is known as excitatory conditioning, with the CS being referred to as a conditioned excitor. It is, however, posssible for a CS to predict the omission of a US, and then it is referred to as a conditioned inhibitor. We shall also examine the techniques, as well as the effects, of such inhibitory conditioning. The final part of the chapter considers the factors that are responsible for associative learning; originally it was thought to occur automatically whenever a CS and US were paired together, but more recent evidence suggests that it takes place only when the second event is unexpected or surprising.

FIRST-ORDER CONDITIONING

Methods of Study

Eye-blink Conditioning.   For eye-blink conditioning the subject, normally a rabbit, is restrained in a stock or harness, and a number of light-weight sensors and transducers are placed near its eye. Rabbits possess an outer and an inner eyelid, and this equipment can permit the recording of a small movement of either. Conditioning consists of the presentation of a relatively brief CS—say a 300-msec tone—followed by the delivery of a mild shock to the cheek. In most cases the intensity of the shock is just sufficient to produce a blink. After a number of CS–US pairings, the CS, which by itself should not make the rabbit blink, is often found to elicit this response. The results from a typical study are presented in the left-hand side of Fig. 4.1, which shows the percentage of trials on which a blink was detected during the CS across successive blocks of 100 trials. The right-hand side depicts the effects of extinction in which the CS is presented but is no longer followed by shock. A term that is frequently used in discussions of learning curves such as those depicted in Fig. 4.1 is the "asymptote", which refers to the part of the curve that is flat and reflects a stable level of responding.

Autoshaping. With autoshaping, a hungry pigeon is placed in a conditioning chamber such as that depicted in Fig. 2.4. At intervals of about 1 min a response key is illuminated for 5–10 sec, and the offset of this stimulus is followed by the delivery of food to a hopper. At first subjects may be unresponsive to the key, but after a few trials they will peck it rapidly whenever it is illuminated. Note this is not an example of instrumental conditioning as the pigeon does not have to peck the key to obtain food. Instead, it is an example of Pavlovian conditioning as the mere pairing of the illuminated key with food is sufficient to engender a CR of keypecking. A typical learning curve produced by this training is presented in Fig. 4.2.

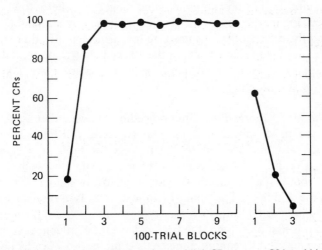

FIG. 4.1.   The acquisition and extinction of an eyeblink CR to a tone CS by rabbits (adapted from Gibbs, Latham, & Gormezano, 1978).

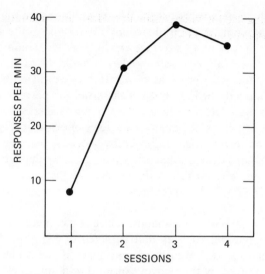

FIG. 4.2.   The rate of keypecking by a group of pigeons for which the illumination of a response key by white light for 10 sec signalled the delivery of food. There were 10 conditioning trials in each session (unpublished study by Pearce).

A similar method has been used with rats, but here the illumination of a bulb, again typically for 10 sec, is used to signal the delivery of food. During the CS the subject will either rear on its hind-legs and possibly sniff at the bulb; or it may approach the magazine where food is to be presented. Figure 4.3 shows the results of a study by Holland (1977) that examined the effects of this training on magazine activity and rearing. The rats were observed twice whenever the 10-sec light was presented, and the percentage of occasions on which a response occurred was taken as the measure of conditioning.

Conditioned Suppression.   In a procedure known either as conditioned suppression or conditioned emotional response (CER), subjects, very often rats, are first trained to lever press for food in a conditioning chamber. Conditioning then consists of pairing a stimulus, such as a light or tone of about 1 min duration, with a relatively mild shock delivered through the grid floor. There may be four such trials in each session, which itself may last for an hour or more.

When it is first presented, the CS will have little influence on the rate of lever pressing. But as conditioning trials continue, so a gradual decline in the rate of responding will be recorded until eventually the lever may not be pressed at all during the CS. As soon as the shock has been delivered, however, responding rapidly recovers to its normal rate and remains at this level until the next trial. It is important to be aware that the cessation of lever pressing has no influence on the outcome of the trial, so that shock is presented irrespective of the animal's behaviour. The decline in responding during the CS is regarded as evidence of successful Pavlovian conditioning.

With this method the measure of conditioning is the extent to which the CS reduces the rate of lever pressing. The slower the response rate during the CS, the more effective is conditioning assumed to be. Since rats vary considerably in the rate at which they press a lever for food, it has not proved useful to look directly at the rate of responding during the CS as a measure of conditioning. Instead, a *suppression ratio* is computed according to the formula $a/(a + b)$. The value of a is determined by the rate of lever pressing during the CS, and b is the rate during a short interval, usually the duration of the CS, immediately prior to CS onset. A ratio of 0.50 indicates that these rates are equal and that conditioning is ineffective, whereas a ratio of 0.00 shows that no responses at all were performed during the CS and that conditioning has been maximally effective. Figure 4.4 (left-hand side) presents the results from a typical study in which the value of the average suppression ratio for a group of subjects declines across successive trials. The right-hand side of this figure shows the effects of extinction.

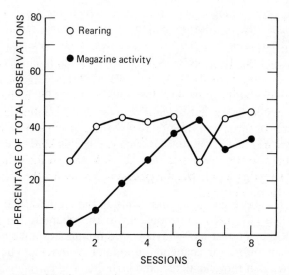

FIG. 4.3.   The observed frequency of rearing and magazine approach by rats during a 10-sec light that signalled food. There were 4 trials in a session (adapted from Holland, 1977).

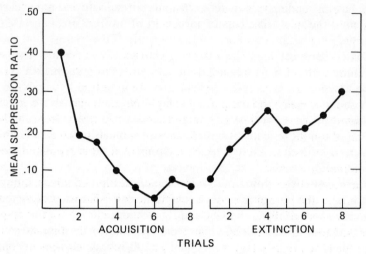

FIG. 4.4.   Acquisition and extinction of conditioned suppression by rats to a 60-sec CS that was paired with footshock (adapted from Hall & Pearce, 1979).

The foregoing examples provide only a sample of the many available techniques of Pavlovian conditioning. It is impossible to discuss all of them here, but before leaving this discussion one method that has already been mentioned merits some comment. With taste aversion conditioning an animal, after consuming a flavour, is made ill by being injected with a mild poison such as lithium chloride, and this produces a marked aversion to the flavour. This technique possesses a number of characteristics that set it apart from many other methods of conditioning. It is often extremely effective with only a single trial, and very long intervals between the CS and US can be employed with little detriment to learning. Nonetheless, in most respects the effects of this procedure resemble those of other methods of conditioning, and for this reason it has proved an extremely useful tool for the study of the general principles of associative learning.

The Need For Control Procedures

The examples above give some indication of the methods that can be used to engender a CR. In the introduction to this chapter, however, it was argued that our interest in Pavlovian conditioning lies not so much in the opportunity it offers for changing an animal's behaviour, but because it demonstrates that they can detect and be influenced by regularly occurring sequences of stimuli. Although the reported findings suggest this has taken place, there are a number of alternative accounts that must be discounted before we can conclude that a CR is a manifestation of associative learning. This point is made particularly forcefully in an experiment by Sheafor (1975).

Two groups of thirsty rabbits received training in which they were presented with a brief tone and a squirt of water into the mouth. In each session Group T–W received a single conditioning trial in which the tone preceded the water, whereas for Group T/W the tone and water were separated by an interval of 12 min and their order varied from session to session. After 48 sessions of this training all subjects received a further 40 extinction sessions in each of which the tone alone was presented twice at an interval of 12 min.

The results from this study are presented in Fig. 4.5 which shows, for each group, the percentage of trials with the tone that were accompanied by a movement of the jaw. For Group T–W the frequency of this response increased to a substantial and consistent level across the first 48 sessions. Since the tone preceded the delivery of water, this jaw movement could be regarded as a CR showing that subjects had detected the relationship between the two stimuli. From this point of view the results from Group T/W are surprising as the tone and water were unpaired and yet substantial jaw movement was also recorded during the tone. The results from the

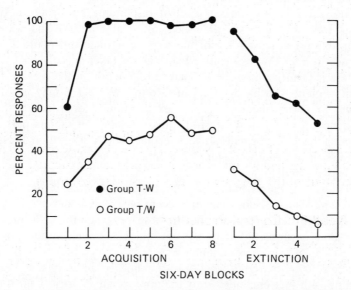

FIG. 4.5.   Percentage of trials on which a jaw-movement was recorded in the presence of a tone, as a function of 6-day blocks in acquisition (1 tone/day) and extinction (2 tones/day). During acquisition the tone and water were paired for Group T–W and unpaired for Group T/W (adapted from Sheafor, 1975).

second, extinction phase are summarised in the right-hand side of Fig. 4.5. For both groups this treatment resulted in a gradual decline in the frequency of jaw movements during the tone.

The findings for Group T/W in both stages are worrying as they indicate that a response that can be considered to be a CR occurs to the tone even when it is not paired with water. In these circumstances it would clearly be unwise to regard the existence of jaw movement as evidence that rabbits had learned that the tone was a signal for water, and it becomes necessary to consider when a response can be safely used to indicate such learning.

One solution to this problem is to treat a control group in much the same way as Group T–W, by giving it the same exposure to the tone and water, but these events should not be consistently paired. If pairing the tone and water does produce a CR because of associative learning, then this response should be stronger in Group T–W than the control group. According to Rescorla (1967), one way of treating such a control group is to present the CS and US randomly with respect to one another; he referred to this as the truly random control. An alternative method, which was employed for Group T/W, is to ensure that the CS and US are never paired. The considerable level of responding by this group to the tone indicates that it would be unwise to attribute all the jaw-movements elicited by this stimulus in Group T–W to associative learning. Nevertheless, the substantially greater level of responding by Group T–W than Group T/W does indicate that the pairing of the tone and water was responsible for at least some of the responding, and this is the necessary evidence to infer that associative learning has taken place.

There is insufficient space to speculate in depth on the reasons for the jaw movements during the tone in Group T/W, but it may be of some interest to know Sheafor's (1975) explanation. He proposed that the experience of water in the test chambers resulted in rabbits persistently expecting this US. Normally, this expectancy does not result in a response, but one can be readily triggered if a relatively salient stimulus such as a tone is presented.

Whatever the merits of this account, the point to stress is that a response that resembles a CR does not only occur when a CS and US are paired. Occasionally, such a response may be observed when the CS is presented, either alone or unpaired with respect to the US. In view of this possibility the best way of being certain that a response is a consequence of associative learning is to compare the level of responding produced by a conditioning schedule with that engendered by the appropriate control. Unfortunately the use of control groups is time-consuming, and they are not always employed. Yet, without them, the conclusions that can be drawn from an experiment will be limited.

Now that the basic procedures for studying associative learning have been introduced, we can examine the nature of this learning. For the sake of clarity the effects of excitatory and inhibitory conditioning will be considered separately.

EXCITATORY CONDITIONING

The Structure of Excitatory Learning

The premise on which this chapter is based is that animals are able to learn that one stimulus reliably signals another. This point of view, which is by no means novel—see for example Konorski (1967)—can be elaborated within the framework of animal memory developed in the previous chapters. Suppose that a tone is repeatedly paired with an electric shock. Initially all that will happen is that these stimuli will excite representations of themselves in memory. As a result, it is now believed that an association or excitatory link will develop gradually between representations of the tone and shock and that information about this relationship is stored in LTM. Subsequent presentations of the tone, by virtue of this association, will then excite a representation of the shock, and this in turn will elicit a response. This response will appear before the shock is delivered and can be regarded as a CR. One way of describing these ideas is shown in Fig. 4.6.

If the above account should seem either obvious or trivial, then bear in mind that for a long while Pavlovian conditioning was conceptualised in a rather different way. The S–R theorists mentioned in Chapter 1 believed that it resulted in an association being formed between a representation of the CS and the centre responsible for the performance of the CR (see Fig. 4.6). The CS was thus presumed to elicit the CR directly without the animal in any sense expecting the US that was shortly to be presented. Given this traditional view, a considerable number of experiments have been conducted to support its intuitively more appealing alternative. To give some indication of the principle behind these studies two examples are described.

Holland and Straub (1979) used a 10-sec noise to signal the delivery of food to two groups of rats. After a number of sessions of this training the onset of the noise resulted in subjects moving towards the magazine in anticipation of the food (see left-hand panel of Fig. 4.7). On each of the next four days, rats in Group E (experimental) were permitted 5 min unrestricted access to the food pellets in their home cages before being injected with lithium chloride to condition an aversion to the pellets. This conditioning was successful because on the fourth session subjects

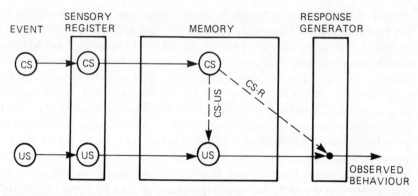

FIG. 4.6. Two possible accounts of what is learned during Pavlovian conditioning; the solid arrows are permanent connections, the dashed ones are a consequence of conditioning. A CS and US can be detected by a sensory register, and this leads to active representations of these events being formed in memory. Whenever the US representation is active, it will produce a response by exciting a centre in the system concerned with response generation. According to one account, conditioning will result in the growth of a CS–US association so that the CR will be an indirect consequence of the CS activating the US representation. The alternative S–R account assumes that conditioning strengthens a CS–R association and thus allows the CS to excite the CR directly.

consumed very few of the pellets. The treatment for Group C (control) was similar except that the lithium chloride injections and free access to food were unrelated so that the liking for the pellets was unaffected. Finally, both groups were returned to the conditioning chambers where the noise was again presented but this time without food. As revealed in the right-hand panel of Fig. 4.7, the tendency of Group E to approach the magazine on the test session was considerably less than for Group C.

These results are entirely consistent with the claim that associations between representations of the CS and US underlie performance in Pavlovian conditioning. On the test session the noise for Group E should activate a representation of food. Since, however, the taste aversion training had resulted in subjects rejecting the food, the activated representation of this US is unlikely to make them approach the magazine. After all, there is little point in going to a place that delivers food associated with illness. For Group C, on the other hand, the representation of food should be just as effective as on the final session of appetitive conditioning, and these rats should be very willing to go to the magazine during the noise.

Perhaps even more striking evidence that Pavlovian conditioning enables the CS to activate a representation of the US comes from a study by Holland and Ross (1981). This employed the ingenious technique of conducting taste aversion training with a representation of food serving as the CS. Rats were first conditioned with a 10-sec tone signalling food. In the next stage of the experiment two groups were presented with the tone, but this was not accompanied by food. Instead, for the experimental group the tone was followed by an injection of lithium chloride; nothing followed the tone for the control group. If a CS can excite a representation of the US, then the tone should excite a representation of food in the second stage of the experiment. For the experimental group, inducing illness after the activation of this representation will provide the opportunity for the growth of an association between representations of the food and illness, and reduce the attractiveness of food. To test this prediction in a final stage of the experiment, Holland and Ross (1981) allowed their subjects free access to the food pellets that had been paired with the tone and discovered that the experimental group showed the greater reluctance to eat them. Thus even though food was never paired directly with illness, it appears that an aversion was acquired to it by associating its representation with illness.

At the same time as supporting a particular theoretical account of Pavlovian conditioning, the foregoing results are extremely difficult for S–R theory to explain. According to this theory the only way to alter the responses elicited by a CS is to pair it with an event that elicits a different response. This could be another US, or no US at all. In the first study mentioned, after initial conditioning the CS was not presented again until the test phase, and there was thus no opportunity for Group E to learn a new response to the noise. As a consequence this stimulus should have

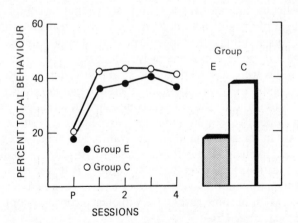

FIG. 4.7.   The amount of magazine activity by two groups of rats during a noise CS on a preexposure (P) session, when it was presented alone, and on each of four conditioning sessions when it signalled food (left-hand side). The histograms show the amount of magazine activity during the noise for a test session after the food pellets had been paired with illness for Group E, but not for Group C (adapted from Holland & Straub, 1979).

elicited the same response in both groups on the test session. Similarly, in the second study both groups received the same experience with food pellets, and S–R theory thus incorrectly predicts that they should have treated them similarly on the test session. It is the failure to confirm these predictions that provides compelling evidence that S–R theory is inadequate as an explanation for the effects of Pavlovian conditioning.

The Nature of CS-activated Representations

Having established that associative learning enables one stimulus to activate a representation of another, it is meaningful to ask what information is retrieved by this process. Much of the theorising concerning this issue draws from the work of Konorski (1967), a Polish researcher who worked for a while in Pavlov's laboratory. Konorski (1967) has suggested that unconditioned stimuli possess two different properties: specific and general. Specific characteristics are those that make the US unique, the place where it is delivered, its duration, intensity, and so on. General properties, on the other hand, are those that the US has in common with other stimuli. One general characteristic that Konorski (1967) held to be particularly important is the affective property of a US. Food, water, and an opportunity to mate all differ in detail, but they share the common appetitive feature that—given the appropriate motivational state—animals will actively search for them. Conversely, electric shock, illness, and loud noise are very different, yet they all possess the common aversive characteristic that animals will do their best to minimise contact with them.

In the light of this distinction, Konorski (1967) suspected that a CS may be capable of activating either specific or general information about the US or indeed both sorts simultaneously. Moreover, when activated these representations were assumed to lead to rather different CRs. A general representation of a US is supposed to elicit a *preparatory* CR consisting of a state of arousal and restlessness, accompanied by a tendency to approach the CS in appetitive conditioning and to withdraw from it in aversive procedures. On the other hand, the activation of a specific representation of a US is said to elicit precise *consummatory* CRs relevant to the receipt of the US in question: for example, the eyeblink CR that is recorded when a CS signals the imminent delivery of shock to the cheek of a rabbit. Hence it is quite likely that in some cases a CS will elicit a consummatory CR and in others a preparatory CR.

Specific Representations.   The evidence that a CS can excite a specific representation of the US comes from at least two sources. There is, first of all, the frequent observation that the form of the CR is precise and reflects the characteristics of the US. Hence, in rabbit eye-blink conditioning, it is only the eye adjacent to the place where shock is applied that shows a reliable CR. This suggests that precise information about the place where the US is to be applied can be retrieved by the CS.

For the second source of evidence we can turn to another study by Holland and Ross (1981) which, again, conditioned an aversion to food by pairing its activated representation with illness. One CS, A, was paired with peppermint-flavoured pellets and another, B, was paired with wintergreen-flavoured pellets. CS A was then presented without the peppermint pellets and followed by an injection of lithium chloride. We have already seen that this should condition an aversion to the food pellets, and the issue of concern is with the specificity of the CR. If the representation of food that CS A activates is general, then subjects should be wary of consuming both peppermint and wintergreen pellets and possibly any other food they are given. Alternatively, if CS A activates a very specific representation of the peppermint pellets, then the aversion should be confined to this flavour. In support of this latter prediction Holland and Ross (1981) found on a final test session that rats were considerably less willing to eat peppermint- than wintergreen-flavoured pellets.

Taken together, these separate lines of evidence strongly suggest that at least in certain cicumstances a CS is capable of arousing a specific memory of the US. We now turn to examine findings that indicate that US representations—at least those of the same affective value—possess common, more general attributes.

General Representations.   One reason for believing that general representations of the US can be associated with the CS comes from the finding that different USs can support similar CRs, presumably because their representations contain the same sort of information. Thus Bakal, Johnson, and Rescorla (1974) have found that a very loud noise or an electric shock to the feet both result in conditioned suppression when paired with a CS. Similarly, birds will approach and peck a key when its illumination signals such different events as food, water, or warmth (Moore, 1973; Wasserman, 1973). In these cases it is likely to be the common motivational properties of the USs that are reponsible for the similar CRs they support. It is noteworthy that in some of these studies the precise topography of the CR appears to be influenced by the nature of the US: Pigeons will peck an illuminated key as if they are trying to eat it when it signals food, but when it signals water their responses are more akin to those that accompany drinking. This suggests that the representations associated with the CS in autoshaping possess both general and specific attributes.

A second reason for believing that a CS can activate a general representation of the US comes from studies showing that conditioning can sometimes be facilitated if the CS has previously been paired with a different US of related affective value. Pearce, Montgomery, and Dickinson (1981), for instance, conducted rabbit eye-blink conditioning in which, for Group E, a brief light signalled shock to the cheek; Group C did not receive this training. Then, in the test phase of the experiment, both groups were conditioned with the light signalling shock to the opposite cheek. Acquisition of an eyeblink CR in these circumstances was considerably more rapid for Group E than Group C, which suggests that the original conditioning with the light resulted in it retrieving information that was not entirely specific to the cheek where the US was applied. The implication of this study, and this is certainly the view advocated by Konorski (1967), is that once an association has been formed between a CS and the general properties of a US, this facilitates the learning necessary for the occurrence of specific CRs, such as eyeblink, when the US is applied elsewhere.

This concludes our discussion of first-order conditioning. But before leaving the topic of excitatory conditioning, we should consider two additional techniques for training animals to perform a CR in the presence of a CS. These are different to all of the above studies, because they do not depend on the CS being paired directly with the US.

Serial Conditioning

In serial conditioning a sequence of stimuli precedes the US—for example, a tone might be followed by a light, which, in turn, would be followed by food. Despite being rather distant from the US, the initial element of the sequence will often elicit a CR, although it may be weaker than the response observed in the presence of the element that is closer to the US. One interesting feature of serial conditioning is revealed in a study by Holland and Ross (1981), who trained rats with the sequence light–tone–food. The normal response to a light that signals food, as noted previously, is rearing or magazine approach; for a tone it is either head-jerking or magazine approach. After a number of sessions of serial conditioning it was found that during the light there was little magazine activity but instead this response was replaced by head-jerking. This led Holland and Ross (1981) to suggest that during serial conditioning the presence of the first element causes animals to anticipate the second one and to respond as if it were actually present.

Second-order Conditioning

Two different types of conditioning trial are administered in higher- or second-order conditioning. Initially, first-order conditioning is conducted in which a neutral stimulus, CS1, is paired with a US until a stable CR is recorded. At this point additional trials are introduced in which a new stimulus, CS2, precedes CS1, but the US is omitted. With sufficient training a CR can be observed during CS2 even though this stimulus itself is never paired with the US.

Pavlov (1927) was the first to report this effect, although a relatively recent example will be described (Rashotte, Griffin, & Sisk, 1977). Pigeons first received autoshaping in which the illumination of a key by white light for 6 sec signalled food; additional trials were then introduced in which the key was illuminated by blue and then white light, for 6 sec of each colour. Food was not presented on these second-order trials. Figure 4.8 shows, for the second-order conditioning stage, the percentage of trials in any session on which at least one peck was directed towards these stimuli. The success of second-order conditioning is revealed by the increase in responding to CS2.

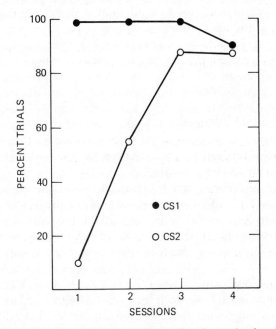

FIG. 4.8.   Number of trials in each second-order conditioning session for which at least one peck was recorded to the previously trained white CS1 and to the second-order blue CS2 (adapted from Rashotte et al., 1977).

Very often second-order conditioning results in CS2 eliciting much the same response as that originally elicited by CS1; a study by Leyland (1977), however, indicates that this need not always be true. First-order conditioning involved the use of a tone as a signal for food to hungry pigeons. On second-order trials a key-light was followed by the tone. As it is physically impossible to peck a tone, it should not be surprising to discover that this conditioned response was not performed during first-order conditioning. A high rate of key-pecking was nonetheless recorded during the key-light second-order CS.

On the basis of the evidence just cited, it is natural to expect second-order conditioning to result in much the same sort of learning as that involved in first-order conditioning. Hence pairing a second-order CS (CS2), with one that has already been paired with a US (CS1) might be expected to result in the growth of CS2–CS1 associations. As a consequence, the occurrence of CS2 should be capable of activating a specific representation of CS1, which, in turn, should activate a representation of the US and elicit a CR. There is certainly some evidence to support this proposal, but there is also some that contradicts it.

First the evidence that favours this analysis. In one study Rescorla (1979) conducted autoshaping with two groups of pigeons by pairing red and yellow keylights with food on different trials. It was then found that second-order autoshaping progressed more rapidly when a third stimulus, CS2, was paired consistently with one of the first-order stimuli than when it was followed by each of them on separate trials. Quite why this result was obtained is not clear, but fortunately this is not of pressing importance. The main point to be drawn is that pairing CS2 with different first-order stimuli disrupted conditioning. Such a disruption can only take place if the subjects were able to identify that the first-order CS varied from one higher-order conditioning trial to the next. And this depends upon CS2 being capable of retrieving an accurate representation of the stimuli it has been paired with on previous trials.

A further indication that second-order conditioning involves the development of CS1–CS2 associations comes from the study by Rashotte et al. (1977) mentioned earlier, which carried out second-order autoshaping with pigeons using blue (CS2) and white (CS1) keylights. An outline of the various stages of the experiment can be found in the upper half of Table 4.1.

After second-order conditioning, Rashotte et al. (1977) gave Group E a series of extinction trials in which the white key-light (CS1) was presented alone. This training was intended to abolish its association with food, and it was soon found that pecking at the white key declined to a very low level. When the blue key-light (CS2) was again shown for the final test trials, it should still activate a representation of white, by virtue of the prior

TABLE 4.1
Summary of the Stimuli Employed in the Stages
of the Second-order Conditioning Studies
by Rashotte et al.[a] and by Rizley and Rescorla[b]

	First-order conditioning	Second-order conditioning	Extinction	Test
Group E	White→Food	Blue→White	White	Blue
Group C	White→Food	Blue→White	—	Blue
Group E	Tone→Shock	Light→Tone	Tone	Light
Group C	Tone→Shock	Light→Tone	—	Light

[a]Rashotte et al. (1977): upper two rows.
[b]Rizley and Rescorla (1972): lower two rows.

second-order conditioning. However, activation of this representation should no longer excite a memory of food, and pecking at blue should not take place. For Group C, which did not receive the extinction training with white, the presence of both an effective blue–white and a white–food association should allow blue to activate a representation of the food and engender a high rate of responding. In keeping with this analysis it was found on the test session that Group C responded significantly more rapidly than Group E in the presence of CS2.

Evidence to the contrary, that second-order conditioning does not enable CS2 to retrieve specific information about CS1, is provided by Rizley and Rescorla (1972). The design of their experiment is very similar to that of Rashotte et al. (1977) and is presented in the lower panel of Table 4.1. The methods differed principally in that Rizley and Rescorla (1972) used conditioned suppression. Two groups of rats received first-order conditioning with a 10-sec tone signalling shock, and second-order conditioning in which a 30-sec light was followed by the tone and no shock. Group E was then given extinction training with the tone. Although this treatment abolished the CR to the tone, the subsequent presentation of the second-order light CS elicited a very strong CR, which did not differ in magnitude from that performed by Group C. This finding makes it difficult to believe that a light–tone association was formed during second-order conditioning, for if it had been, extinction with the tone should have reduced the CR recorded during the light. Moreover, this outcome is not unique: Holland and Rescorla (1975) have obtained a similar effect with rats using appetitive conditioning.

One explanation for this outcome is that second-order conditioning resulted in an association being formed between CS2 and the general representation of the US activated by the presentation of CS1. A similar view has been expressed by Rizley and Rescorla (1972). Thus in their study it is conceivable that the tone aroused a CR of fear, for want of a better word, which was associated directly with the light. If this account is correct, then manipulations of the tone–shock association should not influence the light–fear association and hence leave unaffected the prior second-order conditioning.

What then determines the nature of the associations that are formed during second-order conditioning? According to Rescorla (1980), one answer to this question is the similarity of CS1 and CS2. When the stimuli are similar, such as the illumination of a key by different colours, then a CS2–CS1 association will be formed. When the stimuli are very different, for example if they are from different modalities, then CS2 will be associated with the more general representation of the motivational state that is aroused by the CS that follows it. Of course, this account is incomplete. It does not explain why stimulus similarity should be so important in determining the outcome of second-order conditioning. And as it stands, it leads to the incorrect expectation that first-order conditioning will favour associations between the CS and a general representation of the US because these stimuli are so different.

INHIBITORY CONDITIONING

Methods of Study

Associative learning has been considered thus far as a process that allows animals to discover that one stimulus signals another. There are now also good reasons for believing they can also learn that a stimulus signals the omission of an event such as a US. The term inhibitory conditioning is used when this learning has taken place.

Hearst and Franklin (1977) placed pigeons in a chamber containing a food hopper and two response keys. The keys were illuminated one at a time for 20 sec in a random sequence, with an interval averaging 80 sec between successive trials. During this interval food was occasionally delivered to the hopper, but food was never available when a key was lit. To examine the effects of this training the position of the subject in the chamber was continuously monitored. At first they were indifferent to the key lights, but as training progressed there was a marked tendency to move away from a key whenever it was illuminated. This finding suggests that pigeons are capable of learning that stimuli signal the omission of food and that they may withdraw from such stimuli. One technique, therefore, for inhibitory conditioning is to ensure that the US is delivered in the absence but not the presence of the CS.

There were a number of groups in this study that differed in the frequency with which food was delivered during the intertrial interval. When this frequency was relatively high, the movement away from the lit key was stronger than when food was infrequent. This effect can be seen in Fig. 4.9 which shows changes in a measure called an approach–withdrawal ratio across sessions for the groups. A ratio of 0.50 indicates that birds were unaffected by a lit key, whereas a ratio of 0.00 indicates a very strong movement away from this stimulus.

A second method for inhibitory conditioning is demonstrated in a study by Zimmer-Hart and Rescorla (1974), who used a tone to signal shock for conditioned suppression training. Trials in which the tone was paired with shock were intermixed among trials in which it was presented with a light, and this compound was not followed by shock. At first, the magnitude of conditioned suppression during the compound was much the same as that in the presence of the tone (see Fig. 4.10), but as training progressed, the presence of the light on compound trials counteracted the suppressive effects of the tone. This pattern of responding suggests animals learned that the light signalled the omission of shock and that this opposed the properties of the tone.

The Detection of Conditioned Inhibition

Before examining in detail what this learning might consist of, and how it is effective, we shall first consider a problem concerned with the detection of inhibitory conditioning. A stimulus that has been used to signal the

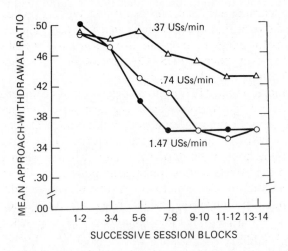

FIG. 4.9.   Mean approach–withdrawal ratio recorded in the presence of a 10-sec keylight for groups of pigeons that received food at the rate of 0.33, 0.74, or 1.48 presentations per min in the absence but not the presence of this stimulus (adapted from Hearst & Franklin, 1977).

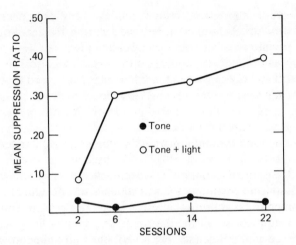

FIG. 4.10. Mean suppression ratios for rats given excitatory conditioning with a tone intermixed among trials with a light–tone compound followed by nothing (adapted from Zimmer-Hart & Rescorla, 1974).

omission of a US, either appetitive or aversive, is referred to as a conditioned inhibitor. Unfortunately, such stimuli rarely elicit a CR on their own. The study by Hearst and Franklin (1977) is unusual in this respect because their subjects did move away from the key light, but frequently a conditioned inhibitor by itself has no effect at all on behaviour. To return to the study by Zimmer-Hart and Rescorla (1974), had they presented the light alone rather than in compound with the tone, then it would have had very little influence on the rate of lever pressing. How then can we be certain that animals have learned anything about this stimulus? One answer to this question, at least for the Zimmer-Hart and Rescorla (1974) study, would be to point to its effects on the compound trials. But on these trials it is possible that the subjects learned nothing about the light itself; they may merely have learned that the configuration of the light and tone together was followed by nothing. It is in order to refute this sort of explanation and to show that a conditioned inhibitor can have properties of its own that two techniques have been developed to reveal the existence of conditioned inhibition: the summation and retardation tests (Hearst, 1972; Rescorla, 1969).

The Retardation Test. This test involves the direct pairing of the conditioned inhibitor with the US for which it had previously signalled the absence. If inhibitory conditioning was successful, then it should disrupt this excitatory conditioning. A formal explanation of this effect is elaborated shortly, but for the moment it should not be too surprising.

A demonstration of a successful retardation test is provided by Pearce, Nicholas, and Dickinson (1982). After receiving training similar to that employed by Zimmer-Hart and Rescorla (1974), Group E was given conditioned suppression training in which the inhibitory CS was paired with shock. Group C also received these pairings but without any prior training. The course of excitatory conditioning with the stimulus is depicted in Fig. 4.11. Evidently the retardation test was successful because conditioning progressed more slowly for Group E than Group C. One important point to note is that on the first test trial the CS had no influence at all on responding in Group E. On this basis there would be little reason for believing that it had acquired any special properties as a result of the prior training. This emphasises the need for special tests to reveal the effects of inhibitory conditioning.

The Summation Test.   The experiment by Zimmer-Hart and Rescorla (1974) revealed that a stimulus can acquire properties that counteract the CRs normally elicited by an excitatory CS. It was suggested that this effect is due to the stimulus serving as a signal for the omission of the US. If this is correct, then these properties of the stimulus should be evident if it is presented in conjunction with any other CS that has been paired with the US in question. A demonstration of this transfer constitutes a successful

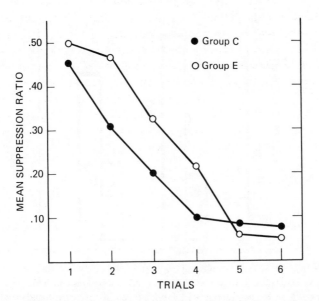

FIG. 4.11.   Acquisition of conditioned suppression to a CS that was novel (Group C) or one that had previously signalled the omission of shock (Group E) (adapted from Pearce et al. 1982).

IAC-E*

summation test, and an example can be found in another conditioned suppression study by Pearce, Nicholas, and Dickinson (1982).

Rats were first trained with three types of trial: a tone paired with shock, a clicker paired with the same shock, and a light–clicker compound followed by nothing. Eventually a strong CR was observed in the presence of the tone and the clicker, but not during the clicker–light compound. In order to test whether the influence of the light on the clicker could transfer to the tone, a single test session was administered. Trials in which the tone was presented alone were intermixed among trials with the light–tone compound. The results in the right-hand pair of histograms of Fig. 4.12 show that the strength of the CR, as indexed by the suppression ratio, was substantially greater to the tone than to the compound. For purposes of comparison, the left-hand pair of histograms show the difference in responding to the clicker and the clicker–light compound for the final session of the prior training. Evidently the influence of the light transferred very well from the clicker to the tone, and this constitutes a successful summation test for conditioned inhibition.

For reasons that need not be considered here—but see Rescorla (1969)—the ideal method for determining whether a stimulus is a conditioned inhibitor is to conduct both the retardation and the summation

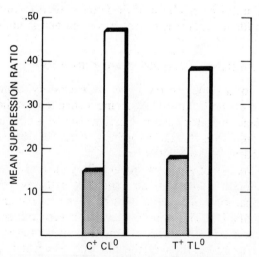

FIG. 4.12.   Mean suppression ratios on the final session of training for a group of rats that had received clicker–shock (C+) trials intermixed among trials in which a clicker–light compound was followed by nothing (CL°, left-hand pair of histograms), and on a test session when they were given a tone that had previously signalled shock (T+), and a compound composed of the tone and light (TL°, right-hand pair of histograms) (adapted from Pearce et al., 1982).

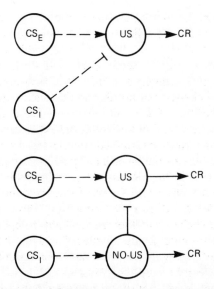

FIG. 4.13.   Two possible models of the learning that occurs during inhibitory conditioning. The arrows and stopped lines, respectively, depict conditioned excitatory and inhibitory links; the solid lines depict permanent links; the dashed lines depict conditioned links; and circles denote representations in memory.

tests. If the stimulus passes both of these tests, then it can be concluded with some confidence that it is indeed a conditioned inhibitor.

The Representation of Conditioned Inhibition

It is natural to assume in the case of excitatory conditioning that representations of the CS and US become associated, as these events are paired. But where inhibitory learning is concerned it is not quite so obvious what is associated with the inhibitory CS. After all, this stimulus is not usually followed by any tangible event.

One possibility is that as a result of signalling the omisssion of a US, the inhibitory CS does not enter into an association with any event. Instead, it acquires a special kind of function that enables it to dampen or inhibit a representation of a US. This point of view has been expressed by Konorski (1948) and Rescorla (1979). Both assume that an excitatory CS is capable of activating a representation of the US with which it is paired. If this excitatory stimulus, CS_E, should be presented in compound with another stimulus and the US is witheld, an inhibitory link is presumed to be formed between the representation of the latter stimulus, CS_I, and the US representation excited by CS_E. This relationship is depicted in the upper half of Fig. 4.13. The subsequent presentation of CS_I will then serve to dampen the US representation that is activated by any excitatory CS with which it is concurrently paired. A consequence of this dampening will be to reduce the strength of the excitatory CR. Of course, if CS_I should be paired with the US in a retardation test, then, although an association will grow between a representation of CS and the US, the existence of the inhibitory link will initially prevent the CS from activating the US representation, and a CR will not be recorded.

A crucial implication of this account is that a conditioned inhibitor should not have any response-eliciting properties of its own. An inhibitory link will permit it only to modulate the strength of CRs whenever the US representation is activated. Very often, conditioned inhibitors do not influence behaviour when they occur by themselves, but as we have seen this is not always true. In the Hearst and Franklin (1977) experiment a conditioned inhibitor was shown to elicit withdrawal. In other studies, it has been found that rats will consume relatively large volumes of a flavoured solution that has previously signalled the omission of a lithium chloride injection (Batson & Best, 1981; Best, Dunn, Batson, Meachum, & Nash, 1985). Findings such as these suggest the need for an alternative account of what is learned during inhibitory conditioning.

In his more recent theorising, Konorski (1967; see also Pearce & Hall 1980) proposed that inhibitory conditioning permits the growth of a conventional association between the CS and what Konorski (1967) called a no-US representation. The activation of this representation was deemed to have two effects. It can dampen any concurrently excited US representations and thus weaken excitatory CRs, and it may also elicit responses in its own right (see lower half of Fig. 4.13). If this account is to be accepted then it is essential to specify what constitutes a no-US representation.

Superficially, the notion of such a representation might seem strange, but a moment's reflection should reveal what is meant by this term. Being told that something is going to happen and then discovering that it will not can often produce strong emotional reactions. The withdrawal of a promised reward, like a large sum of money, might result in frustration or disappointment; whereas an opposite reaction of relief or joy might accompany the news that something unpleasant, like a visit to the dentist, is no longer going to happen. Konorski (1967) considered the no-US representation to be composed of these diffuse reactions, and they are the counterpart to the general US representations formed during excitatory conditioning. It is also conceivable that the no-US representation encodes precise information about the omitted US, and this would be equivalent to the specific component of a US representation. In fact there is evidence to support both proposals.

The outcome of a rabbit eye-blink conditioning study indicates the general nature of a no-US representation (Pearce, Nicholas, & Dickinson, 1981). Inhibitory conditioning was initially performed in which a light signalled shock to one cheek and a light–clicker compound was followed by nothing. Subsequently, to examine the inhibitory properties of the clicker a retardation test was conducted in which it signalled shock to either the same or the opposite cheek to that used during training. The test revealed that excitatory conditioning was disrupted to the same extent irrespective of which cheek was shocked. The implication of this finding is that during inhibitory training the clicker was associated with a no-shock representation that was sufficiently general to disrupt conditioning with a US applied to any location. Perhaps, in this instance the information provided by the no-shock representation was simply that shock would not follow the clicker. If it had been more specific, then the activation of this representation would have disrupted conditioning more when the shock was applied to the original, than to the opposite, cheek.

An indication that, in certain circumstances, inhibitory conditioning can result in the CS being associated with a specific representation comes from a report by Cotton, Goodall, and Mackintosh (1982). Groups of rats received training in which a tone was paired with a moderately strong shock, and a tone–light compound signalled a weak shock. Thus the light signalled a reduction rather than omission of shock. Different groups were then given a summation test in which the light was paired with a clicker that had previously signalled either the strong shock (Group S), or the weak shock (Group W). If the initial training resulted in the light retrieving a general representation signalling, say, relief from an unpleasant event, then its properties should be evident in both groups. In fact it was only in Group S that the light passed the summation test, which implies that it retrieved relatively specific information about the US that was omitted and this restricted the circumstances in which it could function as a conditioned inhibitor. According to Cotton et al. (1982; see also Mackintosh & Cotton, 1985) the information supplied by this inhibitory CS is twofold. There is the general information that it will be followed by a state of relief because it has previously signalled the omission of an anticipated large shock. There is also the specific information that it will be followed by a small shock. This latter information should not prevent the light from passing a summation test for conditioned inhibition when it is paired with a CS that signals a strong shock. But it might well lead to this test being ineffective when the CS has been paired with a weak shock.

At present it is not clear what conditions lead to the development of general or specific inhibitory representations. Nonetheless, the idea that a no-US representation can provide information about the omitted US as well as activate CRs has proved a very useful model for the study of inhibitory learning.

THE RESCORLA–WAGNER MODEL
AND THE CONDITIONS FOR LEARNING

A major conclusion to be drawn from the first part of this chapter is that conditioning results in the growth of an association between representations of the CS and US. Our task now is to identify as precisely as possible the circumstances that are responsible for this learning. For many years it was thought that conditioning would automatically be effective whenever a CS and US were paired, but more recent evidence suggests that this is incorrect. To be successful it is now held that conditioning depends upon the US being unexpected or surprising. The reason for this change lies principally with the discovery of an effect known as blocking. Table 4.2 outlines the stages of a blocking study by Kamin (1969) using conditioned suppression. In the first stage Group E, but not Group C, was given pairings of a noise with shock. For the second stage both groups received identical training for a number of trials in which a compound composed of the noise and a light was paired with shock. Finally, test trials involving the light by itself were given. The suppression ratios at the right-hand side of the table indicate that on the test trials with the light there was virtually no evidence of a CR in Group E, whereas one of considerable strength was recorded for Group C. For Group E therefore the original training with the noise was somehow responsible for preventing, or blocking, learning about the light during compound conditioning.

If conditioning merely depended upon the pairing of a CS and a US, then Stage 2 should have resulted in effective conditioning with the light for both groups. In order to explain his finding to the contrary with Group E, Kamin (1969) proposed that in the first stage of the experiment animals learned that the noise predicted the shock, and this led to the light being followed by an unsurprising US during compound conditioning. The

TABLE 4.2
Summary of the Training Given to the Two Groups
in Kamin's (1969) Study of Blocking

	Stage 1	Stage 2	Test
Group E	Noise → Shock	Light + Noise → Shock	Light 0.45
Group C	—	Light + Noise → Shock	Light 0.05

importance of this relationship is made apparent by the following quote (Kamin, 1969, p. 59): "perhaps, for an increment in an associative connection to occur, it is necessary that the US instigate some 'mental work' on behalf of the animal. This mental work will occur only if the US is unpredicted—if it in some sense 'surprises' the animal."

This proposal led to the development of a number of formal theories of learning, all of which in various ways have stressed the importance of surprise in conditioning (Makintosh, 1975a; Pearce & Hall, 1980; Rescorla & Wagner, 1972; Wagner, 1976, 1978, 1981; Wagner & Rescorla, 1972). In order to demonstrate the way in which these theories operate, the remainder of this chapter considers one of them—that proposed by Rescorla and Wagner (1972)—in detail. There is insufficient space to present its successors in such depth, but some of them are discussed in Chapter 6. By way of introduction to the model, a simplified version of it is applied to conditioning with a single CS.

Conditioning with a Single CS

In keeping with the framework developed throughout this chapter, the Rescorla–Wagner model maintains that Pavlovian conditioning results in the formation of associations between representations of the CS and US. The capacity of the CS to activate the US representation and hence elicit a CR is held to be directly related to the strength of the association connecting them. Hence the greater the strength of the CS–US association—or associative strength of a CS as it is often referred to—the stronger will be the CR that it elicits. In order to understand associative learning, therefore, we must discover the factors that are responsible for changes in associative strength.

There are two assumptions that are basic to the Rescorla–Wagner (1972) model: The first is that the repeated pairing of a CS with a US will result in a gradual increase in the strength of the connection between them. This growth, however, does not continue indefinitely but ceases when the associative strength of the CS is equal to a value determined by the magnitude of the US. The second assumption is that on those trials when there is an increase in associative strength, it is not by a fixed amount. Instead, the growth of an association is determined by the difference between the current associative strength of the CS and the maximum possible for the US employed. When this difference is large, such as at the outset of conditioning, there will be a considerable growth of the CS–US association, and a much stronger CR will be recorded on the next trial. But when the CS–US association is already strong because of extended conditioning, the growth of the association will be slight and there will be little change in the CR from one trial to the next.

Equation 4.1 expresses these assumptions formally, and it can be used to determine the change in associative strength that will occur on any trial.

$$\Delta V = \alpha(\lambda - V) \tag{4.1}$$

The term V refers to the strength of the CS–US association and ΔV indicates the change in strength of an association that will take place on any trial. The value of λ is set by the magnitude of the US and reflects the maximum strength that the CS–US association can achieve. The parameter α does not vary during conditioning and has a value between 0 and 1; its function will be made evident shortly. Because associative strength is held to influence directly the strength of the CR, Equation 4.1 can be used to predict changes in responding during the course of conditioning. In other words, this equation can be used to generate theoretical learning curves and, if the theory is correct, then these curves should be similar to those found in reality.

The application of Equation 4.1 is extremely simple. Assume for the present that α is 0.20 and that the CS is novel. On the first trial of conditioning the CS will possess no associative strength (because it has never been paired with the US), and the value of V will be zero. The value of λ can be arbitrarily set at 100. For the first CS–US pairing the growth in the association between representations of these stimuli will be given by Equation 4.2, which is derived by substituting the above values into Equation 4.1.

$$\begin{aligned} \Delta V &= 0.20(100 - 0) \\ &= 20 \end{aligned} \tag{4.2}$$

Thus on the first conditioning trial there will be an increase of 20 units in associative strength. On the second trial the increment in associative strength will be determined by a new set of values. Specifically, it will be determined by Equation 4.3, because the associative strength of the CS will no longer be zero but will instead have a value of 20 units. The effect of this change will be to produce a smaller increment in associative strength on the second than on the first trial.

$$\begin{aligned} \Delta V &= 0.20(100 - 20) \\ &= 16 \end{aligned} \tag{4.3}$$

$$\begin{aligned} \Delta V &= 0.20(100 - 36) \\ &= 12.8 \end{aligned} \tag{4.4}$$

On the third trial (see Equation 4.4), the associative strength of the CS will be 36 (20 + 16) units, and this will result in an even smaller change than on the previous trials. It should now be clear that with continued training the increments in associative strength across successive trials will be progressively smaller and result in the curve depicted by the solid line in the left-hand side of Fig. 4.14. Eventually a point will be reached where the sum of the increments will equal 100; at this juncture the expression $\lambda - V$ will equal 0 and, according to Equation 4.1, no further changes in associative strength will be possible. This equation thus predicts that the growth in associative strength—and hence increase in CR strength—should be extremely rapid on the initial trials but decline and eventually cease with continued training.

Equation 4.1 can be used just as easily to account for extinction. Suppose that subjects have been given sufficient training to ensure that the strength of a CS–US association equals the value of λ (100 units). If we then present the CS without the US, what does Equation 4.1 predict? Before answering this question, the value to be substituted for λ on these nonreinforced trials must be decided. This term refers to the magnitude of the US, and a value of 0 is appropriate to indicate its absence. The associative strength of the CS, however, does have a value and the change in associative strength on the first extinction trial will be given by Equation 4.5.

$$\Delta V = 0.20(0 - 100) \tag{4.5}$$
$$= -20$$

The first extinction trial will therefore result in the CS losing 20 units of associative strength. Repeatedly applying Equation 4.1 for extinction will, because of the declining value of V, produce progressively smaller losses in associative strength, and result in the curve depicted in the right-hand half of Fig. 4.14. Extinction will be complete when the associative strength of the CS has fallen to zero.

The application of Equation 4.1 is not difficult. However, if you feel uneasy with this account of acquisition and extinction, then perform your own calculations to see the effects of changing the values of α and λ on the shape of the learning curve. This will help considerably in the understanding of what is to follow.

A useful feature of Equation 4.1 is that it captures the essence of what Rescorla and Wagner (1972) consider to be the role of surprise in conditioning. In the first part of this chapter it was argued that conditioning results in the CS retrieving a memory of the US before it actually occurs. In a sense, then, the animal is able to anticipate or expect, during the CS, the forthcoming US. Because associative strength, $V,$ determines the degree to which the US representation can be activated, it follows that the value of this parameter is related to the magnitude of the US that is expected. When the value of V is low, only a weak US will be expected, but as its value aproaches λ, so the expectancy will correspond more and more to the US that is presented.

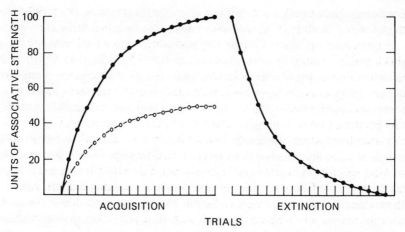

FIG. 4.14.   The changes in associative strength predicted by the Rescorla–Wagner (1972) model during conditioning with a large US ($\lambda = 100$ units: solid line) or a small US ($\lambda = 50$ units: dashed line); and during extinction for a CS that has been paired with a large US.

The implication of this discussion is that the size of the discrepancy ($\lambda - V$) indicates the extent to which the US is unexpected or surprising. The greater the discrepancy between λ and V, the greater the difference between the US that is expected and that which occurs, and hence the more surprising will the US be. We have seen that conditioning, as indexed by changes in associative strength, is fastest when $\lambda - V$ has a large value, which is when the US is most unexpected or surprising. Thus although Equation 4.1 is presented in mathematical terms, it expresses the psychological idea that animals learn most readily about USs that are surprising or unexpected.

A number of factors is known to influence the course of conditioning; some of these are now be described and it is shown how they can be incorporated into the theoretical framework provided by Equation 4.1.

US Intensity.   One objection that might be raised about Equation 4.1 is that it is impossible to know what value should be assigned to λ. This, however, is not a serious problem, as the purpose of developing such equations is not to derive exact, quantitative predictions of the sort: "on trial 4 the CR will be of such a magnitude". Instead, it is concerned more with qualitative statements in which the strength of CR produced by one set of circumstances can be predicted to differ from that recorded in another situation. Suppose we wished to predict the effects of changing the magnitude of the US on conditioning. The fact that we do not know the precise values of λ that should be assigned to USs when they vary in intensity does not matter. All that needs to be said is that this value will be greater for the stronger US. Thus if λ for a strong US is set at 100 units, then a value of 50 units could be employed for one that is weaker.

Equation 4.1 predicts that on the first conditioning trial with the weak shock the increment in associative strength will be $0.20 \times (50 - 0) = 10$ units (using the previously selected value for α). Future increments will decline progressively from this value, and conditioning will cease when their combined value is equal to 50. The dotted line in Fig. 4.14 portrays this predicted growth of associative strength. Comparing this curve with the solid line, which was calculated with $\lambda = 100$ units, then allows us to conclude what the effects will be of conditioning with different magnitudes of US. Specifically a strong US should not only result in the more rapid acquisition of a CR, but this response should be ultimately more vigorous than when a weak US is employed. Note that this prediction will always be true no matter what values are ascribed to λ, providing that its value is greater for the stronger US.

The foregoing analysis is reasonably consistent with experimental findings. For instance, Annau and Kamin (1961), using conditioned suppression, found that both the rate of conditioning and the ultimate level of conditioned responding was greater with a strong than with a weak shock US. When examining Fig. 4.15, which shows the results from their study, bear in mind that a suppression ratio of 0.50 indicates the absence of a CR, whereas one of 0.00 indicates a CR of maximum strength.

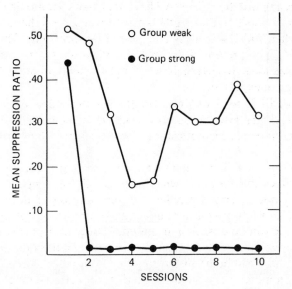

FIG. 4.15.   The acquisition of conditioned suppression to a noise CS by two groups of rats that received either a 0.49-mA (Group Weak) or a 0.85-mA (Group Strong) shock US (adapted from Annau & Kamin, 1961).

CS Intensity.   Very little has so far been said about the the role of α in Equation 4.1. Rescorla and Wagner (1972) suggested that its value is determined by the nature of the CS.

It is now well established that conditioning progresses more rapidly with a strong than with a weak CS, and to accommodate this finding α is set according to the intensity of the CS. With a strong CS its value should approach 1, but with a weaker stimulus α should tend towards 0. Figure 4.16 portrays the acquisition curves predicted by Equation 1 with α set at 0.8 (strong CS, solid line) and 0.2 (weak CS, dashed line). The value of λ was 100 units. It can be seen that the effect of changing the magnitude of α is to alter the rate of conditioning but not the ultimate level of conditioned responding. Because the influence of α is confined solely to determining the speed at which conditioning takes place, it is defined as a learning rate parameter that reflects the *conditionability* or *associability* of the CS.

The results from a study by Kamin and Schaub (1963), which investigated the influence of CS intensity on the acquisition of conditioned

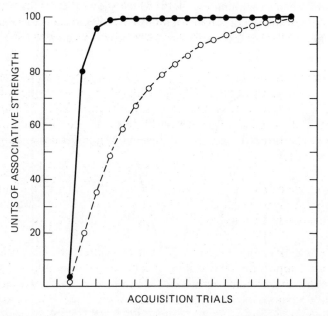

FIG. 4.16.   The changes in associative strength predicted by the Recorla–Wagner (1972) model during conditioning with a relatively intense CS (α = 0.8: solid line) or a weak CS (α = 0.2: dashed line).

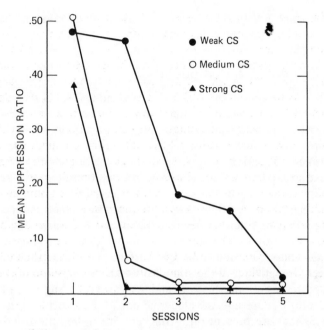

FIG. 4.17. Acquisition of conditioned suppression by groups of rats trained with the same US but with a CS that was weak, medium, or strong (adapted from Kamin & Schaub, 1963).

suppression, are presented in Fig. 4.17. Three groups were conditioned with the same magnitude of US but with different intensities of a white noise CS. For Group High the CS was 81 dB, for Group Medium it was 62.5 dB, and for Group Low it was 49 dB. The rate of conditioning was directly related to the CS intensity, but this factor did not influence at all the ultimate level of responding.

It would be misleading to give the impression that CS intensity never influences the ceiling of responding. Occasionally, it has been found that a weak CS can support only a feeble CR (e.g. Kamin, 1965). Unfortunately a discussion of why this should be is beyond the scope of the present text, but see Mackintosh (1974), pp. 41–45.

Sometimes it may be discovered that two different USs, such as food and water, support the same ceiling of conditioned responding. This would indicate that they should be represented by the same value of λ and thus for a given CS support the same rate of conditioning. On occasion this prediction is not confirmed. To accommodate this possibility, Rescorla and Wagner (1972) proposed that their equation should include a second learning rate parameter, β, which is determined by properties of the US.

The factors that influence the value of β have received scant attention, and no more will be said about this parameter.

Conditioning with a Compound CS

When it comes to conditioning with a compound CS, Rescorla and Wagner (1972) proposed an ingeniously simple modification to Equation 4.1. They retained the principle that conditioning will be most effective with a surprising US—all they did was to extend the factors that can influence surprisingness. Equation 1 stipulates that it is the discrepancy between the associative strength of a single CS and λ that determines how surprising the US will be. Rescorla and Wagner (1972) rejected this notion and instead proposed that it is how well the US is predicted by all the stimuli combined on a given trial that determines whether or not it is surprising. In other words, the value of V to be substituted into Equation 1 is not determined by the associative strength of a CS; instead, it reflects the sum of the associative strengths of all the stimuli present on a conditioning trial.

To capture this notion Rescorla and Wagner (1972) suggested Equation 4.6. The term $\overline{V}$ represents the algebraic sum of the associative strengths of all the CSs that are present on a trial, and it can be said to indicate the extent to which they collectively predict the US. This term also indicates the strength of the CR that can be expected in the presence of these stimuli. The values of V_A, V_B, ..., V_X, are determined by the associative strengths of the elements of the compound.

$$\overline{V} = V_A + V_B + \cdots + V_X \tag{4.6}$$

Equation 4.7 shows how this collective associative strength influences conditioning with CS A on a single compound conditioning trial. To understand the effects of this trial on the other stimuli that are present, this equation would have to be used again for each CS in turn. If the intensities of these stimuli are different then the value of α must change each time the equation is used.

$$\Delta V_A = \alpha_A (\lambda - \overline{V}) \tag{4.7}$$

Blocking.   It is a relatively simple matter to understand the way in which this equation explains blocking. Consider again the study by Kamin (1969), referred to in Table 4.2, in which conditioning was conducted with a noise (N) prior to compound conditioning with the noise and a light (L). At the end of the first stage of training for Group E the associative strength of the noise will be at the asymptotic value of λ (100 units, say). Equation 4.7 can now be rewritten as Equation 4.8, which shows the increment in associative strength to the light on the first compound trial. The novelty of this stimulus will ensure that V_L is equal to 0 for this trial.

$$\Delta V_L = \alpha_L[\lambda - (V_N + V_L)] \tag{4.8}$$
$$= \alpha_L[100 - (100 + 0)]$$
$$= 0$$

It is evident that on the first—or for that matter any—trial of Stage 2 there will be no change in the associative strength of the light. A rather different state of affairs will hold for the control group, because on the first compound trial both the light and noise will be novel, and the values of V_L and V_N will be zero. Equations 4.9a and 4.9b describe the increments in associative strength that can be expected with these stimuli on the first trial.

$$\Delta V_L = \alpha_L[\lambda - (V_L + V_N] \tag{4.9a}$$
$$= \alpha_L[100 - (0 + 0)]$$
$$= \alpha_L \cdot 100$$

$$\Delta V_N = \alpha_N[\lambda - (V_L + V_N)] \tag{4.9b}$$
$$= \alpha_N[100 - (0 + 0)]$$
$$= \alpha_N \cdot 100$$

For these subjects the noise and—of more importance—the light will both gain in associative strength, and the latter stimulus will elicit a stronger CR on the test trial than its counterpart in Group E. According to the Rescorla–Wagner model, therefore, blocking is effective because the pretraining with the tone will ensure the US is accurately predicted by the compound. The lack of surprisingness of the US will then prevent the development of a light–US association.

Overshadowing. Some further thought about Equations 9a and 9b should reveal that conditioning with the noise and light will cease when their combined associative strengths equal λ. As a result neither V_L nor V_N will alone reach this value, which they would do if they were paired independently with the US. The Rescorla–Wagner model thus predicts that when animals are conditioned with two stimuli in a compound, each will gain less associative strength than if they were separately paired with the same US. In these circumstances the presence of one CS is said to *overshadow* learning about the other. Pavlov (1927) was the first to report this effect, and it has been demonstrated on many subsequent occasions (e.g. Kamin, 1969).

An interesting feature of the Rescorla–Wagner model is its prediction that the extent to which one stimulus can overshadow another is determined by their relative intensities. Assume that animals are conditioned with a compound comprising a bright light and a quiet noise. As a result α_L in Equation 4.9a will be greater than α_N in Equation 4.9b, and the equations predict that on each trial the growth in associative strength to the light will be greater than to the noise. When conditioning eventually reaches asymptote—that is, when $\lambda = V_L + V_N$—the light will have gained considerably more associative strength than the noise. Compound conditioning with two CSs, therefore, should not necessarily result in each acquiring equal associative strength. Instead, the stimulus that is the more intense will be the one to gain the greater strength. In general, experimental findings conform to this rule, but there are sufficient exceptions to it for at least one author to have been encouraged to seek an alternative explanation for overshadowing (Mackintosh, 1976).

Inhibitory Conditioning.   One of the great advantages of the Rescorla–Wagner model is that it can also be used to understand the effects of inhibitory conditioning. Consider an experiment in which subjects are first given excitatory conditioning with a tone until its associative strength is at asymptotic value, λ (100 units). They then receive inhibitory conditioning in which tone–US trials are intermixed among presentations of a light–tone compound followed by nothing. What will happen to the associative strength of the light as a result of this training?

Equation 4.10 indicates the change in associative strength that can be expected on the first compound trial. The value of λ is zero because of the absence of the US. V_T is equal to 100 because of the pretraining with the tone, and V_L has a value of 0 due to the novelty of the light. It is evident that this compound trial will reduce the associative strength of the light. Because this stimulus does not possess any strength to lose, we must conclude that the training will endow the light with negative associative strength. In fact conditioning will continue until V_L is of a sufficient negative value to cancel out the positive strength of the tone, V_T.

$$\Delta V_L = \alpha_L[\lambda - (V_L + V_T)] \tag{4.10}$$
$$= \alpha_L[0 - (0 + 100)]$$
$$= -\alpha_L \cdot 100$$

Wagner and Rescorla (1972) suggest that any stimulus that possesses negative associative strength will be a conditioned inhibitor, and it is easy to see why this should be. If a stimulus with negative associative strength is paired with a US, then conditioning will at first be without apparent effect, because a number of trials will be needed before the associative strength of the stimulus becomes positive and it can elicit a CR. This effect constitutes a retardation test for conditioned inhibition. As far as the summation test is concerned, bear in mind that Rescorla and Wagner (1972) assume that the associative strength of a compound is made up of the algebraic sum of the associative strengths of the elements (Equation 4.6). If one of the elements has negative associative strength, then the overall associative strength of the compound and the vigour of the CR that is performed in its presence will be less than if that stimulus were absent.

The CS–US Contingency.   One factor that has been shown to be extremely important in determining associative strength during excitatory conditioning is the degree to which the US occurs in the absence as well as in the presence of the CS, as a study by Rescorla (1968) demonstrates. Rats were trained to lever press for food in a conditioning chamber before being given a number of sessions in a different chamber where a 2-min tone CS and shock were presented. The effect of these conditioning sessions was ultimately assessed by presenting the tone to the rats while they were again responding for food in the original chamber.

In each conditioning session, for all subjects the probability of the CS being paired with the US was 0.40—that is, the shock was delivered on an average of 4 out of every 10 occasions that the tone was presented. The groups differed in the probability of being shocked during the interval, averaging 8 min between successive tone trials. For Group 0 no shocks were presented in this interval. For Group 0.40 the probability of shock being presented in each 2-min segment of the interval was 0.40, which meant that the probability of shock during the CS was the same as at any other time in the session. For the two remaining groups the probability of shock during a 2-min segment of the interval was either 0.20 (Group 0.20), or 0.10 (Group 0.10). Thus for these subjects there was a chance of being shocked at any time in the session, but US delivery was more likely in the presence than in the absence of the tone.

The effects of this training were revealed by the magnitude of conditioned suppression evoked by the tone in the four groups on the test session (see Fig. 4.18). The striking finding was that the strength of conditioning differed dramatically among the four groups, even though the tone–shock pairings were identical for all subjects. What appears to be an important determinant of conditioning, therefore, is the difference between the probability of shock when the CS is present and when it is absent. When this difference is large, as in the case of Group 0, then conditioning is very effective. With a smaller difference between these probabilities, conditioning is still effective, but correspondingly weaker (Groups 0.20 and 0.10). Finally, when the likelihood of shock is the same whether or not the CS is present, conditioning does not occur (Group 0.40).

Findings such as these are said to demonstrate the importance of *contingency* in conditioning. When the probability of a shock given the

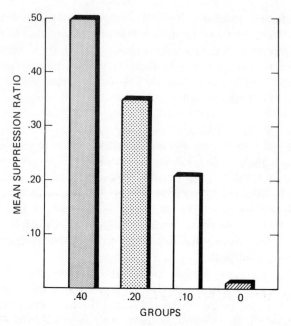

FIG. 4.18.   Mean suppression ratio to the tone CS on the test session for each of the four groups in the study by Rescorla (1968) (adapted from Rescorla, 1968).

presence of a tone is equal to that in the absence of this stimulus, then the contingency between the tone and shock is zero, and conditioning is ineffective. But when the shock is more likely in the presence than the absence of the tone, then there is a positive tone–shock contingency, and excitatory conditioning will take place. A negative contingency between the CS and US can also be imagined in which the likelihood of the US is greater when the CS is absent than when it is present. An example of such a contingency is provided by the study of Hearst and Franklin (1977), discussed a little earlier, in which the probability of food was greater in the absence than in the presence of the illuminated key. The results from this study indicate that when there is a negative CS–US contingency it will result in inhibitory learning.

To account for the importance of the CS–US contingency in determining the outcome of conditioning, Rescorla and Wagner (1972) point out that a CS is necessarily presented in a context which itself can be construed as a stimulus. Even with a single CS, then, conditioning is conducted with a compound in which the experimental context provides the additional stimulus. To return to Rescorla's (1968) study, for some subjects shocks were delivered during the interval between successive presentations of the CS, and this will enable the contextual stimuli to acquire associative strength. The context should then function in a manner analogous to the pretrained element in the earlier example for blocking, and block conditioning to the CS whenever it is presented. It also follows from the model that the more associative strength the blocking stimulus has, the more effective it will be in restricting conditioning to the target CS. Hence the model correctly predicts that increasing the associative strength of the context by increasing the probability of shock in the absence of the CS will reduce conditioning to this stimulus.

By assuming that the contextual cues can gain in associative strength when they are paired with a US, it is also possible for the model to explain why a negative CS–US contingency should result in inhibitory conditioning. In the study by Hearst and Franklin (1977), the delivery of food in the absence of the keylight will result in the growth of a context–food association. Whenever the keylight is presented against this excitatory context, the absence of food will result in it effectively undergoing training for conditioned inhibition.

Evaluation of the Rescorla–Wagner Model

A great benefit of the Rescorla–Wagner model is that the manner in which it is formulated ensures that it generates testable predictions. The success of the model is revealed by the surprising number of these predictions that have been confirmed. For instance, consider an experiment in which two stimuli, A and B, are separately paired with the same US until V_A and V_B both equal λ. What will happen if the stimuli should then be presented together in a compound accompanied by the same US? With the help of Equation 4.7 spend a few moments calculating the effect of the compound trials on the associative strengths of A and B.

Because both A and B are paired with the US on compound trials, intuition, at least, suggests that this training should not weaken the original learning. According to the model, however, our intuition would be wrong. Compound conditioning is, in fact, predicted to reduce to some extent the associative strength of A. and B. Somewhat surprisingly this suggestion that extinction, albeit incomplete, can take place even though the CS and US are paired has been confirmed in a number of studies (Kremer, 1978; Wagner & Rescorla, 1972).

It would be most convenient if the discussion could be closed at this point with the conclusion that the Rescorla–Wagner model provides the ideal account of the conditions of learning. Unhappily, the perfect learning theory has yet to be developed, and there are numerous results that this particular theory is unable to explain.

The model provides a good account for many of the facts of compound conditioning, but not all the effects associated with blocking and overshadowing are consistent with it. A summary of these and related findings can be found in Pearce (1987) and Pearce and Hall (1980). Of particular concern is the discovery that the model does not adequately account for the role of surprise in conditioning. A blocking experiment, using conditioned suppression, by Dickinson, Hall, and Mackintosh (1976), reveals this shortcoming.

A summary of the design is presented in Table 4.3. In Stage 1 two groups received excitatory conditioning in which on every trial a light was followed immediately after its offset by a moderate shock; 8 sec later the shock was delivered again. Both groups were then given compound conditioning with the light and a clicker. For Group C the compound was followed by two shocks, again separated by 8 sec, but for Group E, only the first of each pair of shocks accompanied the compound. Apart from the use of double shocks, the method for Group C resembles the conventional blocking design and, in keeping with most blocking studies, the clicker on test trials was found to produce an insubstantial CR.

The outcome for Group E was rather different, because on the test trials the clicker elicited a reasonably strong CR. Blocking for Group E was thus attenuated, and this must have been due to the surprising omission of the second shock during Stage 2. According to the Rescorla–Wagner (1972) model in this instance effective conditioning with the tone should definitely not take place, and, if anything, it predicts that the CR elicited by the tone should be less in Group E than in Group C. In Chapter 5 two theories that explain why the surprising omission of a second shock might disrupt blocking are discussed.

A further problem with the model relates to the extinction of conditioned inhibition. A conditioned inhibitor is said to possess negative associative strength. According to Equation 7, presenting such a stimulus by itself in a context of zero associative strength will result in it gaining positive increments of associative strength. Provided that sufficient trials of

TABLE 4.3
Summary of the Training Given to the Two Groups
of Rats in the Study by Dickinson et al. (1976)

	Stage 1	Stage 2	Test	
Group E	Light→Sh + Sh	Clicker + Light→Sh	Clicker	0.27
Group C	Light→Sh + Sh	Clicker + Light→Sh + Sh	Clicker	0.45

Note: The effects of blocking were reduced by the surprising omission of one of a pair of shocks (Sh) during compound conditioning.

this nature are given, the gains will eventually counteract the negative strength and leave the stimulus neutral. However, an extensive investigation by Zimmer-Hart and Rescorla (1974) could find no evidence to support this prediction. It appears that a conditioned inhibitor is unaffected by extinction treatment that is more than sufficient to abolish the properties of a conditioned excitor. For a related failure of the model see Baker (1974), and see Rescorla (1979) for a discussion of the ways the model might overcome these difficulties.

Another problem with inhibition is the manner in which it is conceptualised as negative associative strength. There is no objection to this as far as accounting for the retardation and summation tests is concerned. However, we have seen that occasionally a conditioned inhibitor can elicit its own CRs. It is not clear how this can be explained by assuming that inhibition is nothing more than negative associative strength.

SUMMARY AND CONCLUSIONS

This chapter has focussed on Pavlovian conditioning in order to gain some insight into the nature of associative learning and into the conditions necessary for such learning. For a long while it was thought that Pavlovian conditioning resulted in the development of S–R connections in which a representation of the CS is linked to a response that resembles the animal's reaction to the US. More recent evidence has shown that this is not always the case, and it now seems that the CS is associated with a representation of the US, so that whenever the former is presented it activates a representation of the latter and effectively allows the animal to anticipate its occurrence. The growth of the association between representations of the CS and US does not take place automatically whenever the stimuli are paired, but depends upon the US being unexpected or surprising.

According to the Rescorla–Wagner (1972) model, the degree of associative learning on any trial is directly related to the surprisingness of the US. However, this account is not without its shortcomings, and the next chapter considers a number of alternative theories that assume that surprise exerts rather a different influence on conditioning. Despite its failings, one advantage of the Rescorla–Wagner (1972) model is the way in which it is presented. It may seem unreasonable to develop a mathematical equation to describe the behaviour of animals. Nonetheless, once it is accepted that the aim of the model is to make predictions about the relative performance of animals that are treated differently, it can be appreciated that the aims of the model are not unrealistic. Furthermore, by being expressed in such formal terms it has been possible to derive testable predictions from the model, and these have led to experiments that not only revealed novel findings but on occasion prompted the development of alternative theories of learning expressed in a similar fashion.

Turning now to the comparative study of associative learning, there is little to be said at this point. In Chapter 2 a study by Hennessey et al. (1979) that is said to demonstrate successful Pavlovian conditioning in paramecia is described. Given the importance attached to the truly random control in the present chapter, it is of interest to note that in one of their experiments the authors included this condition and found that it engendered a level of responding that was significantly less than when the CS and US were paired. This supports the claim that paramecia are susceptible to Pavlovian conditioning, but whether this means that whenever the CS is presented it excites a representation of the US remains to be seen.

Throughout this chapter, the various phenomena that have been described were found principally with rats, rabbits, and pigeons. It should not be concluded, however, that this bias reflects an impoverished ability for associative learning by other species. There have been relatively few well-controlled studies of Pavlovian conditioning with different animals, but those that have been conducted suggest that the effects described in this chapter will be found in a wide range of species. Two recent examples will serve to support this claim.

Sahley, Gelperin, and Rudy (1981) conducted Pavlovian conditioning with a terrestrial mollusc, *Limax maximus*. Not only was taste aversion conditioning successful, they were also able to demonstrate second-order conditioning and blocking with these animals. Using honeybees, Bitterman, Menzel, Fietz, and Schafer (1983) were able to demonstrate second-order conditioning, inhibitory conditioning, and overshadowing (see also Couvillon & Bitterman, 1982), but attempts to demonstrate blocking have met with less success (Couvillon, Klosterhalfen, & Bitterman, 1983).

There can be little doubt, therefore, that associative learning is to be found in many species and that it is important because it allows them to detect regular sequences of events. One aim of the remaining chapters is to determine whether this learning constitutes the pinnacle of animal intelligence, or whether they possess more sophisticated intellectual processes.

5 Attention

Cognitive psychologists have long acknowledged that selective attention plays an important role in the processing of information by humans. They have pointed out that we are often exposed to more sources of information than we can deal with at once, and that some sort of selection is necessary to enable information from one source to be attended to while other information is being ignored. For instance, while you read this textbook, paying attention to the words will probably lead to the sensations in your feet being ignored. But once these sensations have been mentioned, you may concentrate on them momentarily, and this transfer of attention away from the text will disrupt reading. An experimental demonstration of this effect is provided by Brown and Poulson (1961).

People were asked to listen to repeated strings of 8 numbers. The same sequence was presented successively, except that a randomly selected member of the list was changed from one trial to the next. The task for the person was to listen to the sequence and identify the new item. Not surprisingly, perhaps, performance was very accurate when this was all that subjects were required to do. But when they were asked to identify the changed number and at the same time drive a car through the rural lanes of Cambridgeshire, their accuracy declined considerably. Presumably, these people were unable to attend to the task of driving as well as to the list of numbers, and one source of information had to be ignored. It is fortunate for the pedestrians of Cambridgeshire that it was the numerical information that was rejected.

One concern of the present chapter is with the question of whether animals are also selective in their attention. The importance of such a mechanism for animal information processing can be demonstrated by reference to Fig. 5.1. The figure shows STM and LTM interconnected to allow the transfer of information. The novel feature of the figure is the addition of a mechanism for selective attention between the sensory register and STM. The animal is presumed to be exposed to a number of sources of information, but only a limited amount passes into STM. The importance of this attentional mechanism becomes evident when it is acknowledged that many theorists believe that for a stimulus to be learned about, or even to influence behaviour, it must be represented in STM. Hence in DMTS (see Chapter 3), if a pigeon does not attend to the sample, it will not be stored in STM, and accuracy on the task will be poor. Alternatively, should a CS be rejected by the attentional mechanism on a conditioning trial, then its absence from STM will prevent the growth of a CS–US association. A complete understanding of the learning and memory processes of animals can be achieved, therefore, only when the principles that determine whether or not an animal will attend to a stimulus have been fully elaborated.

Most theorists now accept the general features of Fig. 5.1, but there is disagreement about the principles that determine the sort of information that will be allowed through the attentional mechanism. Indeed, this is an area of current debate, and theorists are far from unanimous in their claims concerning the rules that govern the attentional processes of animals. Accordingly, in this chapter a number of different theories of attention are outlined and their strengths and weaknesses summarised. It must be left to future research to decide the ultimate merits of these approaches. Before describing the theories, we must first consider an assumption that they share and some of the procedures that have been used to test them.

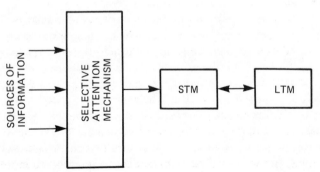

FIG. 5.1.   One possible way in which a selective attention mechanism could restrict the flow of information into memory.

One way of characterising attention is to assume that it is an all-or-none process—that is, animals and people may be regarded either as attending fully to a stimulus or as ignoring it completely. In fact this is a relatively rare theoretical claim and one that is absent from the theories considered later. The more popular view is that the amount of attention paid to a stimulus varies along a continuum, and this determines the extent to which it is represented in STM: The more attention a stimulus receives, the stronger will be its representation. Because the strength of a representation of a stimulus can vary in this manner, the term "salience" is often used to refer to the strength of a representation. The aim of a theory of attention is, then, to identify as precisely as possible the factors that determine the salience of stimuli.

METHODS FOR STUDYING ATTENTION

A major problem with the study of attention in animals is that it is impossible to measure directly the strength of a representation. As a consequence, whether or not a stimulus is being attended to, and to what extent, has to be inferred from the subject's behaviour. There are several ways in which this may be achieved.

One possible method, and perhaps the most direct way, is to monitor what is known as the "orienting response" (OR). In his studies of conditioning, Pavlov (1927) noted that novel stimuli often elicit an OR, or as he referred to it, an investigatory reflex that "brings about the immediate response in man and animals to the slightest changes in the world around them, so that they immediately orientate their appropriate receptor organ in accordance with the perceptible quality in the agent bringing about the change, making full investigation of it" (Pavlov, 1927, p. 12). The implication is that the OR is a consequence of the animal attending to the stimulus, and the vigour of this response may well provide an indication of the strength of its representation. As we shall see, at least some observed changes in the OR do seem to be in accordance with changes thought, on other grounds, to underlie attention.

Other methods for determining the amount of attention that a stimulus receives are notably less direct and rely on the assumption that animals must attend to a stimulus if they are to learn about its consequences, or if it is to control their behaviour. Hence it has been suggested that the conditionability of a stimulus is not solely determined by its intensity, as the Rescorla–Wagner (1972) model stipulates, but by the strength of its representation in STM. If this is correct, then the conditionability of a CS, or its associability with a US, provides an indication of the amount of attention it is receiving.

IAC-F

THE INVERSE HYPOTHESIS

As we noted at the outset of this chapter, the main rationale for introducing the concept of attention is the assumption that we are constantly exposed to more stimuli than we can efficiently cope with. Our resources are limited, and we must therefore concentrate on some stimuli at the expense of others. This argument leads naturally to the notion that attention is selective, because we can only attend to a limited number of stimuli at any one moment. According to the "inverse hypothesis", the more we attend to one stimulus, the less we attend to others.

Some version of the inverse hypothesis seems an inevitable consequence of a theory of attention, and it is not surprising that most early theories incorporated it (e.g. Sutherland & Mackintosh, 1971). These theories were developed principally to account for the findings from studies of discrimination learning. In these experiments animals were exposed to two stimuli—say a black triangle and a white square—and were required consistently to approach one of them for reward. Very often these experiments provided evidence of overshadowing and blocking by showing that animals would learn a great deal about the significance of one dimension, brightness perhaps, and very little about the other (Sutherland & Mackintosh, 1971). Such findings were originally thought to provide strong support for the inverse hypothesis, by suggesting that animals principally attend to, and hence learn about, one dimension at a time. As we saw in the previous chapter, however, the Rescorla–Wagner (1972) model can quite adequately explain this sort of finding without referring to the inverse hypothesis. As an alternative, this model assumes that animals will learn about both dimensions at the same time but at different rates according to their relative intensities. Moreover, although it may make sense to talk of the necessity for selective attention when animals are briefly exposed to complex stimuli, it makes less sense when it is acknowledged that in most discrimination studies the stimuli are relatively simple and exposed for a reasonable time.

A further reason for questioning the value of the inverse hypothesis derives from studies that have shown a subject's experience with a stimulus to be important in determining the amount of attention it receives. Such an outcome is beyond the inverse hypothesis, which stipulates that attention to one stimulus is inversely related to the number of other stimuli available.

An experiment by Kaye and Pearce (1987) shows how the simple experience of being presented repeatedly with a stimulus might influence the attention paid to it. The measures of attention were the conditionability of the stimulus and the strength of the OR directed towards it. Two groups of rats were placed in a conditioning chamber containing a light bulb and a food dispenser. For the first 12 sessions nothing happened for Group Novel, whereas for Group Familiar the bulb was illuminated for 10 sec at regular intervals in each session. Both groups were then given a single pretest session in which the light was occasionally illuminated for 10 sec.

Figure 5.2 shows a typical OR to the light that was performed at the outset of training by Group Familiar. But as the left-hand panel of Fig. 5.3 shows, with repeated exposure to the light the frequency with which this response occurred declined progressively across the 12 sessions. In the extreme right of this panel the strength of the OR for both groups is presented for the pretest session. Not surprisingly, it was considerably more vigorous in Group Novel than in Group Familiar, which suggests that the groups differed in the amount of attention they paid to the light. In order to test this conclusion, all subjects were then conditioned with the light serving as a signal for food. If the repeated exposure to the light had resulted in a loss of attention to it by Group Familiar, then for these subjects conditioning should progress relatively slowly. The right-

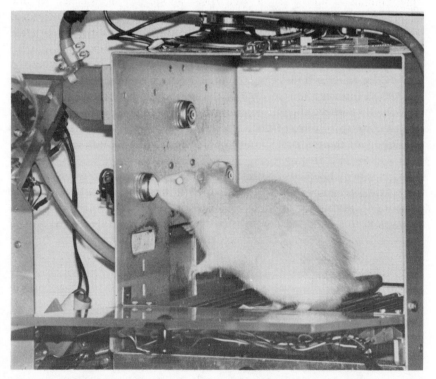

FIG. 5.2. A typical orienting response by a rat to an illuminated bulb (from Kaye, 1983).

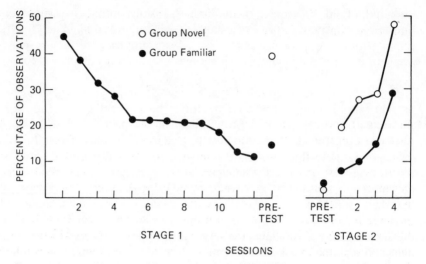

FIG. 5.3. The left-hand panel shows the frequency of the OR by rats to a light during 12 sessions of exposure, Group Familiar, and during a single pretest session when this stimulus was first shown to Group Novel. The right-hand panel shows, for both groups, the amount of magazine activity in the presence of the light that was recorded during the pretest session and during the next four conditioning sessions (adapted from Kaye & Pearce, 1987).

hand panel of Fig. 5.3 shows the strength of the CR of magazine activity during the light for both groups on the preconditioning session, when there was no difference, and on each of the four sessions of conditioning. It is evident that, as predicted, conditioning was more rapid in Group Novel than in Group Familiar. Hence, extended exposure to the light reduced its conditionability in Group Familiar. This effect is known as latent inhibition (see Lubow, 1973).[1]

The principal conclusion to be drawn from these findings is that the past experience of an animal can play an important role in determining the amount of attention a stimulus receives. The inverse hypothesis is unable to explain this outcome, and it is partly for this reason that it has gained

---

[1]The term "latent inhibition" might imply that the disruption in conditioning to which it refers is the same as that produced by conditioned inhibition. But this is incorrect, for two reasons: In Chapter 4 it is proposed that inhibitory conditioning depends upon the CS being followed by the omission of an expected US. Latent inhibition, on the other hand, can develop in the absence of any expectancy for the US. Furthermore, latent inhibition has been found to disrupt inhibitory conditioning (e.g. Reiss & Wagner, 1972). Such an outcome should not occur if latent and conditioned inhibition were the same; it is, however, entirely consistent with the view that latent inhibition reflects a loss of attention to the CS.

little popularity. The next theory to be considered places considerable importance on the influence of experience on attention.

WAGNER'S THEORY

In Chapter 3 we considered briefly a theory by Wagner (1976, 1978, 1979) that was concerned with the memory processes of animals. Wagner (1981; Wagner & Larew, 1985) has now developed his ideas further, and the result is a new model of animal memory, which he refers to as SOP, because it is concerned with the "Standard Operating Procedures" in memory. The theory is both complex and comprehensive, and it is thus not possible to consider it in the detail it deserves in the space available. The SOP model does, however, bear on some of the issues with which we are concerned in this chapter, and it is on this aspect of the theory that we shall focus. The purpose of the following discussion is to give an overview of SOP as it relates to the attentional processes of animals, and this will of necessity lead to an oversimplified account of the model.

The SOP model assumes that the memory of a stimulus can be in three different states (see Fig. 5.4). There is an inactive state that is similar to saying it is stored in LTM. When in this state, information is not modifiable, nor can it influence an animal's behaviour. The remaining states can be regarded as being components of STM and are referred to as A1 and A2. It could be said that when a stimulus is in the A1 state, it will be the centre of an animal's attention, but when in the A2 state, it will be at the periphery of the field of attention. In keeping with our earlier claim that a stimulus must be fully attended to if it is to be learned about readily, Wagner (1981) has proposed that excitatory and inhibitory conditioning is possible only when the CS is represented in the A1 state. The OR to a stimulus will also presumably be strongest in these circumstances.

Information can reside more or less indefinitely in the inactive state, but only for a short while in the active states. More specifically, when information is in the A1 state, it will decay rapidly to the A2 state and then revert rather more slowly to its inactive state. As a result of this relationship the model correctly predicts that conditioning will be more effective with an intermediate rather than short- or long-duration CS (e.g. Smith, 1968). When the CS is too short, conditioning will be poor because there will have been insufficient time for a representation of the CS to be excited from the inactive to the A1 state. And when the CS is too long, the A1 representation that is essential for successful conditioning will have decayed into the A2 state and no longer be capable of entering into associations. Thus, expressed informally, conditioning with an intermedi-

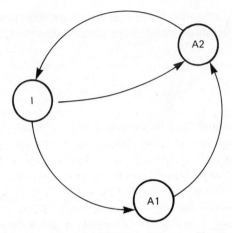

FIG. 5.4. The relationship between the A1, A2, and inactive (I) states of a representation, as envisaged by the SOP model. When in the inactive state, a representation can be excited to the A1 state by presenting the stimulus to which it corresponds. The A2 representation of a stimulus can be formed either as a result of decay from the A1 state (self-generated representation), or directly from the I state by presenting a stimulus with which it is associated (retrieval-generated representation). Representations are assumed to decay rapidly from the A1 to the A2 state, and then more slowly from the A2 to the inactive state (adapted from Wagner, 1981).

ate duration CS is so successful because it is at this point that the stimulus will most fully occupy the animal's attention.

A further feature of the SOP model, and one of particular relevance to the present chapter, is the proposal that a representation can be excited to the A1 state from the inactive but not from the A2 state. Thus if an animal is shown a stimulus for which a representation already exists in the A2 state, then an A1 representation of the stimulus will not be activated, and it will effectively be ignored. The two possible routes by which a stimulus can gain access to the A2 state, and thereby influence attention, will be considered separately.

Self-Generated A2 Representations

The first route has already been mentioned and consists simply of presenting the stimulus by itself. To understand the effects of this treatment, imagine an experiment in which a relatively brief stimulus is presented twice to an animal. On the first presentation it will excite its inactive representation to the A1 state, and the animal will attend to the stimulus fully. When it is turned off, the A1 trace that it leaves will rapidly decay to the A2 state, which will then gradually decay to an inactive state.

If the stimulus should then be presented again before the decay from the A2 state is complete, it will be barely noticed because it will be unable to excite an A1 representation. However, if the second presentation of the stimulus is delayed until the previously formed A2 representation has decayed completely, then it will be able to excite an A1 representation and gain the animal's full attention.

In an experiment based on this design by Whitlow (1975) (see Chapter 2, this volume) rabbits were presented with a pair of identical tones, and it was discovered that the reaction to the second of them was much less when the interval between the members of a pair was short than when it was long. This finding is consistent with the SOP model if it is accepted that the response measure employed by Whitlow (1975), vasoconstriction, is an index of the degree to which the tone excited an A1 representation. Although Wagner (1981) does not comment on this possibility, it gains support from authors such as Sokolov (1963), who view this type of response as a component of the OR.

Additional support for the SOP model can be found in an experiment by Best and Gemberling (1977). Rats were exposed to a flavour, which was then presented some time later as the CS for taste aversion conditioning. For one group, the interval between the flavours was 3.5 hours, for another it was 23.5 hours. A control group received just the conditioning trial with no prior exposure to the flavour. On the following day all subjects were given a test trial in which they were allowed to drink the flavoured solutions. Figure 5.5 summarises the results of this test by showing the amount of solution consumed by the three groups. Conditioning was

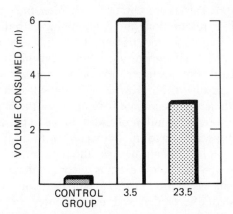

FIG. 5.5. Mean volume of flavoured solution consumed on a test trial that followed a single flavour-aversion conditioning trial. Two groups were given a single exposure to the flavour, either 3.5 or 23.5 hours prior to the conditioning trial, whereas conditioning for the control group was conducted with a novel flavour (adapted from Best & Gemberling, 1977).

evidently effective with the control group, and with the group exposed to the flavour 23.5 hours before conditioning, as they consumed relatively little. In comparison, conditioning was far less effective for the group exposed to the flavour 3.5 hours before the conditioning trial. This poor conditioning, according to the SOP model, is due to the original exposure to the flavour leaving a memory trace in the A2 state that persisted until the conditioning trial. When the flavour was then presented for this trial, it would be unable to excite an A1 representation of itself, and conditioning should be ineffective. The results from the other group that was exposed to the flavour suggest, not surprisingly, that 23.5 hours is sufficient to allow the A2 trace to decay and permit normal conditioning with a representation in the A1 state when the flavour was again presented.

Retrieval-Generated A2 Representations

The second route by which a stimulus can gain access to the A2 state, and thus influence attention, is made possible by associative learning. For successful excitatory conditioning, the SOP model requires the simultaneous rehearsal of representations of the CS and the US while they are both in the A1 state. Future presentations of the CS will then be able to excite a representation of the US directly into the A2 state. This is referred to as a retrieval-generated representation, as it is not excited by the US directly but by a CS with which it is associated. One obvious example of the influence of retrieval-generated representations is provided by blocking. When conditioning is conducted with a novel stimulus in compound with an already established CS, the CS will retrieve a representation of the US into the A2 state. This representation will then prevent the US from activating an A1 representation, and conditioning with the novel stimulus will not be possible. What may perhaps be rather less obvious is that a similar account can be developed to explain latent inhibition. Repeatedly presenting a neutral stimulus in a conditioning chamber will, according to the SOP model, result in the growth of a context–stimulus association. Consequently, whenever the animal is returned to the chamber, the sight of it will retrieve a representation of the stimulus to the A2 state. Should the stimulus then be presented in conjunction with a US, learning about this relationship will be difficult, because the representation of the CS will be in a state that does not allow excitatory conditioning.

The experiments by Whitlow (1975) and by Best and Gemberling (1977) have also revealed effects that can be attributed to the influence of retrieval-generated A2 representations. In his study with rabbits, Whitlow (1975) discovered that the response to a repeatedly presented tone was greater on the first than on subsequent sessions of testing. This relatively long-term instance of habituation was attributed to the growth of a context–tone association during the first session. Subsequent placement of the rabbits in the apparatus should then retrieve an A2 representation of the tone and make them less responsive to it whenever it occurred. Thus the SOP model predicts that habituation is the result of the interaction of both short-term (self-generated) and long-term (retrieval-generated) processes.

For the study by Best and Gemberling (1977), inspection of Fig. 5.5 reveals that conditioning with Group 23.5 was somewhat less effective than for Group Control. The interval of 23.5 hours between the first exposure to the flavour and the conditioning trial makes it unlikely that this disruption was due to the influence of a self-generated representation. It is quite possible, however, that the preexposure trial fostered the growth of a context–flavour association. This would then disrupt conditioning by ensuring the presence of a retrieval-generated A2 representation of the flavour at the time of the conditioning trial. See alsu Westbrook, Bond, and Feyer (1981) for a similar finding.

Some Novel Predictions

One measure of the value of any theory is the degree to which it generates novel experimental research. In this respect Wagner's (1976, 1978, 1981) theorising has been most successful: A wide range of studies has been designed to test the theory, often with positive results.

We have already seen that according to the theory the repeated experience of a stimulus in a specific context will result in the growth of a context–stimulus association and be responsible for a loss of attention to that stimulus. But such a loss need not be permanent. Suppose the stimulus is subsequently presented in a different context with which it is not associated. The new context will be unable to excite an A2 representation of the stimulus, and it should be attended to fully when it is first presented. The theory predicts therefore that latent inhibition and habituation will be specific to the context in which the stimulus was exposed. Note that this prediction is confined to the influence of retrieval-generated representations. The more transient effects of self-generated A2 representations should be found in any context, as they depend simply on the recent occurrence of the stimulus concerned.

As far as both latent inhibition and habituation are concerned, there is evidence showing that these effects are specific to the context in which the stimulus was exposed. Lovibond, Preston, and Mackintosh (1984), for example, reported that exposure to a stimulus is more likely to disrupt future conditioning in the same than in a different chamber, whereas Evans and Hammond (1983) found that once habituation has occurred in one context, it is possible to observe dishabituation simply by presenting the stimulus in a different environment.

A related prediction concerns the influence of exposing animals to an experimental context after they have repeatedly been exposed to a stimulus in it. The original exposure will result in the development of a context–stimulus association. Then, just as presenting a CS without a US can weaken a previously formed CS–US association, so a context–stimulus association should be weakened by placing subjects in the apparatus without the stimulus. Such extinction will prevent the context from exciting an A2 representation of the stimulus, so that it should be be attended to when it next occurs. In support of this prediction Wagner (1978, pp. 203–4) cites an experiment in which two groups of rabbits were exposed to a series of tones for a single habituation session. One group was then placed into the apparatus for two sessions, in the absence of the tone. Animals from the other group remained in their home cages for this stage. Finally, both groups were returned to the apparatus for a test of their reaction to the tone. Subjects given exposure to the context without the tone, thus presumably weakening the context–tone association, responded more on these test trials than did those that had spent the previous stage in their home cages.

In contrast to the above successes, it must be acknowledged that there have been failures to support the theory. Latent inhibition is said to be due to the growth of context–CS associations, and a period of exposure to the apparatus alone after the prior exposure to the CS should weaken these associations and disrupt latent inhibition. Despite a number of tests of this prediction, it has met with very little success (Hall & Minor, 1984). In addition, presenting a stimulus to which subjects are habituated in a different context should produce dishabituation, but this does not always occur (Hall & Channell, 1985; Marlin & Miller, 1981). Further results that are inconsistent with Wagner's theorising will also be mentioned later in this chapter. Despite these conflicting findings, the success with which the theory accounts for many of the phenomena associated with latent inhibition and habituation means that it would be unwise to ignore it as an account for the attentional processes of animals.

STIMULUS SIGNIFICANCE

One class of stimuli to which an animal might be expected to attend are those that signal events of biological significance. The animal that rapidly detects a signal for food or danger, for instance, is more likely to survive than one that ignores these stimuli. Given this line of reasoning, various accounts that assume that animals are most likely to attend to stimuli that predict important events have been developed.

Hunting by Search Image

One of the first to suggest that animals will attend selectively to stimuli of significance was Von Uexküll (1934), who coined the phrase "hunting by search image". This is meant to imply that when animals are searching for food, their perceptual systems are biased to facilitate the identification of a particular type of food, at the expense of not recognising other types. Provided that the food being attended to is in plentiful supply, this should be an efficient strategy for gaining nourishment.

Support for this proposal comes from an experiment by Bond (1983). He placed a mixture of two different types of grain on a gravel-based background. When the grains were conspicuous with respect to the background, pigeons showed no bias in their choice of grain. A marked bias for one type of grain over another was shown, however, when they were both difficult to distinguish from the background. Thus, if identification of food is difficult, pigeons attend selectively to the features of a single food type to facilitate its discovery. (See also Dawkins, 1971a,b.)

Acquired Distinctiveness of Cues

A number of years prior to this study, Lawrence (1949, 1950) proposed that a similar process might be involved in animal discrimination learning. He suggested that the cues that were relevant to the solution of the discrimination would gain in distinctiveness or salience.

In one of his experiments, rats were placed into the start box of the apparatus sketched in the left-hand side of Fig. 5.6, and they had to jump

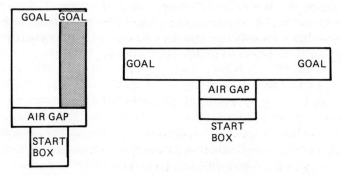

FIG. 5.6. Plan of the mazes used in the study by Lawrence (1949).

over a gap into one of the arms. On any trial one arm was black and the other was white, one arm was narrow and one was wide, and, finally, one was rough and the other smooth. The position of these features varied independently and randomly from trial to trial. For one group brightness was relevant to the solution of the discrimination, so that food was always available in, say, the black but not the white arm. Texture and width were the relevant dimensions for two additional groups. Because subjects could not see the food before they jumped, they had to learn which feature signalled its presence and select the correct arm on the basis of this information.

Lawrence (1949) proposed that when solving this discrimination, subjects not only learn to approach the correct stimulus, they also learn to pay more attention to the relevant stimulus dimension than to the other dimensions. Hence if black is the correct stimulus, then subjects will eventually pay a lot of attention to brightness and relatively little to texture and width.

A moment's reflection should indicate that attractive as this notion might be, it is not very easy to test. After all, just because a rat approaches a black arm consistently does not mean it is attending to some stimuli at the expense of others. In order to test his views, therefore, Lawrence trained the three groups on an additional discrimination, in which black and white were the relevant stimuli for all. If subjects previously trained on this dimension really had learned to attend to brightness, then they should solve the new problem rapidly, whereas those attending to different dimensions because of their previous training should be rather poor at learning the new task. But here, again, a problem arises. Once animals have been trained in a black–white discrimination, the use of the same stimuli in a novel task may result in their resorting to their former habits. There is thus a danger that any benefits from the original training may be due to the transfer of responses that have been learned, rather than to attentional factors. Lawrence was well aware of this problem and thought he had overcome it with the following ingenious design.

The apparatus for the second task is depicted in the right-hand side of Fig. 5.6. Subjects were placed into the start box, and they were required to jump over the air gap to the alley, which on some trials was entirely black and on others entirely white. On those trials when the alley was black, running in one direction, say, left, was rewarded, whereas running in the opposite direction was correct when it was white. Animals that pay a lot of attention to brightness from the outset of this task might be expected to learn it more rapidly than those initially attending to width or to texture. In confirmation of his analysis, Lawrence (1949) found that rats previously trained with brightness as the relevant dimension performed better than the other groups on the second discrimination.

For nearly 20 years these results were taken as support for Lawrence's theoretical views, until Siegel (1967) presented an alternative explanation for them. He suggested that during the original task the rat might adopt a strategy of consistently looking at the same arm of the maze. Perhaps it always looked at the left arm; if it was the correct brightness (black), then it would jump towards the arm, otherwise it would jump without hesitation to the adjacent arm. Now, consider how this might influence the second discrimination. Suppose that, first, the subject must learn to go left when the arm is black and right when white. The adoption of the previous habit will lead immediately to perfect performance. Moreover, if the subject must learn the opposite relationship—go right when black, go left when white—then transfer of the previous training will ensure that the rat starts by being wrong on every trial. Siegel (1967) argued that in these circumstances the subjects will soon relinquish their incorrect strategy and adopt the correct one. This was assumed to require fewer trials than for the other groups, because they would not adopt a strategy that was consistently wrong, and the occasional reward it led to would make it harder to extinguish.

In order to test this account, Siegel (1967) repeated Lawrence's experiment and confirmed that rats did adopt the sort of strategy he proposed during the initial task. We must conclude, therefore, that Lawrence's (1949) study does not unequivocally show that animals learn to attend to stimuli that are relevant to the occurrence of reward.

The subtlety of Lawrence's (1949) experiment and the ingenuity of Siegel's (1967) analysis are sufficient justification for discussing this issue in such depth. There is, however, a further point to be drawn from this topic. It is evidently extremely difficult to design an experiment that demonstrates without question an increase in attention to stimuli that signal reward or nonreward. As a result, to my knowledge, there is not a single study whose results cannot be interpreted in some different way. Nonetheless, the principle is attractive, and it has encouraged the development of a number of theoretical accounts for the role of attention in learning (Mackintosh, 1975a; Sutherland & Mackintosh, 1971).

Mackintosh's Theory

Although Mackintosh's theory is meant to apply to any situation, it is easiest to describe by considering its application to Pavlovian conditioning. In keeping with the views expressed by Lawrence (1949), Mackintosh (1975a) assumes that the better a CS predicts a US, the more attention it will receive. It is possible to express this assumption more precisely by using the terms introduced in Chapter 4. If there is a small discrepancy between the associative strength of the CS and the ceiling to conditioning imposed by the US magnitude (λ), then the CS can be considered to be a good predictor of the US, and the attention it receives will be considerable. But if the discrepancy is large, the CS will receive little attention, because it is a poor predictor of the US. In fact, the theory is not quite this simple. To be attended to fully, a CS must not only be a good predictor of the US, it must be a better predictor than all the other stimuli that are present on a trial.[2]

Stimuli may not only gain in attention; they may also lose it and be effectively ignored. This will happen whenever the CS is either equally as good as, or worse than, a predictor of the US than the other stimuli that are present.[3]

The assumption that there will be a loss of attention to a CS when it is no better at predicting the US than the other stimuli that are present on a trial is important because it allows the theory to explain latent inhibition. Mackintosh (1975a) maintains that animals naturally pay a lot of attention to a stimulus when it is novel. But if the stimulus should be presented alone for a number of trials prior to conditioning, then there will be a loss of attention to it because it is just as accurate at predicting the event that follows it—nothing—as the contextual stimuli that accompany it. After a number of preexposure trials, therefore, attention to the the CS will be relatively low, and subjects should condition more slowly with it than if it were novel.

Once conditioning has commenced with a preexposed stimulus, however, it will gain gradually in associative strength. This will result in the CS becoming a better predictor of the US than the contextual stimuli, and as soon as this happens there will be an increase in attention to the CS.

One interesting feature of Mackintosh's (1975a) theory is that it provides a different account of blocking to that considered hitherto. The Rescorla–Wagner (1972) model, as well as Wagner's (1981) SOP model, maintain that blocking is due to the US being fully expected and thus incapable of entering into novel associations. Mackintosh (1975a) has challenged this claim by proposing that blocking is entirely a result of subjects ignoring the stimulus added for compound conditioning.

---

[2]To represent this idea formally, Mackintosh (1975a) proposed that attention to a CS, A, will increase whenever $|\lambda - V_A| < |\lambda - V_X|$, where V_X is the combined associative strength of all the stimuli present on a trial other than A. (The vertical lines either side of the expression $|\lambda - V|$ indicate that its value is always positive.)

[3]Expressed formally, Mackintosh (1975a) is proposing that attention to CS A will decline either when $|\lambda - V_A| > |\lambda - V_X|$, or when $|\lambda - V_A| = |\lambda - V_X|$.

To understand the application of this theory to blocking, it is essential to emphasise that Mackintosh (1975a) rejects the Rescorla–Wagner (1972) account of compound conditioning. As an alternative, the growth of associative strength to a CS is given by Equation 5.1, which is to be applied when the stimulus is presented either in isolation or in conjunction with other stimuli.

$$\Delta V = \alpha(\lambda - V) \tag{5.1}$$

According to this equation conditioning with a CS is completely unaffected by the properties of any other stimuli that accompany it. The value of α reflects the amount of attention that the stimulus receives, and the greater its value, the more rapid will conditioning be. The way in which α is calculated need not concern us here; for present purposes it is sufficient to accept that α will approach 1 when the stimulus is a good predictor of the US relative to other stimuli, and when it is a relatively poor predictor of the US then α will approach 0.

Consider now a blocking experiment in which a tone is paired with a US prior to conditioning with a light–tone compound. On the first compound trial the attention paid to the light will be relatively high because of its novelty, and Equation 5.1 predicts that it will gain in associative strength. Animals will also have the opportunity of discovering on this trial that the light is a much poorer predictor of the US than the tone. As a result, on future conditioning trials they should pay a considerable amount of attention to the tone and very little to the light, which will ensure that they learn relatively little about the relationship betwen the light and the US.

The difference between this account and that provided by the Rescorla–Wagner model for blocking is emphasised by the conflicting predictions they make. As we have seen, the theory of Mackintosh (1975a) asserts that conditioning with the added CS should be normal on the first compound trial. It is only on later trials when the added CS is ignored that the effects of blocking should become evident. In contrast, the Rescorla–Wagner (1972) model predicts that provided the US is fully predicted on the first compound trial, conditioning with the added CS should be impossible.

Unfortunately, the evidence bearing on these predictions is conflicting. In support of his views Mackintosh (1975b) has shown normal conditioning with the added CS after a single blocking trial, but thereafter there was little change in the associative strength of this stimulus. Balaz, Kasprow, and Miller (1982), on the other hand, found very effective blocking with a single compound trial. The reasons for these discrepant findings are beginning to emerge (Dickinson, Nicholas, & Mackintosh, 1983), but they are too complex to be considered here. For our purposes it is sufficient to note that with a simple blocking design it may be difficult to choose between two very different, sophisticated theories.

As a further test of his theory Mackintosh and his colleagues have investigated in detail the influence of surprise on blocking (Dickinson, Hall, & Mackintosh, 1976; Dickinson & Mackintosh, 1979; Mackintosh, Bygrave, & Picton, 1977). One of these studies is described in Chapter 4 (see p. 148), where its results are shown to be incompatible with predictions from the Rescorla–Wagner (1972) model. Essentially the study demonstrated that the surprising omission of one of a pair of shocks after each compound conditioning trial was sufficient to disrupt blocking. According to the theory, this outcome is due to the surprising omission of one shock arresting the decline in attention to the added stimulus, and hence allowing subjects to learn about its relationship with the shock that was presented. A more detailed presentation of this account can be found in Dickinson and Mackintosh (1979).

By assuming that the attention paid to a stimulus is determined by how good it is as a predictor of the US, Mackintosh (1975a) has developed a theory with a wide range of applications. It has led to subtle experiments showing that such phenomena as blocking and also overshadowing (see Mackintosh, 1976) are not as easy to understand as was once believed. It has also pointed to a new way of looking at an effect to be considered shortly, selective association. A major weakness with his theory is that it has proved extremely difficult to demonstrate experimentally that the attention paid to a stimulus will be high if it is the best available predictor of a US. This means that there is little experimental evidence for a basic supposition of the theory. Indeed, in the section on the Pearce–Hall model (p.171) some evidence is cited which suggests that this fundamental assumption may be incorrect.

Selective Association and Learned Irrelevance

An assumption that was once common to many theories of learning is that conditioning will be equally effective, no matter what stimuli are paired together. In a discussion of this topic Seligman and Hager (1972) referred to this claim as the premise of equipotentiality, but, they argued, there is abundant evidence to contradict it. For example, Garcia and Koelling (1966) (see Chapter 1, p. 15, this volume) found that rats associate a novel flavour with subsequent illness much more readily than an auditory–visual compound. This is not simply due to the interoceptive stimulus being more intense and hence a more effective CS than the exteroceptive compound, because the opposite pattern of results was found when the stimuli were paired with shock. According to the equipotentility premise, the ease of conditioning should not be influenced in this way simply by changing the US.

Moreover, this effect is not confined to tastes, illness, or rats. Shapiro, Jacobs, and Lolordo (1980) have demonstrated a similar outcome with pigeons. These animals have little trouble in learning that a red light signals food, but they learn with difficulty when the same stimulus is used to signal shock. Conversely, conditioning with a tone progresses more readily when it signals an aversive rather than an appetitive US. The term "selective association" refers to this general finding that some CS–US relationships can be learned about more readily than others.

One explanation for selective association is that it is due to some stimuli, or stimulus dimensions, being more relevant to the occurrence of biologically significant events than others. In the case of the Garcia and Koelling (1966) study, for example, tastes are likely to provide more reliable information than sound about whether or not a certain food is poisonous. Given such naturally occurring relationships, it would be in the animal's best interests to capitalise upon them by learning rapidly about those that are most reliable. On the other hand, animals may also benefit by being disposed to learn little or nothing at all about those relationships that are unlikely in their natural environment (Seligman, 1970; Seligman & Hager, 1972).

Experiments on selective association thus suggest that during conditioning animals will attend most to those stimuli, or dimensions, that in the past have proved reliable predictors of the US concerned. But how do they know which cues are most relevant for a given US? According to Rozin and Kalat (1971) this knowledge is acquired as a result of evolutionary processes—that is, some members of a species may be innately disposed to learn rapidly about the relationship between tastes and illness and hence more likely to survive, and to pass on this characteristic, than those lacking in this respect.

According to this approach selective association should be evident from birth, and strong support for this prediction is provided in a study by Gemberling and Domjan (1982). Rats were conditioned when they were only 24 hours old either with illness, induced by an injection of lithium chloride, or with electric shock. When illness constituted the US, saccharin—but not being placed in a cardboard box—was an effective CS. The opposite pattern of results was recorded, however, when shock was the US. It is most implausible that anything the animals had learned in their first 24 hours of life was responsible for this pattern of results, and the most likely explanation is that rats are genetically disposed to learn about some relationships more easily than about others.

In addition to innate factors, the discovery of an effect known as "learned irrelevance" suggests that the animal's experience may also contribute to selective association. In a typical study Mackintosh (1973) exposed rats to random presentations of a CS and footshock (Group Random). As the CS was no better a predictor of the US than the contextual stimuli, his theory predicts that attention to the CS will decline. To test this prediction, conditioned suppression training in which the CS and US were paired was then conducted. It is apparent from Fig. 5.7 that conditioning for this group was considerably less effective than for Group Control, in which the CS and US were both novel at the start of conditioning. A third group, Group Water, was also included in this study. These subjects were given random presentations of the CS and water prior to conditioned suppression training in which the same CS was paired with shock. The intriguing finding from this group is that their pretreatment with the CS had a much less diruptive influence on conditioning than for Group Random. The converse of this effect has also been demonstrated: Conditioning with water is disrupted to a greater extent by prior random presentations of the CS and water than of the CS and shock. Here then is an example of selective association that is due to the individual's experience, rather than to its evolutionary history.

To explain this pattern of findings, Mackintosh (1973) proposed that the random pairings of a CS and a US will result in a loss of attention to the CS

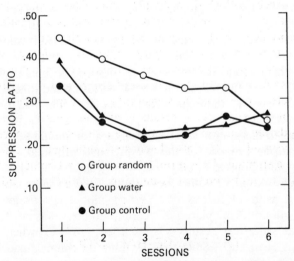

FIG. 5.7. Acquisition of conditioned suppression by three groups of rats trained with a CS that was novel for the start of conditioning (Group Control) or had previously been presented in a random relationship with shock (Group Random) or with water (Group Water) (adapted from Mackintosh, 1973).

that is US-specific. Put informally, learning that a CS is irrelevant to the delivery of shock will lead to animals ignoring it when these events are eventually paired. However, should the CS be used to signal a different US, such as water, then attention to it will be restored, and conditioning will progress normally.

There is, however, an alternative explanation for these findings. The slow conditioning in the test phase of the above studies may have been due to the CS being a conditioned inhibitor, rather than to it being ignored. In the first stage of the experiment, the random presentation of the CS and footshock might be thought sufficient to make the former a signal for the absence of the latter, and this inhibitory learning would disrupt conditioning when they were paired together (see Chapter 4). But this interpretation is unlikely to be correct because the probability of shock in the presence of the CS was identical to that in its absence. Such treatment constitutes a zero contingency between the CS and US, whereas it was indicated in the previous chapter that inhibitory learning depends upon this contingency being negative. In addition, Baker and Mackintosh (1977) have shown that random presentations of the CS and US can also disrupt subsequent inhibitory conditioning with the CS. This outcome is consistent with the claim that animals ignore the CS as a result of the pretraining, and directly opposite to that expected if the CS becomes a conditioned inhibitor because of its random relationship with the US.

The results in this section again point to the importance of attentional factors in governing the behaviour of animals. The principal theoretical claim that has been examined is that animals will pay attention to those stimuli that predict important events. Support for this proposal comes from the finding that when food is hard to identify, pigeons will attend selectively to the features of one sort of food, even though this will lead them to miss other sorts of food. In a rather different vein, experimental studies of selective association suggest that the experience either of an individual, or of its ancestors, results in animals ignoring those stimulus dimensions during conditioning that in the past have proved irrelevant to the US concerned. It has also been suggested that attention will be increased to a stimulus if it is a reliable signal for a US; but although this has proved a useful theoretical assumption, there is little evidence in its favour.

THE PEARCE–HALL MODEL

To introduce the third account of animal attention it may help to return to the experiment of Brown and Poulton (1961), which found that people had difficulty in attending to a string of numbers while driving. There was an additional group in this study consisting of policemen with considerable driving experience. They, too, were required to identify the changed member of the list while driving, but they were able to do both tasks without difficulty, even in urban areas. Perhaps this result should not be too surprising, as the popularity of car radios attests to the ability of many people to drive and attend to an unrelated source of information at the same time. The challenge posed by such results is to provide an adequate theory of attention that can explain them.

According to a number of authors, people have two modes of attention that can operate simultaneously. One of these is assumed to be of limited capacity and is directed towards tasks that are novel or require conscious control. This type of attention is referred to as "controlled" or "deliberate" (Shiffrin & Schneider, 1977; LaBerge & Samuels, 1974). An example of a task that might be appropriate to this type of attention is the number identification task employed by Brown and Poulton (1961). The other type of attention is more *automatic* and directed towards tasks that are very well practiced and the performance of which is more or less habitual. When learning to drive, it can be assumed that the novelty of the task will demand controlled processing and that there will be little spare capacity available for attending to numbers. With practice, however, automatic processes may be responsible for driving, freeing the controlled processing mechanisms to cope with other tasks.

It is within this framework that the Pearce–Hall (1980) model can be most readily understood. This model is based upon the supposition that animals need to attend to a stimulus only while they are learning about its consequences. With Pavlovian conditioning, for instance, attention must be paid to the CS to allow it to gain or lose associative strength. But once conditioning has reached a stable asymptote, there will be no further need for the subject to attend to the CS, and it can be ignored, at least as far as learning is concerned. This type of attention is analogous to controlled processing in humans. Of course, once learning has ceased, then the fact that it may no longer receive controlled processing does not mean that a stimulus will be without influence. If this were true, then a CS that may have gained considerable associative strength would fail to elicit a CR. Instead, it is assumed that once learning has reached a stable asymptote, the CS will be detected, and the appropriate CR triggered, by automatic processes.

Pearce and Hall (1980) say little about this automatic processing, yet it is conceivable that its properties are responsible for the findings of Bond (1983) mentioned earlier. Presumably, for adult pigeons the visual characteristics of grain reliably predict certain gastric consequences and there is no need for controlled processing. The recognition of grain would, instead, be left to a more automatic mechanism that can be biased in certain ways to facilitate the identificaton of food when it is not readily detectable.

Considerably more consideration is given by Pearce and Hall (1980) to controlled attention. We argued that this attention should be directed most to those stimuli that need to be learned about—that is, to those that have recently been followed by unpredictable or surprising consequences. Thus if the US is entirely unexpected on Conditioning Trial n, then on Trial $n +$ 1 the CS needs to be attended to fully so that animals can learn rapidly about its relationship with the US. In contrast, if the US that accompanies a CS is entirely predictable, then there is little need for learning and hence little need for attention to be directed towards the CS on future trials.[4]

Implications for the OR

An experiment by Kaye and Pearce (1984) demonstrates the principles underlying this model. The aim of the study was to test the theory by using the OR as an index of the attention paid to a light CS during conditioning. Three groups of rats first received six 10-sec presentations of this stimulus in a pretest session to assess their reactions to it when novel. Figure 5.8 (left-hand side) indicates that attention to the light for this session was comparatively high. The conditions for the groups then differed for Stage 1 of the experiment, which comprised 14 sessions. In each session, Group None was given a number of exposures to the light entirely in the absence of any US. In these circumstances the events following the light will never be surprising, because from the outset it will not predict a US and none will occur. Accordingly, there will be no need for subjects to attend to the light, and it should very quickly be ignored. Figure 5.8 shows support for this prediction in a rapid decline in the frequency of the OR across sessions.

The second group, Group Continuous, received the same number of

---

[4]To present these ideas formally we used the now familiar discrepancy $|\lambda - V|$, in which λ is determined by the magnitude of the US and V is the associative strength of the CS. The relationship between this discrepancy on Trial n, and the amount of attention paid to the CS on the next trial, α^{n+1}, is given by the equation: $\alpha^{n+1} = |\lambda^n - V^n|$.

On trials when the US is surprising, the value of the discrepancy will be large, and attention to the CS will be high on the following trial. But as the CS becomes a better predictor of the US, there will be a smaller difference between λ and V, and the attention it receives in the future will be reduced accordingly. For this equation to retain the convention that α varies between 0 and 1, it must be stipulated that λ is never greater than 1.

As it is presented, this equation assumes that the attention to a CS is determined entirely by the events of the previous trial. Pearce, Kaye, and Hall (1982) have argued that this assumption is unrealistic and proposed that changes in attention are determined in a more complex manner, which is based upon the above equation.

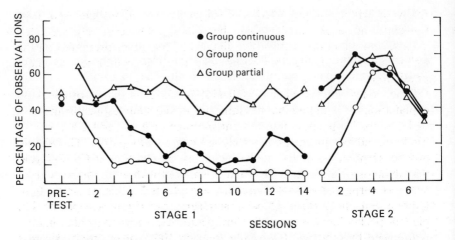

FIG. 5.8. The frequency with which an OR to a light was recorded for three groups in a pretest session: during Stage 1, when the light signalled nothing (Group None), food on every trial (Group Continuous), or food on 50% of the trials (Group Partial); and during Stage 2, when the light signalled nothing for Groups Partial and Continuous, and food for Group None (adapted from Kaye & Pearce, 1984).

presentations of the light as the previous group, but each one was followed by a pellet of food. Initially, the low associative strength of the light will ensure that the food with which it is paired is unexpected, and attention to the light should be considerable. As training progresses, however, the CS will gain in associative strength, and as it becomes a better predictor of the US so attention to it will decline. Thus the model predicts that the OR to the light will be high at the start of conditioning but decline gradually thereafter. Once again, these predictions are supported by the results shown in Fig. 5.8.

The final group, Group Partial, is of particular interest because the light was followed by food on a random 50% of the trials, and on the remaining trials it was followed by nothing. With this schedule rats will be unable to predict what will follow the CS on each trial, and as a result the occurrence of food, or its omission, will consistently be surprising. The effect of this should be to sustain attention to the light no matter how many times it is presented. In confirmation of this prediction Fig. 5.8 shows that the OR to the light was as vigorous after 14 sessions (84 trials) as when it was novel.

For Stage 2 of the experiment the conditioning schedules associated with the light were changed. For Group None the light was paired with food on every trial, whereas for Groups Continuous and Partial food never followed this stimulus. For a while, at least, these changes should ensure that all subjects attend to the light, because for all groups the events that follow it will be unpredicted. As subjects learn about the new rela- tionships, however, the light will be followed by accurately predicted events, and attention to it should diminish. The curves presented on the right-hand side of Fig. 5.8 show that the OR conformed to these predictions.

One benefit of the Pearce–Hall (1980) model is that it provides an explanation for a finding that has hitherto proved troublesome for theories of learning. In general, intermittent pairings of a CS and US result in weaker conditioning than when they are consistently paired. This should not be surprising—all theories of learning predict that a CS will gain maximum associative strength when it is paired with a US on every trial. What is surprising is that there are exceptions to this generalisation. Gibbon, Farrell, Locurto, Duncan, and Terrace (1980) have reported that pigeons peck a key more rapidly during autoshaping when its illumination is followed by food on 50% rather than on 100% of the trials. If, as is usually accepted, the rate of keypecking is taken as an index of associative strength, then these findings stand in marked contrast to both common sense and theoretical predictions.

To explain this type of outcome, Collins and Pearce (1985) proposed that autoshaping with pigeons influences two classes of response, both directed towards the key. One is a CR that will be stronger with continuous rather than intermittent pairings of the CS and US, the other is an OR that is governed by principles embodied in the Pearce–Hall (1980) model. If the CS is always paired with the US, then the CR will ultimately reach a relatively high asymptote. Superimposed upon this responding will be the OR. During the early stages of conditioning this response will be strong because the food accompanying the light will be unexpected, but once subjects have appreciated that food will always follow the light, then the OR will decline, leaving the CR as the major contributor to keypecking. If the CS is only intermittently followed by the US, then the CR will be somewhat weaker than with the continuous schedule. However, as we have just seen, this intermittent schedule will result in a persistent and strong OR being directed towards the keylight. This response may then more than compensate for the difference in the strength of CR generated by the two schedules and lead ultimately to the higher level of responding.

In support of this analysis it can be noted that intermittent CS–US pairings result in stronger responding than continuous pairings only when the CS is provided by an easily identifiable source, such as the illumination of a bulb. It is precisely in these circumstances that the performance of ORs would be expected to augment any CRs directed towards the same source. A more detailed account of this analysis for the paradoxical effects of intermittent CS–US pairings can be found in Collins and Pearce (1985).

Implications for Conditioning

Latent Inhibition. According to Pearce and Hall (1980), animals will pay least attention and hence learn most slowly about those stimuli that have been followed by accurately predicted events, whereas stimuli that have been paired with surprising events should be attended to and learned about readily. To explain the fairly rapid conditioning that occurs with a novel CS, the theory accepts that the attention it receives will be initially high. As training progresses, the CS will gain in associative strength and become a progressively more accurate predictor of the US. This will result in a gradual loss of attention to the CS, and the increments in associative strength will therefore be less on later than on earlier trials. Eventually the CS will accurately predict the US, whereupon it will be ignored completely and no further changes in associative strength will be possible.[5]

The previous discussion of the study by Kaye and Pearce (1984) indicates the way in which this account explains latent inhibition. The repeated presentation of a stimulus by itself will reduce the attention it receives, because it is an accurate predictor of nothing. Should the stimulus then be paired with a US, it will gain associative strength more slowly than if it were novel.

Blocking. The presentation of the Pearce–Hall model so far has been concerned exclusively with the effects of training with a single CS. When applied to compound conditioning, it is assumed that as long as the US is accurately predicted by one stimulus, or a collection of stimuli, then there is no further need for learning and thus no further need for attention to the stimuli present on that trial. As a consequence, Pearce and Hall (1980) stipulate that where conditioning with a compound is involved, attention to a CS will be determined by how accurately the US was predicted by all the stimuli combined on the previous trial involving that CS.[6]

Quite surprisingly, given the difference between them, the Pearce–Hall model now makes exactly the same predictions about blocking as Mackintosh's theory. On the first compound conditioning trial the novelty

---

[5]This relationship between attention and learning can be expressed by the equation $\Delta V = \alpha \cdot S \cdot \lambda$. The terms in the equation should all be familiar, except for S, which is determined by the intensity of the CS. The value of α is given by the equation in Footnote 4. All the parameters can vary in value between 0 and 1.

[6]To take account of this modification for compound conditioning Pearce and Hall (1980) recommend that the equation in Footnote 4 should be replaced by: $\alpha^{n+1} = |\lambda^n - V_T^n|$, where V_T is determined by the combined associative strength of all the stimuli that are present on a trial.

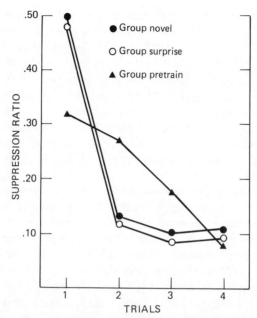

FIG. 5.9. Acquisition of conditioned suppression to a tone by three groups of rats when it was paired with a strong shock for four test trials. The tone was novel at the outset of this training for Group None, but for Groups Pretrain and Surprise it had previously been paired with a weak shock. Group Surprise additionally received two trials with the tone presented alone between the two conditioning stages (adapted from Hall & Pearce, 1982a).

of the added stimulus will ensure it receives attention and that it acquires some associative strength. The subject will also discover on this trial that the stimulus is followed by a US that is totally unsurprising, because its occurrence will be predicted by the other element of the compound. This discovery will ensure that the stimulus is virtually ignored on the next trial, and further changes in its associative strength will be slight.

Latent Inhibition of a CS. The difference in the approaches of Mackintosh (1975a) and Pearce and Hall (1980), however, is brought out very clearly by another set of experiments (Hall & Pearce, 1979, 1982a, 1982b; Pearce & Hall, 1979). In one of these (Hall & Pearce 1982a), three groups of rats received conditioned suppression training in which a tone was paired with a moderately strong shock. Group None received a novel tone at the outset of this stage, and conditioning with it was very rapid (see Fig. 5.9). Prior to the test phase, Group Pretrain experienced a large number of conditioning trials in which the tone was paired with a relatively weak shock. At the start of conditioning with the weak shock animals should attend to the tone as it gains in associative strength; but after a sufficient number of trials, when conditioning has reached asymptote, the tone should be virtually ignored. This low level of attention to the tone should then ensure that conditioning progresses slowly when it is paired with the large shock for the test phase. In other words, the Pearce–Hall (1980) theory predicts that it should be possible to obtain latent inhibition by repeatedly pairing the CS with a US, as well as repeatedly presenting it by itself. In confirmation of this prediction Fig. 5.9 shows that conditioning with Group Pretrain was, indeed, slow for the test stage. Note that the low suppression ratio on the first trial was probably due to the pretraining with the weak shock.

Subjects in Group Pretrain eventually learned about the relationship between the tone and the large shock, albeit gradually, and this can be explained in the following manner: The low attention paid to the tone on the first trial will permit only a limited increment of associative strength. Of more importance, however, is that subjects will also be provided with the opportunity of discovering that the tone is again followed by a surprising US: In the recent past it accurately predicted a small US, and now suddenly it is followed by a large one. Attention to the tone should therefore be restored and enable better learning about the CS–strong shock relationship in the future. To test this account a third group was included in the study, Group Surprise. These subjects received the same initial training as Group Pretrain, but on the test session two "surprise" trials prior to conditioning with the large shock were included. These trials consisted simply of following the tone by nothing and were intended to alert animals to the fact that the CS is no longer an accurate predictor of shock. Such a manipulation should restore attention to the tone and facilitate conditioning with the larger shock in the final stage. The results confirmed this prediction by showing that Group Surprise conditioned more rapidly than Group Pretrain and at much the same rate as Group Novel.

In addition to their relevance to the Pearce–Hall (1980) theory, these findings also have implications for the other theories of attention considered in this chapter. The results of Group Pretrain are relevant to Mackintosh's (1975a) theory, which assumes that a stimulus will receive most attention when it is the best available predictor of a US. Upon the completion of the tone–weak shock pairings this account predicts that subjects in Group Pretrain will pay considerable attention to the tone, and conditioning should be rapid when it is paired with the larger shock. The failure to confirm this prediction seriously challenges a basic assumption of the theory.

The results from Group Surprise have a bearing on the theory developed by Wagner (1981). The way to restore attention to a stimulus according to this approach is to present it in a manner that ensures that it is not represented in the A2 state. We saw earlier that this may be achieved either by exposing subjects to the stimulus in a different context, or by adopting steps to weaken previously formed context–stimulus associations. In the case of Group Surprise, neither of these manipulations was adopted, yet a restoration of attention to the tone was recorded, as revealed by the rapid conditioning in the test phase relative to Group Pretrain. This finding strongly implies that it is how accurately the events following a stimulus are predicted that determines the attention it receives.

It also has to be admitted that the Pearce–Hall model is not without its shortcomings. For example, it follows that once a stimulus is being ignored, the only way to restore attention is to follow it with a surprising event. However, in the discussion of Wagner's theory it was shown that attention to a CS can be restored in a number of other ways. It may be achieved by presenting the stimulus in a new context, or by placing the subject in the original context and witholding the stimulus for a number of sessions. If these effects should prove reliable, then it may be necessary to modify the Pearce–Hall model, perhaps by allowing changes in the context–CS association to influence attention.

Another problem for the theory is posed by Mackintosh's (1973) discovery of learned irrelevance, in which random pairings of a CS and US were found to retard conditioning when they were eventually paired. By being randomly related to the US, the CS may be considered to be an inaccurate predictor of its occurrence. Hence, according to the theory, attention should remain at a high level to this stimulus and facilitate conditioning in the test phase. One possible explanation for the failure to confirm this prediction can be based upon the fact that the random presentations of the CS and US will result in the growth of a context–US association. As a consequence, whenever the US is, by chance, paired with the CS, it will be accurately predicted by the contextual stimuli, and attention to the CS will decline because it is followed by an accurately predicted event.

CONCLUSIONS

The great pity when considering the experiments cited in this chapter is that it is not possible to explain them all with a single theory. It would be a futile exercise to attempt to integrate these different accounts in the absence of further evidence. Indeed, there may well be a grain of truth in each of them, and the attentional processes in animals could be more complex than has hitherto been acknowledged. On a more positive note, the development of these theories has led to the discovery of a wide range of experimental findings that now show the importance of attention in animal cognition. Even if they achieve nothing else, the theories will have been of value.

There has been a marked imbalance in the comparative study of attention. A large number of studies have shown habituation in a wide range of species. Whether these all reflect a loss of attention to the stimuli remains to be seen. Nonetheless, the wide variety of species that demonstrate habituation encourages the view that many different animals possess some sort of attentional mechanism.

In contrast, there have been remarkably few attempts to discover whether changes in the conditionability of stimuli can be obtained with species other than mammals. Lubow (1973) reviews experiments showing latent inhibition in goats, dogs, sheep, rats, and rabbits, but beyond this, studies of latent inhibition are rare. There have been several attempts to demonstrate latent inhibition in pigeons, but these have led to conflicting findings (Mackintosh, 1973; Tranberg & Rilling, 1978); others have had no success in their attempts to show latent inhibition in honeybees (Bitterman et al., 1983) or goldfish (Shishimi, 1985). If future reseach should confirm that changes in attention, as indexed by changes in conditionability, are unique to mammals, then this will be an important discovery. On the basis of the evidence reviewed in the previous chapters we have been unable to identify a major intellectual capacity that is present in some species but not others. It may well be that selective attention, or some aspects of it, is one capacity that does allow us to differentiate between the cognitive processes of species.

6 The Translation of Knowledge into Action

The previous chapters have shown that animals can store information about a variety of stimuli, and that they they can learn about the relationships between them. The processes responsible for the acquisition of this knowledge have also been considered in some detail. But once acquired, knowledge does not remain passively stored inside the animal; instead, it exerts a profound influence on the owner's behaviour. The concern of this chapter is with the way an animal's knowledge is able to influence what it does.

The discussion of associative learning has already hinted at the way in which a simple association controls behaviour. The presentation of a CS, it was said, will excite a representation of the US, and this will lead to the performance of a CR. In the first part of the chapter this account is looked at in some detail. But it is not just knowledge gained as a result of Pavlovian conditioning that determines what an animal does. Thorndike's (1898) pioneering work established that instrumental conditioning is an equally important means of changing behaviour, and many authors (e.g. Skinner, 1938) have always argued that it is far more important. The second part of the chapter discusses in detail the knowledge that is acquired during instrumental conditioning, and the way in which this knowledge is utilised.

PAVLOVIAN CONDITIONING

Two important determinants of the conditioned response are the nature of the US and the properties of the CS. The way in which they influence behaviour will be considered separately.

Influence of the US on the CR

Preparatory and Consummatory CRs.   In Chapter 4 it was shown that Konorski (1967) believed that a CS may activate two different representations of the same US, and these will lead to very different CRs. A representation may contain information about the general, affective properties of the US—that is, the features it has in common with other USs of equivalent motivational quality. Alternatively, a representation may contain specific information, such as where the US is delivered, how large it is, and so forth—in short, all the characteristics that distinguish one US from another. He suggested that when the general representation is activated it will lead to a preparatory CR. Arousal of the specific representation, on the other hand, will lead to a consummatory CR.

Typically, consummatory CRs resemble at least a component of the response to the US. Thus Pavlov (1927) observed that a CS paired either with food or with the delivery of a weak solution of acid into the mouth will elicit salivation. A mild electric shock to the cheek will cause the eye to blink, and so, too, will a stimulus paired with such a shock (e.g. Gormezano, 1965). Pigeons peck a key as if they are trying to eat it when its illumination signals food, but when the US is water the responses directed to the key are more characteristic of drinking (see Chapter 4).

In contrast, preparatory CRs are not so intimately tied to the responses elicited by the US. An appetitive preparatory CR might consist of a general increase in activity, whereas for aversive conditioning it might consist of immobility. This is not to say that these CRs are without direction. Konorski (1967) argued that for appetitive conditioning the preparatory CR will consist of approaching the CS, and that the equivalent response for aversive conditioning is more likely to be withdrawal. Clear support for both claims can be found in a series of experiments by Karpicke, Christoph, Peterson, and Hearst (1977).

Rats were trained to lever press for food in a chamber containing two light bulbs, one near the lever and one further away. While subjects were pressing the lever, the bulbs were occasionally illuminated, and this signalled the imminent delivery of either food (Experiment 1) or electric shock (Experiment 5). There was a decline in instrumental responding when the CS was presented in either study, but the magnitude of this effect was dependent upon the position of the illuminated bulb. When the bulb nearer to the lever signalled food, there was less disruption of lever pressing than when the more distant bulb signalled this US. Presumably a preparatory CR of approaching an appetitive CS is likely to be most disruptive when the CS is far from the lever. In contrast, it was the illumination of the near light bulb that produced the greater reduction in lever pressing during aversive conditioning. In this instance, a tendency to withdraw from a light signalling shock will interfere most with instrumental responding when it is close to the lever.

Compensatory CRs.   Subsequent developments have indicated that Konorski's (1967) account of preparatory conditioning may be too simple. Solomon and Corbit (1974) have suggested that the delivery of a US will immediately arouse what they refer to as an *a*-process. This can be regarded as an emotional state directly related to the motivational quality of the US. An electric shock may excite an *a*-process that involves the physiological changes associated with fear. Thus far the account is not too dissimilar to Konorski's (1967) views, with the *a*-process corresponding to the physiological changes necessary for a preparatory CR. Where the accounts differ is in Solomon and Corbit's (1974) proposal that a US also excites, but rather slowly, a *b*-process that opposes the *a*-process and diminishes reactivity to the US. This leads to the possibility that when a CS and US are paired, the former may become associated with representations either of the *a*- or of the *b*-processes aroused by the latter. Before exploring the implications of this proposal, we must first consider the evidence for the existence of these opposing processes and examine the way they interact.

Church, LoLordo, Overmier, Solomon, and Turner (1966) recorded the change in heart-rate in dogs produced by a series of electric shocks. In keeping with the opponent-process analysis, the shocks were found to have two opposing effects. Whenever the shock was applied, there was an immediate *a*-process reaction of an increase in heart rate, but as soon as the shock ceased the effects of the opponent *b*-process became evident as a temporary reduction in heart rate. With repeated exposure to shock there was a change in this pattern. Shock onset was accompanied by only a modest increase in heart rate, and its offset led to a pronounced decline in the rate of this response. Moreover, it is not only heart rate that is influenced by the repeated exposure to the shock: dogs also seem to be much less distressed by this event after several training sessions (Solomon & Corbit, 1974).

The explanation offered by Solomon and Corbit (1974) for these findings can be understood most readily by referring to Fig. 6.1, which shows the presumed strength of the *a*- and *b*-processes to a stimulus event such as shock after a few (panel A) or many (panel B) trials. The middle

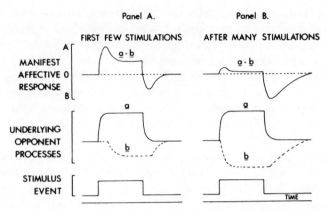

FIG. 6.1.   Panel A: The strength of the *a*- and *b*-processes (middle row) aroused by a stimulus event (bottom row) when it is first presented, and the net reaction to this event that results from subtracting the *b*- from the *a*- process (upper row). Panel B shows these effects when the stimulus event has been presented for many trials (from Solomon & Corbit, 1974).

row shows the effects of these trials on the underlying opponent processes. As far as the *a*-process is concerned, the amount of training has no effect. This response is always aroused rapidly by shock onset and declines equally rapidly following its offset. The amount of exposure does influence the strength of the b-process. At first, this response is rather weak and gains in strength only slowly after the shock is turned on, but when subjects are more familiar with the shock then the magnitude of the *b*-process is considerably greater. Throughout training the decline of the *b*-process is slower than that of the *a*-process.

The upper row of Fig. 6.1 shows the net response that would be observed as a result of the inevitable interaction of the *a*- and *b*-processes. In principle the figure shows the impact of subtracting the *b*-process from the *a*-process and the way this would manifest itself in such measures as heart rate. The curves reflect exactly the changes in reactivity to shock that were reported by Church et al. (1966).

It is reasonable to assume that if, during conditioning, the CS becomes associated with a representation of the *a*-process, then it will elicit a preparatory CR in much the same way as Konorski (1967) envisaged. But what sort of CR could be expected if the CS should become associated with a representation of the *b*-process aroused by a US? One answer is suggested by the work of Siegel (1977) on drug tolerance.

When rats are first injected with morphine, it has a strong pain-killing (analgesic) effect. But with the repeated administration of the drug a tolerance to it develops, so that doses of increasing magnitude are required to obtain the same degree of analgesia. Siegel (1977) has argued that such morphine tolerance can be understood in terms of Pavlovian conditioning. The stimulation accompanying the injection of morphine can be regarded as a CS, and the effect of the drug as the US. In keeping with Solomon and Corbit's (1974) analysis, this latter effect could be of two forms: it might consist of the *a*-process that is responsible for the typical reactions to the drug including analgesia, or it might consist of a *b*-process that opposes these effects. Siegel (1977) has suggested that morphine tolerance develops because the CS becomes associated with the *b*-process. Consequently, after several injections, the sensations produced by the needle (CS) will activate a *b*-process CR that will counteract the subsequent analgesic effects of the injected morphine.

Support for this account can be found in an experiment by Siegel (1977). On each of 6 successive sessions, two groups of rats were injected with morphine shortly before a test for the analgesic effects of the drug. The test consisted of recording the weight that could be applied to a subject's paw before it was withdrawn. After the first injection rats were prepared to tolerate a considerable pressure to their paw. But with the repeated administration of morphine a weakening of the analgesic properties was revealed by a decline in the pressure that the rats were prepared to tolerate after each injection of the drug. This pattern of results is depicted in the left-hand panel of Fig. 6.2.

For the next 12 sessions the groups were treated differently. Group M–P–M was treated in much the same way as for the preceding sessions, except the injections contained saline instead of morphine. This training can be regarded as extinction, because the stimuli produced by the injection were no longer followed by morphine, and their association with the *b*-process should therefore be weakened. No injections at all were administered to Group M–Rest–M for this stage of the experiment. Finally, both groups were given 6 further injections of morphine. For Group M–Rest–M there is no reason why the first of these injections should not elicit a substantial *b*-process CR and counter again the analgesic effect of morphine. In contrast, for Group M–P–M a *b*-process CR should not be aroused by the injection, because of the extinction trials, and the renewed administration of morphine should be accompanied by analgesia. The results of pressure tests after these injections, which are shown in the right-hand part of Fig. 6.2, confirmed this analysis.

Findings such as these reported by Siegel (1977) clearly show that properties of the US can influence the CR, but they tell us very little about the circumstances that dictate the sort of CR that will be performed. This lack of knowledge is emphasised by experiments that are very similar to Siegel's (1977) in design, yet they have found that at least a component of the CR resembles the *a*- rather than *b*-process elicited by the drug (Eikelboom & Stewart, 1979; Sherman, 1979). For the present, the factors

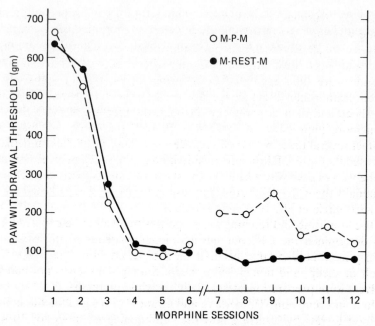

FIG. 6.2.   The mean weight which two groups of rats were prepared to tolerate on their paws shortly after an injection of morphine (M). The left-hand side shows the results for the first six daily trials, the right-hand side shows the results for a further six injections. During the interval between these stages Group M–P–M but not Group M–Rest–M had received saline, placebo (P) injections (from Siegel, 1977).

that determine whether a CR will mimic or oppose the response elicited by the US remain obscure. A similar state of uncertainty holds for the distinction between preparatory and consummatory CRs. Konorski (1967) proposed that the former are more likely when the CS is of relatively long duration, whereas shorter CSs were believed to be responsible for consummatory CRs. Once again, however, there is insufficient evidence to allow an adequate evaluation of these proposals.

Even if the way in which the US influences the CR were fully understood, our knowledge of the factors that determine this response would still be incomplete. This is because the nature of the CS can also influence conditioned responding.

Influence of the CS on the CR

A clear example of the importance of the CS in determining the CR comes from autoshaping. When the illumination of a disc signals the delivery of food to hungry pigeons, then they will peck it rapidly; but when a tone is paired with food the CR is more likely to be an increase in activity. A study by Garcia, Rusiniak, and Brett (1977) provides a more dramatic example of the way the CS can influence the CR. To make them ill, coyotes and wolves were allowed to eat chopped mutton that was wrapped in raw sheep hide and laced with lithium chloride. The effects of this conditioning episode were then examined by allowing the animals to approach live sheep. Rather than attacking them as they normally do, one coyote sniffed the sheep and then turned away retching; the reaction of the wolves was even more impressive, at first they "charged the sheep and made oral contact several times with their characteristic flank attack but immediately released their prey. During the next half hour, the sheep became dominant as the wolves gave way whenever the sheep threatened with short charges. Gradually the wolves withdrew and responded to the sheep like submissive pups" (Garcia et al., 1977, pp. 281–282).

The vomitting and retching are responses that would be expected if the US determined the CR, but the additional reactions of the wolves are clearly influenced by the fact that the CS paired with illness tasted and smelt of sheep, and that the live sheep, finding themselves not eaten by wolves, were prepared to attack their erstwhile predators.

In a different vein, Timberlake and Grant (1975) signalled the delivery of food to rats by inserting into the conditioning chamber for 10 sec a platform on which another rat was strapped. As this event was always followed by food, an account of conditioning that stressed the importance of consummatory CRs leads to the expectation that the experimental subjects would attempt to eat the CS. Happily, there was no evidence of such cannibalism. Instead, whenever the CS was presented, the subject engaged in social behaviour with the restrained rat. This activity included pawing, grooming, and anogenital sniffing. To emphasise the importance that the nature of the CS played in this experiment, it was found that social responses were not directed towards a block of wood when it served as the CS.

Apart from showing that the CS is important in determining the CR, it is difficult to know what other conclusions should be drawn from these studies. Timberlake and Grant (1975) suggest that a signal for food will encourage responses that are normally performed in its presence. Unfortunately this constitutes little more than a restatement of their results, and it has little predictive value. Rats engage in a variety of activities with other rats, including fighting, and it is not at all clear why only a fraction of these were observed when the rat CS was presented.

Limitations of the CR

A common claim concerning conditioned responding is that the CS elicits the CR quite automatically, just as an innate reflex will be triggered by the appropriate releasing stimulus. As a result, whereas properties of the CS and US can influence the form of the CR, it often appears to be quite unaffected by its consequences. Very often this does not matter, because the CR will approximate behaviour that is in the animal's best interests. Signals for food are generally found in close proximity to food itself, and a preparatory CR of approaching an appetitive CS may well lead a hungry animal to its goal. Alternatively, an animal that flees from a signal for an aversive event will very often be fleeing from that event as well. This is not to say that CRs will always benefit the animal; given the appropriate circumstances, it is possible, as the following examples will show, that the automatic occurrence of a CR can lead to maladaptive behaviour.

In one study by Hearst and Jenkins (1974), pigeon autoshaping was conducted in a long conditioning chamber. The delivery of food was signalled by the illumination of a response key located more than 0.6 m from the hopper. After a number of autoshaping trials the pigeons would approach and peck the key as soon as it was illuminated. Pecking then continued until the key light was turned off, whereupon the pigeon frantically rushed down the box to collect the grain that was briefly available at the hopper. Not surprisingly, subjects got very little food to eat as a result of this training. In this example, then, the CS elicited the typical CRs of approach and pecking, and their occurrence prevented the more sensible response of going to the magazine. The automatic, or reflexive, nature of the CRs is revealed by the persistence with which they were performed, even though they interfered with the collection of grain.

A similar outcome has been demonstrated by Williams and Williams (1969) using what is known as an omission schedule for autoshaping. Pigeons were given conventional autoshaping in which the illumination of a response key for 6 sec signalled food. But if the birds pecked the key during a trial, then the light was turned off and food was not presented. Given this arrangement, it would be in the pigeons' best interests never to peck the key. But it seems that the behaviour of these birds is not always governed by their best interests: Even with extended training they all persisted in pecking the key to some extent, thereby receiving only a fraction of the food that was potentially available. The implication of this finding is that even the intermittent pairings of the CS and food were sufficient to sustain a keylight–food association. Illumination of the key would then activate a representation of food and automatically produce a consummatory peck CR and cancel the delivery of food.

The final example of the disruptive influence of CRs is related to a study by Breland and Breland (1961), who experienced considerable difficulty in training a raccoon to pick up a coin and insert it in a money box for food. The problem did not lie with making the subjects pick up the coin, but with making them let go of it again. Boakes, Poli, Lockwood, and Goodall (1978) have suggested that this demonstration of misbehaviour occurs because the coin became an appetitive CS as a result of being paired with food. Consequently, the subject will be compelled to approach the coin whenever it is visible (preparatory CR) and perhaps attempt to eat it (consummatory CR). On this basis it is quite understandable why the raccoons were unwilling to release the coin.

Boakes et al. (1978) conducted an analogous study with rats that were required to drop ball bearings into a hole for food. After a number of training sessions (p. 118):

> the ball was carried to within a centimeter or so of the hole, either directly or with occasional stops en route to mouth the ball. A rat would then sit by the hole, repeatedly alternating between putting the ball in its mouth and turning it in its paws, before eventually dropping it in the hole. Occasionally, some rats showing this pattern would rapidly retrieve the ball from the hole before it rolled out of reach. A further two rats, R10 and R11, had a curious style of delivery with the ball. With the ball between their forepaws they would extend forward to the far side of the hole before dropping the ball. Anthropomorphically, it was as if this manoeuver allowed them to avoid seeing the ball disappear.

Pavlovian conditioning has the potential for allowing animals to learn a great deal about sequences of events that occur regularly in their environment. But if the only way this knowledge can influence behaviour is through a restricted range of reflex-like reponses, then, as the above studies demonstrate, its full benefits could not be realised. It now seems that in addition to exciting stereotyped CRs, Pavlovian conditioning can exert a more flexible influence on what an animal does by modulating the vigour of instrumental responses. Before investigating this possibility we must first focus on the nature of the instrumental learning process.

INSTRUMENTAL CONDITIONING

When a hungry rat is first placed into a chamber containing a lever and a food dispenser, it may press the lever infrequently. But if each press on the lever results in the delivery of food, then it will soon rapidly perform this response. This change in behaviour produced by presenting an event such as food after a specific response is called "instrumental conditioning". The term "positive reinforcer" is used to refer to any appetitive event that sustains instrumental responding. It is also possible for an increase in the frequency of an instrumental response to result from the omission of a stimulus, like electric shock, and here the event is referred to as a "negative reinforcer".

Two separate questions can be asked about the acquisition of an instrumental response. At a fundamental level there is the issue of whether it involves any processes additional to those found in Pavlovian conditioning. I shall argue, in fact, that there is a basic difference between Pavlovian and instrumental conditioning: The former involves learning that one stimulus signals another, whereas with the latter animals learn about the response. Such a distinction leads directly to the second issue, which is that of identifying the nature of this learning about the response.

Learning about Responses

The first important question to answer is whether instrumental conditioning does actually involve processes other than those of simple Pavlovian conditioning. It may seem absurd to suppose otherwise, as Pavlovian conditioning produces such a limited range of reflexive responses and may, as we have seen, lead to maladaptive behaviour. But it is not quite as easy to dismiss a Pavlovian account of instrumental conditioning as one might think.

Consider again the hungry rat that is placed into a conditioning chamber with a lever. While exploring the apparatus, it might accidentally depress the lever, and food will be delivered. The stimuli perceived by the animal immediately prior to the food will therefore be those related to the lever, and an association might be formed between representations of the lever and food. When the subject next looks at the lever, a representation of food will be activated and elicit a preparatory CR of approaching the lever. If this should result in the lever being pressed, then food will again be delivered. The lever–food association will be further strengthened and lead to an increase in the likelihood of the rat approaching the lever in the future.

How accurate is this account? Although during the early stages of training rats often operate a lever by biting it—a response that resembles a consummatory CR—observation of a well-trained rat executing a rapid and efficient series of lever presses before moving to the magazine to collect food makes a Pavlovian account implausible. There is, in addition, experimental evidence that shows even more clearly the inadequacy of a Pavlovian interpretation of instrumental conditioning.

A certain amount of difficulty has been reported in training rats to perform such stereotyped responses as scratching and face-washing to obtain food (Shettleworth, 1975). Nonetheless, the frequency of these responses can be increased by instrumental conditioning, and this finding is difficult to explain if all that animals are capable of is stimulus–stimulus learning. Pearce, Colwill, and Hall (1978), for example, increased the frequency with which a rat scratched itself by presenting food every time this response was performed. It is unreasonable to regard this increase in scratching as being due to the performance of a consummatory CR, because the response bears no similarity to any activities normally directed towards food. Moreover, scratching is unlikely to be a preparatory CR, because in no meaningful sense does it prepare the animal for food, nor does it bring the rat into contact with external stimuli that signal this US. Scratching is therefore very unlikely to be a Pavlovian CR, and by default we must conclude that some sort of learning other than the growth of a CS–US association was responsible for the increase in its frequency as a result of being paired with food.

Studies employing what is known as the bidirectional control also suggest that animals can learn about their responses. This method was used by Grindley (1932), who conducted an experiment with the apparatus depicted in Fig. 6.3. A guinea pig was placed into the harness, and when it was facing forwards a buzzer sounded. The buzzer remained on until the guinea pig turned its head in a specified direction, say, to the right. The buzzer was then switched off, and a carrot, fixed to the lever, was raised in front of the subject, who was allowed a single bite before the carrot was lowered. After an interval of a few minutes the buzzer was again switched on for the start of the next trial. At first it took as long as 100 sec for the

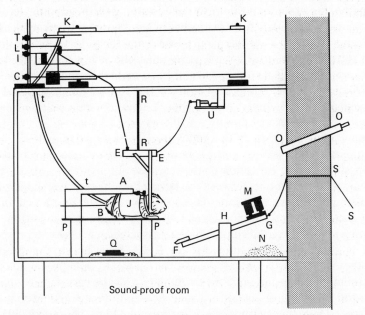

FIG. 6.3.   A sketch of the apparatus used by Grindley (1932) for instrumental conditioning with guinea pigs. A piece of freshly cut carrot was fixed to the lever at the point marked F (adapted from Grindley, 1932).

correct response to be made after the onset of the buzzer, but with training the guinea pig learned to turn its head within a second or two of hearing the buzzer.

There is no doubt that this training provided the opportunity for Pavlovian conditioning, with the buzzer serving as the CS and the carrot as the US. It does seem unreasonable, however, to regard the response measured by Grindley (1932) as a CR. After all, turning the head is unlikely to be a consummatory CR, as it could not possibly facilitate the consumption of the carrot, which was delivered directly in front of the guinea pig. This response is also hard to describe as a preparatory CR, because it is unrealistic to suppose that it enabled the subject to approach the sound of the buzzer. But even if we ignore these arguments, a further stage of the experiment allows us to conclude with confidence that the response Grindley (1932) trained was not a CR.

In the second stage of the experiment the subject was trained in exactly the same manner as before, except that it had to turn its head in the opposite direction to obtain a reward. Despite some initial difficulty, the guinea pigs soon learned to perform this response swiftly whenever a trial started. Now, if it is assumed that looking to the right was a CR elicited as a result of subjects learning that the buzzer signalled a carrot, then some alternative learning process must have been responsible for the subsequent strengthening of the opposite response of turning the head to the left. The most obvious candidate for this process is that it is one that permits animals to learn about their own behaviour. Thus when the same technique can be used to train opposite responses, then it can be safely concluded that at least one of them is a consequence of instrumental learning.

Grindley's (1932) study may point to the conclusion that animals are capable of instrumental learning, but it does not tell us of what this learning consists. According to S–R theory (see Chapter 1), instrumental learning involves the formation of an association between the stimuli that are present when the response is performed and the central mechanism responsible for the execution of the response. In Grindley's (1932) study the association might be between the buzzer and the centre responsible for head-turning. Future presentations of this stimulus should then automatically elicit the correct response. The alternative view is that instrumental learning involves the development of an association between the response and its reinforcing consequences, an R–US association. To return to Grindley's (1932) experiment, the association would be between the centre controlling head turning and a representation of the carrot.

In the following discussion we shall first consider two issues that have confronted S–R theory since it was first formulated by Thorndike (1911) as the Law of Effect. One of these is concerned with the way it explains how motivational factors, like a change in deprivation level, can influence the execution of an S–R habit; the other concerns the problem of explaining the way in which a stimulus, such as the buzzer in Grindley's (1932) experiment, controls instrumental behaviour. These are not by any means the only problems to have confronted S–R theory, nor are the solutions that we consider the only ones to have been proposed. The main purpose in focussing on these issues is that they cover some of the more important points in the development of S–R theory. They also serve to introduce some of the problems that led to the development of an alternative, expectancy theory of instumental learning.

S–R Theory

The most attractive feature of S–R theory is its simplicity. All that is necessary for learning to occur is for a reward to follow a response, and the S–R association will be strengthened. Moreover, once an S–R association has been formed, the response will automatically be performed, almost reflexively, whenever the stimulus is presented. There is, unfortunately, a price to be paid for this simplicity: It leads to instrumental responding being very inflexible. Various factors are known to influence the vigour or frequency with which a response is performed; they include deprivation level, the quality of the positive or negative reinforcer, and whether or not the animal is in the presence of Pavlovian CSs. To take a simple example, it is well established that, up to a point, the hungrier a rat is, the more rapidly will it run down an alley (Cotton, 1953) or press a lever (Clark, 1958) for food. In its most fundamental form S–R theory is unable to explain these or any other motivational effects, as all it stipulates is that given a particular stimulus, a certain response will occur.

Drive Theory.   Theorists have obviously been aware for a long time of these deficiencies, and various attempts have been made to overcome them. One extremely influential attempt was provided by Hull (1943) who suggested that motivational effects are mediated by activity in a drive centre. Drive is a central state that is excited by needs and energises behaviour. It was proposed that the greater the level of drive, the more vigorous will be the response that the animal is currently performing. Thus if a rat is pressing a lever for food, then hunger will excite drive, which, in turn, will invigorate this activity.

A serious shortcoming of Hull's (1943) account is the claim that drive is non-specific: It was held to be enhanced by an increase in any need of the animal. A number of curious predictions follow from this basic aspect of his theorising. For example, the pain produced by electric shock is assumed to increase drive, so that if animals are given shocks while lever-pressing for food, they should respond more rapidly than if shock were omitted. By far the most frequent finding is that this manipulation has the opposite effect of decreasing appetitive instrumental responding (e.g. Boe & Church, 1967). Conversely, the theory predicts that enhancing drive by making animals hungrier should facilitate the rate at which they press a lever to escape or avoid shock. Again, it should not be surprising to discover that generally this prediction is not confirmed. Increases in deprivation have been found, in this respect, to be either without effect (Misanin & Campbell, 1969) or to reduce the rate of such behaviour (Leander, 1973; Meyer, Adams, & Worthen, 1969).

Two-Process Theory. In response to this problem more recent theorists have proposed that animals possess two drive centres. One is concerned with energising behaviour that leads to reward, the other is responsible for invigorating activity that minimises contact with aversive stimuli. They may be referred to, respectively, as the positive and negative motivational systems. A number of two-process theories that share these general characteristics have been proposed, although they differ in detail (Estes, 1969; Gray, 1975; Konorski, 1967; Rescorla & Solomon, 1967).

The assumption that there are two motivational systems rather than a single drive centre allows these theories to overcome many of the problems encountered by Hull's (1943) theory. For example, it is believed that deprivation states like hunger and thirst will increase activity only in the positive system, so that a change in deprivation should not influence the vigour of behaviour that minimises contact with aversive stimuli such as shock. Conversely, electric shock should not invigorate responding for food as it will excite only the negative system.

A theoretically important feature of two-process theory is its assumption that a Pavlovian CS can excite activity in the appropriate motivational system. This proposal follows readily from the point made earlier that a CS is capable of activating a general representation of the US. Konorski (1967) has specifically stated that the arousal of such a representation is equivalent to an increase in activity in the positive system, for appetitive conditioning, or in the negative system, for aversive conditioning. Because of this feature a prediction of two-process theory is that presenting an appetitive CS to an animal while it is responding for food will enhance the level of activity in the positive system and thus enhance the vigour of the instrumental response.

A good example of support for this prediction is provided by Lovibond (1983). Hungry rabbits were first trained to operate a lever with their snouts in order to receive a squirt of sucrose into the mouth. The levers were then withdrawn for a number of sessions of Pavlovian conditioning in which a clicker signalled the delivery of sucrose. In a final test stage subjects were again able to press the lever, and while they were doing so the clicker was occasionally operated. The effect of this appetitive CS was to increase the rate of lever pressing both during its presence and for a short while after it was turned off. Of course, two-process theory stipulates that a similar effect should also be observed with aversive conditioning, and there is also evidence to support this prediction. Rescorla and LoLordo (1965) found that the presentation of a CS previously paired with shock enhanced the rate at which dogs responded to avoid shock.

In contrast to these successful tests of two-process theory there have been findings that may appear to contradict it. For instance, occasionally an appetitive CS has been found to suppress appetitive instrumental behaviour. Indeed, this is precisely the result reported by Karpicke et al. (1977) that was considered earlier in this chapter. The explanation offered for this finding was that the visual CS elicited consummatory CRs that were incompatible with instrumental lever pressing. Hence the appetitive CS might well have enhanced activity in the positive system but at the same time approach to the CS would have prevented its manifestation as a high rate of lever pressing.

Very often an animal will be confronted with a situation in which activity in the positive and negative systems is aroused simultaneously. For example, it may be exposed to one stimulus that signals reward and another indicating danger. In these circumstances, instead of the two systems working independently, it is presumed that they are interconnected by mutually inhibitory links, so that activity in one will inhibit the other (Dickinson & Pearce, 1977).

To understand this relationship, consider the effect of presenting a signal for shock to a rat while it is lever pressing for food. Prior to the signal the level of activity in the positive system, perhaps determined principally by hunger, will be solely responsible for the rate of pressing. When the aversive CS is presented, it will arouse the negative system, which, in turn, will inhibit the positive one and lead to a reduction in the vigour of instrumental responding. As soon as the aversive CS is turned off, the inhibition will be removed and the original response rate restored. Thus by assuming the existence of inhibitory links, two-process theory can provide a very simple explanation for conditioned suppression. It occurs because the aversive CS reduces the positive motivational support for the instrumental response.

Two-process theory evidently supplies a reasonable explanation for the way in which a Pavlovian CS influences instrumental responding. Despite this success, as a complete account of instrumental behaviour two-process theory has serious shortcomings. One weakness is that it is contradicted by findings from some discrimination learning studies.

Suppose a rat has been trained to press a lever for food in a conditioning chamber. Discrimination training might then consist of exposing the rat to alternating periods of light and darkness and rewarding those responses that occur during the light. At first, the rat will behave in accordance with its previous training and respond at a more or less consistent rate throughout the session. But as discrimination training progresses, the majority of its responses will be confined to those intervals when the light is on. With this training the light said to be a discriminative stimulus (S^D). Figure 6.4 provides a summary of this training and its effects.

An obvious feature of discrimination training is that although it is responding by the rat that is responsible for the delivery of the food, this will occur only in the presence of the S^D. Discrimination training therefore provides an opportunity for Pavlovian conditioning, in which the discriminative stimulus would serve as the CS and the instrumental reward as the US. According to two-process theory this conditioning will take place, and moreover it will be responsible for the discrimination shown by the rat. By signalling the presence or absence of food, the alternating periods of light and dark will respectively enhance and reduce activity in the positive system and produce corresponding changes in the rate of lever pressing.

One strategy for testing this interpretation has been to measure concurrently both Pavlovian CRs and instrumental responses while animals are learning a discrimination. If successful discrimination depends upon the S^D becoming a Pavlovian CS, then both types of response should be observed in the presence but not the absence of this stimulus. Experimental tests of this prediction have a history that dates back to at least the work of Konorski and Miller (1930), but the findings have been conflicting. On some occasions a good correspondence between the two classes of response has been recorded (Konorski, 1967, p. 369; Miller & DeBold, 1965). On other occasions the frequency of one response has been poorly, or even inversely, related to frequency of the other (Ellison & Konorski, 1964).

In general these experiments have involved the measurement of such consummatory CRs as salivation, which Konorski (1967) attributes to the arousal of a specific representation of the US. But we have already seen

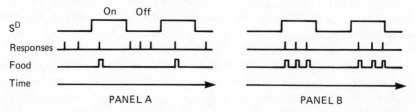

FIG. 6.4.   A record of events that may occur during appetitive instrumental discrimination training. Panel A shows the pattern of responses at the start of training. The pattern of responding that characterises the effects of extended training is shown in Panel B.

that according to Konorski (1967), a Pavlovian CS must excite a preparatory CR if it is to invigorate instrumental responding. As there is no good reason for believing that consummatory CRs always indicate the strength of preparatory conditioning, it should not be surprising that the results from these concurrent measurement studies are not always consistent with predictions from two-process theory. If such studies are to be of value, what is needed is a more direct measure of the degree to which a CS can excite activity in a motivational system. To my knowledge this measure does not yet exist, and we must therefore look to alternative means for testing the interpretation of discrimination learning offered by two-process theory. A related argument can be found in Rescorla and Solomon (1967).

One alternative method has been developed by Holman and Mackintosh (1981; see also Goodall and Mackintosh, 1987), and the results from their studies, which are based on Kamin's (1969) blocking design, do not support two-process theory. A group of rats was given discrimination training in which trials with a single stimulus, A, and a compound, AB, both signalled the availability of reward for lever pressing. Subsequent testing revealed that this resulted in B acquiring very little discriminative control over responding. According to two-process theory the more frequent pairings of A than of B with reward will result in A gaining considerable associative strength, which will block Pavlovian conditioning with B. When B is then presented by itself, it will fail to elicit a preparatory CR and exert little influence on lever pressing. A second group was included in the study to test this analysis. This was treated in much the same way as the first group, except that when A was presented alone it signalled free food, rather than the availability of food for lever pressing. Such a change should not prevent A from becoming a Pavlovian CS, and this stimulus should again block learning about B. In fact when B was subsequently presented alone it was apparent that this stimulus had acquired considerable discriminative control over the instrumental response.

This failure of Pavlovian conditioning with A to block discrimination learning with B is important, because it indicates that the knowledge acquired about a CS is different to that acquired about an S^D. We shall be in a better position to consider what it is that animals do learn as a result of an instrumental discrimination once we have looked at an alternative to the S–R theory of instrumental conditioning. For the present, the principal conclusion to be drawn from this study is that its findings are inconsistent with the account offered by two-process theory for discrimination learning. Thus, whereas two-process theory might provide an adequate account of the way in which a Pavlovian CS can influence instrumental responding, it is unable to account for all aspects of instrumental conditioning.

Expectancy Theory

When a rat performs an instrumental response, it seems reasonable to believe that it has some knowledge of what the outcome of its actions will be. The acquisition of such knowledge, however, lies beyond the scope of S–R theories of instrumental conditioning, which assert that animals learn only to make a response in the presence of a given set of stimuli. Admittedly, two-process theory allows the discriminative stimulus to signal the delivery of the US, but this does not mean the animal can anticipate reward on the basis of the responses it makes. Many theorists find it difficult to accept that animals do not know what the outcome of their actions will be, and they have therefore suggested that R–US associations, or expectancies, form the basis of instrumental learning (Bolles, 1972; Dickinson, 1985; Mackintosh & Dickinson, 1979).

Evidence for Expectancy Theory.   In order to demonstrate support for expectancy theories of instrumental conditioning, Adams and Dickinson (1981) trained two groups of rats to lever press for sucrose pellets. Then for one group, but not the other, an aversion was conditioned to the pellets by pairing their consumption with an injection of lithium chloride. To assess the impact of this treatment both groups were then permitted to press the lever again, but this time sucrose pellets were not available. Before describing the outcome of this test, we shall examine the predictions made by an S–R and R–US account of instrumental learning.

The R–US account states that the original instrumental training will permit the growth of a response–sucrose association. On the test session the control group will therefore know that responding produces sucrose pellets, and, because these are still attractive, subjects should respond enthusiastically for them. As far as the experimental group is concerned the previous taste aversion training will lead to a different outcome. The animals will not only know that responding produces pellets, they will also know that consumption of the pellets is followed by illness, and this should make them reluctant to respond in the first place.

The prediction made by S–R theory concerning this experiment is quite different. As a result of the instrumental conditioning an association will be formed between the stimuli present when the response was made, the experimental chamber, and the response itself. The sight of the chamber in the future should then automatically elicit the response. Because the lever was absent for the taste aversion training, there is no reason to suppose that this conditioning should influence the previously formed S–R association. Hence, on the test session, the sight of the apparatus cues should again automatically elicit the instrumental response, and to the same degree in both groups.

The clear difference in the predictions made by the two theoretical approaches makes it particularly frustrating to discover that the experiment yielded conflicting results. If the initial instrumental training was restricted to 100 lever presses, then on the test session the rate of responding was significantly slower by experimental than control subjects. But if 500 responses were permitted during the initial training, then the groups did not differ on the test session. These results are summarised in Fig. 6.5. Faced with such contradictory outcomes Adams and Dickinson (1981) concluded that R–US associations underlie the acquisition and early stages of instrumental training, but with extended practice their learning becomes transformed into an S–R habit. At present, relatively little is known about the reasons for this transition in the representation of instrumental learning or, in fact, whether it always takes place (Adams & Dickinson, 1981; Colwill & Rescorla, 1985).

It may strike the reader that the results from the groups receiving restricted instrumental training can be explained by a two-process version of S–R theory. During their instrumental training animals might acquire

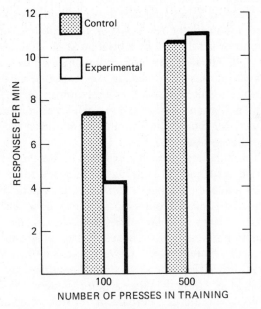

FIG. 6.5.   Mean number of responses per minute made by groups of rats during the first 5 minutes of a test session in which lever pressing was not rewarded. The groups had earlier received a sucrose pellet after each of either 100 lever presses (left-hand pair of histograms) or 500 lever presses (right-hand pair of histograms). Between the two stages of the experiment the experimental (E) but not the control (C) groups had received taste aversion conditioning with the sucrose pellets (adapted from Dickinson, 1980).

context–sucrose associations which would then energise the response by exciting activity in the positive motivational system. Pairing the pellets with illness will reduce the capacity of the context to exert this influence and result in a low rate of responding in the test session. To evaluate this possibility, Adams and Dickinson (1981) repeated the above experiment, with restricted training, but while the rats were lever pressing for food they also received free food pellets of a different flavour. When taste-aversion training was conducted with the pellets used as the instrumental reward, it produced a typically low rate of responding in the extinction test session, but this effect was not observed when the other food pellets had been paired with illness. That is, in order to influence the vigour of instrumental responding, it is insufficient to devalue a US that has simply been presented in the experimental context. Instead, the US must be the reward for lever pressing. On the basis of these findings Adams and Dickinson (1981) concluded that after restricted training instrumental performance is governed by R–US associations.

A further indication that instrumental conditioning may be due to R–US learning comes from a somewhat surprising result reported by Pearce and Hall (1979; see also St. Claire Smith, 1979). The experiment required rats to lever press for food on a variable interval schedule, so that only a few responses were followed by reward. For an experimental group each rewarded response was followed by a brief burst of white noise before the food was delivered. The noise did not accompany nonrewarded responses. The clear finding from this study (see Fig. 6.6), was that the presence of the brief burst of noise resulted in a substantially lower rate of lever pressing by the experimental than control groups, which either received similar exposure to the noise (but it always followed nonrewarded responses) or no exposure to the noise at all.

We argued that the most plausible explanation for these findings is one that assumes that instrumental learning involves the formation of R–US associations and that their strength determines the vigour of instrumental responding. For the control groups the response alone signalled reward, and this should foster a relatively strong R–US association. This association might be weaker for the experimental group, however, as reward was preceded by two events, the response and the brief stimulus. In Chapter 4 it was shown that when two stimuli simultaneously signal a US, then the associative strength they acquire is less than if they are individually paired with the US. Perhaps in our study the stimulus exerted a similar overshadowing influence on the growth of the R–US association and, therefore, curtailed its influence on performance.

Theoretical Interpretation. The foregoing results demonstrate that R–US associations can play an important role in instrumental behaviour,

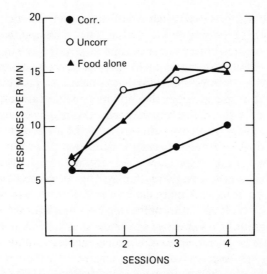

FIG. 6.6. The rate of lever pressing for three groups of rats that received a burst of noise after each rewarded response (Corr), after some nonrewarded responses (Uncorr), or no noise at all (Food Alone) (Adapted from Pearce & Hall, 1979).

but little has been said about the way in which they exert their influence. This is a difficult issue and one that has not yet been fully resolved.

As far as Pavlovian conditioning is concerned, the manner in which knowledge influences behaviour is quite straightforward. Pairing a CS with a US is assumed to result in the growth of an association between internal representations of the CS and the US. Future presentations of the CS will then automatically activate a representation of the US, which, in turn, will lead to the execution of the CR. The way in which knowledge is translated into action is similarly straightforward for S–R theory. The perception of the appropriate stimulus will excite the response centre with which it is connected and elicit the instrumental behaviour.

For expectancy theory the factors controlling response generation must be more indirect and complex. Animals may learn that many different responses lead to a variety of outcomes, but this does not indicate at all how they decide which response to perform. I may know, for example, that walking in one direction leads to a restaurant and in another to a public house, yet this knowledge by itself is insufficient to make me perform these responses. Obviously I also need to be in the appropriate motivational state before I act. But how can a motivational state cause a response associated with a reinforcer to be performed?

One answer to this question can be found in a version of two-process theory advocated by Mowrer (1960a,b). In many respects this account is similar to the two-process theory summarised previously, but with an additional feature. The sensations produced when an animal responds are assumed to be associated with any change in positive or negative activity they precede. Thus training a rat to lever press for food will cause an association to be formed between the sensations produced by lever pressing and the increase in positive activity produced by food. When the rat next presses the lever, the feedback from this response will excite a CR of increased activity in the positive system. Mowrer (1960a,b) further assumes that animals are constantly initiating a wide range of responses. Only those that lead to increased activity in the positive system or decreased activity in the negative system will be completed. In this way the animal will select responses that lead it to reward and away from aversive stimuli. I suspect it is the cumbersome proposal that animals are continuously initiating a variety of responses that has led to the neglect of this particular theory. Nonetheless, it is an ingenious account, and it would be interesting to see it developed further. A related account of instrumental learning has been developed by Estes (1969) and this, too, has had little theoretical impact.

Dickinson (1980, 1985; see also Adams & Dickinson, 1981; Mackintosh & Dickinson, 1979) has proposed a more radical solution to the above question. A feature of much of human behaviour is that it is purposive— that is, we think of a goal and then pursue various means in order to achieve it. Suppose I decide to go to the cinema; this will lead to a number of actions: I might look in a newspaper to see what films are on, I might try to arrange for a babysitter, and so forth. In every case the activity will be initiated with the overall purpose in mind of going to the cinema. In S–R accounts of instrumental learning this purposiveness is completely lacking: The response is always elicited by the stimuli that are present, rather than being selected because it will lead to a goal. Mowrer's (1960a,b) theory is little better in this respect as the genesis of the response is virtually random; only once it has been initiated can it be considered to be goal-directed. But even here the goal is rather nebulous, being simply to increase activity in the positive system or reduce it in the negative one.

Dickinson (1985) sees much of animal behaviour as being more purposive than has hitherto been acknowledged by many accounts of instrumental learning. He, therefore, accepts that animals learn about the relationship between their behaviour and its consequences but denies that this knowledge is encoded in the form of R–US associations whereby activation of a response centre will automatically excite a representation of the US. The main reason for this denial is that although such associations will allow the animal to anticipate the US while it makes the reponse, there is no additional mechanism that makes the animal respond in the first place. In view of this shortcoming Dickinson (1980; see also Mackintosh &

Dickinson, 1979) has proposed that knowledge about responses and their consequences is stored in a fundamentally different way to that used, say, for Pavlovian conditioning. Instead of instrumental conditioning resulting in the development of associative links between internal representations of responses and reinforcers, it may at times result in the formation of propositions.

A proposition can be defined as the smallest unit of knowledge that can be stored as an independent assertion. Hence, if animals have been trained to lever press for food, then they will learn the proposition "lever pressing produces food". Of course it is not being claimed that this information is encoded in anything that resembles human language. Indeed we can say very little about the way in which propositions are represented.

One advantage of encoding knowledge propositionally is that different propositions can be combined in a way that readily allows knowledge to be translated into action. Mackintosh and Dickinson (1979) have suggested that this may be achieved by inferential reasoning, as the following quote from Adams and Dickinson (1981, p. 162) indicates:

> We might, for instance, choose to characterise the steps in this process in the following form:
> "I want food."   [motivational proposition]
>   therefore
> "Perform an action that causes food."   [motivational command]
> "Lever pressing causes food delivery."   [knowledge proposition]
>   therefore
> "Press the lever."   [action command]

This analysis is undoubtedly purposive. The entire process commences with the identification of a goal, and the remaining arguments are concerned solely with achieving it. The account also presumes that animals learn about the consequences of their actions for which, we have already seen, there is a measure of experimental support. This approach thus fulfills Dickinson's aim to develop a purposive account of animal behaviour, and it is not inconsistent with certain experimental facts.

A further advantage of this approach is that it allows us to understand the role of the discriminative stimulus in instrumental behaviour. According to Mackintosh (1983, pp. 110–112), discriminative stimuli exert their control because, rather than excite a representation of the US, they excite a representation of the response–reinforcer relationship that is effective in their presence. This representation cannot be of the kind where the two events are connected by an associative link, because as we have just seen, this would not be sufficient to initiate the response. As an alternative, the knowledge about the response–reinforcer relationship is said to be encoded propositionally. The presence of a discriminative stimulus will thus activate a proposition and make it available for the inferential process that is essential for the translation of instrumental knowledge into action. As the knowledge acquired as a result of discrimination training is so different to that acquired during Pavlovian conditioning, it is hardly surprising that a Pavlovian CS is unable to influence learning about a discriminative stimulus (Holman & Mackintosh, 1981).

In closing this discussion of expectancy theory of instrumental conditioning, two comments need to be made. First, we should acknowledge that very little is known about the inferential processes that are said to be responsible for translating knowledge into action. As a consequence it is not possible to specify how a change in a deprivation state, and how the presence of a Pavlovian CS, can influence this process and modify the vigour of instrumental activity. It is also not at all clear how the various stages of the inferential process should be characterised. Second, although most theorists are happy to accept that animals store information in the form of connections between representations of events such as stimuli or responses, there is far from complete acceptance of the claim that they can also store information propositionally. Thus far, the justification for this claim has been the failure of any other account to provide an adequate explanation for instrumental conditioning. A concern of the next section will be to look for more direct evidence that instrumental knowledge can be stored propositionally.

LEARNED HELPLESSNESS

One line of evidence that suggests that instrumental learning may be represented propositionally comes from studies of escape and avoidance conditioning. On the basis of experiments to be described shortly, Maier and Seligman (1976) have proposed that experience of uncontrollable electric shock teaches animals that their behaviour is ineffective. Such learning is then held to interfere with future conditioning, in which they have to respond in order to escape or avoid shock. This claim is important because it is extremely difficult to envisage how the knowledge that behaviour is ineffective can be represented by an associative link. Associative links allow animals to store the information that one event will be followed by the occurrence or omission of another; they do not permit the storage of knowledge about more complex relationships, where responding is unrelated to the delivery of a US. Of course, there would be little difficulty in representing such a notion propositionally.

The proposals of Maier and Seligman (1976) are not just relevant to our understanding of instrumental learning. On the basis of their experimental work they have developed a sophisticated theory known as the learned helplessness hypothesis. This not only provides a comprehensive account of the way uncontrollable events influence the cognitive, emotional, and motivational processes of animals, it has also been of value in understanding human depression (Seligman, 1975). In addition to examining the evidence that suggests that animals can learn that their behaviour is ineffective, the following account will also provide a brief summary of this influential hypothesis.

A typical learned helplessness study involves three groups, and in an experiment by Seligman and Maier (1967) the subjects were dogs. For the first part of the experiment animals from Group Escape and Group Yoked were placed into hammocks and occasionally given an electric shock. By pressing a panel with its nose, a dog in Group Escape could turn off the shock. Each member of Group Yoked was paired with a master in Group Escape in such a way that it received the same pattern, duration, and intensity of shocks that was delivered to the master. The only difference between the two groups was that the yoked subjects were unable to influence these shocks. Group Naive did not receive any shocks during this part of the experiment.

Upon the completion of this training all subjects received escape/avoidance conditioning. For each trial a warning signal was presented for 10 sec; it was then followed by an electric shock unless the dog responded during the signal by moving to the other end of the apparatus. The shock then remained on either for 50 sec or until the animal made an escape response, also of moving to the other end of the apparatus. It was found that Group Yoked was unable to learn either to avoid or escape the shock. By comparison, dogs in Groups Naive and Escape learned within a few trials to cross to the other side of the apparatus soon after the warning signal was turned on. The time taken to respond on each of the first 10 trials is shown for the three groups in Fig. 6.7.

The principal difference in the treatment of Groups Escape and Yoked was in the degree of control they originally had over the delivery of shock. Both groups received the same preexposure to shock, but only Group Escape could influence the amount of this exposure. Maier and Seligman (1976) therefore proposed that the poor escape/avoidance of Group Yoked was due specifically to their experience of uncontrollable shock. The purpose of the learned helplessness hypothesis was to explain this outcome. In essence it asserts that uncontrollable shock can have three different effects: motivational, emotional, and cognitive.

The motivational component of the hypothesis states that exposure to uncontollable aversive events reduces the tendency of animals to initiate responses. So one explanation for the poor performance of Group Yoked

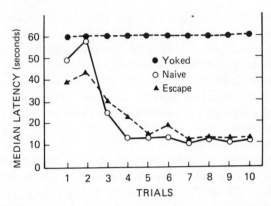

FIG. 6.7.   The median response latency in a shuttle box for groups of dogs previously given inescapable shock (Group Yoked), escapable shock (Group Escape), or no shock (Group Naive) (from Maier & Seligman, 1976).

is that subjects lacked the motivation to move across the conditioning chamber. The following observation of Maier and Seligman (1976), concerning the response of a dog treated similarly to those in Group Yoked, makes this point very clearly: "Such a dog's first reactions to shock in the shuttle box are much the same as those of a naive dog. He runs around frantically for about 30 sec, but then stops moving, lies down and quietly whines" (Maier & Seligman, 1976, p. 4).

The emotional influence of uncontrollable shock manifests itself in a variety of ways. Overmier and Seligman (1967), for instance, noticed that in some circumstances uncontrollable shock exerts a temporary influence, and in others a more permanent influence, on future behaviour. The transient effects were attributed to emotional processes that are typically short-lasting. Using rats, Weiss (1971) has found that exposure to uncontrollable shock can produce weight loss, enhanced defacation (presumably the latter contributes to the former), and stomach ulcers. All of these are symptoms of heightened emotionality.

The cognitive component of the hypothesis states that after exposure to uncontrollable events subjects may in the future have greater difficulty in learning about the relationship between their behaviour and its consequences. Why this should be so is made clear by the next quotation: "animals as a consequence of exposure to inescapable shock, acquire the expectancy that their behaviour is independent of either the onset or offset of shock. This expectancy is presumed to transfer to the shock escape task" (Jackson, Alexander, & Maier, 1980, p. 2). It will then disrupt learning, because "having learned that shock termination is unrelated to behaviour proactively interferes with learning the relation between responding and shock in the escape task" (Jackson et al., 1980, p. 2).

As already mentioned, it is difficult to understand how the knowledge that relief from shock is unrelated to behaviour can be represented in terms of associative links, yet it lends itself very readily to being expressed in propositions. Should Jackson et al.'s (1980) proposal prove correct, therefore, the existence of a cognitive deficit after exposure to inescapable shock will at least lend support to a propositional account of the instrumental learning process.

Despite the many demonstrations of learned helplessness, very few provide a clear indication that uncontrollable shock can produce a cognitive deficit. The problem with demonstrating such a deficit is that very often poor escape/avoidance behaviour can be attributed to the motivational deficit produced by exposure to inescapable shock. In the majority of learned helplessness experiments, which includes those just described, the measure of learning has been the speed at which the correct response is performed in the test stage. As a consequence, a demonstration of learned helplessness could be due either to a reluctance to initiate responses, or to a difficulty in learning about them. To avoid this ambiguity, Jackson et al. (1980) used choice rather than speed of responding as the measure of learning.

After receiving escapable shock, inescapable shock, or no shock at all, rats were placed in one arm of a three-arm Y-maze. Shock was then passed through the grid floor and remained on until the subject moved to the adjacent left arm. A short while later the shock was again turned on, and the same escape response of moving to the adjacent left arm was required. The delivery of shock resulted at first in animals often going to the incorrect arm (adjacent right) and perhaps even returning to the original arm before they responded correctly. With continued training, however, the number of trials on which an error occurred rapidly declined (see Fig. 6.8). In support of the helplessness hypothesis the group that made the most errors, and hence had most difficulty in learning the escape response, was the one exposed to inescapable shock. There is no obvious reason for suspecting that the number of errors should be influenced by the subject's willingness to initiate responses. On the other hand, a difficulty in learning about the relationship between responses and their outcomes would be very likely to increase the number of incorrect choices in this procedure. Thus the results of Jackson et al. (1980) constitute some of the clearer support for the cognitive component of helplessness theory.

The learned helplessness hypothesis provides a comprehensive analysis of an intriguing phenomenon. But it would be misleading not to mention the fact that there has been considerable debate both about the hypothesis and about the evidence on which it is based. A number of authors have developed alternative explanations for the effects of inescapable shock (e.g. Glazer & Weiss, 1976; Levis, 1976), whereas others have demonstrated that predictions from the theory are not always confirmed (Bracewell & Black, 1974; Glazer & Weiss, 1976; Irwin, Suissa, & Anisman, 1980). Although it now seems clear that exposure to inescapable shock can result in cognitive, motivational, and emotional deficits, we should acknowledge that this experience can also have a number of other effects, and that these deficits do not always result from learned helplessness training.

The outcome from at least some studies of learned helplessness is very difficult to explain in terms of association formation. In contrast, the findings can be readily understood if it is accepted that animals utilise propositions to represent at least some of their knowledge. Such a conclusion supports the proposal of Mackintosh and Dickinson (1979) that at least some of the knowledge acquired during instrumental conditioning is propositional in nature. I suspect that there will soon be a considerable growth of interest in the role that propositions play in animal cognition.

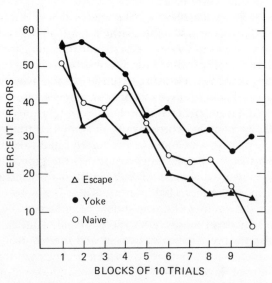

FIG. 6.8.   The mean percentage of trials with one or more errors across successive blocks of 10 trials in a three-arm maze for groups of rats that had been exposed to inescapable shock (Group Yoke), escapable shock (Group Escape), or no shock (Group Naive) (from Jackson et al., 1980).

THE COMPARATIVE ANALYSIS
OF INSTRUMENTAL CONDITIONING

We have seen in this chapter that instrumental conditioning can be successful with dogs, rats, and guinea pigs. How do other species fare when they must respond in a certain way either to gain reward or to minimise contact with an aversive US? Although there are many experiments relevant to this question, we shall look only at a selected few. The results from these studies reveal that the behaviour of a remarkable range of animals can be altered by methods of instrumental conditioning. In many cases, however, the interpretation of these experiments is ambiguous because the results do not allow us to identify the learning that forms the basis of this change in behaviour.

Demonstrations

Planarians are unsegmented flatworms. They possess a primitive nervous system that includes a collection of neurons that might be regarded as a sort of brain. Many might be astonished to discover that a protracted and occasionally bitter controversy has developed over the issue of whether or not these creatures can be instrumentally conditioned. In a review of many of the experiments that have been conducted with this species, Corning and Riccio (1970) conclude that the clearest demonstration of instrumental conditioning can be found in a set of studies by Wells (1967).

Naive planarians were placed into a piece of apparatus known as the Van Oye maze, which consists of little more than a jar of water. At first the planarians remained on the bottom of the jar, and they did not move from there when a piece of meat attached to a length of wire was lowered below the surface of the water to a depth of about 30 mm. In the following stages of the experiment the meat was again lowered into the jar, but this time to just below the surface. After a while the worms crawled up the side of the jar, and along the undersurface of the water, and ultimately they made contact with the meat. The meat was then gradually lowered into the jar so that the worms had to crawl down the wire to reach it. With this training the subjects were reliably crawling from the bottom of the jar to the meat, even when it was 30 mm below the surface. Thus as a result of instrumental training, Wells (1967) conditioned planarians to perform a response for food reward.

The nervous system of ants is very much more sophisticated than that of a planarian, and it appears that they can be trained in a correspondingly more complex instrumental task. Schneirla (1929) trained ants to pass

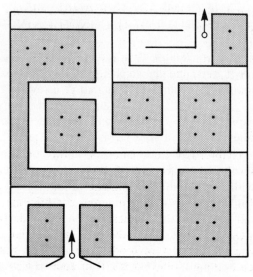

FIG. 6.9.   Plan of a maze used to train ants (adapted from Schneirla, 1929).

through mazes of the sort depicted in Fig. 6.9 in order to get from their nest to food, or vice versa. At first the ants made numerous errors, turning in the wrong direction at choice points, and many took more than 200 sec to complete the maze. After as few as 16 training trials there was a marked improvement in performance: Ants now made one or two errors and completed the maze within 40 sec. The common fly can also be trained to find its way through a complex maze (Platt, Holliday, & Drudge, 1980).

Instrumental conditioning has also been successful with another invertebrate, the octopus. Dews (1959) taught three subjects, Albert, Bertram, and Charles, to pull a vertical lever, hinged at the top, for food. Suspended from the bottom of the lever was a distinctive cross that moved in the current of water passing it. All three octopuses learned to pull the lever, although attempts to train them to repeat this response for a single reward were not paticularly successful: Once they had pulled the lever towards themselves with their tentacles they were most reluctant to release it for the next response, until food was delivered.

Turning now to vertebrates, Macphail (1982) has summarised many demonstrations of instrumental conditioning with fish, reptiles, amphibians, and mammals. Thus sharks have been trained to push an underwater panel for food (Clark, 1959), alligators will respond correctly in a simple discrimination to escape from heat (Davidson, 1966), indigo snakes will press a panel for water (Kleinginna, 1970), desert iguanas will respond similarly to maintain their temperatures within a restricted range (Kemp, 1969), and toads were able to learn in a single trial to avoid bumblebees after being stung while eating one (Brower, Brower, & Westcott, 1960). There is no need to add mammals to this list of examples—experiments already mentioned in this chapter demonstrate their susceptibility to instrumental conditioning.

Interpretation

Earlier in this chapter an explanation in terms of stimulus–stimulus learning was developed to account for the instrumental conditioning of lever pressing with rats. Although it was shown that this type of account is inappropriate for all studies of instrumental conditioning, it might well apply to at least some of the studies just mentioned. In the octopus experiment, for example, the sight of the cross at the end of the lever might regularly precede the delivery of food. Consequently, pulling the lever might have been nothing more than a CR of approaching and contacting the cross CS. This may seem far-fetched, but it is noteworthy that Dews (1959) was unable to condition the octopuses when the cross was absent. To take a rather different line of argument, in any form of maze some cues will be more closely related in time to food than others, and will therefore become better signals for reward. Accurate performance in a maze may then depend on subjects approaching those stimuli that they have learned are most closely related to food (see Deutsch, 1960, for an account of maze learning in these terms). Thus the performance of Schneirla's (1929) ants or Wells' (1967) planarians may have been due to the occurrence of Pavlovian approach CRs rather than to any instrumental learning.

The obvious counter to this type of interpretation is to employ the bidirectional control, or to condition a response that it would be unreasonable to regard as a CR. Such an approach is rare, and there exists only a handful of studies that unambiguously demonstrate that non-mammals are capable of response learning.

Van Sommers (1962) placed a single goldfish into a tube of water in which the level of oxygen could be varied. When a red light was on, the fish had to remain in one end of the tube to ensure a rich supply of oxygen; when a green light was on, the fish had to move to the opposite end for the same reward. That the fish were able to learn opposite responses to these stimuli suggests that at least one was not a CR and that it was strengthened by an instrumental response-learning process.

One of the clearer demonstrations of response learning by pigeons is reported by Jenkins (1977). A subject was placed in a conditioning chamber, and whenever an 8-sec burst of white noise was sounded it had to wave its head to and fro, interrupting two photocell beams, in order to gain food. As there was not a localisable CS to attract the pigeon to the correct position or to make it move its head, the most plausible explanation for this finding is that the bird learned to perform a response of moving to a certain location and then waving its head.

Although the two studies demonstrate response learning in non-mammals, we can say little about the nature of this learning. Subjects may have acquired R–US associations and anticipated the reward for which they were responding. Alternatively, as the Law of Effect stipulates, the reward may have strengthened an S–R association. Vey little research has been undertaken to distinguish between these alternatives, although there is one study that suggests that R–US learning is responsible for instrumental conditioning in pigeons (Hall, 1982). Nor has any suggestion yet been made that instrumental learning in non-mammals is encoded propositionally.

A Response Learning Analysis of Pavlovian Conditioning

The impression may well have been created by the organisation of the book so far that stimulus–stimulus learning is a more fundamental process than response learning. It would be a mistake to accept this view without question. Greater emphasis has been placed on Pavlovian than on instrumental conditioning because of the insights it has provided into the processes of associative learning. One theoretical possibility that has hitherto been ignored is that response learning constitutes the basic learning process, and that many species are incapable of stimulus–stimulus learning. This argument has been advocated most forcefully by Bitterman (1975). He regards fish, among other species, as being capable only of instrumental learning, which for him consists of the formation of S–R associations.

In order to examine this claim a technique must be found that enables us to determine whether or not an animal is capable of stimulus–stimulus learning. Fortunately a procedure that can be used for this purpose does exist—the omission schedule employed by Williams and Williams (1969) for autoshaping.

Many autoshaping experiments have shown that pigeons will peck a response key whenever it is illuminated if this signals the delivery of food. Thus far it has been unquestioningly accepted that this behaviour is due to the formation of a keylight–food association. But an alternative explanation is possible. Suppose that when the key is first illuminated the pigeon approaches and by chance pecks it. This response will be followed by food when the light is turned off, and according to the Law of Effect a keylight

(S)–keypeck (R) connection will be strengthened. On the next trial the sight of the illuminated key will elicit a tendency to peck at it, so that the food at the end of the trial will further strengthen the S–R bond. Note that this interpretation does not depend on the pigeon being requird to peck the key in order to obtain food. It is just that after the pairing of the first response with food, the pigeon is mistakenly led into believing, as it were, that key pecking is responsible for the delivery of food.

With an omission schedule for autoshaping, food is not delivered on every trial but only on those trials when a peck does *not* occur. As a result, pecking will never be followed by food and there will be no opportunity for reward to strengthen accidentally a keylight–keypeck association. If the foregoing account is correct, then autoshaping with the omission schedule should be ineffective in generating response to the key. In fact, Williams and Williams (1969) found a relatively high rate of responding with this method. The single, acceptable explanation for this outcome is that the intermittent pairing of the keylight CS with food permitted the development of a CS–US association that was responsible for the CR.

A reasonable rate of responding with the omission schedule thus provides compelling evidence that the subject is capable of stimulus–stimulus learning. How do species other than pigeons fare with this schedule? In the case of mammals there is ample evidence that they are capable of stimulus–stimulus learning. For example, pairing a CS with water for rabbits (Gormezano & Hiller, 1972) or with food for rats (Holland, 1979) on an omission schedule will still elicit a CR on about half the trials. For other species the evidence is not available: Experiments with the omission schedule have not been conducted, or, if they have, the results have been hard to interpret (e.g. Brandon & Bitterman, 1979).

The arguments developed in this section are complex and difficult to present clearly. It is therefore a pity that the rewards for pursuing them have been slight. We can be reasonably certain that goldfish, pigeons, and mammals are capable of response learning, and that pigeons and mammals are capable of stimulus–stimulus learning. We also know that very many animals are capable of associative learning. However, until many more experiments have been conducted, often using sophisticated techniques, it will not be clear of what this associative learning consists.

7

Problem Solving
and Reasoning

A major concern so far has been with understanding the fundamental processes of animal cognition. In the remainder of this book I intend to examine whether these basic processes are responsible for all aspects of animal intelligence. This chapter explores their role in problem solving; Chapter 8 studies the way in which these processes contribute to communication and language learning.

Animals can be said to have solved a problem whenever they overcome an obstacle to attain a goal. The problem may be artificial, such as having to press a lever for reward or deciding which of two doors to pass through to obtain food. Alternatively, the problem might be one that occurs naturally—for example, an animal might find itself in unfamiliar territory and have to choose a route to its nest.

Despite the range of potential problems that can confront an animal, Thorndike (1911) maintained that they are all solved in the same manner. Animals are assumed to behave more or less randomly until by "trial and error" the correct response is made and reward is forthcoming. As we have seen already, one effect of the reward is to strengthen the accidentally occurring response and to make its occurrence more likely in the future. This account may explain adequately the way cats learn to escape from puzzle boxes, but is it suitable for all aspects of problem solving?

To many authors, learning by trial and error provides an inadequate account for the ability of animals to solve problems. Instead, animals are said to be capable of the more sophisticated process of reasoning. According to Deutsch (1960), "we talk of reasoning when the animal has to combine two sets of information in some way in order to find a conclusion" (p. 101). Reasoning is typically regarded as being either deductive or inductive. Deductive reasoning is said to have occurred when the conclusion necessarily follows from the sets of information that have been combined—for instance, if you are told that *A* is bigger than *B*, and *B* is bigger than *C*, then of necessity it follows that *A* is bigger than *C*. Thus the defining characteristic of deductive reasoning is that provided it has been conducted correctly, there can be no disagreement with the conclusion to which it leads. With inductive reasoning the conclusion that is derived is a possible consequence of the information on which it is based, but it is by no means certain. It rains very often in Wales, and if the sky is overcast when I get up then I conclude that it will rain shortly. The combination of these sets of information usually leads me to the correct conclusion, but there are times when I am wrong. On the day in question it might snow.

To identify a particular line of reasoning as inductive or deductive does not explain how the conclusion was reached. Instead, the identification more or less reveals the degree of confidence we may have in the conclusion. There is ample evidence suggesting that animals are capable of both inductive and deductive reasoning. The principal issue that must be addressed is to determine how it is achieved.

ASSOCIATIVE MODELS OF REASONING

A simple, perhaps even trivial, example of reasoning is provided by Pavlovian conditioning. The salivation that occurs when a dog hears a bell signalling food can be viewed as the integration of two sets of information: (1) that bells in the past have signalled food, and (2) that the present trial is like the previous trials. The combination of these facts leads naturally to the conclusion that food will be delivered on the current trial. Of course, the process that is responsible for the salivary CR is probably a lot simpler than this interpretation implies, as it can be achieved by the bell activating a representation of food. The purpose of raising this mundane example, however, is to show that with even a simple associative model of learning it is possible to account for certain examples of apparent reasoning.

Associative explanations for reasoning can be quite flexible if it is acknowledged that associations containing common elements can be integrated. A demonstration of this possibility is provided by sensory preconditioning. Rizley and Rescorla (1972) first presented rats with the sequence of a light followed by a tone for a number of trials. Then, in the next stage the tone was paired with shock. Finally, the light was presented alone, and it was observed to elicit a substantial CR, although it had never been paired with shock itself. Thus the knowledge that the light signals the tone, and that the tone is paired with shock, can be said to have been combined to produce the conclusion that the light will be followed by something unpleasant. The explanation offered by Rizley and Rescorla (1972) is far less prosaic and almost certainly more realistic than this interpretation. During the first stage of training they proposed that subjects acquired light–tone associations and in the second stage tone–shock associations. The subsequent presentation of the light would then activate a representation of the tone, which, in turn, would activate a representation of shock and lead to an aversive CR being recorded.

This type of effect has also been observed with instrumental conditioning. In the previous chapter we saw that rats are reluctant to press a lever for sucrose if, after instrumental training, the sucrose is paired with illness. Presumably, the separate stages of training resulted in the growth of lever press–sucrose, and sucrose–illness, associations. The combination of this information would then lead rats to anticipate that lever pressing will be followed by illness and make them unwilling to press the lever.

A related outcome has been demonstrated in studies of conditioned reinforcement. Many experiments have shown that animals will learn to press a lever for the presentation of a brief stimulus if the stimulus has previously been paired with a positive reinforcer such as food (e.g. Hyde, 1976). This acquisition of conditioned reinforcing properties by the stimulus can be readily understood if it is accepted that the training results in the growth of a stimulus–food and a lever press–stimulus association. Once these associations have been integrated, animals will be led to expect, incorrectly, that lever pressing will result in food, and this should produce a temporary increase in the vigour of the response.

Interpretations of reasoning in terms of the integration of associations can also be applied to studies of maze learning, as an experiment by Gaffan and Gowling (1984) demonstrates. A single group of rats was trained in the maze depicted in Fig. 7.1. On some trials subjects were placed into the start box, S1, and after passing along the runway, R1, received food in the goal box, G1. On other trials they were placed into S2 and had to pass along R2 to reach the goal, which, although located in the same place as G1, was constructed from walls of a different brightness and was thus identified as G2. The second stage of the experiment began once subjects were running rapidly from the start to the goal boxes. On a number of sessions rats were placed directly into G1 and fed, or into G2 without food. In the test phase of the experiment, the animals were again placed into the

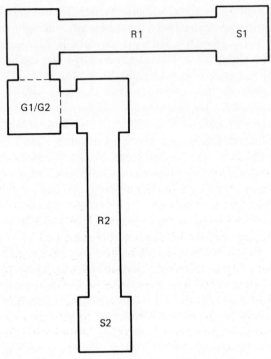

FIG. 7.1.   Plan of the maze used by Gaffan and Gowling (1984)—not to scale (adapted from Gaffan & Gowling, 1984).

start boxes and the time taken to run to G1 and G2 was recorded. During training there was no difference in these times, but during testing running to G1 from S1 was significantly faster than to G2 from S2.

These results can be said to demonstrate reasoning in rats. The knowledge acquired as a result of being either fed or not in the goals, combined with the knowledge of the structure of the maze, would lead to the conclusion that food would be available in the goal after leaving S1 but not S2. To understand how this reasoning might be achieved associatively, assume that the initial training resulted in the development of S1–G1 and S2–G2 associations, which is not unreasonable as rats repeatedly experienced in succession the stimuli of each pair. In the second stage they would then form G1–food and G2–no-food associations. When placed into S1 for a test trial, a representation of G1 and then food would be activated and lead to swift running to the goal. Placement into S2, on the other hand, should not activate a representation of food, and approach to the goal should be relatively slow.

COGNITIVE MAPS

The foregoing discussion suggests that as a rat passes through a maze, it learns associatively about the relationship between one component and the next. A currently popular proposal is that the intellect of many animals goes one step beyond this process of association formation, by integrating the knowledge of a familiar area or apparatus into a cognitive map (Tolman, Ritchie, & Kalish, 1946; O'Keefe & Nadel, 1978). It would not be too misleading to suggest that this map is rather like an aerial view or plan of the space that is being represented, and its possession would be a tremendous asset for solving problems. Thus, if an animal should find itself in a novel location, then by using the map it could deduce the most direct route to a familiar place. Alternatively, if a frequently used route to a goal is blocked, then by consulting a cognitive map it should be possible to identify an alternative path that leads to the same end.

Very often, the claim that animals possess a cognitive map leads to the same predictions as an associative account of reasoning. The results of Gaffan and Gowling (1984) would also be expected if the rats had formed a cognitive map of the mazes in which they were trained. But if an animal does possess a cognitive map, then in certain circumstances it should be at an advantage to one that is incapable of storing information in this way. The following experiments show how this advantage may be used in the selection of a novel route to a goal and in making a detour round an obstacle.

The Selection of a Novel Route

Tolman, Ritchie, and Kalish (1946) placed a hungry rat into the maze shown on the left-hand side of Fig. 7.2 at point A; it then had to pass points C, D, E, F, and G to reach the goal containing food. Once subjects were practiced at running along this route, they were placed again at A for a trial in which the maze had been modified to the form depicted on the right-hand side of the figure. On this occasion the original exit from the maze was blocked, and 18 alternative exits were added. Tolman et al. (1946) argued that if animals had formed a cognitive map of the maze during pretraining, then on the test trial they should be able to deduce from it the direction of the goal relative to the arena and select the exit that most closely corresponded with this direction. On this basis animals were expected to leave the arena through Exit 5. A different outcome is anticipated by an associative account of problem solving. The original experience with the maze will allow the rats to associate the various units of the maze, but nothing more. On the test trial the rats should pass directly

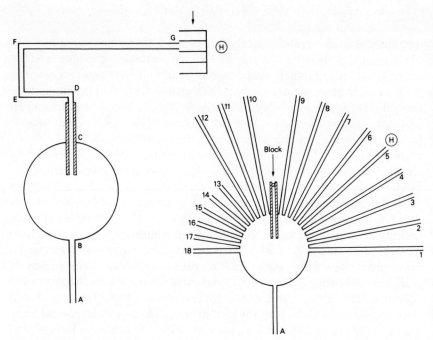

FIG. 7.2.   Plan of the mazes used in the two stages of the experiment by Tolman et al. (1946). Throughout the experiment a light bulb was located at H (from Tolman et al., 1946).

to the blocked exit and then be at a loss to know what to do next. The lack of knowledge of the direction of the goal from the arena will leave the subject at the mercy of trial-and-error responding. Thus one advantage of a cognitive map over a simple associative method for representing know-ledge is that the former alone will permit the subject to deduce correctly a novel route to a goal.

In support of the claim that rats possess cognitive maps, it was found that the majority of subjects on the test trial left by Exit 5. Unfortunately, Tolman et al. (1946) have identified a serious shortcoming with this experiment. Throughout the study there was a light bulb, H, suspended over the goal, and it was visible from all points of the maze. During their training, rats may have associated the light with food, and on the test trial selected the path that led most directly to this appetitive CS. Accordingly, the experiment demonstrates how a cognitive map might aid problem solving, but it does not confirm that animals solve problems in this way.

A study by Morris (1981) provides one of the better attempts to overcome the difficulty encountered by Tolman et al. (1946). To avoid the problem of giving the location of the goal away by a specific cue, a vat (1.3 m in diameter) of milky water was used as the maze, and a platform submerged just below the surface was the goal. After being placed into the vat for several trials, rats soon learned to swim directly to the platform, provided that it remained in the same position from one trial to the next. To explain this successful detection of the invisible goal, Morris (1981) argued that as a result of their initial training subjects formed a cognitive map. This might represent the position of the platform in the vat and also include features of the experimental room. When placed into the vat, the subject would have to identify its location on the map and then deduce the direction in which to swim to reach the platform.

As a test of this argument, rats were trained to swim to the platform from a specific point on the edge of the vat. The position of the platform was also constant for this training. They were then divided into three groups for testing. Group Control received the same treatment as for the previous stage; Group New-Place was placed at the original point of release and had to find the platform in a new location; and Group Same-Place was required to swim from a novel starting point to the platform, which was not moved. The routes taken by each rat from the time it was released until the platform was discovered are shown in Fig. 7.3.

The control group performed the task without difficulty and swam directly to the platform. The performance for Group New-Place suggests that their problem was very difficult. After a period of swimming around the original location of the goal, the behaviour of these animals was essentially without direction until they came upon the goal by chance. This finding confirms that there were no hidden cues to give away the position of the platform. The results for Group Same-Place lie in-between these

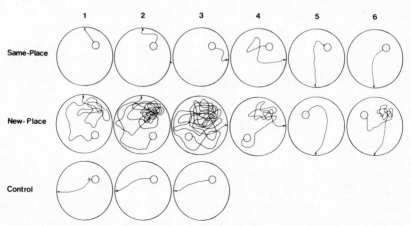

FIG. 7.3.   A vertical view of the routes taken on the first test trial by all the rats in the three groups of the study by Morris (1981) (from Morris, 1981).

extremes. It is apparent that these subjects located the platform without too much difficulty, which Morris (1981) regards as evidence that they possessed a cognitive map.

A careful inspection of Fig. 7.3 suggests, however, that this conclusion may be unwarranted. Apart from Subject 1, all the animals in Group Same-Place started off by swimming in the wrong direction, and there is no obvious reason why the possession of a cognitive map should result in this incorrect behaviour. Admittedly, the rats soon corrected their course, but this does not provide compelling evidence for the use of a cognitive map. During their training rats will doubtless approach the platform from many angles, and they may well learn a variety of routes to the goal. The landmarks of these routes would be provided by the various configurations of external cues, and success in finding the platform would depend on nothing more than learning to swim in a certain direction relative to a specific landmark. In other words, learning to find the platform may involve nothing more than the growth of a number of S–R connections. On the test trial Group Same-Place might set off in a randomly determined direction and swim until a familiar landmark was perceived. At this point they could adjust their course and swim towards the platform. I am not sure how seriously this account should be taken. Nonetheless, it does suggest, if nothing else, that even with a well-designed experiment it is difficult to demonstrate convincingly the existence and operation of a cognitive map.

With this caution in mind we can turn to a study by Gould (1986), which examined whether or not honeybees possess a cognitive map. In principle the study was not too dissimilar to that by Morris (1981). Bees were trained to fly from a hive (see the map in Fig. 7.4) to a feeding station at A. For testing they were then transported in a dark container to a novel place, B, where they were released. All subjects left B in the direction of A and all arrived at A. Moreover, the time taken by many of them suggests that they barely deviated from the straight line between these points. The explanation developed by Gould (1986) for these findings is very similar to one above offered by Morris (1981): The honeybees were assumed to have a cognitive map of the area around the hive and used it to deduce the direction in which they must fly from B in order to go to the food. It is also important to note that when the bees were released from B, the slope of the field was such that they could not see any of the features surrounding A. Thus it is unlikely that the bees solved this problem by approaching a landmark associated with the goal, as was the case for the study by Tolman et al. (1946). In addition, as there is no reason for believing that the honeybees had learned to go directly from B to A for food, an explanation for these findings in terms of following a previously learned route is also unacceptable (Gould, 1986). Although the subjects of this study were

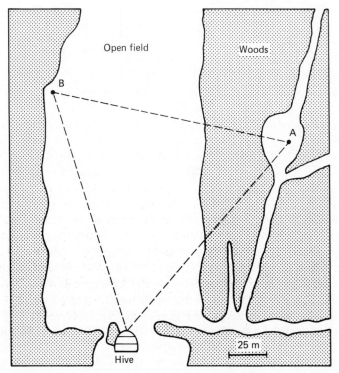

FIG. 7.4. Map of the area used by Gould (1986) for his study with bees (adapted from Gould, 1986).

invertebrates, it provides some of the better evidence that the choice of a novel route can be guided by a cognitive map.

Detour Studies

A second strategy that may demonstrate the operation of a cognitive map is first to show the animal a goal and then to place it some distance away behind a barrier. If the subject should select the correct, shortest route to the goal, then this may be because it possesses a cognitive map of the problem area and uses it to determine how to respond.

Figure 7.5 shows the sort of apparatus used by Kohler (1925), who was one of the first to study detour problems. The subject was placed behind the bars at S and could see food being placed on the other side at F. When dogs were tested, their behaviour depended very much on the distance of food from the barrier. If the food was some distance away, then the dog would immediately run in a smooth loop around the barrier to collect it.

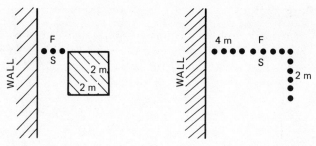

FIG. 7.5.   Plan of the apparatus used in the detour studies by Kohler (1925), not to scale. The dogs were placed initially near S and food was near F (adapted from Kohler, 1925).

When the food was placed by the fence, then the dog would run directly towards it and stay there even though it was inaccessible.

Similar findings have been reported by Chapuis, Thinus-Blanc, and Poucet (1983) in a more recent set of experiments. The barriers were of various shapes that permitted the dogs to pass via two routes to the goal (see Fig. 7.6). When the barrier was opaque, the shorter route was usually taken, which can be easily explained if it is assumed that the dogs possessed a cognitive map of the problem space. In the light of Kohler's (1925) findings it is interesting to note that when the barrier was transparent then the more direct route to the goal was preferred. Thus in Fig. 7.6 (IV), the path marked with a ⋆ was preferred to the other one when the barrier was opaque, but this preference was reversed when a clear barrier was used. It would seem that when the goal is either close or visible, subjects are drawn towards it, and this can interfere with solving the problem.

Kohler (1925) also tested chickens with his detour problem, but they never achieved the success shown by dogs. Instead, they persistently tried to reach the food by pushing through the barrier, as Kohler (1925) comments: "Some particularly ungifted specimens keep on running up against the fence a long while even in the simplest predicaments" (p. 20). Indeed, it seems as if these animals were successful only when their attempts to pass through the barrier led them by chance to pass around it.

Chickens, at least, appear to be very poor at solving detour problems, and their performance does not inspire much confidence in any claim that they might possess cognitive maps. Furthermore, although some of the behaviour by dogs is consistent with the claim that they do possess such maps, this conclusion does not necessarily follow from the above reports. In the study by Chapuis et al. (1983), subjects were first taken on a lead from the starting point around both ends of the detour. This would allow them to discover the shortest route to the goal from the starting point, and their successful performance, with opaque barriers, might reflect nothing more than the products of this learning. In the case of Kohler's (1925) dogs, no indication of their previous training or experiences is given. They may have encountered, therefore, many natural detour problems and solved them by trial and error. The transfer of any learning about these previous successes to the test trial would then account for the animals' behaviour.

Once again, however, some of the better evidence for the existence of cognitive maps comes from bees. These insects possess a sophisticated method of communication that permits a forager returning to the hive to indicate the distance and direction, as the crow flies, of the source of food it has just collected (see Chapter 8). Von Frisch (1950) was interested in the information that was conveyed when the forager took a detour while returning to the hive from the food source. The detour was forced by the presence of a mountain that was too high for bees to cross directly.

On returning to the hive, Von Frisch (1950) expected the bees to indicate the direction and distance either of the first or of the second part of its journey. Instead it communicated the direct route to food, despite never having passed along it. One interpretation of this finding is that in the course of taking their detour subjects formed a cognitive map of the area between the hive and food. With the aid of this map they could then deduce the direction of food from the hive and indicate this information to the other bees.

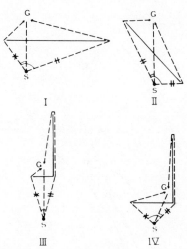

FIG. 7.6.   Plan of the barriers (——) and of the routes (– – –) taken by Breton Spaniels when passing around them from a starting point (S) to reach food (G) (from Chapuis et al., 1983).

The final source of evidence for the existence of a cognitive map in animals comes from another study with honeybees. Gould (1984) cites a study by Dyer in which foragers were trained to collect food from a boat at the point marked "lake station" in Fig. 7.7. On returning to the hive they were unable to attract any recruits when their dance indicated where the food was located. When the boat was moved to the "shore station", however, foragers returning to the hive from it were able to send substantial numbers of recruits to collect food. The obvious explanation for these findings is that bees possess a map of the area around the hive, and when the direction and distance of food is communicated to them by a forager, they identify its position on this map. Because food, for bees, is never found in the middle of lakes, it would be foolish to leave the hive when the map indicated this to be its predicted location. On the other hand, when food is indicated as being on the far side of the lake, then it makes good sense to search for it. Provided that this result is reliable and not open to alternative interpretation, then it provides compelling evidence that bees, at least, possess cognitive maps.

One justification for attributing an experimental outcome to the existence of a cognitive map is that it provides a parsimonious, or simple,

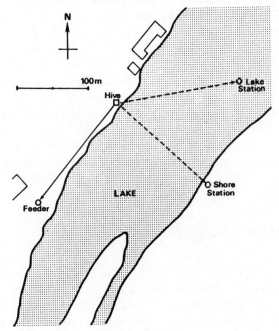

FIG. 7.7.   Map of the lake and surrounding area used for the study by Dyer (from Gould, 1984).

account of the animal's behaviour (Menzel, 1978; Morris, 1981). This simplicity is evident in our account of some of the above studies with bees. The ease of invoking a cognitive map as an explanation, however, is partly illusory; the explanation seems simple only because it directs attention away from certain very important questions. If it is accepted that an animal posesses a cognitive map, then we need to know how it is constructed, how the animal knows where it is located on the map, and how the map is used to determine the route that is taken. Until these questions can be answered satisfactorily, accounts of behaviour in terms of cognitive maps must be seen as incomplete. At present we are a considerable distance from answering any of them.

HOMING

Some of the most remarkable feats of animal problem solving are revealed by studies of homing. This term refers to the ability of animals to return to their nest or loft when they have been taken some distance from it and released. Very often this journey involves travelling across unfamiliar territory. Matthews (1955) has reported that a Manx shearwater released from Boston, Massachusetts flew more than 3,000 miles in 12½ days to return to its nest in South Wales. The albatross has been known to home successfully over distances of greater than 4,100 miles (Kenyon & Rice, 1958). The feats of the most famous homing bird, the pigeon, do not compare with these reports in terms of distance, but the fact that they can return to their loft on the same day that they are released some 600 miles away is no small achievement (Keeton, 1974). It is appropriate to consider homing at this point, as a number of accounts claim that it is achieved by the use of a map.

A variety of explanations for successful homing have been developed, many, if not all, of which are inadequate. The following review of these accounts will focus on pigeons because it is with this species that most information has been gained.

The Use of Landmarks

Homing is vey much more successful after pigeons have been allowed to explore the area around their loft. This may permit them to identify its location relative to prominent landmarks. Should they then be released from within sight of these landmarks they will be able to use them to guide their journey towards the loft. A study by Keeton (1974) provides one reason for questioning this account. He took great care to ensure that pigeons were released more than 50 miles from familiar territory. It is highly unlikely that they could perceive any familiar landmarks when released, yet they were able to home without difficulty.

In a more ingenious test of this hypothesis Schlicte and Schmidt-Koenig (1971) fitted pigeons with frosted contact lenses that allowed light to pass through, but the identification of landmarks was restricted to 6 metres. In spite of this enormous handicap, when the pigeons were released 80 miles from their loft they rapidly oriented in the correct direction, and a number actually managed to return. It is well worth reporting Keeton's (1974) observations of the behaviour of the successful birds on their return home, because they strongly imply that the use of landmarks is not important for homing (p. 91):

> It was a truly remarkable sight. The birds flew considerably higher than normal, and they did not swoop in for a landing on the loft like normal pigeons. Instead, they came almost straight down in a peculiar helicoptering or hovering flight. Being unable to see the loft itself, they landed in yards or fields in the vicinity, where we picked them up and carried them to the loft.

Retracing the Outward Route

While it is being transported to the release site, a pigeon might acquire information about the terrain through which it passes. By integrating this information into a cognitive map, the bird could then determine the correct direction in which to fly from the point of release. A number of techniques have been developed to test this possibility, including transporting pigeons in slowly rotating light-proof drums. But perhaps the best evidence against this account is that pigeons can home efficiently even when they are deeply anaesthetised on the journey to the release site (Walcott & Schmidt-Koenig, 1973). It is highly unlikely that pigeons learn much about the terrain through which they pass while asleep.

Map and Compass Hypothesis

According to Kramer (1952), pigeons possess a map that allows them to determine the direction in which they must fly in order to return home. To be of any value this information must be converted into a bearing that relates to the environment. This could be achieved, Kramer (1952) argued, if pigeons have a compass. For example, if it was inferred from the map that home lies due west of the release point, the use of a compass would then permit the subject to determine the direction in which it should fly. Obviously pigeons do not possess compasses of the sort that can be purchased in shops, nor do they employ directions like due west, but the position of the sun appears to provide an excellent substitute. In fact, quite a lot is now known about the compass component of Kramer's hypothesis, whereas the map component is poorly understood.

The compass is assumed to operate in the following way: On being released, the pigeon observes the position of the sun and incorporates this information with the time of day, provided by an internal clock, to compute any direction it requires. Suppose it needs to fly in a direction that is equivalent to south, then this can be readily computed by extrapolating from the present position of the sun to where it should be at mid-day. Admittedly, this is a complex calculation, but it does not appear to be beyond the capability of pigeons, as experiments on clock-shifting have shown.

An internal clock is generally considered to be set according to the light–dark cycle. Thus by maintaining pigeons in an artificial environment with a light–dark cycle that is out of phase with the external cycle, it should be possible to change the internal clock and influence the accuracy of the sun-compass. In a clock-shift experiment, then, pigeons are maintained for a while in conditions where the lights might come on at midnight and be turned off at midday. Assuming that dawn is at 6 a.m., the internal clock will eventually be ahead of real time by 6 hours. If the pigeon is then released at, say, 9 a.m. real time, the internal clock will inform it that the time is 3 p.m. This will lead the bird to infer that the direction of the sun is equivalent to southwest, where in reality it will be southeast, and any computations involving this information will make the bird fly at right angles to the correct route home. A number of experiments have confirmed predictions of this sort (Keeton, 1969), which strongly implicates the involvement of the sun and the internal clock in homing.

Does this mean that pigeons can home only when the sun is shining? Not at all; accurate homing has been reported when the sky is overcast and, on occasions, at night (Keeton, 1974; Lipp, 1983). An obvious candidate for the source of compass information in these circumstances is the earth's magnetic field. Attempts to test this possibility have involved the placement of magnets, or coils that generate magnetic fields, on pigeons in the hope of distorting their magnetic sense. At first these manipulations did not disrupt homing, but Keeton (1974) has argued that this might be because the experiments were conducted on clear days when the sun-compass can be used to home successfully. In support of this argument Keeton (1974) has reported that carrying magnets can disrupt homing on overcast days. There is also a suggestion that homing is poor at times of magnetic storms, which presumably distort the information normally supplied by magnetic fields (Gould, 1982). However, interference from magnetic fields does not disrupt homing on sunny days (Lednor & Walcott, 1983), and, given the uncertainty over the ability of pigeons to detect magnetic fields in the laboratory (see p. 43), the role of a magnetic sense in homing remains uncertain.

In contrast to the support for the compass component of Kramer's hypothesis, the evidence for the map component is much weaker. Kramer (1952) actually said rather little about this aspect of his model, which is perhaps not surprising. Because pigeons are capable of homing from a totally unfamiliar location, it is implausible that their success depends upon a map which they can have had no opportunity to acquire. As it stands, then, the map and compass hypothesis must be regarded as an incomplete account of homing.

Bicoordinate Navigation

Imagine that a pigeon is able to perceive two separate stimulus sources from its loft, and that it can also detect these sources from the release site. The direction and intensity of the sources will be different for these locations, and if the pigeon is sensitive to these differences then it will be in possession of sufficient information to compute the correct course home by means of bicoordinate navigation. The obvious advantage of this means of homing is that it can readily explain successful homing from unfamiliar territory. And a major obstacle is the specification of stimulus sources that can be detected over many hundreds of miles. As far as the pigeon is concerned, a number of possibilities have been examined. In Chapter 2 it was shown that they can detect infrasound, which is capable of travelling vast distances from where it originates. In addition to the eath's magnetic field, there has also been the suggestion that pigeons can detect lines of coriolis force, which change in intensity across the earth's surface (Yeagley, 1947, 1951). Both of these would be ideal candidates for bi-coordinate navigation. Finally, a group of Italian researchers (e.g. Papi, Ioale, Fiaschi, Benvenuti, & Baldaccini, 1978) have suggested that smell might play an important role in homing over distances. None of these possibilities, however, has gained universal acceptance (see Keeton, 1974; Able, 1980; Gould, 1982, for reviews), and bicoordinate navigation should be seen as a possible rather than a likely explanation for homing.

After reviewing the results from a large number of pigeon homing studies, Gould (1982, p. 211) concluded that "We probably now have nearly all the pieces of the puzzle before us (and, doubtless, several utterly irrelevant ones as well), but for the immediate future, at least, the nature of the animal map sense seems likely to retain its status as the most elusive and intriguing mystery in animal behaviour". On the basis of the evidence reviewed previously, there can be little reason for disagreeing with him.

Migration

Able (1980, p. 286) defines migration as "oriented, long distance, seasonal movement of individuals". It thus differs from homing, as migration need not be oriented towards a specific goal. Although this may make feats of migration less mysterious than homing, they are often just as spectacular. The Arctic Tern, for instance, spends a fortnight each year at the north pole, slightly longer at the south pole, and the rest of the year travelling between the two.

In many cases of migration generations of the same species undertake much the same journey. It is thus possible, as Gwinner (1972) has noted, that the direction and duration of migration is under endogenous control and does not depend at all upon the acquisition of a map. The orientation of migration, therefore, might be in a direction determined by a geographical feature such as the stars (see the discussion of Emlen, 1972, on p. 54). The duration of the journey could be determined either by an internal clock, or when the energy reserves are depleted. Provided that the subject travels at a reasonably constant speed, these factors alone should be sufficient to ensure that it arrives at much the same place as its forefathers (see Able, 1980, for a review). This is not to deny that learning plays a role in migration—it very likely does, but in a way that supplements this more fundamental mechanism.

An experiment by Perdeck (1958) indicates the importance of both endogenous factors and learning in determining the orientation of migration. Starlings were taken from where they were born in Holland and released for migration from Switzerland. When juveniles without any experience of migration were released, the direction of their migration was appropriate for a release site in Holland rather than Switzerland. On the other hand, the adults that were released took account of their displacement and flew towards their usual winter quarters. Presumably this adjustment was possible because of information acquired during the course of previous migrations.

INSIGHT

An early objector to Thorndike's (1911) account of problem solving was Kohler (1925). Thorndike's experiments were so restrictive, he argued, that they prevented animals from revealing their capacity to solve problems by any means other than the most simple. During the First World

War Kohler was fortunate enough to be on the Canary Islands, where he conducted a number of studies that were meant to reveal sophisticated intellectual processes in animals. We have already considered some of his work on detour problems, but he is best known for his experiments that, he claimed, demonstrate the importance of insight in problem solving. Many of his findings are described in his book *The mentality of apes,* which documents some remarkable feats of problem solving by animals.

Kohler (1925) believed that a major step in solving any problem is that of insight. Unfortunately it is rather difficult to know what he meant by this term—apparently it is not easy to translate from the the German word *Einsicht* that Kohler (1925) used. For writers in English on this topic insight is generally regarded as a period of thought followed by a flash of inspiration, when the solution suddenly occurs to the problem-solver. This is rather different from Thorndike's (1911) account of problem solving in which the correct solution is said to be arrived at by chance.

Kohler (1925) cites many instances of what he considers to be evidence of insight in animals. The following three examples might help to convey the meaning of the term. Incidentally, the first of these also provides a further demonstration of a successful solution to the detour problem.

In one experiment, a dog watched Kohler throw some food out of a window before shutting it. The dog "jumps once against the window-pane, then stands a moment, her head raised towards the window, looks a second at the observer, when all at once she wags her tail a few times, with one leap whirls round 180°, dashes out of the door and runs round outside, till she is underneath the window where she finds the food immediately" (p. 26).

In another study, Sultan, whom Kohler (1925) regarded as the brightest of a number of apes he worked with, was in his cage, in which there was also a small stick. Outside the cage was a longer stick, which was beyond Sultan's reach, and even further away was a reward of fruit (p. 151):

> Sultan tries to reach the fruit with the smaller of the sticks. Not succeeding, he tries a piece of wire that projects from the netting in his cage, but that, too, is in vain. Then he gazes about him (there are always in the course of these tests some long pauses, during which the animal scrutinises the whole visible area). He suddenly picks up the little stick once more, goes to the bars directly opposite to the long stick, scratches it towards him with the auxiliary, seizes it and goes with it to the point opposite the objective which he secures. From the moment that his eyes fell upon the long stick, his procedure forms one consecutive whole. . . .

Finally, Kohler (1925) hung a piece of fruit from the ceiling of a cage housing six apes, including Sultan. There was a wooden box in the cage (p. 41):

All six apes vainly endeavoured to reach the fruit by leaping up from the ground. Sultan soon relinquished this attempt, paced restlessly up and down, suddenly stood still in front of the box, seized it, tipped it hastily straight towards the objective, but began to climb upon it at a (horizontal) distance of 1/2 metre and springing upwards with all his force, tore down the banana.

In all of these examples there is a period when the animal responds incorrectly; this is then followed by activity which, as it is reported, suggests that the solution to the problem has suddenly occurred to the subject. There is certainly no hint in these reports that the problem was solved by trial and error. Does this mean, then, that Kohler (1925) was correct in his criticism of Thorndike's (1911) theorising?

Unfortunately it is a most frustrating experience reading Kohler's book, because the majority of his experiments are difficult to interpret. The very fact that six apes may be simultaneously engaged in the same problem means it is virtually impossible to understand the problem-solving abilities of any individual. Furthermore, all of his subjects had played with boxes and sticks prior to the studies just described. It is thus possible that the absence of trial-and-error responding was due to the prior experience of the animals. Sultan may, by accident, have learned about the consequences of jumping from boxes in earlier sessions, and he was perhaps doing no more than acting on the basis of his previous learning. This criticism of Kohler's (1925) work is by no means original. Birch (1945) and Schiller (1952) have both suggested that without prior experience with sticks and so forth, there is very little reason for believing that apes can solve Kohler's problems in the manner just described.

An amusing experiment by Epstein, Kirshnit, Lanza, and Rubin (1984) also shows the importance of past experience in problem solving and, at the same time, raises some important issues concerning the intellectual abilities of animals. Pigeons were given two different types of training. They were rewarded with food for pushing a box towards a spot randomly located at the base of a wall of the test chamber. Pushing in the absence of the spot was never rewarded. They were also trained to stand on the box when it was fixed to the floor and peck for food at a plastic banana suspended from the ceiling. Attempts to peck the banana when not standing on the box were never rewarded. Finally, on a test session they were confronted with a novel situation in which the banana was suspended from the ceiling and the box was placed some distance from beneath it. Epstein et al. (1984) report that (p. 61):

At first each pigeon appeared to be "confused"; it stretched and turned beneath the banana, looked back and forth from banana to box, and so on. Then each subject began rather suddenly to push the box in what was clearly the direction of the banana. Each subject sighted the banana as it pushed and readjusted the box as necessary to move it towards the banana. Each subject stopped pushing it in the appropriate place, climbed and pecked the banana.

This quite remakable performance was achieved by one bird in 49 sec, which compares very favourably with the 5 min it took Sultan to solve his similar problem.

There can be no doubt from this study that the prior training of the pigeon played an important role in helping it solve the problem. Even so, the study clearly reveals that the pigeons performed on the test session in a manner that extends beyond trial-and-error reponding. The act of pecking the banana might have been acquired by trial-and-error learning, and so, too, might the act of moving the box around. But the way in which the box was moved to below the banana does not seem to be compatible with this analysis. This report, as well as those of Kohler (1925), implies that the novel act from its initiation to its conclusion was directed towards the achievement of a specific goal; and, if this is true, then it lies beyond the scope of any trial-and-error analysis.

The description by Epstein et al. (1984) of the pigeons' behaviour bears a striking similarity to Kohler's (1925) account of Sultan's reaction to the similar problem. It might be thought, therefore, that it would be appropriate to account for the pigeons' success in terms of insight. In truth, this would not be a particularly useful approach as it really does not offer an account of the way in which the problem was solved. Other than indicating that the problem was solved suddenly and not by trial and error, the term insight adds very little else to our understanding of these results.

Unfortunately I am unable to offer, with confidence, any explanation for these findings. But one possibility is that during their training with the blue spot, pigeons learned that certain responses moved the box towards the spot, and that the box by the spot was a signal for food. The integration of these associations would then result in them pushing the box towards the spot. During their training with the banana, one of the things they may have learned is that the banana is associated with food. Then, for the test session, although they would be able to push the box towards the blue spot, generalisation from their previous training might result in them pushing the box in the direction of another signal for food, the banana.

DISCRIMINATION LEARNING

A Theoretical Analysis

One popular approach to the study of problem solving with animals has been to confront them with a discrimination learning task. With such a problem the subject is typically presented with a pair of stimuli, and approach to one but not the other will lead to reward. With sufficient training animals will approach the correct stimulus on the majority of trials. As long ago as the 1930s authors such as Krechevsky (1932) and Lashley (1929) proposed that such successful performance depends on subjects testing hypotheses; for example, "Go left", "Approach black", etc. It now appears that, at least for simple procedures, this interpretation is incorrect. But before the evidence against it can be presented it will be helpful to develop an associative account of discrimination learning. There may be some disagreement about the details of this account, but the general principles it embodies are currently very popular.

The apparatus depicted in Fig. 7.8 is a version of the jumping stand that has been used in numerous studies of discrimination learning. In this example the stimuli, horizontal and vertical stripes, were situated behind ledges. At the start of a trial a rat is placed on the central platform and required to jump onto a ledge in front of a stimulus window. If the animal has chosen the correct ledge, then it will be able to push down the stimulus and collect a small amount of food. Jumps to the incorrect ledge never lead to food. In order to ensure that the animal is solving the problem by learning to approach the vertical stripes, the location of the stimuli changes from one trial to the next in a quasi-random sequence.

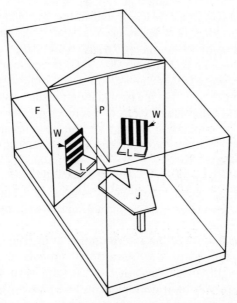

FIG. 7.8.   Sketch of a typical jumping stand used for studies of discrimination learning (from Sutherland, 1964).

An associative account for the solution to this sort of problem can be developed with the Rescorla–Wagner (1972) model (see Chapter 4). To demonstrate this account, consider the case in which animals must learn to approach the horizontal (H) stripes and avoid the vertical (V) ones. On the first trial the rat may, by chance, jump to H on the left side and be rewarded. There will then be a growth in associative strength to H, as well as to the other left-side stimuli (L). For the second trial H might be on the right-hand side, and a degree of conflict will be engendered when the subject is placed upon the platform. The associative strength of the L stimuli will elicit a weak tendency to go left, and the associative strength of H will encourage the conflicting response of jumping to the right. Given that the associative strengths of H and L are equal—and this will be true if they are of equal salience—the rat will be forced again to choose randomly. If it should jump to the right, then the reward it receives will increase the associative strength of H and the other stimuli on the right-hand side (R). From this point the associative strength of H will be greater than any other stimulus in the apparatus; subjects will therefore consistently approach it, and always receive food. On the second trial the rat might, of course, jump to the left and not receive any food. There will be a loss of associative strength by the L stimuli, so that on Trial 3, H will possess the greatest associative strength and control responding thereafter.

The first point to make concerning this analysis is that it is unduly simple. It implies that rats should be capable of learning a discrimination in a jumping stand within a few trials, and to my knowledge this has never occurred. When they first learn even a simple discrimination in this apparatus, rats require about 60 trials before they are performing accurately (Sutherland & Mackintosh, 1971). A common explanation for this poor performance is that when solving a discrimination, animals often adopt a position preference. One explanation for such a strategy is that the salience of the cues that identify position is much greater than of those the experimenter is manipulating (H and V). Such a relationship will ensure that initially the position cues gain the greater associative strength and control the subject's choices. As training progresses, however, the more consistent relationship with reward of H (or V) than the position cues will eventualy result in it gaining the greatest associative strength. At this point the position preference will be abolished, and H will be approached on every trial.

An important feature of this interpretation of discrimination learning is that it is incremental—that is, reward will produce a slight growth in associative strength on all rewarded trials, until asymptote is reached. Conversely, there will be a decrement in associative strength on nonre-warded trials. The account is also non-selective; it maintains that if there is a change in associative strength, then it will be to all the stimuli that are present on that trial. The solution to a discrimination problem is thus seen to be the result of a gradual increase in the associative strength of the correct stimulus, and a gradual loss by those that are incorrect.

Hypothesis Testing

In contrast to this incremental analysis, Lashley (1929) and Krechevsky (1932), among others, considered discriminations to be solved by animals suddenly discovering the correct solution. Krechevsky (1932), for example, thought animals would formulate a single hypothesis for solving the problem, and if this should ultimately prove inadequate, then it would be rejected in favour of another. Thus in the jumping stand the rat might start off with the incorrect hypothesis, "Jump to the left", and only when this had proved unsatisfactory would it test an alternative rule such as "Jump to horizontal".

Attempts to choose between these contrasting accounts of discrimination learning focussed on the influence of the first few trials on the ultimate solution of the problem. An incremental, associative account places great importance on these trials; each reward will increase the associative strength of the correct stimulus and lead the subject a step nearer to perfect performance. According to Lashley (1929) and Krechevsky (1932), however, the events of the first trials may have no influence on learning about the correct hypothesis. Suppose, for example, animals initially adopt the incorrect hypothesis of "Go left"; while they are responding according to this rule, they will learn nothing at all about the merits of the correct rule.

An early experiment to differentiate between these opposing views was performed by McCulloch and Pratt (1934), using apparatus that has long since fallen from popularity—presumably because it must have required considerable patience in training rats to use it. The subject was placed in a box in which there were two strings, one attached to a heavy weight (75 g), the other to a light weight (25 g). In order to gain food, one control group had to pull the string tied to the heavy weight a distance of 100 cm; a second control group had to perform the same response with the light weight. Pulling the incorrect string was never rewarded. Surprisingly, an average of only 68 trials was needed to train these groups. A mixture of the above training was given to the experimental group. These rats first received 28 trials in which pulling the light but not the heavy weight was rewarded, followed by a reversal in which pulling the heavy weight led to food. This final stage of training required 64 trials.

Neither control group showed any sign of learning the discrimination after 28 trials. If discrimination training does involve the use of hypotheses, then it follows that the correct one had not been used up to this point.

Indeed, it looks as though something nearer 60 trials is required before rats hit upon the rule "Pull a specific weight". For the experimental group, therefore, their experience on the first 28 trials should have no influence on the evaluation of this hypothesis, and suddenly reversing the requirements of the task will have no effect on the speed of selection of the correct hypothesis. In other words, the experimental group should still evaluate the correct hypothesis after about 60 trials in the apparatus and therefore solve the problem approximately 30 trials after the reversal. That they needed twice this number lends little support to the notion that discrimination learning progresses by testing one rule after another.

McCulloch and Pratt's (1934) findings are, on the other hand, entirely consistent with an associative account of discrimination learning. The control groups can be expected to respond correctly once the associative strength of the correct weight has been incremented to a value that is greater than for any other stimulus. This appears to need about 60 trials. For the experimental group, the initial 28 trials in which pulling the heavy weight was not rewarded will leave this stimulus, at best, with zero associative strength. As a consequence, after the implementation of the reversal subjects will at least require as many trials as the control groups to solve the discrimination, and this, in fact, was the result recorded.

The success of this account, together with the failure of such views as those espoused by Krechevsky (1932), has led most theorists to accept that simple discrimination learning is based upon association formation. But the debate has not stopped here. A variety of methods for discrimination training have been developed to examine whether in special circumstances animals can be forced to use more sophisticated mental processes when solving problems. The following section examines critically the results from some of these studies.

Serial Reversal Learning

Reversal learning results from training in which animals must change the preference formed in a previous discrimination. Rats may, for example, be required first to approach a white but not a black stimulus for food. Once they have learned to do this, reversal training would then consist of rewarding responses to black but not to white. Serial reversal learning consists essentially of continually training animals in this manner, so that they are repeatedly acquiring a preference for one stimulus and then being asked to reverse it.

An experiment by Mackintosh and Holgate (1969) demonstrates clearly the effects of this training with rats. Using apparatus that results in faster learning than the jumping stand, subjects were initially trained in a simple discrimination in which they had to go consistently to a compartment of a certain brightness for food. The results in Fig. 7.9 show that on average nearly 20 errors were made before this problem was solved. At this juncture the first reversal was initiated, and reward was made available for approaching the compartment of a different brightness. Subjects found this problem quite difficult and made more than 30 errors. The number of errors made on subsequent reversals declined gradually from this level, and eventually only one or two incorrect responses were recorded for each problem.

The accuracy on the later reversals is important because it is difficult to explain with the account of discrimination learning that we have developed so far. Such an account can explain the learning of the original discrimination, just as it can explain the large number of trials to master the first reversal. When the reversal is initiated, subjects will continue to respond to the previously rewarded stimulus until their preference for it has extinguished. Once this has occurred, the subject can approach the other stimulus and start to learn the new discrimination. One explanation for the improvement in learning of the subsequent reversals is that more attention was paid to the discriminative stimuli (see Sutherland & Mackintosh, 1971), but it would be unreasonable to look to this process to explain all the improvement. Reports by Dufort, Guttman, and Kimble (1954) with rats, and Schrier (1966) with rhesus monkeys, indicate that with sufficient training a reversal can be reliably mastered after just one error. On the first trial of a reversal subjects will follow their previous training and select the incorrect stimulus. By attending fully to the relevant stimuli on this trial, it is possible that the absence of a reward will reduce the associative strength of the previously correct stimulus to a level where

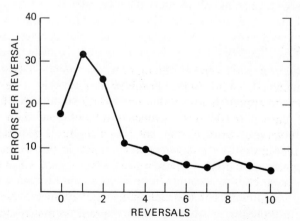

FIG. 7.9.   The number of errors per reversal for a group of rats given serial reversal training; 0 = original discrimination (adapted from Mackintosh, Wilson, & Boakes, 1985).

it is no longer preferred; but this does not explain why animals should consistently approach the other stimulus on the next trial.

How then can these results be explained? One possibility is to propose that the stimuli controlling the animal's behaviour are not those with which it is currently confronted. Instead, the outcome of the previous trial might serve this function (Hull, 1952). To return to the study of Mackintosh and Holgate (1969), these events would be of four kinds: on the previous trial the animal may have been rewarded for approaching either the dark (D+) or light (L+) compartment; or it may have ben nonrewarded for approaching these stimuli (D−, L−). If the animal has learned in the presence of the memories of either D+ or L− to approach the dark compartment, then on all trials but the first of a reversal, it will be rewarded. Similarly, approach to white will be rewarded in the presence of memories of either L+ or D−. By forming associations between the memory of the outcome of one trial and the response that is required on the next trial, animals should then be able to perform accurately on all trials except the first of each reversal.

This argument is complicated, but I believe it is worth taking seriously. A number of experiments that involved Delayed Matching to Sample were described in Chapter 3. In these studies, subjects were required to store information when a sample stimulus was turned off, and to use this memory to choose between two comparison stimuli that were presented some time later. It does not seem too unreasonable to assume that the memory processes responsible for successful performance in those experiments can also operate during serial reversal learning. In support of this claim, it is interesting to note that it predicts that accurate performance on each discrimination is more likely with short rather than long intervals between successive trials. If the interval between trials is too long, then the memory of the events on one trial will have faded from memory before the next trial commences and be unable to elicit the correct response. A number of studies confirmed this prediction by showing better serial reversal learning with massed rather than spaced trials (North, 1959; Stretch, McGonigle, & Morton, 1964; Williams, 1971).

Accurate performance on a serial reversal problem does, then, reveal something more about the problem-solving abilities of animals than is shown by more conventional discrimination training. It is quite clear that this performance cannot be explained by association formation, where the stimuli concerned are those confronting the animal, even when attentional processes are taken into account. In order to account for successful serial reversal learning in terms of association formation, it must be assumed that the memory of the events of one trial serves as a cue for the response on the next trial. This conclusion also appears to be true for another technique of discrimination training, which examines the formation of learning sets.

Learning Sets

Harlow (1949) was the first to use this technique. His subjects, usually rhesus macaque monkeys, were initially trained in a simple discrimination in which reward was consistently associated with one stimulus but not the other. After a number of trials with one pair of stimuli, they were discarded, and a new pair was introduced. Training then continued as before for the same number of trials, whereupon the stimuli were eliminated from the study and replaced by yet another novel pair. Harlow (1949) discovered that after training monkeys in this way with several hundred different pairs of stimuli there was a gradual improvement on each discrimination. Ultimately, although accuracy was necessarily at chance level on the first trial with a novel pair, on the second trial performance was very nearly perfect—Fig. 7.10 shows the accuracy for the first 6 trials of a discrimination at various stages of training. With growing experience of the different problems, the success on the second and subsequent trials of each shows a progressive improvement.

To explain this improvement, it is not possible to use the account that was developed to explain serial reversal learning, as this will be effective only when the same pair of stimuli is used throughout the experiment. Nonetheless, a slightly more complex version of this account can be used to explain Harlow's (1949) findings. All that we need to assume is that

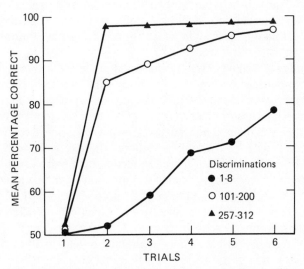

FIG. 7.10.   The mean percentage of correct responses on the first 6 trials for blocks of different discriminations given at various stages in a study of learning set formation (adapted from Harlow, 1949).

animals identify the discriminative stimuli not so much by their physical attributes but by whether or not they were selected on the previous trial. Suppose that by chance a choice on the first trial of a problem resulted in reward; then to obtain reward on the next trial the memory of reward must control approach to the item identified as the one that was previously chosen. On the other hand, if reward was not presented on the first trial, reward on the second trial can be obtained if the memory for nonreward controls approach to the previously nonselected item. Thus if animals can remember at the start of a trial the outcome of the previous trial, and if they also identify stimuli on the basis of whether or not they have been previously selected, then they should be able to master learning sets.

The success of this strategy obviously depends on animals remembering a good deal of information from one trial to the next. There is, therefore, some encouragement to be gained from the finding that learning set performance is most accurate when the interval between successive trials is short (Bessemer & Stollnitz, 1971; Kamil & Mauldin, 1975).

Transitive Inference

When told that A is bigger than B, and that B is bigger than C, few adults have difficulty in reaching the conclusion that A is bigger than C. This type of reasoning, which allows us to combine knowledge about specific relationships in order to infer another relationship, is known as transitive inference. The results from several discrimination learning experiments suggest that animals, too, may be capable of solving transitive inference problems, although the way in which they arrive at the solution is not yet clear.

In a study by Gillan (1981; see also McGonigle & Chalmers, 1977) three female chimpanzees first received training with 5 containers, A, B, C, D, and E, each of which was a different colour. A pair of containers was presented to the subject on each trial and her task was to identify the one in which food was hidden. The trials were of the following sort: A+ B−, B+ C−, C+ D−, D+ E−, where + denotes the container with food. The spatial relationship between the members of each pair varied irregularly, so that the only way that the four discriminations could be learned was on the basis of colour. After a number of training sessions performance on all discriminations was consistently accurate, which can be taken to indicate that subjects preferred A to B, B to C, C to D, and D to E. To examine whether these relationships can be combined to lead to a novel inference, Gillan (1981) then gave test sessions that included, for the first time, the pair B and D. If chimpanzees are capable of transitive inference then combinining the knowledge that B is preferred to C with the knowledge that C is preferred to D should lead to the conclusion that B is preferred to

D. One chimpanzee, Sadie, performed perfectly on this test by choosing B in preference to D on all 12 test trials. The results for the other two chimpanzees were not so consistent. Nonetheless, the success of Sadie shows that at least one chimpanzee can solve transitive inference problems.

This clear demonstration of transitive inference raises the question of how it was achieved. The first point to make is that it is not easy to explain these findings in terms of association formation. During training both B and D were equally often paired with reward and nonreward, depending on the stimulus with which they were currently paired. It would thus be unreasonable on this basis to account for Sadie's success by assuming that the associative strength of D was greater than that of B.

An alternative approach is to assume that chimpanzees have a means of encoding information that allows them to represent the relationship between each pair and also to combine this information. One way of achieving this, as we saw in the previous chapter, might be by the use of propositions. These could be of the form "B is preferred to C" and "C is preferred to D", so that their integration would lead to the correct conclusion. Fortunately we do not have to worry about presenting this account in detail, because there is already evidence that suggests it is wrong. McGonigle and Chalmers (1986) studied transitive inference in squirrel monkeys using a similar method to that of Gillan (1981). Test trials included novel pairs of items that were either closely or distantly related on the transitive series. As fewer propositions would have to be combined to infer the relationship between close rather than distant pairs, subjects should be quicker at choosing between closely related items. In fact, choice of the correct item was faster when the members of a pair were distantly related, with the result, paradoxically, that choices between pairs that had never been given during training—B and D, for example—were made more swiftly than those between pairs that were familiar, B and C, or C and D.

It is noteworthy that this finding is also often true for humans (Anderson, 1980), which raises the prospect that people and chimpanzees solve transitive problems in the same way. According to Anderson (1980, pp. 78–82), when people experience a number of individual relationships then a representation is formed in which the items are organised into a sequence that corresponds to the transitive series. The representation is said to be analogical, so that their position in the sequence corresponds directly to how closely they are related in the series. Hence in the experiment by Gillan (1981), the effects of the training might have been represented as the sequence A–B–C–D–E. To solve a specific discrimination, all that would be necessary for the chimpanzee is to identify the items in the list and select the one that is to the left of the other. Anderson (1980) has suggested that in this type of task it is easier to identify the relative position of the represented items when they are further apart, and this would account for the findings of McGonigle and Chalmers (1986). How such a sequence can be formed in the first place remains to be discovered.

An ability to cope with a transitive series may not be confined to chimpanzees and monkeys, as a study by Straub and Terrace (1981) reveals. Pigeons were trained in a chamber in which there were 6 response keys arranged in a 3×2 matrix. Trials commenced with the illumination of four keys, each by a different colour (A, B, C, and D). The same colours were used consistently across successive trials, but the keys on which they were presented varied randomly. The four keys remained illuminated throughout a trial, and in order to obtain food they had to be pecked in the correct sequence—say, A–B–C–D. Those with little experience of training pigeons may be surprised to discover that this is not an easy task for them to learn. Even with extensive pretraining, birds needed as many as 5,000 trials with the four stimuli before they reached even a modest criterion of success.

Upon completion of this training, Straub and Terrace (1981) presented novel test trials on which only two or three keys were illuminated. Transitive inference is revealed by the discovery that birds would still respond correctly when one of the stimuli, say B, was omitted. Without being able to combine the information that pecks to A must precede those to B with the information that pecks to B must precede those to C, subjects would not correctly peck C after responding to A. Unfortunately, Straub and Terrace (1981) did not report the time it took pigeons to make each response, but it would be of some interest to discover whether, after responding to A, subjects were swifter at responding to C on ACD trials than to B on trials when all four keys were illuminated. Such an outcome would suggest that the mechanisms underlying transitive inference in monkeys and pigeons are the same.

Relationships as Discriminative Stimuli

Sameness. In Chapter 3 several experiments that used a method known as delayed matching to sample were described. The subject would be presented with a sample stimulus, and, a short while after it had been turned off, two comparison stimuli were shown, only one of which was the same as the sample. To gain reward, the subject had to choose the comparison stimulus that was the same as the sample. At the time we were interested in this technique as a method for stuying animal memory, but it has also been used to study another aspect of animal cognition, especially when the sample and comparison stimuli are presented simultaneously. In this format the procedure is simply referred to as matching. Discriminations based on this design are of interest because the subject might solve

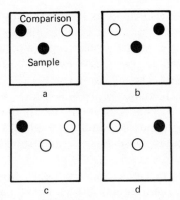

FIG. 7.11.   The four possible configurations of sample and comparison stimuli that can occur in a matching study.

them on the basis of a relationship, rather than on the presence of a specific stimulus. And as we shall see shortly, this, in turn, has important implications for our understanding of the thought processes of animals.

The theoretically interesting account for successful matching is that animals can appreciate that the sample and comparison stimuli are the same, and that this relationship controls the choice of the correct comparison. As is so often the case, however, there are alternative accounts for successful matching, and these must be discounted before we accept that animals can detect and respond to a relationship.

A plausible account for matching can be developed in terms of configural learning. The four panels in Fig. 7.11 depict the possible configurations of stimuli that will confront an animal during a typical matching problem. The sample stimulus is in the middle of the panel, and the two comparisons are at the top. To respond correctly, the left-hand comparisons in panels *a* and *d* must be chosen, and so must the right-hand stimuli in panels *b* and *c*. Note that these are the only possible trials, and that each panel contains a different configuration of sample and comparison stimuli. In order to solve the problem, then, all the animal must do is to associate a specific response with each configuration. For example, configuration *b* would be associated with the response of approaching top-left. Once the four associations have been formed, the problem should be solved successfully on every trial.

In order to test this account of matching, it would be necessary to introduce a new set of sample and comparison stimuli. As there will have been no opportunity to associate the configurations of these stimuli with the correct choices, this change will result in a marked loss of accuracy if such associations are responsible for matching. On the other hand, if the original training resulted in subjects learning to respond according to the relationship between the sample and comparison stimuli, then changing their physical properties should not disrupt responding. Even when the stimuli are novel it will be possible to identify the comparison that is the same as the sample and respond correctly.

Experiments with chimpanzees (Nissen, Blum, & Blum, 1948), rhesus monkeys (Mishkin, Prockop, & Rosvold, 1962), and dolphins (Herman & Gordon, 1974) have found that after sufficient training on a variety of matching discriminations, these animals can respond correctly on the first trial with a novel set of stimuli.

Pigeons experience very much more difficulty with matching problems, but an experiment by Santiago and Wright (1984) has shown, with patient training involving many thousands of trials, that they, too, may learn to respond on the basis of the sameness relationship. On each trial a subject was shown two photographic slides in an experimental chamber, which also contained a red and a green response key. When the slides were identical, then pecks to the red key were rewarded; when they were different, responses to the green key resulted in reward. Much of this training was conducted with a pool of 210 different slides, but eventually test trials were introduced with novel slides. Performance on these trials was significantly better than would be expected on the basis of chance, although it was not as good as with the original training slides.

Second-order Relationships.   In the Santiago and Wright (1984) study a subject was presented with two stimuli, X and Y, and had to decide whether they were the same or different. It is possible to take this method a step further. Instead of being concerned with whether or not two stimuli are physically identical, animals can be asked whether the relationship between one pair of stimuli is the same as or different to that between another pair. Thus a subject might be confronted with the pairs AA and BB, or, alternatively, AX and BY, and be expected to indicate same in both cases. In the former instance both pairs contain the same stimuli and in the latter both pairs are composed of different items. Conversely, given AX and BB, the response should indicate that the relationship between the two pairs is different. Success on this type of task would indicate the sophisticated ability of being able to perceive the relationship between relationships.

Premack (1983b) reports an experiment based upon this principle in which naive chimpanzees were unable to solve this problem, even after 15 sessions of training. This should not be too surprising in the light of his claim that children under 6 also find it difficult. To reach any firm conclusions on the basis of a single study would be foolish, but this finding begins to suggest that we are reaching the limits of animal intelligence.

Analogical Reasoning.   If we are reaching the limits of animal intelligence, then it may be a frontier only for untutored animals. Premack (1983b) reports that after receiving language training, which will be described in the next chapter, Sarah, a chimpanzee, had little difficulty in solving the above problem. An even more impressive demonstration of her capacity to perceive complex relationships is provided by the way she was able to reason analogically (Gillan, Premack, & Woodruff, 1981).

A typical analogical reasoning test for humans would consist of a question like "As dog is to puppy, so cow is to ... ?" In order to reply correctly, it is necessary to identify the relationship between "dog" and "puppy" and then to select the word that bears the same relationship to "cow": "calf". Analogical reasoning, then, is the ability to judge the equivalence of the relationships between two different sets of stimuli. From the present point of view this capacity is interesting because its existence in any animal would indicate that they can identify relationships that extend beyond sameness and difference.

The stimuli used to study analogical reasoning by Sarah were of two basic types: In several experiments she was presented with a matrix of geometric shapes similar to those shown in the left-hand upper panel of Fig. 7.12. Her task was then to select from the bottom row a single shape and place it in the vacant space in the matrix so that the relationship in the right-hand column matched that in the left-hand column. In this example the correct shape is the small triangle containing a dot. Sarah was able to perform a variety of problems based on this design with considerable ease. The other stimuli that Sarah was tested with consisted of household objects that were familiar to her. The example in the lower panel of Fig. 7.12 is similar in principle to that in the panel above, and in this instance the correct item to be placed in the space is the can opener. Given her success with the geometric shapes, it may not be surprising to learn that Sarah was also very good with this sort of problem.

Interpretation.   According to Premack (1983a,b) the explanation for Sarah's success lies in the difference between imaginal (concrete) and abstract representations. In Chapter 2 it was argued that a majority— perhaps all—of the stimuli an animal remembers are stored as concrete representations. This term implies that the representation is in some sense a copy of the stimulus to which it relates. Premack's (1983a) use of the term "imaginal" emphasises this point by suggesting that the memory of a stimulus is an image of it. Such a system may be adequate when an animal is concerned with storing information about specific events, but it fails when details of a more abstract nature must be stored.

To address this issue Premack (1983a,b) focusses on the relationship of sameness and argues that it can hold at a number of levels. At the most

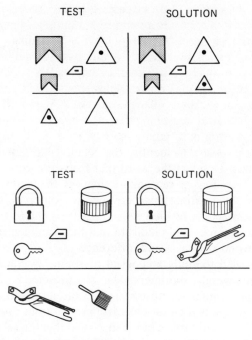

FIG. 7.12.   Two examples of the problems given to the chimpanzee, Sarah, in a study of analogical reasoning (adapted from Gillan et al., 1981).

fundamental, there is the similarity that pertains to objects that are physically identical. In these circumstances they will produce identical concrete representations, which, it is proposed, will result in a reaction of similarity if they are perceived together. Premack (1983b, p. 128) does not specify what this reaction consists of, but it might not be too far-fetched to suggest that when a stimulus is perceived a representation of it will be stored temporarily. If the stimulus, or one that is identical to it, should then be presented again a short time later, it will correspond to this representation and, for want of a better word, it may elicit a sensation of familiarity. In the absence of such a representation the stimulus might be accompanied by a sensation of novelty. Wagner's (1976, 1978, 1981) theory is one framework into which these ideas could be accommodated. In the case of physical identity, then, the sensation of familiarity could provide a concrete stimulus for use in solving simple matching problems. For the task summarised in Fig. 7.11, a subject might look first at the sample and then at a comparison. If the latter should elicit a reaction of familiarity, then this could serve as the discriminative stimulus controlling the correct response. Thus, according to Premack (1983b), success on matching tasks, even with novel stimuli, does not require particularly sophisticated intellectual mechanisms.

At another level, Premack (1983a,b) argues, there is the similarity between relationships. Thus we can talk about the similarity of a dog–puppy to a cow–calf relationship even though there is no physical correspondence between the stimuli concerned. Indeed, this absence of any physical similarity is the obstacle for the development of a concrete representation of this relationship. If we accept for the moment Premack's (1983a) suggestion that a concrete representation is an image, then this point can be clarified because it is so difficult to conceive of what an image of an adult–infant relationship might consist. Moreover, even if such an image can be brought to mind for dog and puppy, it is unlikely to be the same as for cow and calf, and at the imaginal level these relationships would be regarded as different. These limitations of concrete representations led Premack (1983a) to propose that all relationships, apart from those of physical similarity and difference, are represented in an abstract code. Premack (1983a) himself says very little about how the abstract code is formed, or about the information it may contain, but the absence of an obvious alternative method for storing information about relationships means that his ideas merit serious consideration.

A further proposal of Premack (1983a) is that most animals are capable of forming concrete representations, but in addition primates possess the capacity to form abstract representations. For primates without language training this capacity is said to be poorly developed, yet it is a capacity they all share. Once primates have received language training, however, their capacity to use an abstract system for storing knowledge is presumed to be considerably enhanced. And it is for this reason that Sarah was able to identify second-order relationships and to perform so well on the analogical reasoning test. These claims are based on slender evidence, and they are undoubtedly controversial. Nonetheless, the issues being considered are important and will have to be examined further if the study of animal cognition is to progress.

CONCLUSIONS

Possibly the least controversial conclusion to be drawn from this chapter is that Thorndike (1911) was wrong in his claim that animals are constrained to trial and error when problem solving. The accuracy of Sadie with her transitive inference problem, or the the purposeful way in which the pigeons of Epstein et al. (1984) moved the box around their chamber, are but two instances where animals have behaved rationally in a novel situation. Such orderly responding would not be expected if the only reaction to a new problem was to behave randomly.

Rather more uncertainty, however, surrounds the issue of explaining how these problems are solved. There is no denying that associative learning theory can explain many of the findings we have considered, especially when it is acknowledged that associations involving common elements can be integrated to lead to a novel response to a familiar stimulus. The question that remains is whether all the results we have considered can be explained in these terms.

There have been a number of findings which, as they are presently understood, challenge the view that animal intelligence is restricted to the formation of associations between concrete representations. There are the results by Von Frisch (1950) and Gould (1986; see also Gould, 1984) which suggest that honeybees have a cognitive map; there are the demonstrations of insight and transitive inference by pigeons and chimpanzees; and, finally, there is Sarah's skill at analogical reasoning. But although we can readily acknowledge the problem posed by such findings for associative learning theory, we are unfortunately some way from fully understanding how they should be explained.

8

Communication and Language

The most important intellectual capacity possessed by humans is that of language. By use of the spoken word we are able to live together in large and more or less harmonious social groups; we can teach our children an enormous range of skills; and we can also express our feelings and our thoughts. By use of the written word we have benefitted from the knowledge acquired by others over a period of more than 2,500 years. Some can also use the written word to create great works of art. Without these and many other benefits of language our lives would be quite different. Indeed, it may not be too far-fetched to say that without language our lives would differ little from those of other animals.

For a variety of reasons it has been argued that language is unique to humans (Chomsky, 1957; Macphail, 1982). The purpose of the present chapter is to examine this claim and its implications in some detail. If it is correct, then there should be marked differences between the ways in which animals and humans communicate. After examining what these differences might be, the discussion will focus on whether they constitute the dividing line between human and animal intelligence.

ANIMAL COMMUNICATION

To define precisely what is meant by animal communication is a surprisingly difficult task that can readily lead to controversy. For present purposes, however, the definition provided by Slater (1983) should suffice.

Communication is regarded as "the transmission of a signal from one animal to another such that the sender benefits, on average, from the response of the recipient" (p. 10). By interpreting this statement loosely, a wide range of species can be said to be able to communicate. Thus one of the simplest creatures, protozoa, can influence the movement of others by secreting a chemical. During courtship the male fruit fly can stimulate the female by producing a sound with its wings. And the chimpanzee can use a range of sounds, facial expressions, and smell to influence the behaviour of other members of its social group.

The variety of information that may be communicated is also considerable. The identity of the sender can often be determined from its signals. This information may be rather general and indicate nothing more than the species of the sender, which is still worth knowing in the case of mating signals; alternatively, the identification can be more precise and allow an animal to return to its social group, or a parent to identify and feed its offspring. The motivational state of the sender can also be inferred from the signals it sends. Aggression in cats is indicated by an arching of the back, and the change in bird song in the spring is a sure sign of the sexual readiness of males. Animals can also communicate about the environment. Many species have an alarm call that indicates the presence of a predator, whereas the honeybee is famous for her ability to transmit information about the location of food.

In some cases the important component of a signal may be a single feature, such as colour. When the male stickleback is ready to breed, its belly turns red. Should he then enter the territory of another male, the sight of this stimulus will immediately elicit aggression. That it is just the colour red that is sufficient to elicit aggression is revealed by Tinbergen's (1953) observation of a stickleback in an aquarium who attempted to attack a red post-office van whenever it passed. But even a single feature can convey a variety of information. For instance, Stellar's jay raises its crest during aggressive encounters with other jays, and, according to Brown (1964), the degree to which the crest is raised is directly related to the ferocity of the opponent. A very large range of intensities of aggression can therefore be signalled by slight adjustments of the crest.

Some of the most complex communication is engaged in by the honeybee. On returning to the hive, a worker gives the food she has collected to the other bees, prior to performing a dance on the vertical surface of a comb. If food is within 50 to 100 m of the hive then, a *round* dance will be observed. The worker remains on the same spot and starts to turn, once to the left, once to the right, and so on for half a minute or more. A sketch of the dance can be seen in the left-hand side of Fig. 8.1. This dance indicates to the other workers that food is nearby and the effect it has on them is described by Von Frisch (1950, p. 56): "During the dance

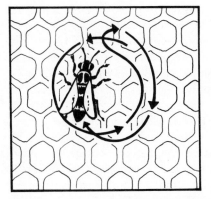 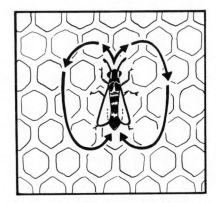

FIG. 8.1.   The round dance (left-hand side) and the waggle dance (right-hand side) of the honeybee (adapted from Von Frisch, 1974).

the bees near the dancer become greatly excited; they troop behind her as she circles keeping their antennae close to her body. Suddenly one of them turns away and leaves the hive. Others do likewise, and soon some of the bees appear at the feeding place".

When the food source is more than 100 m from the hive then the returning worker performs a *wagging* dance (see the right-hand side of Fig. 8.1). After running a short distance in a straight line while wagging the abdomen rapidly, the bee turns through 360° to the left, and in doing so returns to the start of the straight run. She then again runs in the same straight line, wagging her abdomen, but this time at the end of it turns to the right. By repeating this routine, the waggle dance creates a figure-of-eight pattern. The impressive feature of the wagging dance is that it tells the other workers both the direction and distance of the food. Distance is revealed by the rate at which the bee turns during the dance. This relationship is shown in Fig. 8.2, where it can be seen that the greater the distance of food from the hive, the fewer turns are incorporated into the dance in a given time. The graph was constructed from the observation of 3,885 dances performed after the bees had returned from food situated between 100 and 6000 m from the hive. Apparently these experiments were "rather strenuous and exciting" (Von Frisch, 1950, p. 73). More recent evidence suggests that additional information about the distance of food is provided by sounds emitted by the returning forager (Wenner, 1964).

The way in which the direction of food is indicated is particularly ingenious. The wagging dance is performed on the vertical surface of a comb, with the direction of the wagging run being at a constant angle to the vertical. This angle corresponds directly to the angle, at the hive, between

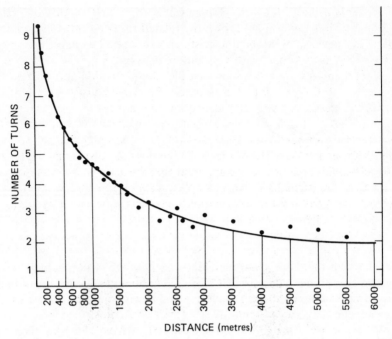

FIG. 8.2.   The relationship between the number of turns of the waggle dance and the distance of the feeding place (adapted from Von Frisch, 1950).

the direction of the food supply and the direction of the sun (see Fig. 8.3). Thus by observing the orientation of the waggle dance on the comb, the workers can calculate the direction they must fly from the hive, relative to the sun, in order to reach food.

The above examples constitute only a fraction of what is known about animal communication, yet they serve to demonstrate many of the characteristics of the way in which animals exchange information.

COMMUNICATION AND LANGUAGE

A Definition of Language

To determine the degree to which animal communication falls short of language, it is first essential to define what is meant by this term. Several authors have done this by listing a set of criteria that an act of communication must fulfill if it is to be regarded as language (Anderson, 1985; Hockett, 1960). Although this list is by no means exhaustive, it provides a useful framework for evaluating the linguistic skills of animals.

1. Arbitrariness of Units. Language is composed of discrete units, words, which in general are arbitrarily related to the events to which they refer. It is because of this characteristic that different languages are able to refer to the same object with very different words.

In certain cases, such as alarm calls, animal communication is also composed of discrete units; but in others the signal consists of a coherent unified pattern, as with the dance of the honeybee. As far as the arbitrariness of the signal is concerned, some instances of communication manifest this property, and some do not. Two examples that fail to meet this criterion are sketched in Fig. 8.4. The dogs are displaying aggression and submission, and it is quite apparent that the actions are related to the state they are signalling. An example of a more arbitrary relationship between a signal and the information it conveys is provided by Seyfarth,

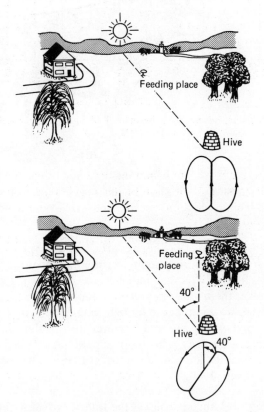

FIG. 8.3.   The way in which the waggle dance indicates the direction of a food source. The angle between the orientation of the dance and the vertical is the same as that between the sun and the food source, as measured at the entrance to the hive (adapted from Von Frisch, 1974).

FIG. 8.4. The postures of dogs displaying submission (top) and aggression (bottom) (adapted from Darwin, 1872).

Cheyney, and Marler (1980). They report that adult vervet monkeys give different alarm calls when they sight a python, a leopard, or an eagle. On hearing the "snake call", other members of the group look down, the "eagle call" makes them look up, and the "leopard call" results in fleeing to the trees. There is no good reason for believing that the precise form of the calls is determined by the nature of the predator—rather, it is more likely that the two are arbitrarily related. In support of this claim it has been found that infants must learn to some extent the significance of these calls (Seyfarth & Cheney, 1980).

2. Semanticity. Language allows the transfer of information from one person to another because every word has a specific meaning. We shall presume that a signal, for an animal, has meaning if it can activate a representation of the event to which it relates. Hence, for the vervet monkey, hearing any of the three alarm calls may excite a representation of a snake, eagle, or leopard, and this may then be responsible for the subsequent response. On the other hand, it is possible that the reception of these calls does nothing more than elicit a specific response, which is performed without the monkey knowing the nature of the predator it is avoiding. In this instance the signal is effective, but it would be unreasonable to assume that the monkey knows its meaning. Unfortunately this uncertainty in interpreting how signals are effective applies to the majority of communication between animals.

One possible exception to this generalisation is provided by the honeybee. It may be recalled from the previous chapter that Gould (1984) found that bees would leave the hive in the direction of food when the returning forager indicated that it was beside a lake, but they would not leave the hive when they were informed that food was near the middle of the lake. Such an outcome suggests that the forager's dance does not serve simply as a stimulus eliciting flight from the hive. Instead, honeybees appear to interpret the meaning of the dance—possibly by identifying the potential location of food on a cognitive map—and then decide whether it is worth making the journey.

3. Displacement.   Language allows people to communicate about events that are displaced either in time or in space. The bulk of animal communication lacks this property, because a signal is usually an immediate reaction to an internal state, such as an increase in certain hormones, or an external event, such as the sight of a predator. An obvious exception to this claim is the dance of the honeybee in which the precise form of the signal is governed by food that may be several kilometres from the hive.

4. Productivity.   A powerful property of language derives from the fact that it is structured according to rules of grammar, or syntax. By using these rules it is possible to construct an almost infinite number of sentences, each of which can convey a different meaning. The productivity criterion refers to this ability to create a large number of meaningful utterances from a limited vocabulary. Examples of animal communication that meet this requirement are scarce, but they do exist. The way in which Stellar's jay signals the intensity of aggression could be said to demonstrate productivity; so, too, could the way in which the honeybee waggle dance is able to convey information about an almost unlimited number of spatial locations. Nonetheless, in both these cases the range of information that can be transmitted is far more restricted than in human language. In these examples the animals are constrained to communicating about food and aggression. Their rules of production are not sufficiently sophisticated to permit them to converse about a wider range of topics. This may be slightly unfair to the honeybee. It has been discovered that they are also capable of communicating about the merits of potential sites for a new hive (McFarland, 1985, p. 416).

In addition, to my knowledge animal communication has never met the productivity criterion by combining discrete units, and this may be one characteristic that sets human language apart from the natural communication of every other animal. Where productivity is demonstrated by animals, it is always achieved by varying an attribute of the signal, such as its orientation or intensity.

5. Iteration and Recursion. For the sake of completion, brief mention should be made of these two properties of language. Essentially, they allow a sentence to be elaborated by the addition of phrases. Thus, "Alex is crying" can be extended to "Alex is crying because she fell over". There have been no reports of natural communication among animals demonstrating this capacity.

Language and Cooperation

There are good reasons therefore for believing that animal communication differs from human language in a number of ways that are important. But this does not necessarily mean that all animal communication is inferior to language. Much remains to be discovered about the way in which animals communicate, and it is possible that future research will reveal impressive capacities in this respect. Bottlenosed dolphins, for instance, are believed to communicate with whistles that are relatively short and vary considerably in frequency (Richards, Wolz, & Herman, 1984). Rather little is known about the function of these signals, and conceivably they may be manifestations of a system approximating language. We should thus acknowledge the possibility that some animal communication meets all the criteria of language, but this has yet to be revealed because of our inability to translate it.

This argument is extremely difficult to evaluate because it will remain possible until we have understood the way in which all species communicate. There may, however, be a simpler and reasonably effective way of testing it. An important feature of communication is that it allows animals to cooperate. If it could be shown, therefore, that animals can cooperate in complex ways, and that this depends upon communication, then we might conclude that the animals concerned possess something akin to language. Of course, there would still remain the task of understanding the communications that passed between the individuals, but at least we could be reasonably confident that our labours in this respect might reveal something of interest. There have been a few studies of cooperation between animals, both in the laboratory and in a more natural setting, but none has yet revealed clear evidence that animals possess language.

In 1972 the BBC transmitted a Horizon programme that demonstrated cooperation between a male and a female dolphin, possibly by means of an intelligent communication (details of this and related studies can be found in Bastian, 1966; and Wood, 1973, pp. 113–118). The two dolphins were situated in adjacent pools that allowed them to hear but not to see each other. Occasionally, the female was shown either a steady or an intermittent light, and the male was then required to press one of two paddles in order to earn reward for both of them. Presses on one paddle were rewarded when the steady light was shown to the female, otherwise pressing the other paddle led to reward. Despite being unable to see the light, the male eventually responded correctly on the majority of trials. That this success was accompanied by much chattering from the female, which differed in the presence of the two lights, suggests that it may have been achieved by a complex exchange of information between the dolphins.

A more recent study by Boakes and Gaertner (1977) using pigeons suggests, however, that this instance of cooperation might involve a rather simpler process. Two pigeons were trained in much the same way as the two dolphins, except that they were in adjacent conditioning chambers separated by a clear Perspex panel. A trial started with the illumination of a key, by either red or green light, which only one bird, the sender, could see; a screen prevented the other bird, the receiver, from seeing the key (see Fig. 8.5). At the same time two keys in the receiver's chamber were illuminated in white. Pecks to one key by the receiver delivered food to both pigeons when the sender's key was red, whereas if the sender's key was green, then food was presented after pecks by the receiver to the other key. Neither bird received food on any trial in which the receiver responded incorrectly. With practice the birds received food on most trials even though, it must be emphasised, the receiver could not see the colour projected onto the sender's key. To account for this success we must accept that the sender and receiver are cooperating to solve the problem. But in what way did the cooperation take place?

The explanation offered by Boakes and Gaertner (1977) for their findings is complex and difficult to present clearly. First, consider the experiment from the point of view of the receiver. A trial always began with the illumination of the two response keys, but there was no indication of which was the correct one to peck. When confronted with this sort of problem, animals sooner or later adopt a position preference of always pecking the same key. Such a preference will ensure that the receiver gains reward on 50% of the trials. Now consider the problem from the sender's point of view. At first, before the receiver has adopted a position preference, a light turns on either red or green, and sometimes it is followed by food and sometimes not. But as soon as the receiver develops a consistent position habit, one colour (say, red) will always be followed by food, and the other will never be paired with food. As a result, our knowledge of autoshaping predicts that the sender will approach and peck the key when it is red but not when it is green. Now return to the receiver. At this stage of the experiment, there are some trials when it will see the sender moving forwards, to a key that the receiver is unable to see, and pecking rapidly. These trials will be rewarded if the receiver retains its position preference. On other trials the sender will do very little, and if the receiver persists with its position preference, it will not be rewarded. The receiver is now being given sufficient information to solve the discrimination: On those trials when the sender is active, the preferred key must be pecked, whereas the other key must be pecked if the sender is relatively inactive.

Despite its complexity, this ingenious analysis gained considerable support from observations of the birds' behaviour throughout the experiment. Moreover, it is surely more plausible than accounts that assume that pigeons engage in intentional communication in order to cooperate in the above task. In the case of the dolphins, it is not clear

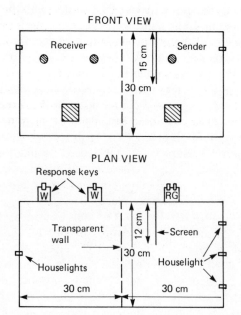

FIG. 8.5.   Front and plan views of two adjacent chambers used for communication between pigeons (from Boakes & Gaertner, 1977).

whether the male adopted a position preference during his training; but if he did, then the different sounds emitted by the female might be no more examples of intentional communication than were the sender pigeon's autoshaped keypecks. The female dolphin might have associated one stimulus with food and the other with none, and produced appropriate Pavlovian CRs accordingly. Until this possibility is discounted, we need look no further than the account offered by Boakes and Gaertner (1977) to explain the accurate behaviour of the dolphins.

The next study that might be cited as evidence of animals being sophisticated communicators was conducted in a relatively naturalistic setting. Menzel and Halperin (1975) housed a small group of chimpanzees beside an outdoor enclosure in cages that prevented them from seeing into the enclosure. One member of the group (a "leader") was then carried to a spot in the enclosure where it was shown some hidden food before being returned to its cage. A second "leader" was then treated similarly, except that it was shown a toy in a different location. After several minutes all the animals were released into the enclosure, and their activity was recorded. Chimpanzees enjoy playing with toys, but they have a much greater preference for food, and it is thus understandable that on most trials the majority of the group went first to the hidden food and then to the toy. As the location of each item was known by a single member of the group, the signals they transmitted must have informed the others of where the objects could be found and of their relative value. It is tempting to speculate that this information was transferred by means of a complex conversation, but this is unlikely, as the following quote reveals (Menzel & Halperin, 1975, p. 654):

> Usually each leader took a few steps toward the goal object that we had shown him (or her) earlier, and then stopped and looked back at the rest of the group. If the other leader was setting out or trying to recruit followers more vigorously than he (which usually occurred if the goal was a more highly preferred one), he often abandoned his own goal, accompanied the other leader, and then led the group to the second goal.

Thus it is nothing more than the vigour with which a leader moves towards a goal that indicates to the other members of the group what the goal might be. The conclusion to be drawn from the studies considered in this section therefore is that cooperation merely depends upon the behaviour of one animal serving as a stimulus that elicits a certain response from the other. There have been other studies of cooperation between animals (Epstein, Lanza, & Skinner, 1980; Lubinski & MacCorquodale, 1984; Savage-Rumbaugh, Rumbaugh, & Boysen, 1978), but there is little reason for believing that their results challenge this conclusion (Epstein et al., 1980).

CAN AN APE CREATE A SENTENCE?

The evidence reviewed thus far provides scant support for anyone wishing to claim that animals possess an intellectual skill akin to language. There remains, however, one line of enquiry to be considered before we can reach any firm conclusions about their linguistic abilities: This consists basically of teaching them an artificial language; although it may reveal little about the way they communicate naturally, such an approach should indicate the linguistic potential of the animals concerned. There is little doubt that animals can be taught certain features of a language, but there is much dispute as to where the limit of this ability lies. Indeed, the question posed as the title for this section, which is taken from an article by Terrace, Pettito, Sanders, and Bever (1979), captures very precisely a major theoretical issue that currently occupies this area of research.

During the present century there have been a number of attempts to teach language to all of the great apes: chimpanzee, orangutan, and gorilla. After a brief account of the methods that have been used and the results they have produced, we shall examine critically the conclusions that have been drawn from these studies.

Training Methods

One of the earliest attempts to teach an ape language was by William Furness (1916), and the rewards for his endeavours were slight. For many hours he attempted to teach a female orangutan to speak English, but she was able only to pronounce "papa", "cup", and "th". These were used as the trainer intended, and the ape is reported to have uttered the words "cup cup" shortly before dying of influenza. Some years later Hayes and Hayes (1951; Hayes, 1961) raised a chimpanzee, Vicki, as if she were a human child, but again despite careful training she was able to speak just four words: "mama", "papa", "cup", "up".

This virtual failure to teach apes to speak is due in part to the fact that their vocal tracts are incapable of producing all the sounds of human speech. Figure 8.6 shows the vocal tracts of a human and a chimpanzee. The structures between the lips and the larynx are of great importance in producing speech, and it is apparent that they differ greatly for the two species. This difference places a considerable limitation on the range of sounds that the chimpanzee can produce—for example the vowel sounds [a], [i], and [u] are said to be impossible for it to pronounce (Lieberman, 1975). Nevertheless, they should be able to articulate some speech sounds and acquire a rudimentary form of spoken language. Passingham (1982) has argued that their inability to do so rests with their failure to imitate the

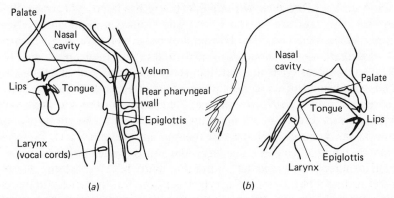

FIG. 8.6.   The adult vocal tract of a human (left-hand side) and a chimpanzee (right-hand side) (adapted from Lieberman, 1975).

speech that they hear. Why chimpanzees should differ so much from children in this respect has yet to be determined.

A possible means for overcoming this barrier to teaching apes a language is to use a medium for communication that does not involve speech. This was the strategy adopted by Gardner and Gardner (1969) who trained a chimpanzee, Washoe, to communicate with her hands in much the same way as deaf people do. In fact Washoe was taught Ameslan, which is the principal method for conversation among deaf people in North America. Just as spoken words can be broken down into one or more units—phonemes—so words in Ameslan are constructed from a combination of one or more gestures, cheremes. Each chereme consists of a configuration of the hands placed in a specific position and making a particular action. The words can then be combined to produce sentences by the use of grammatical rules, which differ to some extent from those governing English. Because it possesses these features, Ameslan meets all the requirements for language that were enumerated previously.

By using a variety of techniques, considerable success was achieved with Washoe. At the age of five, after four years of training, she was able to sign 132 different words, which included nouns ("sweet", "key"), pronouns ("me", "you"), and verbs ("tickle", "open"). She was also able to combine these words into strings of up to five in length and used them to give commands to her trainer: "you tickle me", "open key food" (an instruction to open the refrigerator). Washoe was capable of replying to questions posed by her trainer in Ameslan. Thus on one occasion her trainer asked her "What's that?" in the presence of a swan, and was told "Water bird". Following this pioneering work, there have been other attempts to teach apes Ameslan. The most systematic of these has been by Terrace (1979; see especially Terrace et al., 1979), who trained a chimpanzee, Neam Chimpsky—nicknamed Nim. During the course of his training he learned 125 different signs and was observed to combine them into more than 19,000 utterances. Throughout the study a record was kept of these combinations and of the context in which they occurred.

Premack's (1971, 1976) solution to the problem of the ape's reluctance to speak was to create an artificial language in which the words were plastic objects, which varied in shape, size, colour, and texture. Sarah, Premack's brightest chimpanzee, became proficient in the use of about 130 words; these included nouns ("Sarah", "apple", "knife"), verbs ("wash", "draw", "give"), adjectives ("brown"), quantifiers ("all", "none"), conditionals ("if", "then"), etc. To create a sentence, the words, which had a metal backing, could be placed in a vertical column on a magnetic board (see Fig. 8.7). In order for the sentences to be acceptable, the words had to be placed in a grammatically correct sequence.

On some occasions words were placed on the table beside the magnetic board, and the chimpanzee was expected to construct a sentence. If it was correct, then the trainer would place a word representing "correct" on the board, praise the subject verbally, and perhaps give her a jelly bean or similar reward. On trials when the sentence was wrong, an "incorrect"

FIG. 8.7.   One of the chimpanzees, Elizabeth, trained by Premack. The message on the board says, "Elizabeth give apple Amy" (adapted from Premack, 1976).

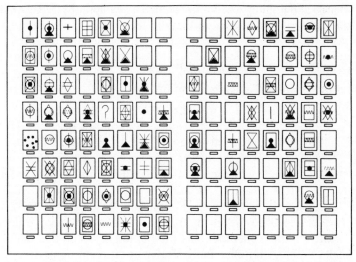

FIG. 8.8. The arrangement of lexigrams on a keyboard. Blank spaces were nonfunctioning keys, or displayed photographs of trainers (from Savage-Rumbaugh et al., 1983).

token was placed on the board, and the trainer might say "No, you dummy".

At other times the trainer placed a sentence on the board, and if it was an instruction the subject was supposed to obey it—for example, "Sarah give Mary apple". The sentence could also take the form of a question. Two coloured cards might be placed one on top of the other, on the table, and a sentence on the board would ask "? red on green" (is red on green?). The subject was then required to reply by placing a token for either "yes" or "no" on the board.

Premack's technique has been developed a step further, in a project supervised by Rumbaugh (1977), in which the symbols serving as words—or lexigrams, as they were called—were displayed on a keyboard connected to a computer. Pressing a key resulted in its symbol being projected onto a screen above the console. To create a sentence, the chimpanzee, originally Lana, had to press a sequence of keys that resulted in the display of a string of lexigrams. The sentence had to be structured according to a set of grammatical rules, known as Yerkish, which are not too dissimilar to those governing English. Hence, in order to receive a drink, Lana had to press the lexigrams for "Please machine give juice", in that sequence. Figure 8.8 shows a selection of lexigrams as they are typically arranged on a keyboard. The purpose of the computer was to keep a record of Lana's statements and to dispense films, slides, music, food, sweets, and liquids, when requested. The computer screen could also be used to present instructions to Lana in lexigrams.

Assessment of Language Training with Apes

Discreteness and Displacement

Of the various criteria that were listed as requisites for language, there are good demonstrations both of displacement and of discreteness being met by apes using an unnatural system of communication. Discreteness is revealed by the use of specific gestures or symbols to represent words, and displacement is revealed by conversations involving objects that are not in view. An excellent example of such a conversation is provided by Savage-Rumbaugh, Pate, Lawson, Smith, and Rosenbaum (1983). They tested two chimpanzees, Austin and Sherman, who were trained to communicate with an experimenter by a method based on that devised by Rumbaugh (1977). After examining a table of different items of food, the chimpanzee had to walk around a partition to a keyboard, from where the food could not be seen. He then had to request one of the items and wait for permission from the trainer to collect it. Once permission had been granted the chimpanzee returned to the table, picked up the specified food, and took it to the trainer, where it was shared. By requesting food that was out of sight, the subject is clearly communicating about a spatially displaced object.

Semanticity

Considerable effort has been expended in establishing whether or not apes know the meaning of the words they use. It would be as well to establish at the outset, therefore, what precisely is implied when we say that a word means, or symbolises, something else. In the discussion of natural communication by animals it was proposed that a signal has meaning if it excites a representation of the event to which it relates. There seems to be no good reason why this should not also apply to the gestures and symbols used in the artificial languages taught to apes. Thus when it is claimed that Washoe knows the meaning of the sign for "apple", then it is implied that the sign, when performed either by Washoe or her trainer, can activate a representation of apple for her. Perhaps at this point it is worth drawing attention to the fact that this capacity is not beyond the laboratory rat. An experiment by Holland and Straub (1979) was cited in Chapter 4 in which a noise signalled the delivery of food, and it was clearly demonstrated that the noise by itself could activate a representation of the food.

Given that rats are capable of learning what a tone "means", it might be anticipated that apes should experience little difficulty in understanding the meaning of the signs used for their training. However, as Savage-Rumbaugh et al. (1983; Savage-Rumbaugh, 1984) have argued, in at least some cases the training of the apes has been such as to minimise the likelihood of them learning the meaning of their signs. Consider one aspect of Sarah's training. She would be seated at her table in the presence of a banana, and if she wrote the sentence "Mary give Sarah banana", the symbol for correct was placed on the board, followed by praise and perhaps something like a jelly baby (Premack, 1976, pp. 26). On other trials an apple might be visible, and she would have to request this fruit in order to be given much the same rewards. Thus the effect of this training might be to make the meaning of the symbols for apple and banana ambiguous, as they were each paired with a variety of rewards. This problem is not unique to Sarah's training. To teach Lana the word "banana", she was given a tray with a slice of banana on it. Using the appropriate lexigrams, the experimenter then constructed the sentence "?What name of this". If she then replied correctly "Banana name of this" she could request from the computer any reward she wanted, including banana. This training might have taught her the meaning of the word banana; it is just as likely, however, that she learned to press a certain lexigram in the presence of a banana as an instrumental response that led to reward. There is reasonable support for this interpretation. Savage-Rumbaugh et al. (1983) report that if a chimpanzee is trained in the above manner and then confronted with a table covered with different foods, it will say something like "banana, lollipop, apple, sweet, me, apple, gimme, lollipop". They argue that this chaotic statement indicates that chimpanzees have not learned the meaning of the words they are using. Instead, they have merely learned to press lexigrams as instrumental responses for gaining reward.

It seems that this analysis may also apply to Nim's use of words (Savage-Rumbaugh, 1984). He was quite capable of signing correctly "apple" or "banana" when these fruits were presented one at a time, but when they were given together he was unable to respond correctly if requested to give the trainer an apple. This confusion would not be expected if he understood the meaning of the words he used.

Despite these and other findings (see for example Savage-Rumbaugh et al., 1983, pp. 473–474), there is clear evidence that chimpanzees learn the meaning of at least some of their words. A simple demonstration is provided by Sarah, whose training with the word "brown" consisted solely of being told that "Brown colour of chocolate" in the absence of any chocolate. When she was then given four disks of different colours, she responded correctly to the command "Take brown" (Premack, 1976, p. 353). Unless the symbol for chocolate was capable of activating a representation of chocolate, she would not know to which colour the word brown referred.

A more complicated experiment, which demonstrates that Austin and Sherman had understood the meaning of certain nouns, is reported by Savage-Rumbaugh, Rumbaugh, Smith, and Lawson (1980). The chimpanzees were separately given a mixed collection of foods and tools and required to sort them into two trays according to these categories. The experiment then progressed through a number of additional training stages, each with its own test trials, which were conducted with novel objects. For the second stage, the experimenter held up an object, and the subject had to identify it by pressing the appropriate category key on the computer console. For the third stage the experimenter held up a photograph, and for the fourth a lexigram, and again the chimpanzees had to press a key on the console to categorise the objects that they represented.

Even with this last stage of the experiment both Sherman and Austin performed with a very high level of accuracy on the test trials. Savage-Rumbaugh et al. (1980) maintain that this performance can best be explained by assuming that the lexigrams excited a representation of the objects to which they related. The information that was then made available by this representation would be sufficient to enable the lexigram to be categorised correctly. Note that the relationship between the lexigrams and the objects was quite arbitrary. It was therefore impossible to identify the category to which the lexigram belonged by reference only to its physical attributes.

An interesting feature of this experiment is that when it was conducted with Lana she was unable to progress beyond the first stage, which again suggests that she did not know the meaning of the lexigrams she used. To understand the success of Austin and Sherman, it is necessary to point out that they were trained in a rather different manner to Lana. To teach them the meaning of a new lexigram for food they were shown a collection of foods, and the use of the symbol would allow them to have access to the food to which it related. Consequently, responding with the symbol could not be regarded as a means for acquiring any reward; instead, its use was always followed by the same, unique reward. Savage-Rumbaugh et al. (1983) regard this training as being much better suited to teaching the meaning of symbols, and the evident competence of Austin and Sherman in the above task supports them in this respect. Perhaps a simpler method for endowing symbols with meaning would be to employ Pavlovian conditioning. The symbol could be presented to the subject, followed a short while later by the object to which it refers. To my knowledge this technique has never been attempted with apes, but its success with rats suggests that it is worth a try.

Productivity

Very often the meaning of a sentence is not just governed by the words it contains; the order in which they occur is also very important. "Jessica hit Tim" is thus completely different in meaning to "Tim hit Jessica", even though both sentences contain the same words. This is possible because all sentences are constructed according to grammatical rules. Not only do these rules constrain the way a sentence can be constructed or interpreted, they also enable a speaker to create an almost unlimited number of meaningful statements from a finite vocabulary. Given the importance of grammar to language, it is understandable that a considerable amount of interest has been directed at the issue of whether or not apes can master these rules. In the following discussion their ability in this area will be considered separately for language comprehension and production.

Comprehension. For some of her training Sarah was required to respond on the basis of information provided in the following form of sentence: "Debby give apple Mary ⊃ Sarah insert cracker dish", which is an instruction for Sarah to put a biscuit in a dish if Debby gives Mary an apple. After training with a variety of such sentences, she responded to them correctly, even when novel. Because of the statement's complexity, her success might be taken as evidence that she had used grammatical rules to decode it. Premack (1976) points out, however, that instead of understanding the sentence, Sarah's training could have taught her an alternative means for solving this problem. In all the sentences of this sort that she was given, the first part was always true; in the above example Debby, as a matter of course, gave Mary the apple. Thus, to receive reward, it was only necessary for Sarah to fulfill the command in the second half, and there was no reason for her even to look at the first half. A better test of Sarah's linguistic abilities would have been to examine her response on probe trials in which the "if" condition was not true. Regrettably, as is so often the case with good ideas, this one did not occur to Premack (1976) until it was too late to test it.

Even in the absence of this test it might be said that Sarah understood grammatical rules, because in the above example she did put the biscuit in the dish. But Sarah had received extensive training with instructions such as "Sarah insert cracker dish", and she may simply have learned to perform the appropriate action in the presence of a certain configuration of shapes in order to gain reward.

It is impossible to analyse here the training behind all the sentences that have been given to apes. Suffice it to say that, as far as comprehension is concerned, those sentences that have been claimed to reveal the use of grammatical rules by apes are generally open to alternative explanation (Ristau & Robbins, 1982). As a consequence, we must conclude that, as yet, there is no compelling reason for believing that apes can use rules of grammar to understand a sentence.

Production.   While being rowed across a pond by Fouts (1975), her trainer, Washoe was shown a swan and asked "what that?" Despite never having been taught the phrase, she replied "Water bird". On another occasion, Washoe's trainer Susan Nichols placed a doll in a cup and asked the ape to sign about it. Washoe's reply is quite impressive: "Baby in my drink".

These constitute but two of many examples where an ape has provided a novel utterance that is appropriate to the situation in which it occurred. Moreover, as they consist of a string of words that, for English, are correctly structured, it seems as if Washoe can use grammatical rules to produce sentences. Or does it? Terrace et al. (1979) have argued that they do not justify any sophisticated claims about the linguistic ability of apes.

As far as the water-bird example is concerned, it is not inconceivable that Washoe was replying to the question by identifying, first, a body of water and, second, a bird. "Before concluding that Washoe was relating the sign *water* to the sign *bird,* one must know whether she regularly placed an adjective (*water*) before, or after, a noun (*bird*). That cannot be decided on the basis of a single anecdote, no matter how compelling the anecdote may seem to an English speaking observer" (Terrace et al., 1979, pp. 895–896). On examining a film of the "Baby in my drink" incident, Terrace et al. (1979, p. 898) discovered that, perhaps unwittingly, Susan Nichols pointed first to the doll and then to the cup before Washoe started her reply. This information, rather than rules of grammar, was possibly responsible for the way in which Washoe structured her answer.

Lieberman (1984, pp. 240–241) has suggested that these arguments of Terrace et al. (1979) are unduly harsh. He also cites several other examples of novel utterances by chimpanzees, which, he maintains, are harder to discount as examples of rule-governed sequences: "smell fruits" (citrus fruits), "hurt fruit" (a radish), and "drink fruit" (a watermelon). But once again, although these examples are consistent with a rule such as "adjective before noun", they do not confirm that the chimpanzee was using a rule to generate them. These phrases may have occurred equally often in the reverse order, which would not be expected from a grammatical chimpanzee. I am not sure how seriously this possibility should be taken. It is offered merely to show the difficulty there is in forming conclusions about the grammatical skills of animals when isolated examples are drawn from a large body of multi-word utterances.

In addition to analysing the utterances of apes trained by other researchers, Terrace et al. (1979) also conducted a thorough examination of the strings of words produced by Nim. In total, over an 18-month period, Nim signed 19,203 multi-word utterances, of which there were 5,235 different types. Despite this number and variety, the experimenters were unable to conclude that these statements were structured according to a set of rules.

One problem was posed by the limited variety of certain classes of utterance. For example, when the word "more" was used in a two-word utterance, it consistently occupied the first position. Unfortunately, Nim knew no other words to express recurrence, and it is therefore impossible to determine whether this particular pattern reflects a grammatical rule or, more fundamentally, a habit of starting statements with "more". Another difficulty is that Nim often copied the signs of the trainer. He may thus have created grammatically correct sequences by cheating.

It is also instructive to compare the multi-word utterances of Nim with those of children. The term "mean length of utterance" (mlu) refers to the average length of all multi-word utterances made by an individual. It is apparent from Fig. 8.9 that for a normal child, as well as for one that is deaf and using Ameslan, there is a sharp increase of mlu with age. In stark contrast, Nim's mlu was maintained at much the same value of about 1.5 throughout his training. If Nim had mastered the rules of grammar, then they would have allowed him to produce increasingly longer sentences. A further difference between Nim and children is that for the latter a long utterance is more informative than a short one. Thus "Sit Daddy" might be elaborated to "Sit Daddy chair". This was very rarely true for Nim, who generated long utterances principally by repeating words. The following utterance by Nim makes it hard to believe that he was grammatical in his use of language: "Give orange me give eat orange me eat orange give me eat orange give me you" (from Terrace et al., 1979, p. 895).

Despite these arguments, there is no doubt that apes can produce reliably statements that are grammatically correct. Sarah would consistently write sentences of the form "Give Sarah grape" to indicate that she was to receive, and not give, a grape. But it remains to be determined whether or not these reflect a mastery of syntactic rules. Instead of using rules, an alternative strategy would be for Sarah to remember each of the strings of symbols that had previously led to reward, and the situations in

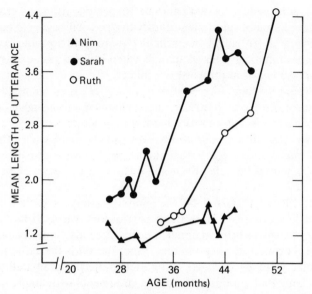

FIG. 8.9.   The change in the mean length of utterance with age for a normal child, Sarah, a deaf child, Ruth, and Nim (adapted from Terrace et al., 1979).

which they were effective. In other words, the sight of a grape might have served as a discriminative stimulus controlling the response of placing a number of shapes in a fixed sequence.

The principal conclusion to be drawn from this evaluation of the ape language studies is that, as yet, there is no clear evidence that an ape can create a sentence (see also Ristau & Robbins, 1982). But it would be foolish to assume without reservation that apes will never conquer this apparent barrier between the intelligence of humans and animals. The work of Savage-Rumbaugh (1984) and her colleagues (Savage-Rumbaugh et al., 1980; Savage-Rumbaugh et al., 1983) with Austin and Sherman makes it plain that the method of language training plays a critical role in determining the linguistic skills of apes. Perhaps we still have to discover the correct techniques for teaching them how to construct a sentence. In addition, because of the detailed way in which the study was conducted and analysed, it is natural to place considerable emphasis on Nim's failure to acquire grammatical skills. A word of caution, however, is required when interpreting the performance of this subject. Undoubtedly the intellectual abilities of the individual chimpanzees vary, as they do for humans. Nim may not have been an especially gifted subject, and it would be unwise to regard his results as representative of chimpanzees in general. To support this point, it is noteworthy that Nim had a succession of trainers, which resulted in his repeatedly forming and then breaking close attachments. The influence of these emotional disturbances on his intellectual development is difficult to assess (see Lieberman, 1984, pp. 244–246).

LANGUAGE TRAINING WITH OTHER SPECIES

Attemps to teach language to animals have not been confined to the apes. This training has also been conducted with other species, notably a parrot and dolphins. In this section the methods employed for this research, and the results it has revealed, are briefly examined.

A Parrot

Parrots are famous for their capacity to mimic human speech, although normally they say only a few words. In a series of articles Pepperberg (1981, 1983, in press), has shown that they can, in fact, acquire a relatively large vocabulary of spoken words, which can be combined to form meaningful multi-word utterances. Her single subject is an African grey parrot, Alex, who was tutored in English. He was trained first to speak the names of objects (e.g. "paper", "key", "grain", "chair", "back", "gym"). Of some interest is the fact that the manner in which correct responses were rewarded differed from that used in the majority of studies with apes. Whenever Alex named an object, he was praised and then allowed to eat it or to play with it. The method of training is also of interest. Alex would be in a position that allowed him to see two trainers. One trainer then asked the other, who adopted the role of a parrot, to name an object; if the trainer's reply was correct, then he or she was praised and expected to play with it. Merely as a result of watching these interactions, Alex soon entered into the proceedings, as the following extract from a typical session shows. *I* and *B* refer to Irene Pepperberg and a trainer, Bruce Rosen; *A* is Alex, the parrot (after Pepperberg, 1981).

I: Bruce, what's this?
B: Pasta. (loudly)
A: (interrupting) ah-ah.
B: Do you want this, Alex? What is it?
A: Pah-ah.
B: Better . . .
A: Pah-ah.
B: No. Irene, what's this?
I: Pah-ah.

B: Better!

I: Pas-ta. (emphasising the "s" and "t")

B: That's right, tell me what it is again. (offers pasta)

I: Pasta! (takes pasta) Pasta! (Alex stretches from his perch on top of the cage, appears to reach for pasta)

A: Pa!

I: Better . . . what is it?

A: Pah-ah.

I: Better!

A: Pah-ta.

I: Okay, here's the pasta. Good try.

Training in this manner soon became more elaborate, so that Alex's speech eventually included colours, shapes, and numbers, which were often combined with object names. Thus when shown a piece of computer paper for the first time, he was able to identify it as "Four-corner paper". On other trials an object such as a blue triangle might be presented accompanied by the question "What colour?" or "What shape?" His answers were correct with an accuracy that was far in excess of that predicted by chance. These findings are particularly impressive when it is appreciated that Lana was unable to respond correctly on this sort of problem (Savage-Rumbaugh et al., 1983).

Intriguing as these findings may be, they do not show that Alex was capable of understanding or creating sentences. As an alternative, his sentences may have been the product of rote learning sequences of sounds that were produced in the presence of the appropriate discriminative stimuli. Evidence that Alex's linguistic skills might extend beyond this interpretation comes from his use of the phrase "Wanna go". When his training started Alex was unhappy in novel places and consequently spent most of the time in his cage or his gym, a collection of rods and ropes. When in his cage he was often asked "Wanna go gym?" and this frequently produced a squeaky "yeah" in reply. After a while he spontaneously uttered the phrase "Wanna go gym" and was immediately carried to it. He even modified this phrase to "Wanna go gym–no" when he was in the gym and appeared to want to leave it (as indicated by stretching towards something else).

As he gained in confidence Alex would sit on chairs, shelves, and a trainer's knee. During this time he often heard the names of these perches, but care was taken to ensure that he never heard them in conjunction with the phrase "Wanna go". Despite this constraint, Alex started to say phrases like "Wanna go chair". And if he was taken to a different place he responded either with a "No" or with a repeat of the request.

These findings indicate that Alex is capable of generating novel, meaningful, multi-word utterances (although it is arguable that "wanna go" should be regarded as a single word). Unfortunately the limited number of these utterances makes it difficult to be sure of their origins. They may have been the production of a primitive grammar that contains a rule of the form: "Wanna go" is followed by an object. Alternatively, they may have been produced by chance and strengthened because of the reward that followed.

Dolphins

Herman, Richards, and Wolz (1984) have presented a carefully documented report of an investigation into the linguistic ability of two dolphins. But it must be noted that whereas the training for apes, as well as that for Alex, involved both the comprehension and the production of sentences, only the former was tested with the dolphins.

Herman et al. (1984) trained two bottlenosed dolphins, Akeakamai and Phoenix, to behave in specific ways according to sequences of signals. For Akeakamai the signals were gestures performed by a person standing by the pool in which the dolphins were tested (see Fig. 8.10). The signals for

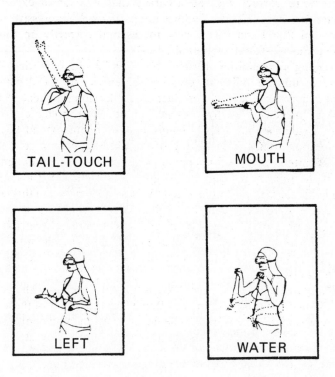

FIG. 8.10. Examples of some of the gestural signs used for the sentence comprehension studies with a dolphin, Akeakamai (adapted from Herman et al., 1984).

TABLE 8.1
The Comprehension Vocabulary of a Dolphin, Akeakamai

Objects

window	net	basket	person
speaker	ball	pipe	frisbee
water	hoop	fish	surfboard
phoenix			

Actions

tail-touch	(go) through
pectoral touch	spit (squirt water from mouth at object)
mouth (grasp with mouth)	fetch (take one named object to another named object)
(go) over	in (place one named object in or on another named object)
(go) under	toss (throw object)

Agent

Akeakamai (prefix for each sentence)

Modifiers

left	right

Other

no	yes	erase

Source: After Herman et al. (1984).

Phoenix were short discrete noises generated by a computer. The training for the two animals differed in a number of other respects, and for the sake of brevity the account that follows concentrates on Akeakamai's treatment and results.

Table 8.1 shows the words that Akeakamai responded to correctly. The list includes objects, actions, agents, and modifiers. After preliminary training, she was instructed in the comprehension of two-word sentences. Examples of these and the longer sentences that were eventually used can be seen in Table 8.2 together with the rules of the artificial syntax that governed their construction. The table also includes a translation of the sentences. Thus two-word sentences were structured according to the rule of object before action, which means that "Phoenix over" is an instruction for Akeakamai to jump over Phoenix. On the most recent test reported, Akeakamai responded correctly to 85% of the possible sentences that can be constructed from this language.

One enormous advantage of this type of training is that it is possible to conduct test trials that provide unambiguous results. For example, during the course of her training Akeakamai was tested with 193 novel sentences when all the objects mentioned in Table 8.1 were in the pool. The objects thus provided no clue as to how she should respond, yet her performance on these trials was very much more accurate than would be expected on the basis of chance. The most plausible explanation for this outcome is that she had understood the rules that structured the artificial language and could use them to interpret novel sequences of signals. Support for this important conclusion can be found in other aspects of Akeakamai's performance.

After experiencing many two- and three-word sentences, Akeakamai was suddenly given one containing four words, and she responded correctly. The implication of this finding is that she was able to use the rules relevant to the shorter sentences to understand a more complex syntactic structure. This is precisely the sort of skill that should be demonstrated by an animal that is grammatically competent.

The sample of sentences in Table 8.2 makes it apparent that in some cases their meaning is very much dependent on word order. Although composed of the same signals, the string "Pipe hoop fetch" is a very different instruction to "Hoop pipe fetch". Despite this added complexity Akeakamai was able to react appropriately when given a novel sentence of this sort. In fact, the likelihood of responding correctly was the same as for

TABLE 8.2
The Rules of Syntax for the Gestural Language
for a Dolphin, Akeakamai

Rule	*Examples*
2-word	
Object + Action	Basket toss (Throw the basket)
	Window tail-touch (Touch a window in the tank with your tail)
3-word	
Modifier + Object + Action	Left person mouth (Touch the person on your left with your mouth)
IO + DO + Action	Pipe hoop fetch (take the hoop to the pipe)
	Hoop pipe fetch (take the pipe to the hoop)
4-word	
IO + Modifier + DO + Action	Ball right frisbee fetch (Take the frisbee on your right to the ball)
Modifier + IO + DO + Action	Right basket pipe fetch (Take the pipe to the basket on your right)

IO = Indirect object.
DO = Direct object.
Source: After Herman et al. (1984).

equivalent sentences with which she was familiar. Once again, such an outcome strongly suggests that she understood the grammatical rules of her language.

The dolphins also demonstrated that they were able to meet some of the other requirements of a linguistic ability. Mastery of the displacement criterion was revealed on numerous occasions. On some trials the instruction related to an object that was hidden from view (spatial displacement), and the dolphin had to find it before responding. On other trials the command was issued as much as 30 sec before the objects to which it related were thrown into the pool (temporal displacement). Neither of these variants caused much difficulty. A rather different version of this type of test consisted of placing all the objects but one in the pool and then giving a two-word sentence that related to the missing object. Akeakamai would often search for up to nearly a minute for the missing item and then stop, without responding to the other objects. She also rapidly learned to press a paddle to indicate that the designated item was missing.

The way in which dolphins are able to react to sophisticated commands is most impressive and suggests at least a rudimentary understanding of grammatical rules, but some caution is needed when drawing conclusions from this study. As a component of language, production is certainly of equal importance to comprehension and, as yet, there is no evidence that dolphins can produce even the simplest sentence. The study by Herman et al. (1984) suggests that further attempts at language training with dolphins are worthwhile, but the eventual outcome of this research remains uncertain.

THE REQUIREMENTS FOR LEARNING A LANGUAGE

Language Acquisition Device

From the point of view advocated by Chomsky (1972), the reason for the absence of a clear demonstration of linguistic competence by animals is quite simple. The languages of the world share a striking similarity in the way in which their grammars operate. This suggested to Chomsky (1972) that humans possess an innate device for generating a "universal grammar", from which the grammars of these languages are derived. As apes and other animals do not naturally use language, it would be reasonable to conclude that they do not possess such a device, and this would explain their limitations in sentence construction. Macphail (1982) has also argued that language is a uniquely human phenomenon, but for reasons that are rather different from those of Chomsky (1972). After considering much of the evidence summarised previously, he concluded: "humans acquire language (and non-humans do not) not because humans are (quantitatively) more intelligent, but because humans possess some species-specific mechanism (or mechanisms) which is a prerequisite of language-acquisition" (p. 312).

Attractive as these arguments may be, it may be too early to accept them without reservation. Currently very little is known about the properties of the device that is said to provide humans with their universal grammar. We should, therefore, be cautious in accepting the existence of such a device until we know what it is and how it operates. Furthermore, Chomsky's (1972) proposals have not gone unchallenged. Anderson (1985), for example, maintains that there are constraints on the way in which our cognitive processes operate, and these, in turn, are responsible for the structure of language. Thus it is natural to think of the subject of an action before considering the object, and this constraint may explain why, for three-word sentences, the majority of the world's languages place the subject before the object (Greenberg, 1963). If there are grounds for doubting the existence of a specific language acquisition device, then we should also doubt the claim that its absence is the reason for the inability of apes to produce a sentence.

A further troublesome feature of the views of Chomsky (1972) and Macphail (1982) is the implication that certain, possibly complex, biological structures governing language acquisition are unique to humans. On the basis of evolutionary considerations, this is most unlikely. It is beyond question that some species possess characteristics that are absent in others, but, to my knowledge, there is not a single species that possesses a complex characteristic, such as a language acquisition device, which has nothing in common with the characteristics of other species. Instead, it appears to be the rule that a number of species manifest the same characteristic, but to varying degrees. The possession of a language acquisition device by humans may be the exception to this rule; however, until there is very good reason for believing this to be so, such a claim should be regarded cautiously.

One final point: Even if humans are unique in possessing a language acquisition device, it does not necessarily follow that non-humans will be forever doomed to being incompetent linguistically. They may, given the appropriate training, acquire rudimentary skills in this respect.

Motivation

The claim that humans possess an innate language acquisition device is not, therefore, wholly justifiable, and even if it were, it is not obvious that in its absence animals would be incapable of learning a language. There may, however, be another barrier that restricts animals in their use of language: They may simply be unwilling to communicate with humans—that is, their linguistic shortcomings may be due to a motivational rather than intellectual deficit.

There can be little doubt that young children are extremely willing communicators. In the early stages of language development, they frequently point to objects and name them without any prompting (Locke, 1980). At a later stage they will often initiate a conversation that bears no relevance to what has just been said. Apes, in contrast, have shown themselves to be much more reluctant to engage in spontaneous acts of communication. Hence, rather than to start a conversation, a high proportion of Nim's utterances were imitations of the trainer's previous signs, which is relatively rare in children (Terrace, 1979). Acts of spontaneous pointing and naming are also reported to be uncommon for many language-trained apes (Savage-Rumbaugh, 1984).

Despite what has just been said, there are a number of reports that suggest that apes, given the appropriate circumstances, may well engage spontaneously in communication. The clearest of these concerns Austin and Sherman. Some time after they had taken part in the categorisation experiment described previously, they began to name objects without being asked to do so. Thus one of the apes would name an object on the keyboard—for instance, "blanket"—and then point to it or give it to the trainer. This behaviour was not specifically trained but, maintains Savage-Rumbaugh (1984), was a consequence of the unique type of language training they had received. On this basis, then, it is likely that an unwillingness to communicate will not prove an impenetrable barrier for training apes to use language.

Some observations by Gardner and Gardner (1974) are also consistent with this interpretation. They noticed that Washoe often signed to herself in play, or when looking through a book. "Washoe also signed to herself about her ongoing or impending actions. We have often seen Washoe moving stealthily to a forbidden part of the yard, signing *quiet* to herself" (Gardner & Gardner, 1974, p. 20).

More recently, Savage-Rumbaugh, McDonald, Sevcik, Hopkins, and Rubert (1986) have reported some preliminary findings from a study with a male—Kanzi—and a female—Mulika—Pygmy Chimpanzee. These chimpanzees are a different species from those that are normally studied and are reputed to be much brighter. Of interest to the present discussion is the finding that once he had been trained to use lexigrams, the majority of Kanzi's multi-word utterances were spontaneous. Again, this confirms that at least some apes are willing communicators. And on the basis of the slender evidence that is available, it appears that Alex the parrot will also communicate spontaneously.

Thought

Language and thought are intimately related. Without the capacity to think, people would have little need for a language, as they would not have any ideas to communicate; and without certain mental processes we would be unable to produce grammatically correct sentences that are comprehensible by others. Ultimately, therefore, the constraints upon language use by animals may be imposed by the limitations of their thought processes. Discussions of the nature of animal thought are rare, principally because so little is known about them. It is, however, possible to identify some thought processes that are essential for language and to ask whether they are possessed by animals.

Sentence Production.   Turning first to sentence production, two aspects of thought would seem to be essential. The language user must be able to construct sentences according to certain rules. For example, to express the idea in three words that "Tim likes Alex", it is necessary to know that the subject of an English sentence precedes the verb, which, in turn, comes before the object. The construction of a sentence also requires that the user is capable of forming categories. Unless certain types of events can be identified as subject, object, and so forth, it is impossible to place the words in the right order.

We have already seen from the language training studies with apes that they can produce gramatically correct sequences of symbols, but there is little evidence to suggest they were constructed according to a set of rules. One much simpler process for producing these sequences can be expressed in terms of S–R theory. Suppose that an animal is required to pick up three shapes (A, B, and C) from a table one at a time and place them in the correct sequence on a board for reward. If the animal has received extensive training with this problem, then the sight of all three shapes on the table might serve as the discriminative stimulus for the response of picking up A and placing it on the board. The sight of A on the board could then serve as the discriminative stimulus for picking up B, and so on. Thus by assuming that animals can form chains of S–R connections it is possible to understand how, in certain circumstances, they can correctly order a sequence of symbols. But this is insufficient for language, because it would not allow the user to create novel meaningful utterances. For this to be achieved the animal must possess the skill of being able to apply rules.

Surprisingly, some of the clearest evidence that animals can produce sequences by using rules, albeit simple ones, comes from pigeons. In Chapter 7 a study by Straub and Terrace (1981) is mentioned in which pigeons learned to peck a matrix of four simultaneously illuminated keys (of colours A, B, C, and D) in a particular sequence for reward. According to an S–R chaining analysis the sight of all four keys might serve as the discriminative stimulus for pecking A, and the sensory feedback from making this response, and all future responses, could then function as the discriminative stimulus for pecking the next member of the series. Where this account runs into difficulty is with explaining the results from test trials in which only two or three of the keys were illuminated simultaneously. Assume that pigeons are presented for the first time with the colours A, C, and D. The sight of A might elicit a peck towards it, and the consequent sensations might elicit a tendency to peck B; but in the absence of this stimulus there will be nothing to guide the pigeon towards the selection of C rather than D, and the choice between them should be random. According to Straub and Terrace (1981), the best explanation for the success of their pigeons on these tests is one that assumes that pigeons can use rules of the form "Peck A first" or "Peck D last". Once these have been learned, they should allow accurate performance with an incomplete matrix of illuminated keys.

Animals may therefore be able to use rules to construct sequences, but this skill will be of little use for language if the object of each rule is a specific item. What is necessary is for animals to be able to formulate rules about categories, so that they can be applied to all members of that category.

In Chapter 2 several studies indicating that pigeons can form categories are cited (e.g. Herrnstein, 1984). For example, once a pigeon has been trained to peck a key whenever it sees a picture of water, then it will do so even in the presence of an unfamiliar picture of water. In general, the categories that have been studied are of objects that share common physical attributes—trees, a particular person, etc.—and this may be insufficient for language. The rules of grammar require that the categories are more abstract, so that events can be classified as subject or object, for example.

Studies of learning set formation suggest that animals may be able to categorise stimuli on a basis other than their physical attributes. In Chapter 7 it is suggested that learning set formation depends upon subjects classifying objects on the grounds that they were either selected or rejected on the previous trial. Here, then, is a suggestion that animals can categorise stimuli, not just by their physical attributes, but by the way they have treated them in the past.

A more impressive demonstration of category learning is possibly provided by the Savage-Rumbaugh et al. (1980) study considered earlier in this chapter. They trained Austin and Sherman to identify whether objects were food or tools, and one interpretation of the chimpanzees' success on this task is that they were able to form categories according to the rather abstract notion of an object's function. There is, however, an alternative explanation for Austin and Sherman's performance. Conceivably the sight of food, or a lexigram for food, elicited a response such as salivation. As with learning sets, therefore, the objects could be categorised on the basis of whether they were associated with a specific response, rather than on the basis of more abstract principles. The evidence that animals can form abstract categories is thus better described as encouraging rather than convincing. But even if animals can form abstract categories, this skill would only be of help in producing sentences if the category could be incorporated into a rule that generated a grammatically correct sequence. Whether animals possess this capacity remains to be discovered.

The Representation of Knowledge.   We can now turn to the question of whether animals are capable of representing ideas that merit communication by language. All transitive sentences convey information about the relationship between a subject and an object—for instance "Alex likes Tim". The same can also be said for intransitive sentences, except that here the relationship is implied: The sentence "Jessica fell over "can be interpreted as an expression of a relationship between Jessica and the ground. In order to produce a sentence, therefore, it may be necessary for an animal to be able to represent objects and, more importantly, be aware of the relationship between them.

The extent to which animals are capable of comprehending relationships is dealt with in some detail in Chapter 7. According to Premack (1983a,b), the ability to represent any but the most fundamental relationships depends upon the possession of an abstract mental code. If his argument is correct, then it follows that language training will only be successful with animals that possess this code because without it they would be incapable of comprehending the relationships on which all sentences are based. Sarah's success with analogical reasoning tasks suggests that she is capable of understanding a wide range of relationships. At present, however, there are no demonstrations of this skill in species other than the chimpanzee.

On the basis of the slender evidence that is available, it would seem that there are reasonable grounds for believing that some animals possess at least the fundamental thought processes necessary for language comprehension and production. If further research should confirm this conclusion, then future attempts to train animals in the use of language may well be more successful than their predecessors. I am certain that humans will always be superior to animals in their use of language, but I suspect that with improved training techniques this difference will be less than authors such as Chomsky (1972) and Macphail (1982) have implied.

9 Concluding Comments: The Distribution of Intelligence

In the opening chapter of this book two contrasting views of the way in which intelligence is distributed throughout the animal kingdom were developed. One of these makes the assumption that intelligence is related to brain size or, more precisely, to a cephalisation index (K) which is based on a ratio of the weight of the brain to that of the body. The other, which has been referred to as the null hypothesis (Macphail, 1985), asserts that apart from humans all vertebrates are of equal intelligence. We are now in a position to evaluate these very different proposals.

INTELLIGENCE AND BRAIN SIZE

The suggestion that a cephalisation index can provide an indication of intelligence is attractive; after all, it is presumably in the brain that most of the information processing by animals takes place. Moreover, there have been occasional reports that claim to demonstrate a high correspondence between intelligence and some measure of brain size.

Consider, for example, the results from a number of different studies of learning set formation that are plotted in Fig. 9.1. The figure shows, for a variety of species, the accuracy on the second trial of a discrimination, as a function of the number of problems that have been given. The obvious feature of this figure is that the species can be ranked according to their skill at forming learning sets. And this ranking is of interest because as

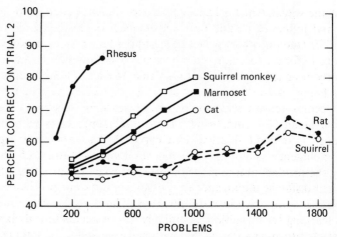

FIG. 9.1.   The mean percentage of correct responses on the second trial of a discrimination, as a function of the number of discrimination problems given, for 6 different species (from Warren, 1965).

Passingham (1982) points out, it corresponds with an index of brain size that is related to the cephalisation index of the species concerned (Riddell, 1979). If it is now assumed that the ability to form learning sets is related to intelligence (McFarland, 1985), then the pattern of results depicted in Fig. 9.1 suggests that intelligence does depend on brain size.

There are, however, at least two reasons why this conclusion may not be justified: First, Macphail (1982) and Warren (1973), among others, have argued that results such as those summarised in Fig. 9.1 can be very misleading. Comparing the speed at which species form learning sets is hampered not only because they possess different perceptual skills and motivational processes, but also because the apparatus in which they are trained is necessarily different. These differences, rather than variations in intelligence, may well be responsible for the pattern of results summarised in Fig. 9.1.

To emphasise this point it is worth considering the results from two learning set experiments with dolphins. When a single bottlenosed dolphin was trained with a series of visual discriminations in which the stimuli differed in shape, Herman, Beach, Pepper, and Stalling (1969) found very little evidence for the formation of a learning set. In contrast, Herman and Arbeit (1973) had little difficulty in training another dolphin to form a learning set when the discriminations involved auditory stimuli. Indeed, by the end of her training, the dolphin was responding with an accuracy of greater than 85% on the second trial of each new discrimination. Thus for dolphins the way in which a learning set experiment is conducted can have a profound influence on the outcome it reveals. This conclusion is also bound to be true for other species. Consequently, when an animal shows a reluctance to form a learning set, we should be aware that this may be due to a poorly designed experiment, rather than to a lack of intelligence by the subjects being tested.

The second reason why the study of learning sets may not be a justifiable means for comparing animal intelligence rests with the way intelligence is defined. I argue in Chapter 1 that instead of regarding animal intelligence as a unitary mechanism it may be more useful to see it as being the product of a number of different cognitive processes. Species could then differ in intelligence by possessing different processes, which themselves may operate in different ways. The use of a single measure, such as learning set formation, is unlikely to test adequately all aspects of information processing by an animal, and any index of intelligence it produces will almost certainly be inaccurate. Indeed, if it is accepted that animal intelligence depends upon a collection of capacities that can differ in both degree and kind from one species to the next, then it may not be possible to rank them neatly according to their intelligence. How, for example, would a bee with its sophisticated skills of communication be placed with respect to a bird that can remember the location of thousands of buried pine seeds? Perhaps all we can hope to achieve is to identify and understand the cognitive processes of the species with which we are interested.

Thus even if it were possible to devise a test, or a battery of tests, that could be fairly applied to a range of species, it is unlikely that the outcome would allow us to rank them according to their intelligence. Once this conclusion is acknowledged, then it is no longer meaningful to try to correlate brain size with intelligence as it is defined here.

THE NULL HYPOTHESIS

After reviewing a large body of experimental findings Macphail (1982) concluded that all vertebrates (with the exception of humans) are of equal intelligence. Implausible as this proposal may seem, Macphail (1982, 1985) cites an impressive body of evidence in its support. This includes the results from many studies of instrumental and Pavlovian conditioning, as well as recent instances of birds revealing skills that had previously been demonstrated only by primates. One example he quotes is the "insight" displayed by the pigeons who moved a box in order to climb on it to peck a banana (Epstein et al., 1984). Another example is Alex the parrot trained by Pepperberg (1981, 1983, in press). He also argues, as we did for the study of learning sets, that when a difference is revealed between two species on a task, then this could be due to poor experimental design rather than to their intelligence.

This latter argument is important because it makes the Null Hypothesis logically impossible to refute. No matter how many times an animal fails to solve a certain problem, it will always be possible for an advocate of the Null Hypothesis to blame this failure on the experimenter rather than the intelligence of the animal. Nonetheless, it may be worthwhile searching for evidence that is inconsistent with the hypothesis, if only to embarrass it by making it implausible. In the following discussion we focus on a specific prediction of the hypothesis that the intelligence of rats and goldfish is the same.

When a rat is repeatedly exposed to a neutral stimulus, subsequent conditioning is slower than with a novel stimulus. This effect is known as latent inhibition and is said to reflect a loss of attention to the familiar stimulus. Although there is little difficulty in demonstrating latent inhibition with many mammals, to my knowledge it has never been demonstrated with goldfish. Indeed, Shishimi (1985) specifically tested them for latent inhibition and was unable to detect it either with excitatory or with inhibitory conditioning, and when both appetitive and aversive unconditioned stimuli were used. This failure also occurred whether the stimulus was auditory or visual. There seem to be strong grounds for concluding, therefore, that latent inhibition cannot be found with goldfish and that the attentional processes of rats and goldfish differ in some important way.

Of course, the possibility remains that Shishimi (1985) did not design his experiments properly. With mammals, at a minimum about 20 trials of exposure to the stimulus are necessary before latent inhibition can be demonstrated. Perhaps goldfish need more exposure than this, and even the 160 trials employed in one of the studies by Shishimi (1985) were insufficient to produce latent inhibition. Despite this word of caution, the procedures for both generating and detecting latent inhibition in mammals are very simple, and it would be surprising if the various techniques used by Shishimi (1985) were inadequate.

There is, moreover, another source of evidence based on a different experimental design, which also suggests that the attentional processes of rats and goldfish differ. Chapters 4 and 5 show that, for rats, the effects of blocking can be modified by the surprising omission of a US after each compound conditioning trial. Although there is some dispute about the interpretation of blocking, at least two theories (Mackintosh, 1975a; Pearce & Hall, 1980) attribute the effects of the surprising events to their influence on attentional processes. Accordingly, if the mechanisms of attention for goldfish and rats do differ, they might be affected in different ways when a US is unexpectedly omitted after a blocking trial. In support of this prediction Gonzalez (1985) has demonstrated blocking with goldfish and found that it is not at all disrupted by the unexpected omission of a US during compound conditioning.

A further suggestion that rats and goldfish differ intellectualy comes from an article by Mackintosh, Wilson, and Boakes (1985). Given the appropriate training conditions, these animals can be shown to be equally efficient at learning a simple discrimination and reversing it. But if they are given repeated reversal training with the same pair of stimuli, rats show a much greater improvement across these reversals than fish. Figure 9.2 shows this pattern of results for a spatial discrimination (Mackintosh & Cauty, 1971). The similarity of the performance at the outset of the experiment suggests that the demands of the task were equivalent for both species, so that it is difficult to attribute the subsequent divergence in the speed of their reversal learning to perceptual, motivational, or other theoretically trivial factors. As an alternative, the possibility is raised that rapid reversal learning depends upon an intellectual process that is different for rats and goldfish. To understand what this process might be, remember that in an earlier discussion (see p. 240) the suggestion was made that rapid reversal learning depends upon animals being able to

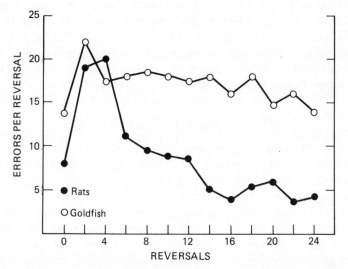

FIG. 9.2.   Number of errors per reversal for groups of rats and goldfish that were given serial reversal training in a study by Mackintosh and Cauty (1971), 0 = original discrimination (adapted from Mackintosh et al., 1985).

remember the outcome of the previous trial. If this is correct, then the implication of the results by Mackintosh and Cauty (1971) is that the memory processes of rats are more efficient than those of goldfish.

Insufficient is known about the memory processes of goldfish to permit a detailed evaluation of this suggestion, but it gains plausibility from studies of alternation learning. In an alternation task an animal may be required to go down an alley for food that is available at the end on alternate trials. If the animal can remember the outcome of the previous trial, then it should be able to anticipate whether or not reward will be delivered on the present trial. Although such anticipation can be readily demonstrated with rats, by discovering that eventually they run faster on rewarded than on nonrewarded trials, a similar effect is very much harder to reveal with goldfish. One explanation for this difference is that unlike rats, goldfish are unable to remember whether or not reward was delivered from one trial to the next (see Mackintosh et al., 1985).

Even when they are taken together, these results do not allow us to reject the claim that rats and goldfish are of equal intelligence. In the future, experiments that reveal striking similarities in the memory and attentional processes of rats and goldfish may be devised. Nonetheless, the results we have considered do at least suggest that the cognitive processes of these species are different, and that future work to support this view will be successful. The results also encourage us to expect that with careful experimentation we shall discover differences in the cognitive processes of other species. We may support Premack's (1983a,b) proposal that primates are unique in their possession of an abstract code. We may also find that only a few species are capable of comprehending syntactic rules. In the absence of further evidence, however, these and many other proposals that could be made are nothing more than speculative.

INTELLIGENCE AND EVOLUTION

Quite apart from the experimental evidence, there is another reason for questioning the Null Hypothesis. During the course of evolution the characteristics of a species will be changed according to the demands imposed upon its members by the ecological niche they occupy. This niche can be identified by the relationship of the animal both with other organisms and with its physical environment. Because the problems that confront an animal differ markedly from one niche to another, it is understandable why species differ so profoundly in their characteristics. Of course, it is not just physical characteristics that are influenced in this way; mental processes will also be modified as a result of evolutionary pressures.

One implication of this discussion is that animals occupying different niches will possess different mental processes. For instance, a capacity to communicate about the location of food will be required only by those animals that need to forage for food cooperatively. We should not therefore expect to find this skill in more solitary animals. Alternatively, an ability to construct a cognitive map may be most likely in animals that forage over reasonable distances and must then return to a specific location, such as a nest or hive.

A further implication is that even where animals do have mental processes in common, evolutionary processes may result in their becoming specialised in some way. To avoid starving during the winter, Clark's nutcrackers must remember where they have stored a large number of pine seeds. Obviously the birds that are most likely to survive a winter are those with a large and accurate memory. It is therefore plausible that over successive generations there has been an improvement in the memory capacity of this species. Such an improvement would not be expected in species of birds for which the role played by memory in their survival is less critical.

Studies of learning provide a further indication of the way the characteristics of an ecological niche can influence a specific cognitive process. Many animals are capable of associative learning, but very often it is found that a particular species is disposed to learn more readily about some relationships than about others. Moreover, these relationships, such as that between illness and poison, are those that are most likely to occur naturally and are important to the animal's survival. The associative learning mechanisms could therefore be said to be biased in a way that facilitates the acquisition of knowledge that is most likely to be of importance to the animal. The way in which the white-crowned sparrow is restricted in its song learning provides a further example of the influence of evolution on the learning processes.

On the basis of the foregoing examples and discussion, the argument might be made that Macphail (1982, 1985) is wholly unjustified in proposing that all vertebrates other than humans are of equal intelligence, as they live in such a variety of environments. However, this criticism overlooks the fact that many niches have common characteristics that may be resposible for their occupants possessing similar mental processes (Dickinson, 1980; Revusky, 1977). This point is made in Chapter 1 with the example of Pavlovian conditioning. In many different environments, a stimulus will signal the imminent occurrence of an event that is of significance to the animals that live in them. If these relationships can be learned about, then animals will be able to anticipate and prepare themselves for the events. Such a learning ability would be of as much value to insects as to chimpanzees and we might expect it to be possessed by a very wide range of animals. The evidence reviewed in Chapters 4 and 6 is certainly consistent with this expectation. In addition, a number of authors argue convincingly that the laws governing associative learning in many animals are the same (Domjan, 1983; Roper, 1983). Hence, because they face a common problem of needing to predict what will happen to them, many species appear to possess a similar mechanism of associative learning. This argument does not only apply to associative learning; many other cognitive processes that would be of value to a wide range of species can be identified. We are thus in the position of anticipating, on the basis of evolutionary considerations, that animals will possess similar or different cognitive processes, or a mixture of both. Unfortunately this conclusion is of little help in evaluating accounts of animal intelligence, as it is impossible to study the environment of an animal and then draw accurate conclusions about its intellectual processes. Instead, as we have seen, the way to understand the intelligence of animals is to experiment on them directly.

Before closing this discussion, some attention should be paid to our own species. Occasionally in this book evidence is cited to suggest that the cognitive processes of humans and animals have much in common. The serial position curves obtained by Wright et al. (1984) with pigeons, monkeys, and a human demonstrate that the memory processes of these species are in some respects very similar (see Chapter 2). Further support for this conclusion may be found in the impressive concept-learning skills of pigeons. The attentional processes of humans and animals may also operate in fundamentally similar ways—for both it has proved useful to distinguish between two sorts of attention, which may be referred to as automatic and controlled (see Chapter 5). In studies of problem solving it is striking that a monkey and, occasionally, humans are quicker at choosing betwen two members of a transitive series the more distantly they are related. Sarah's ability to reason analogically also hints at there being something in common in the way humans and animals solve problems. Finally, Premack's (1983a,b) suggestion that primates possess both a concrete and an abstract code for representing knowledge is a claim that has often been made about human cognition (e.g. Anderson, 1980).

How then do the cognitive processes of humans and animals differ? Language undoubtedly provides us with a tremendous intellectual advantage over our fellow creatures, but it is not clear why this is so. The suggestion that there is a language acquisition device that is unique to humans is questioned in Chapter 8. We also saw that some animals possess a number of the cognitive skills that may be considered essential for language comprehension and production. It seems that there must be profound differences between the cognitive processes of humans and animals, but for the present we must withhold judgement on what they might be. We can be sure, however, that as our understanding of animal cognition improves so we shall discover more about the origins of human intelligence and the ways in which it is unique.

References

Able, K. P. (1980). Mechanisms of orientation, navigation, and homing. In S. A. Gauthreaux (Ed.), *Animal migration, orientation, and navigation* (pp. 284–373). New York: Academic Press.

Adams, C. D. & Dickinson, A. (1981). Actions and habits: Variations in associative representations during instrumental learning. In N. E. Spear & R. R. Miller (Eds.), *Information processing in animals: Memory mechanisms*, pp. 143–165. Hillsdale, N.J.: Lawrence Erlbaum Associates.

Anderson, J. R. (1983). Response to mirror image stimulation and assessment of self-recognition in mirror- and peer-reared stumptail macaques. *Quarterly Journal of Experimental Psychology, 35B*, 201–212.

Anderson, J. R. (1980). *Cognitive psychology and its implications*, 1st ed. San Francisco: Freeman.

Anderson, J. R. (1985). *Cognitive psychology and its implications*, 2nd ed. San Francisco: Freeman.

Anderson, J. R., Kline, P. J. & Beasley, C. M. (1979). A general learning theory and its application to schema abstraction. In G. H. Bower (Ed.), *The psychology of learning and motivation*, Vol. 13. New York: Academic Press.

Angermeier, W. F. (1984). *The evolution of operant learning and memory*. Basel: Karger.

Annau, Z. & Kamin, L. J. (1961). The conditioned emotional response as a function of intensity of the US. *Journal of Comparative and Physiological Psychology, 54*, 428–432.

Aschoff, J. (1955). Exogene und endogene Komponente der 24 Stunden-Periodik bei Tier und Mensche. *Naturwiss., 42*, 569–575.

Atkinson, R. C. & Estes, W. K. (1963). Stimulus sampling theory. In R. D. Luce, R. R. Bush, & E. Galanter (Eds.), *Handbook of mathematical psychology*, Vol. 2, pp. 121–268. New York: Wiley.

Baddeley, A. D. (1976). *The psychology of memory*. New York: Basic Books.

Bakal, C. W., Johnson, R. D., & Rescorla, R. A. (1974). The effect of change in US quality on the blocking effect. *Pavlovian Journal of Biological Sciences, 9*, 97–103.

Baker, A. G. (1974). Conditioned inhibition is not the symmetrical opposite of conditioned excitation: A test of the Rescorla–Wagner model. *Learning and Motivation, 5*, 369–379.

Baker, A. G. & Mackintosh, N. J. (1977). Excitatory and inhibitory conditioning following uncorrelated presentations of CS and US. *Animal Learning and Behavior, 5*, 315–319.

Baker, R. R. (1984). *Bird navigation: The solution of a mystery?* London: Hodder & Stoughton.

Balachandran, N. K., Dunn, W. L., & Rind, D. H. (1977). Concorde sonic booms as an atmospheric probe. *Science, 197*, 47–49.

Balaz, M. A., Kasprow, W. J., & Miller, R. R. (1982). Blocking with a single compound trial. *Animal Learning and Behavior, 10*, 271–276.

Banks, W. P. & Flora, J. (1977). Semantic and perceptual processes in symbolic comparisons. *Journal of Experimental Psychology: Human Perception and Performance, 3*, 278–290.

Baptista, L. F. & Morton, M. L. (1981). Interspecific song acquisition by a white-crowned sparrow. *Auk, 98*, 383–385.

Barnett, S. A. (1970). *Instinct and intelligence*. Harmondsworth, London: Penguin.

Bastian, J. (1961). *Proceedings of the symposium on bionic models of animal sonar systems*. Italy: Frascati.

Batson, J. D. & Best, M. R. (1981). Single-element assessment of conditioned inhibition. *Bulletin of the Psychonomic Society, 18*, 328–330.

Baum, M. (1966). Rapid extinction of an avoidance response following a period of response prevention in the avoidance apparatus. *Psychological Reports, 18*, 59–64.

Beatty, W. W. & Shavalia, D. A. (1980a). Spatial memory in rats: Time course of working memory and effect of anaesthetics. *Behavioral and Neural Biology, 28*, 454–462.

Beatty, W. W. & Shavalia, D. A. (1980b). Rat spatial memory: Resistance to retroactive interference at long retention intervals. *Animal Learning and Behavior, 8*, 550–552.

Berthold, P. (1978). Concept of endogenous control of migration in warblers. In K. Schmidt-Koenig & W. T. Keeton (Eds.), *Animal migration, navigation, and homing*, pp. 275–282. Berlin: Springer-Verlag.

Bessemer, D. W. & Stollnitz, F. (1971). Retention of discriminations and an analysis of learning set. In A. M. Schrier & F. Stollnitz (Eds.), *Behavior of nonhuman primates*, Vol. 4, pp. 1–58. New York: Academic Press.

Best, M. R., Dunn, D. P., Batson, J. D., Meachum, C. L., & Nash, S. M. (1985). Extinguishing conditioned inhibition in flavour-aversion learning: Effects of repeated testing and extinction of the excitatory element. *Quarterly Journal of Experimental Psychology, 37B*, 359–378.

Best, M. R. & Gemberling, G. A. (1977). Role of short-term processes in the conditioned stimulus preexposure effect and the delay of reinforcement gradient in long-delay taste-aversion learning. *Journal of Experimental Psychology: Animal Behaviour Processes, 3*, 253–263.

Birch, H. G. (1945). The relation of previous experience to insightful problem solving. *Journal of Comparative Psychology, 38*, 367–383.

Bitterman, M. E. (1965). The evolution of intelligence. *Scientific American, 212*, 92–100.

Bitterman, M. E. (1975). The comparative analysis of learning. *Science, 188*, 699–709

Bitterman, M. E., Menzel, R., Fietz, A., & Schafer, S. (1983). Classical conditioning of proboscis extension in honeybees (*Apis mellifera*). *Journal of Comparative Psychology, 97*, 107–119.

Blough, D. S. (1975). Steady state data and a quantitative model of operant generalization and discrimination. *Journal of Experimental Psychology: Animal Behavior Processes,* **1**, 3–21.

Boakes, R. A. & Gaertner, I. (1977). The development of a simple form of communication. *Quarterly Journal of Experimental Psychology,* **29**, 561–575.

Boakes, R. A., Poli, M., Lockwood, M. J., & Goodall, G. (1978). A study of misbehavior: Token reinforcement in the rat. *Journal of the Experimental Analysis of Behavior,* **29**, 115–134.

Boe, E. E. & Church, R. M. (1967). Permanent effects of punishment during extinction. *Journal of Comparative and Physiological Psychology,* **63**, 486–492.

Bolles, R. C. (1971). Species-specific defense reactions. In F. R. Brush (Ed.), *Aversive conditioning and learning,* pp. 183–233. New York: Academic Press.

Bolles, R. C. (1972) Reinforcement, expectancy and learning. *Psychological Review,* **79**, 394–409.

Bolles, R. C. (1975). *Theory of motivation,* 2nd ed. New York: Harper & Row.

Bond, A. B. (1983). Visual search and selection of natural stimuli in the pigeon: The attention threshold hypothesis. *Journal of Experimental Psychology: Animal Behavior Processes,* **9**, 292–306.

Bookman, M. A. (1977). Sensitivity of the homing pigeon to an Earth-strength magnetic field. *Nature,* **267**, 340–342.

Bracewell, R. J. & Black, A. H. (1974). The effects of restraint and noncontingent pre-shock on subsequent escape learning in the rat. *Learning and Motivation,* **5**, 53–69.

Brandon, S. E. & Bitterman, M. E. (1979). Analysis of autoshaping in goldfish. *Animal Learning and Behavior,* **7**, 57–62.

Breland, K. & Breland, M. (1961). The misbehavior of organisms. *American Psychologist,* **16**, 661–664.

Brower, L. P., Brower, J. Z., & Westcott, P. W. (1960). Experimental studies of mimicry. 5. The reaction of toads (*Bufo terrestris*) to bumblebees (*Bombus americanorum*) and their robberfly mimics (*Mallaphora bomboides*) with a discussion of aggressive mimicry. *Am. Nat.* **94**, 343–355.

Brown, I. D. & Poulton, E. C. (1961). Measuring the spare "mental capacity" of car drivers by a subsidiary task. *Ergonomics,* **4**, 35–40.

Brown, J. L. (1964). The integration of agonistic behavior in Stellar's jay *Cyanocitta stelleri* (Gmelin). *University of California Publications in Psychology,* **60**, 223–328.

Capaldi, E. J., Hovancik, J. R., & Lamb, E. O. (1975). The effects of strong irrelevant thirst on food-rewarded instrumental performance. *Animal Learning and Behavior,* **3**, 172–178.

Cerella, J. (1979). Visual classes and natural categories in the pigeon. *Journal of Experimental Psychology: Human Perception and Performance,* **5**, 68–77.

Cerella, J. (1980). The pigeon's analysis of pictures. *Pattern Recognition,* **12**, 1–6.

Cerella, J. (1982). Mechanisms of concept formation in the pigeon. In D. J. Ingle, M. A. Goodale, & R. J. W. Mansfield (Eds.), *Analysis of visual behaviour,* pp. 241–262. Cambridge, Mass.: M.I.T. Press.

Chapuis, N., Thinus-Blanc, C., & Poucet, B. (1983). Dissociation of mechanisms involved in dogs' oriented displacements. *Quarterly Journal of Experimental Psychology,* **35B**, 213–219.

Chen, C. S. (1967). Can rats count? *Nature,* **214**, 15–17.

Cheng, K. & Gallistel, C. R. (1984). Testing the geometric power of an animal's spatial representation. In H. L. Roitblat, T. G. Bever, & H. S. Terrace (Eds.), *Animal cognition,* pp. 409–424. Hilldale, N.J.: Lawrence Erlbaum Associates.

Chomsky, N. (1957). *Syntactic structures.* The Hague: Mouton.

Chomsky, N. (1972). *Language and mind,* enlarged edn. New York: Harcourt Brace Jovanovich.

Church, R. M. (1978). The internal clock. In S. H. Hulse, H. Fowler & W. K. Honig (Eds.), *Cognitive processes in animal behavior*. Hillsdale, N.J.: Lawrence Erlbaum Associates.

Church, R. M. & Deluty, M. Z. (1977). Bisection of temporal intervals. *Journal of Experimental Psychology: Animal Behavior Processes, 3*, 216–228.

Church, R. M., LoLordo, V. M., Overmier, J. B., Solomon, R. L., & Turner, L. H. (1966). Cardiac responses to shock in curarized dogs. *Journal of Comparative and Physiological Psychology, 62*, 1–7.

Church, R. M. & Meck, W. H. (1984). The numerical attributes of stimuli. In H. L. Roitblat, T. G. Bever, & H. S. Terrace (Eds.), *Animal cognition*, pp. 445–464. Hillsdale, N.J.: Lawrence Erlbaum Associates.

Clark, E. (1959). Instrumental conditioning of lemon sharks. *Science, 130*, 217–218.

Clark, F. C. (1958). The effect of deprivation and frequency of reinforcement on variable-interval responding. *Journal of the Experimental Analysis of Behavior, 1*, 221–227.

Collins, L. & Pearce, J. M. (1985). Predictive accuracy and the effects of partial reinforcement on serial autoshaping. *Journal of Experimental Psychology: Animal Behavior Processes, 11*, 548–564.

Colwill, R. M. (1984). Controlled processing in pigeons. *Animal Learning and Behaviour, 12*, 285–291.

Colwill, R. M. & Rescorla, R. A. (1985). Instrumental responding remains sensitive to reinforcer devaluation after extensive training. *Journal of Experimental Psychology: Animal Behavior Processes, 11*, 520–536.

Cook, R. G., Brown, M. F., & Riley, D. A. (1985). Flexible memory processing by rats: Use of prospective and retrospective information in the radial maze. *Journal of Experimental Psychology: Animal Behavior Processes, 11*, 453–469.

Corning, W. & Kelly, S. (1972). Platyhelminthes: The turbellarians. In W. Corning, J. Dyal, & A. O. D. Willows (Eds.), *Invertebrate learning*, Vol 1. New York: Plenum.

Corning, W. & Riccio, D. (1970). The planarian controversy. In W. Byrne (Ed.), *Molecular approaches to learning and memory*. New York: Academic Press.

Cotton, J. W. (1953). Running time as a function of food deprivation. *Journal of Experimental Psychology, 46*, 188–198.

Cotton, M. M., Goodall, G., & Mackintosh, N. J. (1982). Inhibitory conditioning resulting from a reduction in the magnitude of reinforcement. *Quarterly Journal of Experimental Psychology, 34B*, 163–181.

Couvillon, P. A. & Bitterman, M. E. (1982). Compound conditioning in honeybees. *Journal of Comparative and Physiological Psychology, 96*, 192–199.

Couvillon, P. A., Klosterhalfen, S., & Bitterman, M. E. (1983). Analysis of overshadowing in honeybees. *Journal of Comparative Psychology, 97*, 154–166.

Cox, J. K. & D'Amato, M. R. (1982). Matching-to-compound samples by monkeys (*Cebus apella*): Shared attention or generalization decrement? *Journal of Experimental Psychology: Animal Behavior Processes, 8*, 209–225.

D'Amato, M. R. (1973). Delayed matching and short-term memory in monkeys. In G. H. Bower (Ed.), *The psychology of learning and motivation*, Vol. 7, pp. 227–269. New York: Academic Press.

D'Amato, M. R. & Buckiewicz, J. (1980). Long delay, one-trial conditioned preference and retention in monkeys (*Cebus apella*). *Animal Learning and Behavior, 8*, 359–362.

D'Amato, M. R. & O'Neill, W. (1971). Effect of delay-interval illumination on matching behavior in the capuchin monkey. *Journal of the Experimental Analysis of Behavior, 15*, 327–333.

D'Amato, M. R., Safarjan, W. R., & Salmon, D. (1981). Long-delay conditioning and instrumental learning: Some new findings: In N. E. Spear & R. R. Miller (Eds.),

Information processing in animals: Memory mechanisms, pp. 113–142. Hillsdale, N.J.: Lawrence Erlbaum Associates.

D'Amato, M. R. & Salmon, D. P. (1982). Tune discrimination in monkeys (*Cebus apella*) and in rats. *Animal Learning and Behavior,* **10**, 126–134.

D'Amato, M. R. & Salmon, D. P. (1984). Processing of complex auditory stimuli (tunes) by rats and monkeys (*Cebus apella*). *Animal Learning and Behaviour,* **12**, 184–194.

D'Amato, M. R. & Worsham, R. W. (1972). Delayed matching in the capuchin monkey with brief sample durations. *Learning and Motivation,* **3**, 304–312.

Darwin, C. (1872). *The expression of emotions in man and animal.* London: John Murray.

Davidson, R. S. (1966). Operant stimulus control applied to maze behavior: Heat escape conditioning and discrimination reversal in *Alligator mississippiensis. Journal of the Experimental Analysis of Behavior,* **9**, 671–676.

Dawkins, M. (1971a). Perceptual changes in chicks: Another look at the "search image" concept. *Animal Behaviour,* **19**, 566–574.

Dawkins, M. (1971b). Shifts of "attention" in chicks during feeding. *Animal Behaviour,* **19**, 575–582.

Delius, J. D. (1985). The peck of the pigeon: Free for all. In C. F. Lowe, M. E. Richelle, D. E. Blackman, & C. M. Bradshaw (Eds.), *Behaviour analysis and contemporary psychology,* pp. 53–81. Hove & London: Lawrence Erlbaum Associates Ltd.

Delius, J. D. & Emmerton, J. (1978). Sensory mechanisms related to homing in pigeons. In K. Schmidt-Koenig & W. T. Keeton (Eds.), *Animal migration, navigation, and homing,* pp. 35–41. Berlin: Springer-Verlag.

Deutsch, J. A. (1960). *The structural basis of behavior.* Cambridge: Cambridge University Press.

Deweer, B., Sara, S. J., & Hars, B. (1980). Contextual cues and memory retrieval in rats: Alleviation of forgetting by a pretest exposure to background stimuli. *Animal Learning and Behavior,* **8**, 265–272.

Dews, P. (1959). Some observations on an operant in the octopus. *Journal of the Experimental Analysis of Behavior,* **2**, 57–63.

Dickinson, A. (1980). *Contemporary animal learning theory.* Cambridge: Cambridge University Press.

Dickinson, A. (1985). Actions and habits: The development of behavioural autonomy. In L. Weiskrantz (Ed.), *Animal intelligence,* pp. 67–78. Oxford: Clarendon.

Dickinson, A., Hall, G., & Mackintosh, N. J. (1976). Surprise and the attenuation of blocking. *Journal of Experimental Psychology: Animal Behavior Processes,* **2**, 313–322.

Dickinson, A. & Mackintosh, N. J. (1979). Reinforcer specificity in the enhancement of conditioning by posttrial surprise. *Journal of Experimental Psychology: Animal Behavior Processes,* **5**, 162–177.

Dickinson, A., Nicholas, D. J., & Mackintosh, N. J. (1983). A reexamination of one-trial blocking in conditioned suppression. *Quarterly Journal of Experimental Psychology,* **35B**, 67–79.

Dickinson, A. & Pearce, J. M. (1977). Inhibitory interactions between appetitive and aversive stimuli. *Psychological Bulletin,* **84**, 690–711.

Dimattia, B. V. & Kesner, R. P. (1984). Serial position curves in rats: Automatic versus effortful information processing. *Journal of Experimental Psychology: Animal Behavior Processes,* **10**, 557–563.

Domjan, M. (1983). Biological constraints on instrumental and classical conditioning: Implications for general process theory. In G. H. Bower (Ed.), *The psychology of learning and motivation,* Vol. 17, pp. 215–277.New York: Academic Press.

Dowsett-Lemaire, F. (1979). The imitative range of the song of the marsh warbler,

Acrocephalus palustris, with special reference to imitations of African birds. *Ibis,* **121,** 453–468.

Dufort, R. H., Guttman, N., & Kimble, G. A. (1954). One-trial discrimination reversal in the white rat. *Journal of Comparative and Physiological Psychology,* **47,** 248–249.

Duncan, C. P. (1949). The retroactive effect of electroshock on learning. *Journal of Comparative and Physiological Psychology,* **42,** 32–44.

Eikelboom, R. & Stewart, J. (1979). Conditioned temperature effects using morphine as the unconditioned stimulus. *Psychopharmacology,* **61,** 31–38.

Ellison, G. D. & Konorski, J. (1964). Separation of the salivary and motor response in instrumental conditioning. *Science,* **146,** 1071–1072.

Emlen, S. T. (1970). Celestial rotation: Its importance in the development of migratory orientation. *Science,* **170,** 1198–1201.

Epstein, R., Kirshnit, C. E., Lanza, R. P., & Rubin, L. C. (1984). "Insight" in the pigeon: Antecedents and determinants of an intelligent performance. *Nature,* **308,** 61–62.

Epstein, R., Lanza, R. P., & Skinner, B. F. (1980). Symbolic communication between two pigeons *(Columba livia domestica). Science,* **207,** 543–545.

Epstein, R., Lanza, R. P., & Skinner, B. F. (1981). "Self-awareness" in the pigeon. *Science,* **212,** 695–696.

Estes, W. K. (1969). New perspectives on some old issues in association theory. In N. J. Mackintosh & W. K. Honig (Eds.), *Fundamental issues in associative learning.* Halifax: Dalhousie University Press.

Evans, J. G. M. & Hammond, G. R. (1983). Differential generalization of habituation across contexts as a function of stimulus significance. *Animal Learning and Behavior,* **11,** 432–434.

Farah, M. J. (1985). Psychophysical evidence for a shared representational medium for mental images and percepts. *Journal of Experimental Psychology: General,* **114,** 91–103.

Fouts, R. S. (1975). In R. H. Tuttle (Ed.), *Society and psychology of primates.* The Hague: Mouton.

Fowler, H. & Miller, N. E. (1963). Facilitation and inhibition of runway performance by hind- and forepaw shock of various intensities. *Journal of Comparative and Physiological Psychology,* **56,** 801–805.

Franks, J. J. & Bransford, J. D. (1971). Abstraction of visual patterns. *Journal of Experimental Psychology,* **90,** 65–74.

Furness, W. (1916). Observations on the mentality of chimpanzees and orangutans. *Proceedings of the American Philosophical Society,* **65,** 281–290.

Gaffan, D. (1977). Response coding in recall of colours by monkeys. *Quarterly Journal of Experimental Psychology,* **29,** 597–605.

Gaffan, D. & Gowling, E. A. (1984). Recall of the goal box in latent learning and latent discrimination. *Quarterly Journal of Experimental Psychology,* **36B,** 39–51.

Gaffan, D. & Weiskrantz, L. (1980). Recency effects and lesion effects in delayed non-matching to randomly baited samples by monkeys. *Brain Research,* **196,** 373–386.

Gallup, G. G. (1970). Chimpanzees: Self-recognition. *Science,* **167,** 86–87.

Gallup, G. G. (1983). Toward a comparative psychology of mind. In R. L. Mellgren (Ed.), *Animal cognition and behavior,* pp. 473–510. Amsterdam: North Holland Publishing Co.

Gallup, G. G., McClure, M. K., Hill, S. D., & Bundy, R. A. (1971). Capacity for self-recognition in differentially reared chimpanzees. *Psychological Record,* **21,** 69–74.

Garcia, J. & Koelling, R. A. (1966). Relation of cue to consequence in avoidance learning. *Psychonomic Science,* **4,** 123–124.

Garcia, J., McGowan, B. K., & Green, K. F. (1972). Biological constraints on conditioning.

In A. H. Black & W. F. Prokasy (Eds.), *Classical conditioning I.: Current research and theory*. New York: Appleton-Century-Crofts.

Garcia, J., Rusiniak, K. W., & Brett, L. P. (1977). Conditioning food-illness in wild animals: *Caveant canonici*. In H. Davis & H. M. B. Hurwitz (Eds.), *Operant-Pavlovian interactions*. Hillsdale, N.J.: Lawrence Erlbaum Associates.

Gardner, R. A. & Gardner, B. T. (1969). Teaching sign language to a chimpanzee. *Science,* **165**, 664–672.

Gardner, R. A. & Gardner, B. T. (1974). Comparing the early utterances of child and chimpanzee. In A. Pick (Ed.), *Minnesota symposium on child psychology, 8*. Minneapolis: University of Minneapolis Press.

Gemberling, G. A. & Domjan, M. (1982). Selective association in one-day-old rats: Taste-toxicosis and texture-toxicosis aversion learning. *Journal of Comparative and Physiological Psychology,* **96**, 105–113.

Gibbon, J. & Church, R. M. (1981). Time left: Linear versus logarithmic subjective time. *Journal of Experimental Psychology: Animal Behavior Processes,* **7**, 87–108.

Gibbon, J. & Church, R. M. (1984). Sources of variance in an information processing theory of timing. In H. T. Roitblat, T. G. Bever, & H. S. Terrace (Eds.), *Animal cognition*, pp. 465–490. Hillsdale, N.J.: Lawrence Erlbaum Associates.

Gibbon, J., Farrell, L., Locurto, C. M., Duncan, H. J., & Terrace, H. S. (1980). Partial reinforcement in autoshaping with pigeons. *Animal Learning and Behavior,* **8**, 45–59.

Gibbs, C. M., Latham, S. B., & Gormezano, I. (1978). Classical conditioning of the rabbit nictitating membrane response: Effects of reinforcement schedule on response maintenance and resistance to extinction. *Animal Learning and Behavior,* **6**, 209–215.

Gillan, D. J. (1981). Reasoning in the chimpanzee: II. Transitive inference. *Journal of Experimental Psychology: Animal Behvior Processes,* **7**, 52–77.

Gillan, D. J., Premack, D., & Woodruff, G. (1981). Reasoning in the chimpanzee: I. Analogical reasoning. *Journal of Experimental Psychology: Animal Behavior Processes,* **7**, 1–17.

Glazer, H. I. & Weiss, J. M. (1976). Long-term and transitory interference effects. *Journal of Experimental Psychology: Animal Behavior Processes,* **2**, 191–201.

Gleitman, H. (1971). Forgetting of long-term memories in animals. In W. K. Honig & P. H. R. James (Eds.), *Animal memory*, pp. 1–44. New York: Academic Press.

Gonzalez, R. C. (1985). Personal communication.

Goodall, G. & Mackintosh, N. J. (1987). Analysis of the Pavlovian properties of signals for punishment. *Quarterly Journal of Experimental Psychology,* **39**.

Gordon, W. C. (1981). Mechanisms of cue-induced retention enhancement. In N. E. Spear & R. R. Miller (Eds.), *Information processing in animals: Memory mechanisms*, pp. 319–340. Hillsdale, N.J.: Lawrence Erlbaum Associates.

Gordon, W. C., Frankl, S. E., & Hamberg, J. M. (1979). Reactivation-induced proactive interference in rats. *American Journal of Psychology,* **92**, 693–702.

Gordon, W. C. & Mowrer, R. R. (1980). The use of an extinction trial as a reminder treatment following ECS. *Animal Learning and Behavior,* **8**, 363–367.

Gormezano, I. (1965). Yoked comparisons of classical and instrumental conditioning of the eyelid response: And an addendum on "voluntary responders". In W. F. Prokasy (Ed.), *Classical conditioning: A symposium*, pp. 48–70. New York: Appleton-Century-Crofts.

Gormezano, I. & Hiller, G. W. (1972). Omission training of the jaw-movement response of the rabbit to a water US. *Psychonomic Science,* **29**, 276–278.

Gould, J. L. (1982). The map sense of pigeons. *Nature,* **296**, 205–211.

Gould, J. L. (1986). The locale map of honey bees: Do insects have a cognitive map? *Science,* **232**, 861–863.

Gould, J. L. (1984). Natural history of honeybee learning. In P. Marler & H. S. Terrace (Eds.), *The biology of learning*, pp. 149–180. Berlin: Springer-Verlag.

Grant, D. S. (1975). Proactive interference in pigeon short-term memory. *Journal of Experimental Psychology: Animal Behavior Processes*, **1**, 207–220.

Grant, D. S. (1976). Effect of sample presentation time on long-delay matching in the pigeon. *Learning and Motivation*, **7**, 580–590.

Grant, D. S. (1981). Short-term memory in the pigeon. In N. E. Spear & R. R. Miller (Eds.), *Information processing in animals: Memory mechanisms*, pp. 227–256. Hillsdale, N.J.: Lawrence Erlbaum Associates.

Grant, D. S. (1984). Directed forgetting and intratrial interference in pigeon delayed matching. *Canadian Journal of Psychology*, **38**, 166–177.

Grant, D. S. & Roberts, W. A. (1973). Trace interaction in pigeon short-term memory. *Journal of Experimental Psychology*, **101**, 21–29.

Grant, D. S. & Roberts, W. A. (1976). Sources of retroactive inhibition in pigeon short-term memory. *Journal of Experimental Psychology: Animal Behavior Processes*, **2**, 1–16.

Gray, J. A. (1975). *Elements of a two-process theory of learning*. London: Academic Press.

Greenberg, J. H. (1963). *Universals of language*. Cambridge, Mass.: M.I.T Press.

Grindley, G. C. (1932). The formation of a simple habit in guinea pigs. *British Journal of Psychology*, **23**, 127–147.

Guthrie, E. R. (1935). *The psychology of learning*. New York: Harper.

Guttman, N. & Kalish, H. I. (1956). Discriminability and stimulus generalization. *Journal of Experimental Psychology*, **51**, 79–88.

Gwinner, E. (1972). Endogenous timing factors in bird migration. In S. R. Galler, K. Schmidt-Koenig, G. J. Jacobs, & R. E. Belleville (Eds.), *Animal orientation and navigation*, pp. 321–338. NASA, Washington.

Hall, G. (1982). Effects of a brief stimulus accompanying reinforcement on instrumental responding in pigeons. *Learning and Motivation*, **13**, 26–43.

Hall, G. & Channell, S. (1985). Differential effects of contextual change on latent inhibition and on the habituation of an orienting response. *Journal of Experimental Psychology: Animal Behavior Processes*, **11**, 470–481.

Hall, G. & Minor, H. (1984). A search for context–stimulus associations in latent inhibition. *Quarterly Journal of Experimental Psychology*, **36B**, 146–169.

Hall, G. & Pearce, J. M. (1979). Latent inhibition of a CS during CS-US pairings. *Journal of Experimental Psychology: Animal Behavior Processes*, **5**, 31–42.

Hall, G. & Pearce, J. M. (1982a). Restoring the associability of a preexposed CS by a surprising event. *Quarterly Journal of Experimental Psychology*, **34B**, 127–140.

Hall, G. & Pearce, J. M. (1982b). Changes in stimulus associability during conditioning: Implications for theories of acquisition. In M. L. Commons, R. J. Herrnstein, & A. R. Wagner (Eds.), *Quantitative analyses of behavior: Acquisition*, pp. 221–240. Cambridge, Mass.: Ballinger.

Harlow, H. F. (1949). The formation of learning sets. *Psychological Review*, **56**, 51–65.

Hawkins, R. D. & Kandel, E. R. (1984). Is there a cell biological alphabet for simple forms of learning? *Psychological Review*, **91**, 375–391.

Hayes, C. (1961). *The ape in our house*. New York: Harper.

Hayes, K. & Hayes, C. (1951). The intellectual development of a home-raised chimpanzee. *Proceedings of the American Philosophical Society*, **95**, 105–109.

Hearst, E. (1972). Some persistent problems in the analysis of conditioned inhibition. In R. A. Boakes & M. S. Halliday (Eds.), *Inhibition and learning*, pp. 5–39. Academic Press: London.

Hearst, E. & Franklin, S. R. (1977). Positive and negative relations between a signal and food: Approach–withdrawal behavior. *Journal of Experimental Psychology: Animal Behavior Processes*, **3**, 37–52.

Hearst, E. & Jenkins, H. M. (1974). *Sign tracking: The stimulus–reinforcer relation and directed action*. Monograph of the Psychonomic Society, Austin, Texas.

Hebb, D. O. (1949). *The organization of behavior*. New York: Wiley.

Hennessey, T. M., Rucker, W. B., & McDiarmid, C. G. (1979). Classical conditioning in paramecia. *Animal Learning and Behavior*, **7**, 417–423.

Herman, L. M. (1975). Interference and auditory short-term memory in the bottlenosed dolphin. *Animal Learning and Behavior*, **3**, 43–48.

Herman, L. M. & Arbeit, W. R. (1973). Stimulus control and auditory discrimination learning sets in the bottlenose dolphin. *Journal of the Experimental Analysis of Behavior*, **19**, 379-394.

Herman, L. M., Beach, F. A., Pepper, R. L., & Stalling, R. B. (1969). Learning-set formation in the bottlenose dolphin. *Psychonomic Science*, **14**. 98–99.

Herman, L. M. & Gordon, J. A. (1974). Auditory delayed matching in the bottlenose dolphin. *Journal of Experimental Analysis of Behavior*, **21**, 19–29.

Herman, L. M., Richards, D. G., & Wolz, J. P. (1984). Comprehension of sentences by bottlenosed dolphins. *Cognition*, **16**, 129–219.

Herman, L. M. & Thompson, R. K. R. (1982). Symbolic identity, and probed delayed matching of sounds in the bottlenosed dolphin. *Animal Learning and Behavior*, **10**, 22–34.

Herrnstein, R. J. (1979). Acquisition, generalization, and discrimination reversal of a natural concept. *Journal of Experimental Psychology: Animal Behavior Processes*, **5**, 116–129.

Herrnstein, R. J. (1984). Objects, categories, and discriminative stimuli. In H. T. Roitblat, T. G. Bever, & H. S. Terrace (Eds.), *Animal cognition*, pp. 233–262. Hillsdale, N.J.: Lawrence Erlbaum Associates.

Herrnstein, R. J. (1985). Riddles of natural categorization. In L. Weiskrantz (Ed.), *Animal intelligence*, pp. 129–144. Oxford: Clarendon.

Herrnstein, R. J. & Loveland, D. H. (1964). Complex visual concept in the pigeon. *Science*, **146**, 549–551.

Herrnstein, R. J., Loveland, D. H., & Cable, C. (1976). Natural concepts in pigeons. *Journal of Experimental Psychology: Animal Behavior Processes*, **2**, 285–311.

Herrnstein, R. J. & de Villiers, P. A. (1980). Fish as a natural category for people and pigeons. In G. H. Bower (Ed.), *The Psychology of Learning and Motivation*, Vol. 14, pp. 60–97. New York: Academic Press.

Hinde, R. A. (1970). *Animal behaviour: A synthesis of ethology and comparative psychology*. New York: McGraw-Hill.

Hinde, R. A. & Stevenson-Hinde, J. (1973). *Constraints on learning*. London: Academic Press.

Hockett, C. F. (1960). The origin of speech. *Scientific American*, **203**, 89–96.

Holland, P. C. (1977). Conditioned stimulus as a determinant of the form of the Pavlovian conditioned response. *Journal of Experimental Psychology: Animal Behavior Processes*, **3**, 77–104.

Holland, P. C. (1979). Differential effects of omission contingencies on various components of Pavlovian appetitive conditioned behavior in rats. *Journal of Experimental Psychology: Animal Behavior Processes*, **5**, 178–193.

Holland, P. C. & Rescorla, R. A. (1975). The effects of two ways of devaluing the unconditioned stimulus after first- and second-order appetitive conditioning. *Journal of Experimental Psychology: Animal Behavior Processes*, **1**, 355–363.

Holland, P. C. & Ross, R. T. (1981). Associations in serial compound conditioning. *Journal of Experimental Psychology: Animal Behavior Processes*, **7**, 228–241.

Holland, P. C. & Straub, J. J. (1979). Differential effects of two ways of devaluing the unconditioned stimulus after Pavlovian appetitive conditioning. *Journal of Experimental Psychology: Animal Behavior Processes*, **5**, 65–78.

Hollard, V. D. & Delius, J. D. (1982). Rotational invariance in visual pattern recognition by pigeons and humans. *Science*, **218**, 804–806.

Holman, J. G. & Mackintosh, N. J. (1981). The control of appetitive instrumental responding does not depend on classical conditioning to the discriminative stimulus. *Quarterly Journal of Experimental Psychology*, **33B**, 21–31.

Honig, W. K. (1978). Studies of working memory in the pigeon. In S. H. Hulse, H. Fowler, & W. K. Honig (Eds.), *Cognitive processes in animal behavior*. Hillsdale, N.J.: Lawrence Erlbaum Associates.

Hull, C. L. (1943). *Principles of Behavior*. New York: Appleton-Century-Crofts.

Hull, C. L. (1952). *A behavior system*. New Haven, Conn.: Yale University Press.

Hulse, S. H., Cynx, J., & Humpal, J. (1984). Cognitive processes of pitch and rhythm structures by birds. In H. L. Roitblat, T. G. Bever, & H. S. Terrace (Eds.), *Animal Cognition*, pp. 183–198. Hillsdale, N.J.: Lawrence Erlbaum Associates.

Hyde, T. S. (1976). The effect of Pavlovian stimuli on the acquisition of a new response. *Learning and Motivation*, **7**, 223–239.

Irwin, J., Suissa, A., & Anisman, H. (1980). Differential effects of inescapable shock on escape performance and discrimination learning in a water escape task. *Journal of Experimental Psychology: Animal Behavior Processes*, **6**, 21–40.

Jackson, R. L., Alexander, J. H., & Maier, S. F. (1980). Learned helplessness, inactivity, and associative deficits: Effects of inescapable shock on response choice escape learning. *Journal of Experimental Psychology: Animal Behavior Processes*, **6**, 1–20.

Jenkins, H. M. (1977). Sensitivity of different response systems to stimulus–reinforcer and response–reinforcer relations. In H. Davis & H. M. B. Hurwitz (Eds.) *Operant-Pavlovian interactions*, pp. 47–62. Hillsdale, N.J.: Lawrence Erlbaum Associates.

Jennings, H. S. (1906). *Behavior of the lower organisms*. New York: Columbia University Press.

Jerrison, H. J. (1969). Brain evolution and dinosaur brains. *Am. Nat.* **103**, 575–588.

Jerrison, H. J. (1973). *Evolution of the brain and intelligence*. New York: Academic Press.

Kamil, A. C. (1978). Systematic foraging by a nectar feeding bird, the amakihi (*Loxops virens*). *Journal of Comparative and Physiological Psychology*, **92**, 388–396.

Kamil, A. C. & Mauldin, J. E. (1975). Intraproblem retention during learning-set acquisition in blue jays (*Cyanocitta cristata*). *Animal Learning and Behavior*, **3**, 125–130.

Kamin, L. J. (1965). Temporal and intensity characteristics of the conditioned stimulus. In W. F. Prokasy (Ed.), *Classical conditioning: A symposium*, pp. 118–147. New York: Appleton-Century-Crofts.

Kamin, L. J. (1969). Selective association and conditioning. In N. J. Mackintosh & W. K. Honig (Eds.), *Fundamental issues in associative learning*, pp. 42–64. Halifax: Dalhousie University Press.

Kamin, L. J. & Schaub, R. E. (1963). Effects of conditioned stimulus intensity on the conditioned emotional response. *Journal of Comparative and Physiological Psychology*, **56**, 502–507.

Kaplan, P. S. (1984). Importance of relative temporal parameters in trace autoshaping: From excitation to inhibition. *Journal of Experimental Psychology: Animal Behavior Processes*, **10**, 113–126.

Karpicke, J., Christoph, G., Peterson, G., & Hearst, E. (1977). Signal location and positive versus negative conditioned suppression in the rat. *Journal of Experimental Psychology: Animal Behavior Processes*, **3**, 105–118.

Kaye, H. (1983). *The influence of Pavlovian conditioning on the orienting response in the rat*. Unpublished Ph. D. thesis, University College, Cardiff.

Kaye, H. & Pearce, J. M. (1984). The strength of the orienting response during Pavlovian conditioning. *Journal of Experimental Psychology: Animal Behavior Processes*, **10**, 90–109.

Kaye, H. & Pearce, J. M. (1987). Hippocampal lesions attenuate latent inhibition of a CS and of a neutral stimulus. *Quarterly Journal of Experimental Psychology*, **39B**.

Keeton, W. T. (1969). Orientation by pigeons: Is the sun necessary? *Science*, **165**, 922–928.

Keeton, W. T. (1974). The orientational and navigational basis of homing in birds. *Advances in the Study of Behaviour*, **5**, 47–132.

Kemp, F. D. (1969). Thermal reinforcement and thermoregulatory behaviour in the lizard *Dipsosaurus dorsalis*: An operant technique. *Animal Behaviour*, **17**, 446–451.

Kendrick, D. F., Rilling, M., & Stonebraker, T. B. (1981). Stimulus control of delayed matching in pigeons: Directed forgetting. *Journal of Experimental Analysis of Behavior*, **36**, 241–251.

Kenyon, K. W. & Rice, D. W. (1958). Homing of Laysan Albatrosses. *Condor*, **60**, 3–6.

Kettner, R. E. & Thompson, R. F. (1982). Auditory signal detection and decision processes in the nervous system. *Journal of Comparative and Physiological Psychology*, **96**, 328–331.

Kleinginna, P. R. (1970). Operant conditioning in the indigo snake. *Psychonomic Science*, **18**, 53–55.

Kohler, W. (1925). *The mentality of apes*. London: Routledge & Keegan Paul.

Konorski, J. (1948). *Conditioned reflexes and neuron organization*. Cambridge: Cambridge University Press.

Konorski, J. (1967). *Integrative activity of the brain*. Chicago: University of Chicago Press.

Konorski, J. & Miller, S. (1930). Methode d'examen de l'analysateur moteur par les réactions salivomotrices. *C.r. Séanc. Soc. Biol.*, **104**, 907–910.

Kraemer, P. J. & Roberts, W. A. (1984). Short-term memory for visual and auditory stimuli in pigeons. *Animal Learning and Behavior*, **12**, 275–284.

Kramer, G. (1952). Experiments on bird orientation. *Ibis*, **94**, 265–285.

Krechevsky, I. (1932). Hypotheses in rats. *Psychological Review*, **39**, 516–532.

Kreithen, M. L. (1978). Sensory mechanisms for animal orientation—Can any new ones be discovered? In K. Schmidt-Koenig & W. T. Keeton (Eds.), *Animal migration, navigation and homing*, pp. 25–34. Berlin: Springer Verlag.

Kreithen, M. L. & Keeton, W. T. (1974). Detection of changes in atmospheric pressure by the homing pigeon, *Columba livia*. *Journal of Comparative Physiology*, **89**, 73–82.

Kremer, E. F. (1978). The Rescorla–Wagner model: Losses of associative strength in compound conditioned stimuli. *Journal of Experimental Psychology: Animal Behavior Processes*, **4**, 22–36.

Kroodsma, D. E. (1978). Aspects of learning in the ontogeny of bird song: Where, from whom, when, how many, which and how accurately? In G. Burghardt & M. Bekoff (Eds.), *The development of behavior: Comparative and evolutionary aspects*, pp. 215–230. New York: Garland.

LaBerge, D. & Samuels, S. J. (1974). Towards a theory of automatic information processing in reading. *Cognitive Psychology*, **6**, 293–323.

Lashley, K. S. (1929). *Brain mechanisms and intelligence: A quantitative study of injuries to the brain*. Chicago: University of Chicago Press.

Lawrence, D. H. (1949). Acquired distinctiveness of cues: I. Transfer between discriminations on the basis of familiarity with the stimulus. *Journal of Experimental Psychology*, **39**, 770–784.

Lawrence, D. H. (1950). Acquired distinctiveness of cues: II. Selective association in a constant stimulus situation. *Journal of Experimental Psychology*, **40**, 175–188.

Lea, S. E. G. (1984). In what sense do pigeons learn concepts? In H. T. Roitblat, T. G. Bever, & H. S. Terrace (Eds.), *Animal cognition*, pp. 263–276. Hillsdale, N.J.: Lawrence Erlbaum Associates.

Leander, J. D. (1973). Effects of food deprivation on free-operant avoidance behavior. *Journal of the Experimental Analysis of Behavior, 19*, 17–24.

Ledbetter, D. H. & Bensen, J. A. (1982). Failure to demonstrate self-recognition in gorillas. *American Journal of Primatology, 2*, 307–310.

Lednor, A. J. & Walcott, C. (1983). Homing pigeon navigation: The effects of in-flight exposure to a varying magnetic field. *Comparative Biochemistry and Physiology, 76A*, 665–671.

Lethmate, J. & Ducker, G. (1973). Untersuchungen zum Selbsterkennen im Spiegel bei Orang-utans und einigen anderen Affenarten. *Zeitschrift für Tierpsychologie. 33*, 248–269.

Lett, B. T. (1978). Long delay learning: Implications for learning and memory theory. In N. S. Sutherland (Ed.), *Tutorial essays in experimental psychology*, Vol. 2. Hillsdale, N.J.: Lawrence Erlbaum Associates.

Levis, D. J. (1976). Learned helplessness: A reply and alternative S–R interpretation. *Journal of Experimental Psychology: General, 105*, 47–65.

Lewis, D. J. (1979). Psychobiology of active and inactive memory. *Psychological Bulletin, 86*, 1054–1083.

Leyland, C. M. (1977). Higher-order autoshaping. *Quarterly Journal of Experimental Psychology, 29*, 607–619.

Leyland, C. M. & Mackintosh, N. J. (1978). Blocking of first- and second-order autoshaping in pigeons. *Animal Learning and Behavior, 6*, 391–394.

Lieberman, D. A., Davidson, F. H., & Thomas, G. V. (1985). Marking in pigeons: The role of memory in delayed reinforcement. *Journal of Experimental Psychology: Animal Behavior Processes, 11*, 611–624.

Lieberman, D. A., McIntosh, D. C., & Thomas, G. V. (1979). Learning when reward is delayed: A marking hypothesis. *Journal of Experimental Psychology: Animal Behavior Processes, 5*, 224–242.

Lieberman, P. (1975). *On the origins of language*. New York: Macmillan.

Lieberman, P. (1984). *The biology and evolution of language*. Cambridge, Mass.: Harvard University Press.

Lipp, H. P. (1983). Nocturnal homing in pigeons. *Comparative Biochemistry and Physiology, 76A*, 743–749.

Locke, A. (1980). *The guided reinvention of language*. London: Academic Press.

Logan, C. (1975). Topographic changes in responding during habituation to waterstream stimulation in sea anemones (*Anthopleura elegentissima*). *Journal of Comparative and Physiological Psychology, 89*, 105–117.

LoLordo, V. M. (1979). Selective associations. In A. Dickinson & R. A. Boakes (Eds.), *Mechanisms of learning and motivation*, pp. 367–398. Hillsdale, N.J.: Lawrence Erlbaum Associates.

Lovibond, P. F. (1983). Facilitation of instrumental behavior by a Pavlovian appetitive conditioned stimulus. *Journal of Experimental Psychology: Animal Behavior Processes, 9*, 225–247.

Lovibond, P. F. Preston, G. C., & Mackintosh, N. J. (1984). Context specificity of conditioning, extinction and latent inhibition. *Journal of Experimental Psychology: Animal Behavior Processes, 10*, 360–375.

Lubinski, D. & MacCorquodale, K. (1984). "Symbolic communication" between two pigeons

(*Columba livia*) without unconditioned reinforcement. *Journal of Comparative Psychology*, **98**, 372–380.

Lubow, R. E. (1973). Latent inhibition. *Psychological Bulletin*, **79**, 398–407.

McCulloch, T. L. & Pratt, J. G. (1934). A study of the pre-solution period of weight discrimination by the white rat. *Journal of Comparative Psychology*, **18**, 271–290.

McFarland, D. (1985). *Animal Behaviour*. Bath: Pitman.

McGonigle, B. O. & Chalmers, M. (1977). Are monkeys logical? *Nature*, **267**, 694–696.

McGonigle, B. O. & Chalmers, M. (1986). Representations and strategies during inference. In T. Myers, K. Brown, & B. McGonigle (Eds.), *Reasoning and discourse processes*, pp. 141–164. London: Academic Press.

Mackintosh, N. J. (1973). Stimulus selection: Learning to ignore stimuli that predict no change in reinforcement. In R. A. Hinde & J. Stevenson-Hinde (Eds.), *Constraints on learning*, pp. 75–100. London: Academic Press.

Mackintosh, N. J. (1974). *The psychology of animal learning*. London: Academic Press.

Mackintosh, N. J. (1975a). A theory of attention: Variations in the associability of stimuli with reinforcement. *Psychological Review*, **82**, 276–298.

Mackintosh, N. J. (1975b). Blocking of conditioned suppression: Role of the first compound trial. *Journal of Experimental Psychology: Animal Behavior Processes*, **1**, 335–345.

Mackintosh, N. J. (1976). Overshadowing and stimulus intensity. *Animal Learning and Behavior*, **4**, 186–192.

Mackintosh, N. J. (1983). *Conditioning and associative learning*. Oxford: Oxford University Press.

Mackintosh, N. J., Bygrave, D. J., & Picton, B. M. B. (1977). Locus of the effect of a surprising reinforcer in the attenuation of blocking. *Quarterly Journal of Experimental Psychology*, **29**, 327–336.

Mackintosh, N. J. & Cauty, A. (1971). Spatial reversal learning in rats, pigeons, and goldfish. *Psychonomic Science*, **22**, 281–282.

Mackintosh, N. J. & Cotton, M. M. (1985). Conditioned inhibition from reinforcement reduction. In R. R. Miller & N. E. Spear (Eds.), *Information processing in animals: Conditioned inhibition*, pp. 89–111. Hillsdale, N.J.: Lawrence Erlbaum Associates.

Mackintosh, N. J. & Dickinson, A. (1979). Instrumental (type II) conditioning. In A. Dickinson & R. A. Boakes (Eds.), *Mechanisms of learning and motivation*, pp. 143–169. Hillsdale, N.J.: Lawrence Erlbaum Associates.

Mackintosh, N. J. & Holgate, V. (1969). Serial reversal training and nonreversal shift learning. *Journal of Comparative and Physiological Psychology*, **67**, 89–93.

Mackintosh, N. J., Wilson, B., & Boakes, R. A. (1985). Differences in mechanisms of intelligence among vertebrates. In L. Weiskrantz (Ed.), *Animal intelligence*, pp. 53–66. Oxford: Clarendon Press.

Macphail, E. M. (1980). Short-term visual recognition memory in pigeons. *Quarterly Journal of Experimental Psychology*, **32**, 521–538.

Macphail E. M. (1982). *Brain and intelligence in vertebrates*. Oxford: Clarendon.

Macphail E. M. (1985). Vertebrate intelligence: The null hypothesis. In L. Weiskrantz (Ed.), *Animal intelligence*, pp. 37–51. Oxford: Clarendon.

Maier, S. F. & Seligman, M. E. P. (1976). Learned helplessness: Theory and evidence. *Journal of Experimental Psychology: General*, **105**, 3–46.

Maki, W. S., Brokofsky, S., & Berg, B. (1979). Spatial memory in rats: Resistance to retroactive interference. *Animal Learning and Behavior*, **7**, 25–30.

Maki, W. S. & Hegvik, D. K. (1980). Directed forgetting in pigeons. *Animal Learning and Behavior*, **8**, 567–574.

Malott, R. W. & Sidall, J. W. (1972). Acquisition of the people concept in pigeons. *Psychological Reports,* **31**, 3–13.

Marler, P. (1970). A comparative approach to vocal learning: Song development in white-crowned sparrows. *Journal of Comparative and Physiological Psychology,* **71** (Supplement), 1–25.

Marlin, N. A. & Miller, R. R. (1981). Associations to contextual stimuli as a determinant of long-term habituation. *Journal of Experimental Psychology: Animal Behavior Processes,* **7**, 313–333.

Matthews, G. V. T. (1955). *Bird navigation.* London: Cambridge University Press.

Mazmanian, D. S. & Roberts, W. A. (1983). Spatial memory in rats under restricted viewing conditions. *Learning and Motivation,* **12**, 261–281.

Meck, W. H. & Church, R. M. (1982). Abstraction of temporal attributes. *Journal of Experimental Psychology: Animal Behavior Processes,* **8**, 226–243.

Meck, W. H. & Church, R. M. (1983). A mode control model of counting and timing processes. *Journal of Experimental Psychology: Animal Behavior Processes,* **9**, 320–334.

Medin, D. L. & Schaffer, M. M. (1978). A context theory of classification learning. *Psychological Review,* **85**, 207–238.

Menzel, E. W. (1978). Cognitive mapping in chimpanzees. In S. H. Hulse, H. Fowler, & W. K. Honig (Eds.), *Cognitive processes in animal behavior*, pp. 375–422. Hillsdale, N.J.: Lawrence Erlbaum Associates.

Menzel, E. W. & Halperin, S. (1975). Purposive behavior as a basis for objective communication between chimpanzees. *Science,* **189**, 652–654.

Menzel, R. M. (1979). Behavioural access to short-term memory in bees. *Nature,* **241**, 477–478.

Menzel, R. M. & Erber, J. (1978). Learning and memory in bees. *Scientific American,* **239**, 80–88.

Meyer, M. E., Adams, W. A. & Worthen, V. K. (1969). Deprivation and escape conditioning with various intensities of shock. *Psychonomic Science,* **14**, 212–214.

Miller, G. A. (1956). The magical number seven, plus or minus two: Some limits on our capacity for processing information. *Psychological Review,* **63**, 81–97.

Miller, N. E. & DeBold, R. C. (1965). Classically conditioned tongue-licking and operant bar pressing recorded simultaneously in the rat. *Journal of Comparative and Physiological Psychology,* **59**, 109–111.

Miller, R. R. & Berk, A. M. (1977). Retention over metamorphosis in the African claw-toed frog. *Journal of Experimental Psychology: Animal Behavior,* **3**, 343–356.

Misanin, J. R. & Campbell, B. A. (1969). Effects of hunger and thirst on sensitivity and reactivity to shock. *Journal of Comparative and Physiological Psychology,* **69**, 207–213.

Mishkin, M., Prockop, E. S., & Rosvold, H. E. (1962). One-trial object-discrimination learning in monkeys with frontal lesions. *Journal of Comparative and Physiological Psychology,* **55**, 178–181.

Moore, B. R. (1973). The role of directed Pavlovian reactions in simple instrumental learning in the pigeon. In R. A. Hinde & J. Stevenson-Hinde (Eds.), *Constraints on learning*, pp. 159–186. London: Academic Press.

Moore, R. F. & Osadchuk, T. E. (1982). Spatial memory in a passerine migrant. In F. Pappi & H. G. Wallraff (Eds.), *Avian navigation.* Berlin: Springer-Verlag.

Morgan, C. L. (1894). *An introduction to comparative psychology.* London: Scott.

Morgan, M. J., Fitch, M. D., Holman, J. G., & Lea, S. E. G. (1976). Pigeons learn the concept of an "A". *Perception,* **5**, 57–66.

Morris, R. G. M. (1981). Spatial localization does not require the presence of local cue. *Learning and Motivation,* **12**, 239–260.

Mowrer, O. H. (1960a). *Learning theory and behavior*. New York: Wiley.

Mowrer, O. H. (1960b). *Learning theory and the symbolic processes*. New York: Wiley.

Nissen, H. W., Blum, J. S., & Blum, R. A. (1948). Analysis of matching behavior in chimpanzee. *Journal of Comparative and Physiological Psychology, 41*, 62–74.

North, A. J. (1959). Discrimination reversal with spaced trials and distinctive cues. *Journal of Comparative and Physiological Psychology, 52*, 426–429.

O'Keefe, J. & Nadel, L. (1978). *The hippocampus as a cognitive map*. Oxford: Clarendon Press.

Olds, J. & Milner, P. (1954). Positive reinforcement produced by electrical stimulation of septal area and other regions of rat brain. *Journal of Comparative and Physiological Psychology, 47*, 419–427.

Olton, D. S. (1978). Characteristics of spatial memory. In S. H. Hulse, H. Fowler, & W. K. Honig (Eds.), *Cognitive processes in animal behavior*, pp. 341–373. Hillsdale, N.J.: Lawrence Erlbaum Associates.

Olton, D. S., Collison, C., & Werz, M. (1977). Spatial memory and radial arm maze performance of rats. *Learning and Motivation, 8*, 289–314.

Olton, D. S. & Samuelson, R. J. (1976). Remembrance of places past: Spatial memory in rats. *Journal of Experimental Psychology: Animal Behavior Processes, 2*, 97–116.

Over, R. & Mackintosh, N. J. (1969). Cross-modal transfer of intensity discrimination by rats. *Nature, 224*, 918–919.

Overmier, J. B. & Seligman, M. E. P. (1967). Effects of inescapable shock upon subsequent escape and avoidance learning. *Journal of Comparative and Physiological Psychology, 63*, 28–33.

Papi, F., Ioale, P., Fiaschi, V., Benvenuti, S., & Baldaccini, N. E. (1978). Pigeon homing: Cues detected during the outward journey influence initial orientation. In K. Schmidt-Koenig & W. Keeton (Eds.), *Animal migration, navigation, and homing*, pp. 65–77. Berlin: Springer-Verlag.

Papousek, H. (1977). Entwicklung der Lernfähigkeit im Säuglingsalter. In Nissen (Ed.). *Intelligenz, Lernen und Lernstörungen*. Berlin: Springer.

Passingham, R. E. (1982). *The human primate*. San Francisco: Freeman.

Pavlov, I. P. (1927). *Conditioned reflexes*. New York: Oxford University Press.

Payne, R. B. (1981). Song learning and social interaction in indigo buntings. *Animal Behaviour, 29*, 688–697.

Pearce, J. M. (1987). A model for stimulus generalization in Pavlovian conditioning, *Psychological Review, 94*, 61–73.

Pearce, J. M., Colwill, R. M., & Hall, G. (1978). Instrumental conditioning of scratching in the laboratory rat. *Learning and Motivation, 9*, 255–271.

Pearce, J. M. & Hall, G. (1978). Overshadowing the instrumental conditioning of a lever press response by a more valid predictor of reinforcement. *Journal of Experimental Psychology: Animal Behavior Processes, 4*, 356–367.

Pearce, J. M. & Hall, G. (1979). Loss of associability by a compound stimulus comprising excitatory and inhibitory elements. *Journal of Experimental Psychology: Animal Behavior Processes, 5*, 19–30.

Pearce, J. M. & Hall, G. (1980). A model for Pavlovian learning: Variations in the effectiveness of conditioned but not of unconditioned stimuli. *Psychological Review, 87*, 532–552.

Pearce, J. M., Kaye, H., & Hall, G. (1982). Predictive accuracy and stimulus associability: Development of a model for Pavlovian learning. In M. L. Commons, R. J. Herrnstein, & A. R. Wagner, (Eds.), *Quantitative analyses of behavior: Acquisition*, pp. 241–256. Cambridge, Mass.: Ballinger.

Pearce, J. M., Montgomery, A., & Dickinson, A. (1981). Contralateral transfer of inhibitory and excitatory eyelid conditioning in the rabbit. *Quarterly Journal of Experimental Psychology*, **33B**, 45–61.

Pearce, J. M., Nicholas, D. J., & Dickinson, A. (1981). The potentiation effect during serial conditioning. *Quarterly Journal of Experimental Psychology*, **33B**, 159–179.

Pearce, J. M., Nicholas, D. J., & Dickinson, A. (1982). Loss of associability by a conditioned inhibitor. *Quarterly Journal of Experimental Psychology*, **33B**, 149–162.

Peeke, H. V. S. & Veno, A. (1973). Stimulus specificity of habituated aggression in three-spined sticklebacks (*Gasterosteus aculeatus*). *Behavioral Biology*, **8**, 427–432.

Pepperberg, I. M. (1981). Functional vocalizations by an African Grey parrot (*Psittacus erithacus*). *Z. Tierpsychol.* **55**, 139–160.

Pepperberg, I. M. (1983). Cognition in the African Grey parrot: Preliminary evidence for auditory/vocal comprehension of the class concept. *Animal Learning and Behaviour*, **11**, 179–185.

Pepperberg, I. M. (in press). Interspecies communication: A tool for assessing conceptual abilities in the African Grey parrot (*Psittacus arithacus*). In G. Greenberg & E. Tobach (Eds.), *Language cognition, consciousness: Integrative levels*. Hillsdale, N.J.: Lawrence Erlbaum Associates.

Perdeck, A. C. (1958). Two types of orientation in migratory starlings, *Sturnus vulgaris L*, and chaffinches, *Fringilla coelebs L*, as revealed by displacement experiments. *Ardea*, **46**, 1–37.

Pfungst, O. (1965). *Clever Hans: The horse of Mr Van Osten*. New York: Holt. (German original, 1908).

Platt, S. A., Holliday, M., & Drudge, O. W. (1980). Discrimination learning of an instrumental response in individual *Drosophila melanogaster*. *Journal of Experimental Psychology: Animal Behavior Processes*, **6**, 301–311.

Porter, D. & Neuringer, A. (1984). Music discriminations by pigeons. *Journal of Experimental Psychology: Animal Behavior Processes*, **10**, 138–148.

Premack, D. (1971). Language in chimpanzees? *Science*, **172**, 808–822.

Premack, D. (1976). *Intelligence in ape and man*. Hillsdale, N.J.: Lawrence Erlbaum Associates.

Premack, D. (1983a). Animal cognition. *Annual Review of Psychology*, **34**, 351–362.

Premack, D. (1983b). The codes of man and beasts. *The Behavioral and Brain Sciences*, **6**, 125–167.

Rashotte, M. E., Griffin, R. W., & Sisk, C. L. (1977). Second-order conditioning of the pigeon's key peck. *Animal Learning and Behavior*, **5**, 25–38.

Reed, S. K. (1972). Pattern recogntion and categorization. *Cognitive Psychology*, **3**, 382–407.

Reiss, S. & Wagner, A. R. (1972). CS habituation produces a "latent inhibition effect" but no active "conditioned inhibition". *Learning and Motivation*, **3**, 237–245.

Rescorla, R. A. (1967). Pavlovian conditioning and its proper control procedures. *Psychological Review*, **74**, 71–80.

Rescorla, R. A. (1968). Probability of shock in the presence and absence of CS in fear conditioning. *Journal of Comparative and Physiological Psychology*, **66**, 1–5.

Rescorla, R. A. (1969). Pavlovian conditioned inhibition. *Psychological Bulletin*, **72**, 77–94.

Rescorla, R. A. (1979). Conditioned inhibition and extinction. In A. Dickinson & R. A. Boakes (Eds.), *Mechanisms of learning and motivation*, pp. 83–110. Hillsdale, N.J.: Lawrence Erlbaum Associates.

Rescorla, R. A. (1980). *Pavlovian second-order conditioning.* Hillsdale, N.J.: Lawrence Erlbaum Associates.

Rescorla, R. A. (1981). Within-signal learning in autoshaping. *Animal Learning and Behavior, 9,* 245–252.

Rescorla, R. A. & LoLordo, V. M. (1965). Inhibition and avoidance behavior. *Journal of Comparative and Physiological Psychology, 59,* 406–412.

Rescorla, R. A. & Solomon, R. L. (1967). Two-process learning theory: Relationship between Pavlovian conditioning and instrumental learning. *Psychological Review, 88,* 151–182.

Rescorla, R. A., & Wagner, A. R. (1972). A theory of Pavlovian conditioning: Variations in the effectiveness of reinforcement and nonreinforcement. In A. H. Black & W. F. Prokasy (Eds.), *Classical conditioning II: Current research and theory,* pp. 64–99. New York: Appleton-Century-Crofts.

Revusky, S. H. (1971). The role of interference over a delay. In W. K. Honig & P. H. R. James (Eds.), *Animal memory,* pp. 155–213. New York: Academic Press.

Revusky, S. H. (1977). Learning as a general process with an emphasis on data from feeding experiments. In N. W. Milgram, L. Krames, & T. M. Alloway (Eds.), *Food aversion learning,* pp. 1–51. New York: Plenum.

Richards, D. G., Wolz, J. P., & Herman, L. M. (1984). Vocal mimicry of computer-generated sounds and vocal labeling of objects by a bottlenosed dolphin, *Tusiops truncatus. Journal of Comparative Psychology, 98,* 10–28.

Riddell, W. I. (1979). Cerebral indices and behavioral differences. In M. E. Hahn, C. Jensen, & B. C. Dudek (Eds.), *Development and evolution of brain size,* pp. 89–111. New York: Academic Press.

Riley, D. A. (1984). Do pigeons decompose stimulus compounds? In H. L. Roitblat, T. G. Bever, & H. S. Terrace (Eds.), *Animal cognition,* pp. 333–350. Hillsdale, N.J.: Lawrence Erlbaum Associates.

Riley, D. A. & Roitblat, H. L. (1978). Selective attention and related cognitive processes in pigeons. In S. H. Hulse, H. Fowler, & W. K. Honig (Eds.), *Cognitive processes in animal behavior.* Hillsdale, N.J.: Lawrence Erlbaum Associates.

Ristau, C. A. & Robbins, D. (1982). Language in the great apes: A critical review. *Advances in the Study of Behaviour, 12,* 141–255.

Rizley, R. C. & Rescorla, R. A. (1972). Associations in second-order conditioning and sensory preconditioning. *Journal of Comparative and Physiological Psychology, 81,* 1–11.

Roberts, S. (1981). Isolation of an internal clock. *Journal of Experimental Psychology: Animal Behavior Processes, 7,* 242–268.

Roberts, S. (1982). Cross-modal use of an internal clock. *Journal of Experimental Psychology: Animal Behavior Processes, 8,* 2–22.

Roberts, W. A. (1979). Spatial memory in the rat on a hierarchical maze. *Learning and Motivation, 10,* 117–140.

Roberts, W. A. (1981). Retroactive inhibition in rat spatial memory. *Animal Learning and Behavior, 9,* 566–574.

Roberts, W. A. & Dale, R. H. I. (1981). Remembrance of places lasts: Proactive inhibition and patterns of choice in rat spatial memory. *Learning and Motivation, 12,* 261–281.

Roberts, W. A. & Grant, D. S. (1974). Short-term memory in the pigeon with presentation time precisely controlled. *Learning and Motivation, 5,* 393–408.

Roberts, W. A. & Grant, D. S. (1976). Studies of short-term memory in the pigeon using the delayed matching-to-sample procedure. In D. L. Medin, W. A. Roberts, & R. T. Davis (Eds.), *Processes in animal memory.* Hillsdale, N.J.: Lawrence Erlbaum Associates.

Roberts, W. A. & Kraemer, P. J. (1981). Recognition memory for lists of visual stimuli in monkeys and humans. *Animal Learning and Behavior*, **9**, 587–594.

Roberts, W. A. & Smythe, W. E. (1979). Memory for lists of spatial events in the rat. *Learning and Motivation*, **10**, 313–336.

Robert, W. A. & Van Veldhuizen, N. (1985). Spatial memory in pigeons on the radial maze. *Journal of Experimental Psychology: Animal Behavior Processes*, **11**, 241–260.

Roitblat, H. L. (1980). Codes and coding processes in pigeon short-term memory. *Animal Learning and Behavior*, **8**, 341–351.

Roitblat, H. L., Tham, W., & Golub, L. (1982). Performance of *Betta splendens* in a radial arm maze. *Animal Learning and Behavior*, **10**, 108–114.

Romanes, G. J. (1882). *Animal intelligence*. London: Keegan Paul.

Romer, A. S. (1966). *The vertebrate body*. Philadelphia: W. B. Saunders.

Roper, T. J. (1983). Learning as a biological phenomenon. In T. R. Halliday & P. J. B. Slater (Eds.), *Animal behaviour: Genes, development and learning*, pp. 178–212. Oxford: Blackwell.

Rosch, E. (1973). On the internal structure of perceptual and semantic categories. In T. E. Moore (Ed.), *Cognitive development and the acquisition of language*. New York: Academic Press.

Rozin, P. & Kalat, J. W. (1971). Specific hungers and poisoning as adaptive specializations of learning. *Psychological Review*, **78**, 459–486.

Rumbaugh, D. M. (1977). *Language learning by a chimpanzee: The LANA project*. New York: Academic Press.

Russell, I. S. (1979). Brain size and intelligence: A comparative perspective. In D. A. Oakley & H. C. Plotkin (Eds.), *Brain behaviour and evolution*, pp. 126–153. London: Methuen.

Sahley, C., Gelperin, A., & Rudy, J. W. (1981). An analysis of associative learning in a terrestrial mollusc. I: Higher-order conditioning, blocking, and a transient US pre-exposure effect. *Journal of Comparative Physiology*, **144**, 1–8.

Sands, S. F. & Wright, A. A. (1980). Serial probe recognition performance by a rhesus monkey and a human with 10- and 20-item lists. *Journal of Experimental Psychology: Animal Behavior Processes*, **6**, 386–396.

Santiago, H. C. & Wright, A. A. (1984). Pigeon memory: *Same/different* concept learning, serial probe recognition acquisition, and probe delay effects on the serial position function. *Journal of Experimental Psychology: Animal Behavior Processes*, **10**, 498–512.

Savage-Rumbaugh, E. S. (1984). Acquisition of functional symbol usage in apes and children. In H. L. Roitblat, T. G. Bever, & H. S. Terrace (Eds.), *Animal cognition*, pp. 291–310. Hillsdale, N.J.: Lawrence Erlbaum Associates.

Savage-Rumbaugh, E. S., McDonald, K., Sevcik, R. A., Hopkins, W. D., & Rubert, E. (1986). Spontaneous symbol acquisition and communication by pygmy chimpanzees (*Pan Paniscus*). *Journal of Experimental Psychology: General*, **115**, 211–235.

Savage-Rumbaugh, E. S., Pate, J. L., Lawson, J., Smith, T., & Rosenbaum, S. (1983). Can a chimpanzee make a statement? *Journal of Experimental Psychology: General*, **112**, 457–492.

Savage-Rumbaugh, E. S., Rumbaugh, D. M., & Boysen, S. L. (1978). Symbolic communication between two chimpanzees (*Pan troglodytes*). *Science*, **201**, 641–644.

Savage-Rumbaugh, E. S., Rumbaugh, D. M., Smith, S. T., & Lawson, J. (1980). Reference–The linguistic essential. *Science*, **210**, 922–925.

Schiller, P. H. (1952). Innate constituents of complex responses in primates. *Psychological Review*, **59**, 177–191.

Schlicte, H. J. & Schmidt-Koenig, K. (1971). Zum Heimfindevermögen der Brieftaube bei erschwerter optischer Wahrnehmung. *Naturwissenschaften,* **58,** 329–330.

Schneirla, T. C. (1929). Learning and orientation in ants. *Comparative Psychology Monographs,* **6,** No. 29.

Schrier, A. M. (1966). Transfer by macaque monkeys between learning set and repeated-reversal tasks. *Perceptual and Motor Skills,* **23,** 787–792.

Schrier, A. M., Angarella, R., & Povar, M. L. (1984). Studies of concept formation by stumptailed monkeys: Concepts humans, monkeys, and letter A. *Journal of Experimental Psychology: Animal Behavior Processes,* **10,** 564–584.

Seligman, M. E. P. (1979). On the generality of the laws of learning. *Psychological Review,* **77,** 406–418.

Seligman, M. E. P. (1975). *Helplessness.* San Francisco: Freeman.

Seligman, M. E. P. & Hager, J. L. (1972). *Biological boundaries of learning.* New York: Appleton-Century-Crofts.

Seligman, M. E. P. & Maier, S. F. (1967). Failure to escape traumatic shock. *Journal of Experimental Psychology,* **74,** 1–9.

Seyfarth, R. M., Cheyney, D. L., & Marler, P. (1980). Vervet monkey alarm calls: Semantic communication in a free-ranging primate. *Animal Behaviour,* **28,** 1070–1094.

Shapiro, K. L., Jacobs, W. J., & LoLordo, V. M. (1980). Stimulus–reinforcer interactions in Pavlovian conditioning of pigeons: Implications for selective associations. *Animal Learning and Behavior,* **8,** 586–594.

Sheafor, P. J. (1975). "Pseudoconditioned" jaw movements of the rabbit reflect associations conditioned to contextual background cues. *Journal of Experimental Psychology: Animal Behavior Processes,* **1,** 245–260.

Shepard, R. N. & Metzler, J. (1971). Mental rotation of three-dimensional objects. *Science,* **171,** 701–703.

Sherman, J. E. (1979). The effects of conditioning and novelty on the rat's analgesic and pyretic response to morphine. *Learning and Motivation,* **10,** 383–418.

Shettleworth, S. J. (1975). Reinforcement and the organization of behavior in golden hamsters: Hunger, environment, and food reinforcement. *Journal of Experimental Psychology: Animal Behavior Processes,* **1,** 56–87.

Shiffrin, R. M. & Schneider, W. (1977). Controlled and automatic human information processing: II. Perceptual learning, automatic attending and a general theory. *Psychological Review,* **84,** 127–190.

Shishimi, A. (1985). Latent inhibition experiments with goldfish (*Carassius auratus*). *Journal of Comparative Psychology,* **99,** 316–327.

Siegel, R. K. & Honig, W. K. (1970). Pigeon concept formation: Successive and simultaneous acquisition. *Journal of the Experimental Analysis of Behavior,* **13,** 385–390.

Siegel, S. (1967). Overtraining and transfer processes. *Journal of Comparative and Physiological Psychology,* **64,** 471–477.

Siegel, S. (1977). Morphine tolerance acquisition as an associative process. *Journal of Experimental Psychology: Animal Behavior Processes,* **3,** 1–13.

Skard, O. (1950). A comparison of human and animal learning in the Stone multiple T-maze. *Acta Psychologica,* **7,** 89–109.

Skinner, B. F. (1938). *The behavior of organisms.* New York: Appleton-Century-Crofts.

Skinner, B. F. (1950). Are theories of learning necessary? *Psychological Review,* **57,** 193–216.

Slater, P. J. B. (1983). The study of communication. In T. R. Halliday & P. J. B. Slater (Eds.), *Communication.* Oxford: Blackwell.

Slater, P. J. B. & Ince, S. A. (1982). Song development in chaffinches: What is learnt and when? *Ibis*, **124**, 21–26.

Smith, J. C. & Roll, D. L. (1967). Trace conditioning with X-rays as the aversive stimulus. *Psychonomic Science*, **9**, 11–12.

Smith, M. C. (1968). CS–US interval and US intensity in classical conditioning of the rabbit's nictitating membrane response. *Journal of Comparative and Physiological Psychology*, **69**, 226–231.

Sokolov, Y. N. (1963). *Perception and the conditioned reflex*. Oxford: Pergamon Press.

Solomon, R. L. & Corbit, J. D. (1974). An opponent-process theory of motivation: I. Temporal dynamics of affect. *Psychological Review*, **81**, 119–145.

Spear, N. E. (1973). Retrieval of memory in animals. *Psychological Review*, **80**, 163–175.

Spear, N. E. (1981). Extending the domain of memory retrieval. In N. E. Spear & R. R. Miller (Eds.), *Information processing in animals: Memory mechanisms*, pp. 341–378. Hillsdale, N.J.: Lawrence Erlbaum Associates.

Spear, N. E., Smith, G. J., Bryan, R., Gordon, W., Timmons, R., & Chiszar, D. (1980). Contextual influences on the interaction between conflicting memories in the rat. *Animal Learning and Behavior*, **8**, 273–281.

St. Claire-Smith, R. (1979). The overshadowing of instrumental conditioning by a stimulus that predicts reinforcement better than the response. *Animal Learning and Behavior*, **7**, 224–228.

Straub, R. O. & Terrace, H. S. (1981). Generalization of serial learning in the pigeon. *Animal Learning and Behaviour*, **9**, 454–468.

Stretch, R. G., McGonigle, B., & Morton, A. (1964). Position–reversal learning in the rat: Trials/problem and intertrial interval. *Journal of Comparative and Physiological Psychology*, **57**, 461–463.

Suarez, D. & Gallup, G. G., Jr. (1981). Self-recognition in chimpanzees and orangutans, but not gorillas. *Journal of Human Evolution*, **10**, 175–188.

Sutherland, N. S. (1964). The learning of discrimination by animals. *Endeavour*, **23**, 69–78.

Sutherland, N. S. & Mackintosh, N. J. (1971). *Mechanisms of animal discrimination learning*. New York: Academic Press.

Suzuki, S., Augerinos, G., & Black, A. H. (1980). Stimulus control of spatial behavior on the eight-arm maze in rats. *Learning and Motivation*, **11**, 1–18.

Terrace, H. S. (1979). *Nim*. New York: Knopf.

Terrace, H. S., Petitto, L. A., Sanders, R. J., & Bever, T. G. (1979). Can an ape create a sentence? *Science*, **200**, 891–902.

Theios, J., Lynch, A. D., & Lowe, W. F. Jr. (1966). Differential effects of shock intensity on one-way and shuttle avoidance conditioning. *Journal of Experimental Psychology*, **72**, 294–299.

Thomas, D. A. (1979). Forgetting of a CS attribute in a conditioned suppression paradigm. *Animal Learning and Behavior*, **7**, 191–195.

Thomas, D. R. (1981). Studies of long-term memory in the pigeon. In N. E. Spear & R. R. Miller (Eds.), *Information processing in animals: Memory mechanisms*, pp. 257–290. Hillsdale, N.J.: Lawrence Erlbaum Associates.

Thomas, D. R. & Lopez, L. J. (1962). The effect of delayed testing on the generalization slope. *Journal of Comparative and Physiological Psychology*, **44**, 541–544.

Thomas, G. V., Lieberman, D. A., McIntosh, D. C., & Ronaldson, P. (1983). The role of marking when reward is delayed. *Journal of Experimental Psychology: Animal Behavior Processes*, **9**, 410–411.

Thompson, R. F., Berger, T. W., & Madden, J. (1983). Cellular processes of learning and memory in the mammalian CNS. *Annual Review of Neuroscience*, **6**, 447–491.

Thompson, R. F. & Spencer, W. A. (1966). Habituation: A model phenomenon for the study of neuronal substrates of behavior. *Psychological Review, 73*, 16–43.

Thompson, R. K. R. & Herman, L. M. (1977). Memory for lists of sounds by the bottle-nosed dolphin: Convergence of memory processes with humans? *Science, 195*, 501–503.

Thorndike, E. L. (1898). Animal intelligence: An experimental study of the associative processes in animals. *Psychological Monographs, 2* (4, Whole No. 8).

Thorndike, E. L. (1911). *Animal intelligence: Experimental studies*. New York: Macmillan.

Thorpe, W. H. (1963). *Animal intelligence: Experimental studies*. New York: Macmillan.

Timberlake, W. & Grant, D. S. (1975). Autoshaping in rats to presentation of another rat predicting food. *Science, 190*, 690–692.

Tinbergen, N. (1951). *The study of instinct*. Oxford: Clarendon Press.

Tinbergen, N. (1953). *The herring gull's world*. London: Collins.

Tolman, E. C. (1932). *Purposive behavior in animals and men*. New York: Century.

Tolman, E. C. (1948). Cognitive maps in rats and men. *Psychological Review, 55*, 189–208.

Tolman, E. C., Ritchie, B. F., & Kalish, D. (1946). Studies in spatial learning. I. Orientation and the short-cut. *Journal of Experimental Psychology, 36*, 13–24.

Tranberg, D. K. & Rilling, M. (1978). Latent inhibition in the autoshaping paradigm. *Bulletin of the Psychonomic Society, 11*, 273–276.

Van Beusekom, G. (1948). Some experiments on the optical orientation in *Philanthus triangulum. Fabr. Behavior, 1*, 195–225.

Vander Wall, S. B. (1982). An experimental analysis of cache recovery in Clark's nutcracker. *Animal Behaviour, 30*, 84–94.

Van Sommers, P. (1962). Oxygen-motivated behavior in goldfish (*Carassius auratus*). *Science, 137*, 678–679.

Vaughan, W. Jr. & Greene, S. L. (1984). Pigeon visual memory capacity. *Journal of Experimental Psychology: Animal Behavior Processes, 10*, 256–271.

Von Frisch, K. (1950). *Bees, their vision, chemical senses, and language*. Ithaca, N.Y.: Cornell University Press.

Von Frisch, K. (1974). Decoding the language of the bee. *Science, 185*, 663–668.

Von Uexküll, J. (1934). *Streifzüge durch die Umwelten von Tieren und Menschen*. Berlin: Springer-Verlag. Translated in C. H. Schiller (Ed.), *Instinctive behavior*. London: Methuen.

Wagner, A. R. (1976). Priming in STM: An information-processing mechanism for self-generated and retrieval-generated depression in performance. In T. J. Tighe & R. N. Leaton (Eds.), *Habituation: Perspectives from child development, animal behavior, and neurophysiology*, pp. 95–128. Hillsdale, N.J.: Lawrence Erlbaum Associates.

Wagner, A. R. (1978). Expectancies and the priming of STM. In S. H. Hulse, H. Fowler, & W. K. Honig (Eds.), *Cognitive processes in animal behavior*, pp. 177–209. Hillsdale, N.J.: Lawrence Erlbaum Associates.

Wagner, A. R. (1979). Habituation and memory. In A. Dickinson & R. A. Boakes (Eds.), *Mechanisms of learning and motivation*, pp. 53–82. Hillsdale, N.J.: Lawrence Erlbaum Associates.

Wagner, A. R. (1981). SOP: A model of automatic memory processing in animal behavior. In N. E. Spear & R. R. Miller (Eds.), *Information processing in animals: Memory mechanisms*, pp. 5–47. Hillsdale, N.J.: Lawrence Erlbaum Associates.

Wagner, A. R. & Larew, M. B. (1985). Opponent processes and Pavlovian inhibition. In R. R. Miller & N. E. Spear (Eds.), *Information processing in animals: Conditioned inhibition*. Hillsdale, N.J.: Lawrence Erlbaum Associates.

Wagner, A. R. & Rescorla, R. A. (1972). Inhibition in Pavlovian conditioning: Application of a theory. In R. A. Boakes & M. S. Halliday (Eds.), *Inhibition and learning*, pp. 301–336. London: Academic Press.

Wagner, A. R., Rudy, J. W., & Whitlow, J. W. (1973). Rehearsal in animal conditioning. *Journal of Experimental Psychology, 97*, 407–426.

Walcott, C. (1978). Anomalies in the Earth's magnetic field increase the scatter of pigeon's vanishing bearings. In K. Schmidt-Koenig & W. T. Keeton (Eds.), *Animal migration, navigation, and homing*, pp. 143–151. Berlin: Springer-Verlag.

Walcott, C. & Schmidt-Koenig, K. (1973). The effect of anesthesia during displacement on the homing performance of pigeons. *Auk, 90*, 281–286.

Ward, J. P., Yehle, A. L., & Doerflein, R. S. (1970). Cross-modal transfer of a specific discrimination in the bushbaby (*Galago senegalensis*). *Journal of Comparative and Physiological Psychology, 73*, 74–77.

Warren, J. M. (1965). Primate learning in comparative perspective. In A. M. Schrier, H. F. Harlow, & F. Stollnitz (Eds.), *Behaviour of nonhuman primates: Modern research trends*, pp. 249–281. New York: Academic Press.

Warren, J. M. (1973). Learning in vetebrates. In D. A. Dewsbury & D. A. Rethlingshafer (Eds.), *Comparative psychology: A modern survey*, pp. 471–509. New York: McGraw-Hill.

Wasserman, E. A. (1973). Pavlovian conditioning with heat reinforcement produces stimulus-directed pecking in chicks, *Science, 181*, 875–877.

Weiskrantz, L. & Cowey, A. (1975). Cross-modal matching in the rhesus monkey using a single pair of stimuli. *Neuropsychologia, 13*, 257–261.

Weiss, J. M. (1971). Effects of coping behavior in different warning signal conditions on stress pathology in rats. *Journal of Comparative and Physiological Psychology, 77*, 1–13.

Wells, G. P. (1950). Spontaneous activity cycles in polychaete worms. *Symposium of the Society of Experimental Biology, 4*, 127–142.

Wells, P. (1967). Training flatworms in a Van Oye maze. In W. Corning & S. Ratner (Eds.), *Chemistry of learning: Invertebrate research*. New York: Plenum.

Wenner, A. M. (1964). Sound communication in honeybees. *Scientific American, 210*, 116–124.

Wesley, F. (1961). The number concept: A phylogenetic review. *Psychological Bulletin, 58*, 420–428.

Westbrook, R. F., Bond, N. W., & Feyer, A. M. (1981). Short- and long-term decrements in toxicosis-induced odor-aversion learning: The role of duration of exposure to an odor. *Journal of Experimental Psychology: Animal Behavior Processes, 7*, 362–381.

Whitlow, J. W. Jr. (1975). Short-term memory in habituation and dishabituation. *Journal of Experimental Psychology: Animal Behavior Processes, 1*, 189–206.

Williams, B. A. (1971). The effects of intertrial interval on discrimination reversal learning in the pigeon. *Psychonomic Science, 23*, 241–243.

Williams, D. R. & Williams, H. (1969). Auto-maintenance in the pigeon: Sustained pecking despite contingent non-reinforcement. *Journal of the Experimental Analysis of Behavior, 12*, 511–520.

Wood, F. G. (1973). *Marine mammals and man, the navy's porpoises and sea lions*. Washington, D.C.: R. B. Luce.

Wright, A. A., Santiago, H. C., Sands, S. F., & Urcuioli, P. J. (1984). Pigeon and monkey serial probe recognition: Acquisition, strategies, and serial position effects. In H. L. Roitblat, T. G. Bever, & H. S. Terrace (Eds.), *Animal cognition*, pp. 353–374. Hillsdale, N.J.: Lawrence Erlbaum Associates.

Yeagley, H. L. (1947). A preliminary study of a physical basis of bird navigation. *Journal of Applied Physiology, 18*, 1035–1063.

Yeagley, H. L. (1951). A preliminary study of a physical basis of bird navigation. II. *Journal of Applied Physiology*, **22**, 746–760.

Yerkes, R. M. & Morgulis, S. (1909). The method of Pavlov in animal psychology. *Psychological Bulletin*, **6**, 257–273.

Yodlowski, M. L., Kreithen, M. L., & Keeton, W. T. (1977). Detection of atmospheric infrasound by homing pigeons. *Nature*, **265**, 725–726.

Zimmer-Hart, C. L. & Rescorla, R. A. (1974). Extinction of Pavlovian conditioned inhibition. *Journal of Comparative and Physiological Psychology*, **86**, 837–845.

Author Index

Subject Index

Acknowledgements

The following figures originally appeared in publications of the American Psychological Association and are reprinted here by permission of the author and publisher.

Figure 2.6 (p. 46). Copyright 1984
Figure 2.7a (p. 48). Copyright 1984
Figure 2.7b (p. 49). Copyright 1984
Figure 2.11 (p. 62). Copyright 1979
Figure 2.13 (p. 66). Copyright 1984
Figure 3.3 (p. 79). Copyright 1973
Figure 3.7 (p. 89). Copyright 1983
Figure 3.9 (p. 90). Copyright 1978
Figure 3.12 (p. 105). Copyright 1980
Figure 4.9 (p. 127). Copyright 1977
Figure 6.1 (p. 184). Copyright 1974
Figure 6.2 (p. 186). Copyright 1977
Figure 6.7 (p. 206). Copyright 1970
Figure 6.8 (p. 208). Copyright 1980
Figure 8.8 (p. 265). Copyright 1983

AUG 0 3 1988   **DATE DUE**

NOV 1 9 1989			
NOV 2 0 1989			
GAYLORD			PRINTED IN U.S.A.